STEPHEN LORD worked in banking for 12 years, living in Japan and the USA for most of that time. He loved the travel and living overseas but ultimately opted for camping and travelling under his own steam rather than a life of luxury hotels and sitting in taxis and offices.

He has toured in Asia, North America and Europe on mountain- and touring-bikes. He also enjoys kayak-touring and long-distance walking but always comes back to cycle-touring, believing that the combination of a bike and a tent give unsurpassed freedom. Between trips he's based in London.

Adventure Cycle-Touring Handbook
First edition: May 2006

Publisher
Trailblazer Publications
The Old Manse, Tower Rd, Hindhead, Surrey, GU26 6SU, UK
Fax (+44) 01428-607571
info@trailblazer-guides.com
www.trailblazer-guides.com

British Library Cataloguing in Publication Data
A catalogue record for this book is available from the British Library

ISBN 1-873756-89-5
EAN 978-1873756-898

© **Stephen Lord 2006**
Text, maps and photographs (unless otherwise credited)
The right of Stephen Lord to be identified as the author of this work has been asserted
by him in accordance with the Copyright, Designs and Patents Act 1988

© **Cass Gilbert**: front cover and colour photographs as indicated
© **Robb Maciag**: back cover photograph

Editors: Chris Scott, Henry Stedman & Patricia Major
Series Editor: Patricia Major
Typesetting: Henry Stedman & Anna Jacomb-Hood
Layout: Chris Scott
Proofreading: Jane Thomas
Cartography: Nick Hill
Index: Jane Thomas

Global travel by bicycle is unpredictable and can be dangerous.
Every effort has been made by the author, contributors and the publisher to ensure that
the information contained herein is as accurate as possible. However, they are unable
to accept responsibility for any inconvenience, loss or injury sustained by anyone
as a result of the advice and information given in this guide.

Printed on chlorine-free paper by D2Print (☎ +65-6295 5598), Singapore

ADVENTURE CYCLE-TOURING HANDBOOK

STEPHEN LORD

with contributions by
JEAN BELL, JANNE CORAX, PHILIP DAVIS, SEBASTIAN EISSING
MARK ELLIOTT, EDWARD GENOCHIO, CASS GILBERT
SIMON HILL, FELIX HUDE, ALASTAIR HUMPHREYS, IGOR KOVSE
KENICHI KUROE, MAYA VAN LEEMPUT, ROBB MACIAG
MARK & JULIETTE MCLEAN, TIM MULLINER, STEVE PELLS
LUKA ROMIH & MANCA RAVNIKAR, MICHELE SANNA
CHRIS SCOTT, LUKE SKINNER & ANNA HEYWOOD
PETER SNOW CAO, LAURA STONE, RAF VERBEELEN
IVAN VIEHOFF, ROBIN & HELEEN WIELDERS-BOERMAN
DAVE WODCHIS, PAUL WOLOSHANSKY

TRAILBLAZER PUBLICATIONS

Acknowledgements

This book is much the richer for all the contributions of writing, photos and ideas from cyclists from all around the world. Thank you all for your help.

In particular, Philip 'Five Bikes' Davis and Steve Pells were most generous in helping in many ways and in recounting their experiences and points of view. Philip even lent me his best jokes and Steve was always there to remind me that bikes ride best when they're light. Paul Woloshansky, a professional bike mechanic, kindly edited and proofed the technical stuff and made sure I could tell my Prestas from my Schraders. He also wrote the Canada section and has since learned firsthand about fending off grizzly bears, while bike touring there.

Several Trailblazer writers freely chipped in with wonderful work – thanks very much to Mark Elliott (*Azerbaijan*) for the section on the Caucasus, and to Laura Stone (*Himalaya by Bicycle – a route and planning guide*) for the comprehensive information on the Himalaya and for the colour photos. Chris Scott, whose *Adventure Motorcycling Handbook* inspired this book, played a vital role in knocking the text into shape, plucking out my weak jokes and planting his own more robust ones.

Felix Hude and his cycling buddy Mr Pumpy were real professionals in trying to get their heads round the project, sending me drafts from Bangkok in the middle of their nighttime. Felix's words (see p.138, *The Unknown Road*) capture something wonderful about cycle touring. The other great wonder is the people you meet and the friends you make by cycle touring. I was lucky to meet contributor Janne Corax while in Tibet and narrowly missed running into Beat Heim when he turned off the Friendship Highway to bag another snow-covered 5000m pass. I made a lot of friends in the course of writing this book and hope to meet more of them – hopefully on the road. Although I didn't meet him, Edward Genochio (*The Colonel's Trousers*, p.215) is still out there, aiming to be the first person to cycle solo from Britain to China and back again and had just crossed Tibet (in winter) as we went to press. Good luck for the rest of your trip!

Thanks also to Cass Gilbert for providing the excellent photos. More important than his many talents, Cass is a real gentleman and has been most gracious and helpful to me.

I'm grateful to Annick Lambert for the photo on p.1 and Alan Bradshaw for the Trip Report graphics. Thank you also to Alastair Bland and *The San Francisco Bay Guardian* for the highly-entertaining tale on pp.263-5 which originally appeared in that publication (15 March 2005). And thanks to Apex Cycles of Clapham, London for their help.

Thanks to all at Trailblazer: Bryn for his patience, support and stamina in seeing this project through, Patricia for her thorough work on the tales, Henry for wading into wild and woolly text, Jane for proof-reading and for the index, Anna for her support and helpful comments and Nick for making sense of my map requests. Any aspiring travel writer would be fortunate indeed to have a publisher like Trailblazer.

A request

Every effort has been made by the author and the publisher to ensure that the information contained in this book is as up to date and accurate as possible. Nevertheless things will change; even before the ink is dry. If you notice any changes or omissions that you think should be included in the next edition of this book, please write to the author at stephen@adventurecycle-touringhandbook.com or c/o Trailblazer (address on p.2).

Updated information and a whole lot more at:
www.adventurecycle-touringhandbook.com

Cover photo: On the Manali-Leh Highway, India © Cass Gilbert

CONTENTS

PART 3: TALES FROM THE SADDLE

INTRODUCTION

Adventure cycle-touring

Why are so many people going bike touring these days? A minority pastime during the heyday of the car, cycling has once again become a popular choice for travelling – especially for long overseas trips.

Britain's CTC, the Cyclists' Touring Club, began life over 125 years ago during the first cycle-touring craze in the 1870s. Then, as now, the bicycle offered a revolutionary way of touring: you go exactly where you want, when you want, and all under your own steam. This was before the age of the car and walking or riding a horse were the only other options until the bicycle. In 1885 the Rover Safety Bicycle came along, and for all the innovation since then, most modern touring bicycles would be recognizable to a Victorian, as would their derailleur gears.

Bike touring is undergoing a boom at the moment but it is really one of many periodic rediscoveries. Bicycle design, components and gear are evolving to suit the changing needs and tastes of people. It's a combination of experimentation and using tried and tested designs, such as the 'diamond' frame of the Rover Safety Bicycle. The *Adventure Cycle-Touring Handbook* is all about looking at what people are choosing and using: what kind of bikes, what gear and what destinations are being chosen by today's bike tourers.

There are many reasons for taking a bike on your next long trip. My own guess as to why bike

In 1929 Jean Bell (see p205) cycled across Europe on this gearless, single-brake Belgian bike. Accustomed to solid American tyres he was surprised to discover that those on his new-fangled European bike came with inflatable inner tubes.

touring is back in fashion is that many travellers get burned out by backpacking, which really amounts to travelling by bus and train for most of the time. Buses are certainly fast but they go from one noisy town to another, leaving little possibility of exploring the spaces in between, the places where the bus doesn't stop.

Others use bikes to go even further off the beaten track: they want to go where buses don't go at all and perhaps where other vehicles cannot get to either. Paul Woloshansky built his own racks to carry extra gear after being told all too often: 'There's a prettier way to go but there's nothing out there at all'. Other adventurers, such as Sweden's Janne Corax (see p122), have said the same thing: there were times when there was no other way of getting to where

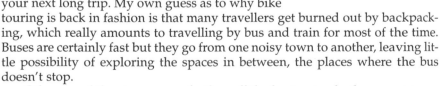

they wanted to go. You couldn't get there on foot and you couldn't get there in a truck. It was possible only on a bicycle.

Half the adventure, though, is in the riding itself. Being out in the fresh air and seeing much more than is possible from a bus or train window is always a good feeling, whether you are wandering around France or riding across India. A lot of today's cycle tourists are interested in the riding but not that interested in bikes. It's a means of transport and a way to carry bags comfortably, while sitting down and enjoying the view. Not everyone is drawn to the high passes of the Andes or the Himalaya but they are all enjoying that same sense of freedom and all that comes with it – unexpected discoveries, off-route detours or an impromptu day off when you find a great place to stay. Trips like these are not as arduous as some expeditions but they are every bit as satisfying – and they are still adventures, for they allow for spontaneity. And if you are carrying a tent and camping gear, you're prepared for just about any eventuality because you've always got a place to spend the night.

This book looks at the possibilities out there, the different styles of travelling and the basic gear and know-how that you need. We also look at some of the more exciting cycling destinations around the world, complete with suggestions as to which routes to take and what you need to plan a trip in that region. The *Adventure Cycle-Touring Handbook* does not set out to tell you exactly where to go: it's your adventure, after all. But it's good to have a general idea of a destination and what you're likely to find when you're there and this is what this book aims to do.

In the final part of this book we include stories from all around the world, not just about the biking but also about the adventures cyclists had on their journeys. It's the old idea that a bike ride isn't just about the riding but also about the places you were able to get to and the people you got to meet – and all because you decided to travel by bicycle.

Planning and preparation

WHAT KIND OF TRIP?

Experienced bike-tourers vary enormously in the extent to which they prepare for a tour. So much depends on the person and their lifestyle. Much more may depend on where you are going and for how long; often, oddly, the shorter trips sometimes demand more planning. A three-week summer tour, for example, might be planned down to each day in order to maximize riding time and see all the sights. Getting into fitness training makes a lot of sense if you have a trip to the Alps planned, or you can expect sore muscles for the first week. It's usually the short tours where you want to do 100km-plus days from the moment you arrive that can be a shock to the system. On a short trip, too, you will want to get your gear just right. It's a bore to waste time shopping for essentials when you should be riding. There is therefore no one answer or magic list which covers all the problems of planning for every bike trip.

If you are setting out on a long ride across a continent, on the other hand, you might instead start the trip off with a low daily mileage and build up stamina gradually. A longer-term traveller can also afford to wait and see what gear and clothing works for them and how much of it they really need. People on long tours often end up sending back a lot of unwanted or unused stuff. It's better to build a collection of touring and camping equipment prior to departure rather than buying everything in one major shopping expedition where you're bound to make mistakes as shop assistants tempt you with camping espresso makers and folding toasters. You're more likely to find out what gear and clothing you like and what you don't really need while on the road. The really long tours are likely to involve all sorts of climates and terrain and therefore changing needs but you can afford to put off those actions or decisions – clothing, kit changes and visa issues – till later in the trip.

The following is a general pre-departure plan of action to help start you off on your adventure:

Pre-departure timetable

Three months before a trip

- Book flights
- Identify what visas/permits are required
- Work out who is going to look after your home/cat/mortgage
- Check your passport (have you at the very least nine months before it expires?)
- Check up on inoculations, etc
- Prepare a basic list of any kit you don't have but think you will need
- If necessary, start thinking about a fitness regime

One month before

- Give your bike/kit some test rides
- Final shopping for spares (allowing time if parts need to be ordered)
- Final service for your bike
- Purchase any medicines (malaria prophylactics etc)

Two weeks before

- Get a bike box from a bike shop
- Start packing
- Tell your wife/husband/partner what you are doing

THE BIG PICTURE: WHY ARE YOU DOING THIS TRIP?

Questions from a bike ride: some answers from my sofa. Everyone I meet asks me the same questions. So here are a few reflections from deep amongst the empty teacups, toast crumbs and general air of lethargic joy that surround me at the moment...

I'd sold the idea to myself so well. The whole package seemed perfect so I grabbed at it and refused to let go. Despite a fantastic group of friends, a flattering job offer, a comfy seat on the gentle conveyor belt of conformity and a girlfriend who, by most accounts, was way out of my league, I decided this was an opportunity I couldn't ignore.

Cycling around the world seemed ideal for me as it would allow me to escape from the looming threat of a normal job. I just couldn't see the sense in plodding all week towards the lone bright light of a Friday night out in a gloomy town. It has taken me time to appreciate that everyone has different dreams and goals and that to judge your own way superior to another's is both arrogant and plain wrong. But I needed to leave England and this seemed the perfect way to do it.

My head was full of luminous visions of Himalayan peaks, Alaskan forests, coconut palms and cheesy sunsets. Every day would be an adventure. Everybody I met would greet me, smiling. Smiling, I would wave back and so would begin wonderful cultural interactions and learning opportunities not available to me queuing for the bus back home. I would be utterly free, with time to potter around the globe living a life of adventure, fun and just enough challenges to keep me high on my patronizing pedestal. For years I'd wanted to be a travel writer. This would be the perfect apprenticeship for me. If I was unable to write a good book after cycling around the world then I'd never be able to do it. In short, the benefits and end products were so appealing that I couldn't wait to get out on the road.

The reality, as anyone who has been following my progress will know, has been rather different. Once on the bike I realized in a wave of terror the grim hopelessness of what I had got myself into. It was too big, too hard. I was too alone. I could never make it. But I could never quit either. I was trapped. The smiling citizens of the world didn't seem to notice me as I rode through their lives. Most were not even smiling. On my first day one smiling citizen called me a w@*#$r! If I had known before I left all that I know now there is no way that I would have had the guts to start. Looking back, I cannot believe that I managed to keep pushing on. Suffice to say it didn't take me long to realize that I wasn't quite as tough as I'd imagined!

Being alone has given me so much time – too much, perhaps – to reflect on these things. Doing this alone was, I still believe, the right decision. It's stress free, it adds to the challenges and leaves you with no excuses if you fail. It opens many doors. However, it is tough, it is more dangerous and there is nobody to pick you up when you're down and struggling to keep life in perspective.

The question that everyone, without exception, asks is the biggest question of all: 'Why are you doing this?' It seems that the answer to the question 'why' is intangible; it's just a feeling of something that you have to do. One of my favourite activities (or inactivities) in life is to slob on a sofa, feet up, and watch football on the telly. But it always feels like such a terrifying waste of precious minutes. Perhaps then, my reason for why I am doing all this is that I'm just trying to earn the right to sit on my sofa!

Alastair Humphreys left the UK in September 2001 for a sponsored charity ride for Hope and Homes for Children. He rode over 50,000 miles on five continents and arrived home in November 2005. His website is 💻 www.roundtheworld bybike.com.

ALONE OR WITH FRIENDS?

Most people don't have to decide whether to set off on their bike trip alone or with a friend; the circumstances of their life will make it very clear that there is, or is not, an obvious companion who is as excited to go as they are. And it is also going to become clear that persuading a reluctant partner to pack up and go with you is fraught with danger. Bike touring is hard work and so are all the non-biking aspects of the trip – finding accommodation, maintaining your health, watching your money, staying in some rough places etc. You will be tested, even if you are going away only for a couple of weeks. Make sure you call for volunteers only and don't press-gang your partner into joining you. But if you are wondering whether to go on a long trip alone or not, the following are some ideas to bear in mind.

Travelling solo

Travelling on your own is harder work than with company; you feel the good times and the bad times all the more because there is no one to share them with. You have to become emotionally self-reliant, calling forth reserves of physical and emotional energy to get you over the hills and through the inevitable hassles. You may know already if you are the type to enjoy a holiday on your own, or the freedom of enjoying your own company may come to you while on the trip. It's not set in stone: you may learn the valuable skills of becoming your own emotional support group while on the road. In fact you will have to, if you have a 'knock-down' experience such as a wallet theft or an accident. Getting over this can take a lot longer when you are on your own, but challenges like these can see you come out of the experience a lot stronger and wiser. These are all good reasons for seeing the trip as a challenge and a chance to grow as you find the resources within you to look after yourself.

Solo travelling is therefore potentially a lot more rewarding in terms of personal growth as well as the freedom you experience. At first you may feel free but quickly tire of having to make every decision, large and small. It is actually a bit of a bore to go through the day thinking 'Shall I stop for a coffee now or in ten minutes?', and until you can still that mental chatter, you are going to feel a little uncomfortable. The urge to talk to others and enjoy their company can overcome shyness in solo travellers and that way you'll find yourself speaking up and making friends. Being on your own, you are far more likely to make the effort, and people are much more likely to befriend you or offer you a meal or a place to stay in the same way that people stop to pick up solo hitchhikers more often than they pick up couples. You will have plenty of quiet nights too, but you'll also get lots of invitations and make many friends on the road. This is especially true among cyclists. Travelling on a bike is an instant conversation piece and other bikers will be on your side. It's very natural to strike up a conversation with other bikers to share information, join them for dinner or ride with them for a few days. In many parts of the world that are popular among cyclists, you will never lack for company.

The last major advantage of travelling alone is that you will never be held back by anyone else's weakness or lack of enthusiasm. You are riding at your own pace, finding it neither fast nor slow, but just right, though it may take a while before you stop pushing yourself and stop measuring yourself by how many miles or 'clicks' you ride each day. Because you are riding where you want at the speed you want, you will never hear a word of complaint and you can slow down and stop whenever you want.

Generally, solo riders travel further each day than couples or groups. There is simply less distraction and not as much reason to hang around. Many otherwise gregarious people take to solo riding quite quickly and would find it difficult to ride with others for more than a few days. The rest, if you'll pardon the self-help claptrap, have to 'learn to be their own best friend'. Once you do that, life on the road becomes a trip with the best riding partner you could hope for.

Despite the many intangible benefits of travelling alone, never fool yourself that it is as safe as travelling with a friend or in a group. If you are planning a great adventure like crossing the Taklamakan Desert in Western China, no doubt you have already developed the skills to make that trip and do not need any advice. However, travelling solo is far less safe, especially so in extreme environments. You have less margin of error, no back-up and little hope of rescue if you get into difficulties. You cannot share essentials like a stove, tools or tent. Be careful not to bite off more than you can chew and even if you are riding on your own, try to get in a group to travel through dangerous or remote areas.

Two's company

You may be planning your trip with your partner or riding buddy and do not need to make a decision about travelling alone or with someone else, but it helps to look at the pros and cons. Travelling with a friend is just like having a long-term relationship back at home – it involves having some limits on your freedom in the hope of greater happiness together. Certainly you are limiting the downsides, because you are there to support each other in times of illness, weakness and loneliness. Having a partner on your trip will give you a lot of support and company at dinnertime every night. Tasks are shared and problems lightened, if not halved. Certainly the weight of the tent is halved, though as discussed later on, a single person is best off with a cosy two-person tent and a couple will appreciate having a two- to three-person tent after just a few days on the road.

Going with a friend is therefore a very practical decision. Safer, easier and a little less intimidating. But like a long-term relationship, you have to be well matched, otherwise it's going to feel like the three-legged race you did at school – slow, ungainly and painful. This is why you need to be on guard against persuading someone to come with you. If they are not as gung-ho as you are, watch out. They may just want to be with you or part of your adventure, but deep inside not be as excited about the trip and be relying on you to take responsibility and make major decisions. At the first sign of trouble a reluctant rider might want to bale out – and besides that trauma, you'll be stuck with a large tent you don't need!

This might be contentious, but the successful couples I have seen on long trips were well matched in terms of abilities and strength. For couples of dissimilar strength but similar aspirations, there are tandems (see p.29). Going with a friend rather than your partner may be a lot easier in that the relationship is simpler and not so demanding. As long as your riding partner is relaxed and easygoing, life will be a lot less stressful. For women, travelling with another woman makes the trip a lot safer.

It is a lot more convenient travelling with other people. There is someone to watch your bike so you can go into a shop or find a toilet in a village. Several times a day the solo rider has to leave his bike to do these necessary things. With a pair of riders, these chores are simpler and safer. I find that two people are less likely to make mis-

Friends on the Friendship Highway, Tibet.

PART 1 – PRACTICALITIES

takes if they share all the major decisions. You are forced to verbalize and rationalize what you decide to do. You have two pairs of eyes to look out for road signs and remember the way. Being able to talk through problems will lead to better decisions.

Differences in strength are common and should not be allowed to divide the two of you. If the stronger rider can learn to be patient, he or she can look at the upside of their position. It's not that they have to wait for their riding partner but that they are being less stressed physically and can afford to take longer breaks while waiting for their partner to catch up, which in turn makes them even stronger. You have to learn to look at the good side of whatever situation you are in, and having to wait for someone is no problem at all. The slower rider needs to stand their ground and not push themselves beyond their limits. It's their trip too and they should not put themselves at risk by overdoing it. Couples and pairs sometimes end up riding a mile apart, but I think this gives up some of the advantages of riding together and introduces the extra hazard of accidentally losing each other. As a couple, it's best to stay within eyesight. A pair of friends might space out a little further than that, but if the slower rider has a puncture or the person in front takes a wrong turn, it is an entirely avoidable but serious hassle to be in. Keeping within eyesight and perhaps having mirrors on your bikes works best to give some time alone during the day and let your friendship recharge a little. If there are still difficulties or differences after all this enforced reasonableness on both sides, a temporary split may not hurt.

Taking a guided tour

We have only 45 minutes at this château and there's another two to see this afternoon!
    Hurried comment from a bike tour group member in the Loire Valley.

Walking down the cobbled streets of the mediaeval Austrian village of Dürnstein, I was confronted by a swarm of guided bike tourists (guided missiles, more like!) buzzing by, none bothering to stop and see the village, even though it's probably the only time in their lives they will have the chance to do so. Guided bike tours tend to offer a lot of activity in their brochures because that's what sells tours to their busy clients on the basis that more is better. If you are reading this book, you are probably of a mind to go touring independently and want the tools and know-how to do it, whereas guided bike tours do everything for you except ride the bike – and even then, many of them have space in the van for you.

Guided bike touring should not automatically be ruled out as inferior, though, just as independent, loaded touring shouldn't be regarded as the ultimate form of travel (though it's well up there!). Have a look at the advantages of a guided bike trip:

- Less organization and research required for the trip
- Probably no need to bring your bike or any gear except clothing
- No need to carry your bags while riding
- A better chance of seeing the best areas without having to ride through the bad ones
- No worries about reservations each night

Those are the good points; everything is done for you and if you're short of time and out of shape, they are significant advantages. If you are working and have only a few weeks, you can pack a lot into a guided tour but whether you see a lot is another matter. You are giving up a lot: the freedom to stop whenever you want and to change your mind or change plans because you met someone, for example, or it rained; and you're also giving up the satisfaction of hauling your own gear and having access to it any time you want. These are all good things.

There are other times, however, when you'll be on your bike, sweating up a long hill loaded to the gunwales and a tour group's sag wagon flies by and perhaps some unloaded and carefree bikers glide past too. Then you might reconsider and think of the reasons why, in some cases, an organized tour makes sense. It may be that, for some rides, you simply cannot carry enough water to make a mountain-bike tour work. The Kokopelli Trail across Utah to Moab is one such trail. It's high desert and, for parts of the route, the only water is in the Colorado River and it's not drinkable no matter what you do to it. At other times, a bike tour organizer or outfitter might have local contacts and expertise that enables them to take you to places you could not get to as an individual. For instance, cycling from Kathmandu to Lhasa (and only in that direction) almost invariably needs group permits. There are also tour groups that let you make the plans and maybe provide a sag wagon too. These outfits might also encourage you to bring your own gear. They will solve your logistical problems and let you keep your freedom and it can be an occasional chance to lighten up from carrying those bags and try something different.

GETTING INFORMATION

The internet has its role to play, particularly around matters of detail, but be careful – a lot of nonsense is written there too. The internet costs nothing and the information you get from it may be worth exactly that.

A few hours spent in the travel section at a bookshop may be a better way to get basic information on countries: what to see, how things work and what they cost, and where to stay in the big cities. Bookshop shelves have never been fuller with travel books and your time may be better spent reading 'offline', considering your options and then filling in the details with research on the internet, especially as regards destinations and roads if you want that level of detail.

Besides internet forums, some governments also keep their information up to date and are surprisingly candid, if a little conservative. The UK's Foreign Office (💻 www.fco.gov.uk) is excellent, while the US Centers for Disease Control and Prevention (💻 www.cdc.gov/travel) is first class for health issues. Don't laugh, but the CIA is actually very knowledgeable in some areas and surprisingly up to date. Try 💻 www.cia.gov/cia/publications/factbook.

Documentation, money and information

PASSPORTS AND VISAS

It's worth repeating that you need to check your passport expiry date. On a long trip, it might be worth starting off with a fresh one. You need lots of space in your passport for visa stamps. It can be a hassle getting those transferred to a new passport en route. Visa research may take some time if you're on a long haul, especially if you're headed to Africa, but that becomes part of the fun as Africa becomes a big board game where you can sometimes move east or west but not to the country to the south, which is where you wanted to go. You can get *most* visas, at least, while travelling and can change direction if your luck runs out. That's normal.

It won't be long before you discover that much of the information on the web is contradictory. As far as visa information goes, that is not entirely surprising because governments themselves are often confused by their own rules and you get different answers and different results depending on where and to whom you apply. The best network of information to get around visa planning problems is the travellers' network, and it works best on Lonely Planet's *Thorn Tree* forum (💻 www.thorntree.lonelyplanet.com); they run 'On Your Bike', a lively section covering bicycle touring. The *Thorn Tree* has been going for years, it's a great place to get up-to-date information about visas and border hassles for the sorts of dodgy countries you might want to visit.

MONEY

Money matters: there's no getting away from it. We travel to get away from material worries and have some time to think on a higher plain, but from the moment you leave home you are a walking safe, carrying your valuables close to your chest or stomach. It is one of the downsides of travelling, wearing your passport and having to be aware of where it is, along with your wallet, all the time. Get some peace of mind by keeping money matters as simple as you can to minimize the risk of loss, otherwise there is going to be too much to think of and you will make a mistake.

Credit cards

Your credit card is there for big purchases such as plane tickets, major gear expenditures and the odd blow-out meal or hotel bill. Otherwise, it shouldn't be used that much, especially in poor countries where it's best kept out of sight to be used in the above cases or only in an emergency.

TWO YEARS ON THE ROAD: ONE COUPLE'S FINANCES

How much did you spend?
Total cost per person per year (all-inclusive) was £4000 [US$7600]. This works out at around £11 a day per person. We budgeted roughly half of this for day-to-day expenses (£5 a day per person). The rest went on a mix of visas, bike parts, postage, sightseeing trips and medical expenses (eg over £100 to visit a good Hong Kong doctor).

Did it vary from place to place?
Yes, a bit: in Europe we spent slightly more although our expenses were almost all on food as we camped each night and did very little sightseeing.

In Russia and Mongolia, we spent less. Food is cheap, camping is free. The big expenses here are the visas and their registration and some 70% duty on imported bike bits. Our Russian friends in Ufa, Omsk and Novosibirsk put us up. This way we could help reduce the expense of cycling in Russia, instead of spending over US$40 a night in business hotels. China is cheap all round, but as we stayed in rooms and enjoyed more tourist activities, our overall bill was just a bit less than in Europe.

Thailand was a bit more expensive. In tourist centres the rooms are cheaper than in Chinese tourist centres, but in the countryside, where we mostly were, hotels are aimed at businesspeople rather than peasants and truck drivers, hence they are twice the price of their Chinese equivalents. There are also so many tempting tourist activities to enjoy.

Where did you get the money from?
This is not a polite question in English society but we are regularly asked this abroad. Hopefully you can see that we are fairly ordinary folk.

Firstly, we sold our house which gave us £17,000 after we had paid back the mortgage. Ju worked as a teacher for six years, some of it part-time, earning on average £17,000 a year and managed to save over £26,000 in that time. Mark worked as an engineer for eight years, earning an average £20,000 per year, but having a more healthy interest in gadgets and beer, he saved £18,000. Mark worked for his company providing documentation and advice and has earned around £10,000 since we set out. He also cashed in a company share option worth £6,000. This amounts to our total funds. There is no secret stash of cash for our return, so we would be unwise to blow it all! For a year before leaving we tried harder to save by buying big sacks of potatoes and making one meal in three a baked-potato-and-butter meal. This was surprisingly effective.

How do you manage the money from abroad?
We have internet banking and most places have cash machines that will take a debit card. This can go wrong if, for example, cards are lost. We have to thank our parents for handling things, such as dealing with banks and paying credit-card bills from our accounts. To do this you need to get the papers signed to give them 'power of attorney'. This has proved vital. It has to be done before you leave on the trip.

Do you realize how lucky you are?
Yes. Most of the folk we meet day to day could not do this sort of thing. Usually they have family commitments. Many are simply too poor or have family memories of extreme poverty that would prevent anyone from selling up their only asset. Having said this, we have met some people who lack the advantages of a Western salary and have nevertheless set off for adventure.

Mark and Juliette McLean left Liverpool in July 2002 and arrived at Mark's uncle's home near Sydney, Australia, in December 2004.
🖥 *www.mark-ju.net.*

Take two credit cards and no more!
Taking more credit cards does not provide much more security overall, it just increases the possibilities for loss and complicates your life. Trips are stressful enough without having to worry about lots of payments. Therefore, take no more than two credit cards and use one for major expenses and keep the other – unused and well hidden – as a backup in case your main card is lost, rejected for some reason or stolen. Make sure you can remember the PIN numbers

for your cards so you can get cash easily from ATMs. The big headache with a credit card is paying bills while you are away. A second headache is the difficulty of seeing the bill before paying it to check what you are being billed for.

There is a trend these days to get just a basic credit card rather than pay extra for services you don't need and a card colour – gold, platinum, etc. I see it differently, I think a prestige card is worth having for the reasons outlined below. Most importantly, you should look for a card that automatically debits charges from your bank account every month, so you are never late with payments and never pay interest: much better than calling home and asking your parents to pay your bills for you. Of course automatic monthly payments require having a good credit limit with your bank but you need that anyway to travel. Travellers are coy about how they get or carry their money, but they aren't travelling on thin air: they've made arrangements so they don't have to carry too much cash.

Getting a 'prestige' card

Prestige cards, ie something more than just plain 'vanilla' credit cards, usually come with travel insurance and better service if you get into trouble. They are more likely to send an emergency card – a temporary credit card enabling you to buy air tickets or pay bills and move on – to an address you give them in the country where you happen to be, rather than sending it to your home address. This is exactly what you want: special attention and service at your time of greatest need. A card with an annual fee and extra benefits will give you an edge if the worst should happen. You will most likely have to get this card through your existing bank but I believe you benefit by putting all your banking eggs in one basket as it gives you more pull with your bank.

Credit card companies care little about individual customers who have no other business with them and are shopping for the best rate. They give minimal service to keep their costs down. Your bank, on the other hand, cares about your business and it's worth getting to know local staff so you can telephone them direct; indeed, it's even worth moving your business to a bank that will deal with you as an individual and not through a call centre. One additional advantage, varying from bank to bank, is the ability to check your credit card purchases when doing internet banking. This is a nice feature, though one has to be a little circumspect about the security of internet cafés, mainly a matter of watching out for people looking over your shoulder. As long as you do not use the internet to order things using your credit card, you are pretty safe if you stick to internet banking due to the latest security features such as randomizing the order of your PIN and passwords when you log on. Be sure to keep emergency phone numbers for lost cards handy.

Debit (ATM) cards

These will probably be your main way to obtain cash in almost every country you visit. Even in the poorest countries, banks in the capital cities will have ATMs (cash machines) and you are bound to be thinking of carrying plenty of cash whenever you are going up-country in places like Uganda or Laos. Start by taking a look at the debit card you've got. Unless it's new and in excellent shape, order a new one with no wear and tear on it and with a long expiry date. A worn-out magnetic strip would render your card useless on a trip. A debit card with a large daily withdrawal limit is what you want, so check your limit is not as low as US$200 or you might have to wait three days in the last town with an ATM just to draw out sufficient cash before heading off into the wilderness. If necessary, ask your bank to increase the daily limit – it does not increase your liability for misuse of the card. The limit set by the ATM where you withdraw cash might be lower than what your bank will give you but it's still worth having a large withdrawal limit.

Debit cards typically charge a small percentage fee for withdrawals but are the most efficient way to access your money. This is because cash withdrawals are much cheaper for banks to manage than physical exchanges of bank notes. You get the wholesale exchange rate when you use a debit card whereas when you exchange cash or travellers' cheques, you get the retail rate, which is much worse. Therefore, do not fret too much over the 2.5% handling fee your bank may charge for withdrawing money overseas. It is a cost of travel and you are probably in a country where costs overall are far less than they are at home. Obviously, if your bank charges a flat fee for cash withdrawals, then take out cash in fairly large amounts to minimize the cost. Your debit card should be protected against fraudulent use just as your credit card is. A thief has to know the PIN number to use it at all, so it is a fairly low risk thing to carry. Safety-wise, it has a huge advantage over all other ways of financing your trip, as it means carrying less cash.

Travellers' cheques

Travellers' cheques are too expensive and inconvenient to be your main source of cash on a trip but they are useful as a backup, something to carry deep in your bags to use when all else fails, and in countries where you do not expect to find ATMs. Travellers' cheques have hidden costs in that you pay the same disadvantageous exchange rate as you would for bank notes whenever you use them and sometimes pay a commission to buy or cash them on top of that. If you are from outside the USA or Eurozone but choose to carry US$ or Euro travellers' cheques due to their greater acceptability, you get hit with that unfavourable exchange rate twice; first when you buy the cheques and again when you cash them. Carrying a large amount of travellers' cheques or cash exposes you to currency fluctuations, so minimize the amount you carry and save them for emergencies.

People like travellers' cheques because of the security – the ability to get a refund if they are stolen. But as with travel insurance, there may be small print in the contract that makes getting a refund difficult or impossible in some circumstances (such as not being able to prove theft) and a delay in getting your hands on the money is inevitable if you are in the back country. Understand the fine print that comes with your travellers' cheques and if you use them, carry them with the idea of diversifying your cash sources so you always have something to fall back on.

Cash

Carrying a bundle of bank notes in hard currency is necessary both in poor countries where you may not see a bank for ages, and as a last-ditch emergency reserve; nothing beats cash.

Carrying a wad of cash adds an extra risk of course, but it gives you ultimate flexibility and can be hidden in your clothing, bags or bike. It's useful for wilderness trips when day after day of small bribes and backhanders may be necessary. The US dollar is still the currency of choice across most of the world – Asia and South America are the most obvious areas where the dollar still rules as a hard currency. It has the edge in Africa too. The Euro is dominant only in Europe, though it has a number of advantages, not least of which is the fact that it is easier to carry a large amount, in terms of value, of Euros, because the notes are thinner and generally available in larger denominations. But weighed against this is the fact that US dollars are usually the currency you need to pay for visas if you are getting them en route.

You will have to hide your cash stash in various places and hopefully not forget where you put it. Hide it in your bags and bike (eg inside the frame) and protect it in plastic bags. Although anyone would think moneybelts (by which we mean a regular-looking belt with a zip on the inside, as opposed to the beige cloth pouch beloved of most backpackers) are obvious ways to carry money and thus vulnerable, travellers report that bandits, muggers or border guards rarely spot money-belts. Even if you have to 'drop trou' in a full-on strip search, your uniformed antagonists don't usually notice that tell-tale zip on the back of a belt.

KEEPING YOUR VALUABLES SAFE

All evidence for the safest way to carry money and valuables is anecdotal, but every time I hear of a theft or pick-pocketing, the most common factor was that the victim was not wearing their money-belt or pouch. It needs to be on your body somewhere, because it is much less safe if carried even in a shoulder bag. Your main stash should never be visible and should be brought out from its hiding place only in your tent or hotel room or on a visit to the bank. Draw out your 'day money' each morning and keep that in a purse. If you want, add your fake wallet with expired credit cards if you are in bandit country. Your purse or wallet needs to be fairly tight against your body so you are aware of it at all times. If you are carrying only 'day money', you can use pockets and not worry too much if you do lose it, but the important stuff should be in a money-belt or neck/waist pouch.

In my own experience, too many times I found I was leaving zipped pockets open till I was pick-pocketed once on a bus in Nepal, when my wallet was in a loose pocket in cargo pants down near my knee. I discovered the loss moments after it happened, raised hell, offered a reward to the crowd gathering round me and got my cash back – though the wallet and cards had already been chucked away by then.

Nowadays I wear Fjällraven trousers with zips **and** strong Velcro for pockets up on the thigh for carrying day money. Trousers with secret pockets are great, but remember eyes are always on you when you go to your pockets, and a pouch behind the waistband is best.

Using ATMs

Withdrawing cash from an ATM overseas is probably no more dangerous than it is back home, possibly less so, but the consequences of a mugging or theft overseas are much worse, so be alert when using ATMs. Just as at home, don't use ATMs at night. Don't wait until you are out of cash and have no choice when or where to get money either: think ahead and withdraw cash during daylight hours, choosing machines inside the bank if you can and looking out for signs of tampering with the machine. Try to have a friend with you when you use them. As the Americans say, the price of liberty is eternal vigilance and this applies to the liberty to travel. Wandering saddhus in India are thoroughly admirable but the rest of us have to use money on our trips and thus can't forget it, not for a moment.

Health precautions, inoculations and insurance

INOCULATIONS

If you have not travelled to developing countries before, a visit to the travel health clinic can be an expensive proposition involving several repeat visits for follow-up doses of vaccines. The good thing is that after your first trip, many of these immunizations are good for several years and you will not need to repeat these courses for subsequent trips.

Medical guidance can be given only by your doctor or health clinic staff and this section provides suggestions only. In some cases, you have choices whether to choose a large and expensive vaccination or just a small booster, as is the case with rabies. Only you can decide, based on your appetite for risk. The World Health Organization (🖥 www.who.int) and the US Center for Disease Control (🖥 www.cdc.gov) have copious information and advice on the matter of disease and information. Much of it will depend on where you travel, but there are a number of immunizations that are good for all travel, no matter where you go. You may well be up to date on some of these immunizations but that first trip to the health clinic is the time to sort out which you have or have not had, and get them all listed on a vaccination certificate so you remember when you had them.

The most common **immunizations** are:
- **Hepatitis A and B** These can now be taken together but are expensive (although the Hepatitis A shot is available free in the UK on the NHS). They need to be started six months before you set off (as the vaccination involves two shots, six months apart). Highly effective and good for ten years, which makes it fair value for peace of mind.
- **Tetanus** The disease itself is omnipresent in spore form and the risk of catching it from dirty wounds is high. Cyclists taking falls are likely candidates and the adult booster jab is one of those you can get and and then forget about for a very long time.
- **Rabies** Cyclists, of course, are an 'at risk' group. The reason to take this vaccination is that once the dog has bitten you you'll need to get to a clinic ASAP for a series of big jabs. Having the immunization before your trip buys you a couple of days of precious time if you are bitten in a remote area (see Igor Kovse's story on p.242).

- **Yellow fever** It's not the jab you need so much as the certificate to say you have been inoculated which is necessary for those countries that require it for entry – mostly in Africa.
- **Typhoid, polio** and **diphtheria** These are vaccinations you may have already had – polio has almost disappeared but is present in countries such as India. Typhoid and diphtheria are uncommon but widespread and typhoid is prone to appearing as an epidemic. These three should be checked off as 'up to date' on your visit to the clinic. Note that typhoid, like any other water-borne disease, is most common during the monsoon season, so make sure your plans take this into account (it's not much fun riding in a monsoon, so you might want to avoid this season altogether!).
- **Japanese B encephalitis** and **meningitis** These are regional diseases and not widespread but can be fatal and therefore worth considering, depending on destination.

AVOIDING OTHER HEALTH HAZARDS

Malaria is the biggest headache for travellers in affected areas. It's a thoroughly unsatisfactory situation – the expense of buying the tablets, the fact that you have to buy them in advance of a trip and carry them with you, remembering to take them while you travel, and the side-effects of using them if you do. The right advice and pills may be hard to find and there is a risk of buying counterfeit medicines and pills in some countries, especially India and Thailand, so you are better off paying full price at home for the pills you need. The prescription is always specific to an area; it's not a good idea to self-medicate based on leftover tablets from a previous trip.

Take malaria seriously – it's one of the world's biggest killers. Reducing your exposure to malarial mosquitoes is very important as malaria prophylactics are not 100% effective and you can never guarantee that you won't be exposed to malaria. Long-sleeved shirts, bandannas and thick socks are all good ideas for clothing in malarial zones. It's hot at first but you will get used to wearing long sleeves and long trousers, and if you take a look at what the locals are wearing, it's probably what they do anyway. Long trousers (along with socks) are also good for numerous other reasons, such as preventing scratches, sunburn and tick bites.

Which repellent you use is a matter of personal choice. Deet has a long shelf life and is very effective in concentrated form. If you have had no reactions to it you are probably safe using a stronger mix rather than the 10% Deet formulas common in Europe that seem pretty ineffective. Where possible, spray it on your clothes rather than your skin, for instance on your socks or on a bandanna that you wear round your neck. Deet is nasty stuff, though, and the more you can use clothing instead of deet, the better off you are. The same is true for permethrin, a chemical that kills insects. You will read suggestions to dip your mossie net in permethrin and there are travellers' clothes that are treated with it, but it is a powerful neurotoxin, a possible carcinogen in humans and is bad for the environment. A long-term traveller would therefore do well to avoid it altogether and to minimize the need to use Deet, too.

SUNBURN AND SUNSTROKE

Sunburn is still under-rated as a risk by light-skinned Westerners who are most at risk from it. Skin-cancer rates are rising and the risk is much higher in tropical zones and areas in the southern hemisphere where the ozone layer has been damaged. Hats and clothing are better solutions than using sun cream, though you need to use both. There's a tendency to think that once you have a good suntan, you don't need to cover up or use cream, but it's not true; incremental doses of UV cause incremental cell damage, leading to an increased risk of skin cancer.

Sunstroke is a related risk. Riding in temperatures up to and over normal body heat is not unusual in much of the world. Sunstroke occurs from overheating. Adequate hydration is an important part of preventing overheating and therefore sunstroke: avoiding riding in the heat altogether is another solution. Recent research proved the blindingly obvious truth that plain water rehydrates the body faster than anything else – including so-called rehydration drinks. Sugar and minerals in those drinks slow down the body's absorption of water. Glucose drinks and oral rehydration solutions are good for recovery from dysentery and diarrhoea that lead to dehydration but are not as helpful for healthy people who have lost fluids. Eating plenty of fruit is the best way of absorbing minerals.

ALTITUDE SICKNESS

If you are going to ride at altitude it's well worth becoming fully acquainted with the two types of altitude sickness and the symptoms of and solutions to them. It's often possible to buy medicine locally (Diamox) and use it before you show symptoms, as guided groups sometimes do. Diamox increases the rate of respiration to support a greater intake of oxygen which, in turn, hastens dehydration, so monitor your fluid intake when using it.

As with all pharmacy items, when buying them in poor countries be as sure as you can that you are buying the real thing by going to a reputable clinic. Clinics in the developing world are often the recipients of donated medicines near the end of their shelf-life; always check the labels for expiry dates.

There is evidence that the greatest number of victims of altitude sickness are people travelling in guided groups, where there is time pressure and possibly peer pressure to continue ascending faster than is safe. The clear implication is that ascending too fast is the cause and that the safest solution is to descend if the symptoms do not rapidly clear up. Avoid reaching for the Diamox too soon and instead pay attention to the fundamentals of altitude. A day or two extra of rest is nothing in the long term yet will make a huge difference in terms of combatting altitude sickness.

DIET AND HEALTH

Additional stress is often placed on the body by cyclists who eat poorly while on a long trip. Inadequate nutrition is the first concern. Your muscles have additional caloric, vitamin and mineral requirements when you ride and your diet may not be up to the task. Reducing your daily distances is the simplest answer but is often not possible. Cramming in extra nutrients is the usual solution but this is fraught with problems. When you ingest too high a dose of water-soluble vitamins, the excess is usually flushed away naturally but there is a risk, particularly with some vitamins like vitamin C, that too much of it can cause kidney stones. There are also cases where the body becomes accustomed to large doses of vitamins and receives no extra benefit, but suffers a deficiency once the mega-dosing stops. It is impossible to overdose from vitamins absorbed from food and this is the best way of getting nutrition. Again, overloading the body is an additional stress.

Piling on the carbs or protein is another form of stress for your body just when it should be resting after a long day's ride. Riders often resort to junk food for quick sugar fixes but sugary foods cause a surge in insulin levels and are another source of fatigue and imbalance. Far better to eat a balanced diet that allows for slow absorption of calories in line with a steady burning of those calories while riding. Try to avoid gimmick biker food products such as energy bars; these are just expensive junk food that ruin teeth and taste buds. Always go for fruits, preferably those you can peel, as well as nuts, seeds and beans and rely on multi-vitamins only in situations where the local diet is limited and inadequate. Trying local food is all part of the experience of bike touring; it's a chance to learn more about food and food culture and talk to people in the process, rather than relying on home-bought foods as if you were on a trip into outer space.

CONCLUSION: TAKE IT EASY

Cyclists' health troubles all have something in common: the sufferers are usually overdoing it. A long-term traveller should never be in a hurry. Overextending yourself puts you in situations where you have to cut corners and over-stress the body: riding in the heat, at altitude, working up a sweat, etc. The truly competent travellers are those who keep a steady, relaxed pace. They stay well within their range and so have a good reserve of stamina and health to fall back on if they really need it. Riding for long distances day after day runs down your body's reserves of energy and nutrients and makes you far more susceptible to illness. Allowing plenty of rest gives your body time to recover and, if necessary, produce extra muscle to cope with the increased work.

Most cycling ailments should be treated early on. Muscle pains may subside as your body adapts but are a warning sign that should be heeded. Joint pains and soreness are indications of overuse, postural problems or evidence that you need to change your bike's set-up. Stay within a comfortable range of exertion in terms of daily duration as well as intensity. Stretched and relaxed muscles are more supple and less likely to suffer damage than weakened or over-stressed muscles that are close to their elastic limit. This suppleness of muscle tissue can be cultivated by stretching and looking after your body and works best when accompanied by a supple and open frame of mind, ready to change plans and adapt to changing situations. This means listening to your body and paying attention to it – the very opposite of a Tour de France 'mind over matter' approach. A bicycle tour, no matter how relaxed, is an intensely physical thing. Try not to see your body as a machine, something distinct from your conscious self. Willpower is an important strength to keep you going on a long ride but use it to tackle the mental pressures of a long ride, not to force your body to keep going when it's telling you to rest.

DEALING WITH DOGS: DIPLOMACY – THEN WAR

Cyclists and postmen provide great delight to dogs but once you get into the countryside and then into poorer countries, dogs seem to have less of a sense of humour and can be downright dangerous. Pyrenean dogs, for instance, are bred and trained to protect sheep; dogs in Turkey play a similar role. These dogs are not pets and aren't playing if they challenge you. Tibetan mastiffs are thankfully rare in that country, but there are plenty of aggressive and underfed cross-breeds. In India, rabies kills around 20,000 people every year, many of whom will have been bitten by dogs.

Many small and medium-sized dogs which are strays or pets take a liking to bikes and will chase and bark but for the most part are not threatening. Speeding away only provides them with a good chase, while getting off the bike and walking spoils the fun and they will quickly lose interest. It's hard to out-run a dog but if a burst of speed helps you avoid the dog in the first place, that should be your first option. Calmness is always the best approach as dogs respond to aggression and it's well known that they can sense fear. Stand facing the dog (the sneaky ones will attack from your rear) but look away, remaining calm. Don't give ground or bend down (except to pick up ammo; see below). You might use your bike as a shield but you should also keep some room in case you need to give a hard kick. If the diplomatic approach fails, choose from the following weapons:

Ultrasonic dog-repellents There are two brands, **Dog-Dazer** and **Dog-off**, and both are available on either side of the Atlantic. They use the same 9v power pack and work on the same principle. Some bikers swear by them but I have found neither gives guaranteed protection, especially against big dogs. Some dogs, especially the old, are deaf or will not hear the ultrasonic sound in high winds. Some are trained to ignore it and a few become more aggressive when they hear it because it is painful to them. If a dog is barking its head off, it's unlikely to hear a Dog Dazer.

Sticks A pretty reliable weapon for a dog-fight. Dogs know that and will likely back off if you wave a stick at them. But you have to carry the stick, which is not so easy – and it needs to be a substantial stick.

Stones An excellent choice but you will have to carry a fair number and keep them handy. Dogs are often deterred by seeing you bend down to pick up stones and getting ready to throw them. Make sure you're a good shot and follow standard army practice by aiming for the ringleader. A catapult might be frowned on by border control or police, but you're hardly like to be locked up for it and it would be an effective but dangerous weapon against dogs.

Sprays These are unlikely to be allowed to cross borders if discovered and are illegal in many countries while being openly sold in sports shops in others. I have seen shepherds' dogs who recognized a spray being aimed at them and backed off. Pepper or CS gas sprays are dangerous things to everyone around them and should be kept secure in case kids or other innocents get hold of them. Watch out for wind direction before firing and choose sprays that emit a jet rather than a mist.

The iron gol A regional speciality suggested by Dave Wodchis and well known by Tibetan dogs – its appearance alone may deter them. Found in markets in Lhasa, the iron gol is a metal bar on the end of a leather belt. A little heavy, and you might want to wear your bike helmet while swinging it around!

What this should tell you is that there is no perfect or foolproof solution to the threat from dogs, partly because all dogs are different and partly because of the risks and disadvantages associated with each. Weapons are always going to be dangerous to *you*, too, except for the Dog Dazer and Dog-off, though these are unreliable and battery-dependent. Be wary of becoming violent and paranoid towards dogs, for they can become a source of additional stress on a long trip.

You must not injure or harm a dog unless your life depends on it. Try dog diplomacy, calmness, ignoring them and acting superior. Don't try friendliness with dogs from the developing world, the health risk is too great. It is wiser to try and ward them off when they are 50 metres away. If the dog snaps or bares teeth or has its back hair up and you get into a fight, my advice both from personal experience and first-hand accounts is that you should fight as if your life depends on it.

What kind of bike?

The range of bikes available these days is more diverse than ever before as bike designs have become ever more specialized. In the old days you might have gone touring on whatever bike you found without a second thought (read Jean Bell's story of his 1929 ride on p.204), but the choice of bikes nowadays is huge. Ride around any city and you will see commuters on mountain bikes, racing bikes, city bikes and hybrids. For short tours you can pick whatever style appeals to you, but on long rides far away from home, this approach won't do. You must choose a bike based on its function as you won't get far on a bike that can't carry you and your gear comfortably and efficiently.

The logical place to start your search is with bikes designed specifically for touring. If your budget or preferences suggest something different, there are other options such as buying an old mountain bike or converting the bike you already have (see p.41), but begin your search by looking at touring bikes and their advantages.

TOURING BIKES

Touring bikes have been around for a long time, though are not as popular as they once were, as a generation of riders has grown up having never ridden a bike with dropped handlebars. However, they're still the choice of experienced touring riders because they have the following three advantages, factors you should consider in any bike you're considering taking on tour.

DO I NEED SUSPENSION?

There are hard-core bike tourers who are impervious to pain and see suspension as a luxury, or worse, a liability as it's mechanically complex, needs maintenance, and is impossible to repair without specific tools. However, mere mortals find suspension forks reduce jarring on the wrists and improve a bike's handling by keeping the wheel in better contact with rough ground. This means reduced stress and risk of injury and after more than a decade of development there are many reliable units out there. Many riders with experience on the world's roughest roads such as Kym McConnell (see his *Tibet Overland*, p.286) actually recommend front suspension for unpaved roads as it works well on washboarded surfaces and saves you and your bike from being rattled to pieces.

In general, though, if you're on a several month-long trip, most of your riding will be on paved roads and you can make do with rigid forks, which when combined with a touring frame, have some give. Avoid fitting a suspension fork to a bike not designed for it; if you want front suspension, buy a bike that is 'suspension-ready'.

The old problems of fitting front racks to a suspension fork have now been solved, but make sure that your particular fork is a reliable and low maintenance unit – some require adjustment or lubrication every 40 hours – that's once a week for a touring rider. Avoid rear suspension altogether – no touring bike would come with it. It's too heavy, complicated, and unsuited to fitting strong rear racks.

Touring Bike Anatomy

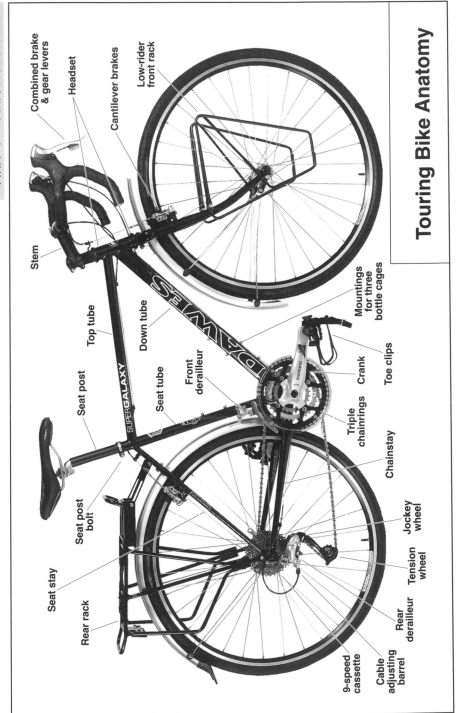

Combined brake & gear levers

Headset

Cantilever brakes

Low-rider front rack

Stem

Top tube

Down tube

Seat post

Seat tube

Front derailleur

Mountings for three bottle cages

Crank

Toe clips

Triple chainrings

Chainstay

Seat post bolt

Jockey wheel

Seat stay

Tension wheel

Rear rack

Rear derailleur

9-speed cassette

Cable adjusting barrel

Comfort You're going to be riding your bike for perhaps 6-8 hours a day, for weeks or possibly months. Comfort will matter to you every second on the road, and touring bikes have frame geometry designed for comfort over long distances – something you may not appreciate until well into your trip.

Frame strength Touring bike frames are designed to carry heavy loads without excessive flexing, while being able to absorb road shock. Sure, mountain bikes often have stiffer frames, but the ride quality is harsher.

Stability Mountain and racing bikes are designed to be nimble, but touring bikes give a much less twitchy ride, especially when heavily loaded, which allows you to spend more time enjoying the views and less time concentrating on steering and balancing. The longer wheelbase also keeps the panniers well clear of your feet while pedalling.

Of these three factors, comfort is probably the most important, though all are vital. A comfortable ride helps avoid neck and wrist injuries that can bring your trip to a premature end. If you're tempted by other types of bike, bear in mind that problems with comfort often don't appear until after a week or more's riding.

Within the world of touring bikes, there are a couple of options to think through before narrowing down your choice. For people who are selling up and going travelling for a year or more, a made-to-order bike makes sense, as the longer the ride, the more critical the three factors and the expense of a custom bike is spread over a longer period. With a bike made to your specifications you also avoid additional expense in upgrading components or gear on a machine not designed to exactly suit your needs.

Over the last few years, touring bikes have adopted styles and componentry from mountain bikes; these machines are sometimes marketed as 'expedition bikes'. This is partly a marketing ploy catering to buyers' rugged aspirations (much as some drivers are attracted to 4WDs), but expedition bikes are also a response to bike tourers wanting to tackle the Himalaya or to ride across Africa rather than spend a week or two riding in the Dordogne. Expedition touring bikes tend to have 26" wheels, not so much for strength as for the ease of finding replacement tubes and tyres, (a wide range of off-road tyres are available in 26"). The gear components on many touring bikes and all expedition bikes are nowadays the same as found on mountain bikes, with extremely low gearing and tough construction.

Brakes too are derived from mountain bikes, though don't expect to find disc brakes on touring bikes yet – the extra complexity makes them unsuitable for touring and they make rack fitting more complex. If you're certain you will only be riding on roads or won't be carrying much gear, a more traditional touring bike with slimmer and taller 700c wheels will ride faster than a 26"-wheel bike, and there is no reason why the 700c cannot be made just as strong. If you have plans to go off-roading or riding extensively in the developing world, then narrow your search to 26" wheel bikes with adequate clearance for tyres up to 2" wide.

MOUNTAIN BIKES

The big sellers in the world of bikes in the past fifteen years have been mountain bikes and it's very common to see them on tour. They have an instant appeal when you first ride one – nippy and responsive, with gear controls and powerful brakes right where you want them. Be wary of this showroom appeal – mountain bikes these days are designed to sell, and often have lighter wheels with fewer spokes than touring bikes. Like running in lightweight trainers, these wheels will give good acceleration but are often not strong enough for loaded touring, where tougher 'boots' are better. A mountain bike will not be quite as fast as a touring bike, but it's a tour and not a race and this may not be a drawback to you.

Wide mountain bike handlebars give you a lot of leverage and control for turning on rough roads or steep hills when you're carrying a heavy load, but tend to be less comfortable for longer trips. The stretched-out riding position can also give neck problems over time. Mountain bike frames are generally strong enough for touring, but it's harder to carry your gear as the chainstays (see diagram p.26) are shorter than on a touring bike, bringing your rack and hence your panniers closer to your pedalling feet. Mountain bikes are also less stable than touring bikes, but adding loaded panniers usually reduces this problem. The gears and brakes (though not necessarily disc brakes) are well suited to loaded touring, so if you find your mountain bike is comfortable on long day rides, test it for a week or so and if it still passes the comfort test, you may well have a tourer.

Shopping for a new mountain bike for touring is becoming harder as the complexity of these bikes increases – they are moving further away from an ideal touring bike, whereas the original mountain bikes were simple and suitable designs. Disc brakes and suspension are not the only question marks – you also need to consider the frame material as mountain bikes nowadays are almost always made from aluminium.

Things to consider
- If the rear tyre is close to the down tube you may have heel clearance problems when fitting a rack and panniers.
- Talking of racks, are there braze-ones (eyelets) to fit racks?
- Does the bike have disc brakes, which may hinder fitting a rack?
- Is the bottom bracket so high you feel unstable while riding?
- Can the handlebars be raised for comfort and are you stretched too far forward for a comfortable riding position?
- Are the wheels or spokes exotic in materials or form, which would be difficult to repair in the field?

If you have problems with racks but everything else checks out, consider using a trailer to carry your gear. See p.53 for your best option.

TREKKING BIKES

Trekking bikes were the first recognition by manufacturers that people were taking their bikes to more remote places and needed something more rugged than a traditional tourer. They are similar to expedition bikes but have been around since the mid-nineties and are a common sight in continental Europe.

The frame design is not that different from a mountain bike but is a little more upright to reduce neck strain, and comes with multi-position handle-bars. Trekking bikes typically come ready for departure on your big tour, with front and rear racks and often mudguards and dynamo lights as well. As a buyer, you save some money by having all these accessories already fitted, though on cheaper models you may want to upgrade crucial items like racks, which may not be as rugged as they look. The Koga-Miyata (see p.33) is the best example of a trekking bike, but there are numerous makes to be found, especially in the Netherlands and Germany.

TANDEMS

'....will speed your relationship along in the direction it's going. Either up or down'
Tandem owner Lee Taylor

Tandems are an interesting possibility for two riders who have equal enthusiasm but unequal physical strength and who want to ride together. As the quote above suggests, a decision to ride a tandem is primarily a relationship issue, as for most people a tandem's good points are outweighed by the bad: expense, weight, and the whole set up.

Tandem attracting attention in Bishkek.
© Cass Gilbert

STEEL vs ALUMINIUM FRAMES

Look in any bike shop in Europe or the USA and it's hard to find a bike made of steel. Yet steel remains the most commonly used material in bike frames around the world – think of all those bikes in India and China, for example. This is a key to how you should think when choosing your bike frame material. The steel used in good quality bikes is known as chromoly or 4130. Chromoly is an alloy containing small amounts of chromium, molybdenum and other elements added for increased strength while leaving it an easy material to weld. It's great for bicycle frames because of its ability to flex and so absorb shock rather than suffering metal fatigue which can lead to failure.

Chromoly steel is therefore the obvious choice for bike tourers who want to wander far. Should you need one, steel welders exist in any small town; aluminium welding is rare and specialized. Whatever the virtues of aluminium – either its looks, or the few ounces saved – it's an unnecessary and entirely avoidable risk.

Aluminium is a great choice for ounce-counting mountain bikers or racers and seems to be preferred by bike manufacturers for the exotic shapes they can form from it. Its stiffness may help minimize frame flex in bikes designed for front shocks, but these are very specialized requirements that should not concern people choosing a touring bike. Nonetheless, aluminium has its followers and companies like Cannondale, which only make bicycles from aluminium, produce bicycles well thought out for touring.

A note of caution: when buying a bike, less knowledgeable sales people may tell you a bike is made from 'alloy', yet either chromoly or aluminium could be referred to as alloys. Chromoly frames are nearly always made of uniform shaped tubing, while aluminium is often made from different gauges, usually wider in diameter than chromoly. The frame material is nearly always identified somewhere on the bike frame; tapping an aluminium frame will give a dull click as opposed to chromoly's more audible ring.

PART 1 – PRACTICALITIES

FOLDING BIKES

Folding bikes are aimed at yachties, motorhomers and of course urban commuters who often take a part of their journey on public transport, but can a folder make a suitable tourer? Realistically, no, in the conventional long distance, self-sufficient sense. Their modest carrying capacity limits their range, and the typical 30-second fold-down time into ingenious bundles of tubes is of little use in a blizzard on the Karakoram Highway. Small wheels are designed for nippy urban manners and compactness, but for longer distances on less-than-perfect roads, a conventional touring bike is far superior.

However, perhaps you love your folder, have the urge to travel but don't want to experience the world by spending weeks pedalling vast distances between cities. A good example would be Inter-railing around Europe, travelling round Australia by bus or plane, or even following the Silk Road or Trans-Siberian Railway (see p.287). Sure, you could buy or rent bikes locally, but having your own folder offers an enviable autonomy, mobility and a touch of smugness! You can store your bike out of sight in your hotel room or tent, avoid airline surcharges and tedious packing regulations, and even hop into a taxi for the boring bits. You have the independence without the sore butt and 1000-mile stare.

Most folding bikes are not up to the rigours of long-range touring, but weighing in at around 11kg, three models are light and compact enough to be genuinely hand portable, while sharing a renowned build quality: Britain's Brompton (below), Germany's Birdy (right) and Bike Friday's New World Tourist (far right).

Tandem riding is of course more companionable and the bikes themselves are faster if the riders are willing to work on their coordination, but in any case, in terms of wind resistance and drag, tandems are more efficient and can be an exciting way to ride. The extra weight creates a lot more stress on the frame, so it's all the more important to get a high quality model that is well thought-out for your trip. Wear and tear is much higher, but stronger components offset that factor. The need for high quality components and frame means that your expedition tandem may cost as much as a decent second-hand car.

There will be a lot more weight on a touring tandem, and less space for two people's gear. Tandem riders sometimes choose to tow a trailer, but that creates a bike that feels as long as a train. The length of a tandem is also going to be a problem when transporting it by air or train, as special bike carriages or designated bike racks have replaced the guard's vans of old. One expensive solution is to buy a tandem fitted with S&S couplings; high quality couplings built into the frame enabling dismantling for transporting. S&S couplings are available on made to order high quality tandems.

For a lot of riders – and that includes many happy couples – a tandem is just too much togetherness for six to eight hours a day. Having separate bikes offers more spontaneity and freedom – the very factors that attract most people to cycling – so you both need to be very sure about tandem riding before buying one, and certainly before undertaking a long tour.

FOLDING BIKES

The Brompton is justly regarded as a prince among folders, while the Birdy gives a slightly livelier ride and a 'big bike' feel, though it's harder-to-retyre 18" wheels are not much larger than the Brompton's 16"s. Bromptons are steel framed, Birdys are aluminium, and although the Birdy has a higher spec and a price up to 50% above a Brompton, both brands are high quality and well thought-out designs. If you are willing to sacrifice some portability, you can get a substantially more capable touring bike in Bike Friday's New World Tourist (far right). Built to order in the US, these 20"-wheel bikes are designed to get round bicycle surcharges common on US airlines while riding just as well as normal tourers. The New World Tourist is Bike Friday's most popular model, coming with various spec levels which add up to between $1000 and $2000. Bike Friday's 'H' style handlebar, effectively a straight bar with bar-ends, works well for touring. A number of touring tandems are also available.

🖳 www.birdybike.com,
🖳 www.bromptonbicycle.co.uk
🖳 www.bikefriday.com.

PART 1 – PRACTICALITIES

RECUMBENTS

Recumbent bikes are a somewhat eccentric choice for a long tour, but they have their devotees and many have gone round the world. The comfort of the seating position is often the prime attraction although your first half an hour on a recumbent will feel like learning to ride all over again. The ergonomics are arguably superior for touring as your weight is distributed over a much wider area, eliminating pressure points and sore wrists.

Recumbents are a natural choice for cyclists who have had repetitive stress injuries such as wrist or neck trouble. Because the rider is leaning back, the view is much better than on an ordinary bike. The only blind spot – and it's a serious one – is the stretch of road immediately in front of the bike which is blocked by your feet. Most recumbents have a smaller front wheel to give better forward visibility and a more upright riding position, but small wheels themselves are more vulnerable to potholes.

Other downsides to riding a recumbent are significant. Even recumbent fans acknowledge that they are slower up hills as they are heavier and you cannot stand on the pedals. They are also more complex than other bikes and their lower riding position and low-speed instability makes driving in traffic a little nerve-wracking. Though not an obvious choice for riding on rough, rutted tracks, these bikes have sometimes performed well in surprising places like Tibet, where their low wind-resistance has proved invaluable. Only look at a recumbent designed for touring – see p.35 for two recommended models.

Choosing a new bike

The longer the trip, the more you are spreading the fixed cost of the bike and the more you need the best quality, especially if you are carrying a lot of gear to last you through all kinds of climate and conditions. If you are going to be on the bike almost every day for a year or two, it makes a lot of sense to get the best you can. High-quality components will pay off in terms of greater reliability and longer service life and a top-notch frame will pay off every second you are on the bike in terms of fit and comfort. This is not an exhaustive list of models by any means, but covers the main styles of bike available in major markets. Current prices are given in the source currency, but these will of course vary and so should only be used comparatively, model to model. Bike components often change from year to year, and even within model years. Reading prices is further complicated in that the same model from the big US-based producers like Trek and Cannondale, though widely available round the world, will be much less expensive in the US than in Europe (something that can be said for a lot of equipment too).

There are no new mountain bikes in this list. Buying an old mountain bike to convert to a touring bike makes a lot of sense, especially financial sense (see p.40), but buying a brand-new mountain bike and trying to adapt it involves extra work and expense for what is often a sub-optimal solution. Many of these bikes have the best of mountain-bike design and technology combined with frame geometry and gear that works best for touring.

Thorn eXp variant (see box opposite).
© Luke Skinner

THORN EXP

Thorn (⌨ www.sjscycles.com) is Britain's – and arguably the world's – top builder of full-on expedition bikes, though it's a tiny market and Thorn's eXps are assembled to order from frames built in-house in six sizes, each with a choice of three cockpit lengths. The rest of the componentry is all à la carte, including the paint job, with an assembled bike including Thorn's own immensely strong chromoly racks going for around £2100. Thorn is adamant that expedition bikes should be built around 26" wheels and using the best chromoly tubing made especially for Thorn in sections which have a tapered internal gauge rather than conventional butted tubing.

Thorn bikes are not just tough but give a really sweet ride even in the toughest cycling conditions. Features are too numerous to list but the forks are the best there are and the frame is incredibly well thought out. An eXp is everything you could want in an expedition bike... if you can afford it. If an

BIKE REVIEW – THORN EXP

Which bike to choose? This was a question which occupied our thoughts a great deal in the months before setting off to cycle 30,000km across Africa. Now, 12,000km and nine months into the trip, we're convinced we made the right choice.

We first came across Thorn at a cycling Expo in London the year before we planned to leave and were immediately impressed by the knowledge of the staff manning the stand. Having contacted all the big players, we'd become accustomed to dealing with salespeople to whom a bike was simply another product to sell. This was something different – people who knew about their bikes and were passionate about cycling.

It soon became clear that these were the bikes for us. Everything from the choice of material for the frame to the tape on the handlebars had been carefully thought about and lovingly assembled. There was an answer to every question and the answers made sense. Despite the frankly horrifying price tag, we took the plunge.

Six weeks later we made the trip out to Bridgwater in Somerset to collect the bikes. We discussed pedals, saddles, spare parts and admired the shiny new paintwork. The bikes we eventually bought were almost identical to the popular eXp but ours, a non-production model, had a slightly longer wheelbase which would enable us to carry heavy, bulky loads of equipment, food and water without the bikes becoming unwieldy.

Over the weeks before departure we took them out for numerous test rides, gradually got used to the SPD pedals (which we'd been persuaded were for the best, despite never having used them before!) and quickly came to realize we'd made a good choice.

The hand-built wheels and Schwalbe Marathon XR tyres have stood the test of Africa's notorious roads, Shimano XT chainsets have performed admirably despite the liberal doses of sand and, above all, every query, however stupid on our part, has been answered thoroughly and quickly. Fingers crossed for the next 18,000km or so!

Luke Skinner

eXp is beyond your means but the idea appeals, consider their Nomad for around £1500 or the 14-speed Rohloff hub gear-equipped (see p.34) Raven starting at around £1200. People have sold their houses to buy Thorns and take off on a world tour; see Mark Mclean's story on p.16. Thorn bikes are only available to order from their factory in Bridgwater, Somerset.

Other specialist possibilities in the UK include Orbit Cycles (🖳 www.orbit-cycles.co.uk), Hewitt's Cheviot (🖳 www.hewittcycles.co.uk), and Roberts (🖳 www.robertscycles.com), whose £1500 Roughstuff is the choice of roving writer Josie Dew. In the US, Rivendell (🖳 www.rivendellbicycles.com) makes the Atlantis, a handsome, traditionally made lugged-frame expedition bike, assembled to each customer's order.

KOGA-MIYATA WORLD TRAVELLER

Dutch manufacturer Koga-Miyata (🖳 www.koga.com) has been making distinctive high-end trekking bikes with aluminium frames for years, and their strongest bike is now the 26"-wheeled World Traveller. These models appeal to people who want a bike that comes fully loaded with the best there is. For around €2000, this bike has everything you could possibly want, including

The Flying Dutchman – Koga-Miyata World Traveller.

lights, mudguards, bottle cages, pump and stand. Componentry is almost entirely high-end Shimano Deore XT; to upgrade a cheaper bike to this standard would cost a lot more. Koga also produces similar models with larger 700c wheels and dropped handlebars if you prefer that style.

Thorn Raven on tour in the Himalaya.

THORN RAVEN

Though Rohloff 14-speed hubs have been around for a few years, sales haven't really taken off – until the Thorn Raven came out. Designed throughout for the Rohloff hub, the Raven might well be the ideal world touring bike, combining Thorn's expedition bike features with the ultra-reliable Rohloff. Long beefy stays and tubes made of oversized chromoly steel and a fork that is the best in the business for touring (a suspension fork is also available) are the foundation, the rest is chosen by the customer. Ravens come in two different lengths as well as different sizes so a perfect fit is guaranteed.

Although the bike has to be ordered from the UK, Thorn routinely ship bikes all over the world and have an excellent reputation for supporting riders on tour who need urgent supplies.

Prices start at £1199 but with Thorn's racks and a few upgrades, expect to pay around £1500/€2250.

Bruce Gordon's Rock 'n' Road Tour Ex has 26" wheels. Note the high-mounted front rack, which is Bruce's own design.

BRUCE GORDON ROCK 'N' ROAD TOUR

Bruce Gordon (💻 www.bgcycles.com) is a small California-based bike builder, designing and building his frames in-house from chromoly steel. The Rock 'n' Road Tour comes with the 700c or the easier-to-find 26" for expedition use (known as the 'Ex' version).

These are top-of-the-range touring bikes available with dropped handlebars, straight bars or a switching system to take either. Bruce's bikes are built to have the strength of mountain bikes and he also designs and supplies some of the strongest chromoly racks in the business. The high-mounted 'Ex' version sits further back than most high-rider front racks to ensure neutral handling. He sells direct; either pick one up or have it shipped and assembled by your local bike shop.

Bruce Gordon has a very loyal clientele and is known for extremely high quality and attention to detail. If the Rock 'n' Road is too expensive, the cheaper Basic Loaded Touring (BLT) is available, still made in-house, with LX spec drivetrain.

HP VELOTECHNIK
STREET MACHINE GTe

Recumbents are a huge step for most of us; a completely different ride from a conventional bike but there are a couple of models that make worthwhile tourers: just make sure you try one out first. The German HP Velotechnik Street Machine GTe (⌨ www.hpvelotech nik.com) is designed for speed, supreme comfort and a surprising ability to carry a lot of gear low down: up to 50kg on two optional racks. The GTe is the latest version of the GT, in aluminium.

Street Machine GT
© Bram Goots

The UK distributor Bikefix recommends using Ortlieb's larger motorcycle panniers on the lower racks (see photo), which hold 24 litres each. The Street Machine GTe has good-quality full suspension and costs around £1600 with both racks, or approximately US$2150 in the USA.

DAWES ULTRA-GALAXY

Cyclists more used to road riding and dropped handlebars should look at this British classic from the long-established Dawes stable (⌨ www.dawes-cycles.co.uk). The Galaxy series has a long history and has been ridden all over the world. Gearing is a little higher than 26″ MTBs as they are more road oriented, but Galaxies are strong enough to handle potholed roads and rough tracks. The Ultra-Galaxy is

Pride of Britain: Dawes Ultra-Galaxy, available in British Racing Green.

made from the finest chromoly: Reynolds 853 steel with a strength-to-weight ratio of titanium but at a fraction of the cost. It's a 700c model so heel clearance won't be a problem, though finding decent tyres in many countries may well be.

The Ultra Galaxy gives a fast, easy and ultra-comfortable ride but if the price is too high the Super-Galaxy (see p.26) is the same bike but equipped with LX, rather than XT, components.

RIDGEBACK PANORAMA

The UK manufacturer Ridgeback (⌨ www.ridgeback.co.uk) recently introduced a fully-equipped, under-£1000 touring bike: the Panorama. It is very much a road bike, featuring 700c

Ridgeback Panorama; enjoy the view.

wheels and road-oriented gearing that is higher than MTB gearing, ie great for high speeds but less suited to long, gruelling ascents pulling heavy loads. The Panorama has a chromoly Reynolds 725 frame and STI shifters – the combined brake and gear shifters found on the Cannondales, Dawes and the Trek 520 – but it also has extra brake levers on the straight part of the bar so your hands are always close to the brakes.

Optima Condor: unusually featuring two 26" wheels as well as full suspension.

OPTIMA CONDOR

Another recumbent alternative is the Optima Condor (💻 www.optima-cycles.nl). This Dutch bike has both front and rear 26" wheels that make it more suitable for off-road riding, though the rider lies in a more prone position due to the pedal height. Nevertheless, one of these bikes has been ridden down the Friendship Highway in Tibet. The riding position looks high but panniers can be fitted fairly low. Admittedly, a Condor is more complex than a conventional diamond-frame bike, and the position of the pedals reduces visibility of the road immediately ahead, but comfort and low wind-resistance make it an interesting choice for a long distance ride.

Trek 520: America's top-selling tourer.

TREK 520

The long-established Trek 520 (💻 www .trekbikes.com) is America's leading road touring bike (much like Britain's Dawes Super Galaxy). With its chromoly frame, 700c wheels and dropped bars, the 520 is fast and comes with good-quality components including a rear rack but no mudguards. For lightweight trips it's an excellent bike, but the high gearing is not well-suited to heavy loads or rough roads. Most Trek dealers, even in the US, don't keep a 520 in stock, but it can be ordered easily enough.

Cannondale's T2000 or their less expensive T800 (💻 www.cannondale .com) are very similar bikes to the Trek 520 but made from aluminium. Alternatively Jamis (💻 www.jamisbikes.com), a smaller but highly-regarded US manufacturer, makes the Aurora, a cyclo-cross influenced steel road bike with the braze-ons necessary for touring.

FAHRRAD MANUFAKTUR T400

Germany's Fahrrad Manufaktur T400 is a well-equipped tourer, with a kickstand, Tubus rear rack, mudguards, pump, dynamo lights and a solid, conservative MTB design and construction. Components are Shimano Deore LX and tyres are top of the line 1.75" Schwalbe Marathon XRs; no need to upgrade those. This brand is easy to find in the German-speaking countries but less easy to source elsewhere. Bikefix in London (🖳 www.bike fix.co.uk) is the UK distributor, with the T400s retailing at around £650 in the UK. Make sure you are comfortable with the 'butterfly'-style handle-

Fahrrad Manufaktur T400 Rohloff

bars before embarking on a long trek, though. The same bike with a Rohloff 14-speed hub gear (see p.43) sells for nearly €2000 in Germany.

SURLY LONG HAUL TRUCKER

You might have some great components on your old bike that you really like, or perhaps you don't like some of the compromises or economies inevitable in a bike whose parts are chosen by someone else. Either way, buying a frame built for touring and then building it up to your spec combines a reliable frame design with your own individual wishes. American bike maker Surly's Long Haul Trucker is a double-butted chromoly frame made with strength, comfort and stability in

Surly Long Haul Trucker frame

mind. Long 18" chainstays, laid-back angles and a tall head tube are the basics, and the trimmings are the braze-ons for racks, down tube shifters, canti brakes and even braze-ons for carrying spare spokes. Surly makes the smaller sizes for 26" wheels and the larger sizes – 22" (56cm) frames and larger – for 700c. The stays are wide enough to take 2.1" tyres for the 26" wheels, or 1.9" on the 700c wheels. Whether you ride with drops or flat bars is up to you or the gear you already have. Surlys are available to order in the UK, Australia, New Zealand and most European countries besides the USA.

BIANCHI VOLPE

An American designed-model after the famous Italian Bianchi marque, the Volpe (🖳 www.bianchiusa.com) has been around since the early 1990s. Cyclo-cross influenced the design which is strong enough for bad roads and good trails (I took mine mountain biking several times) and makes a great light touring bike. These days it

The Bianchi Volpe is a cyclo-cross bike turned loaded tourer

comes with all-terrain 700cx32 WTB All Terrainasaurus tyres on 36-hole Mavic rims well suited to touring, and features braze-ons for a rear rack. The rear mech is Shimano Deore and a suspension seatpost is a nice touch. At 16.7" (42.4cm) the chain stays are on the short side for a touring bike, reflecting its racing origins, but the Volpe comes with slick STI gear shifters. This model may be harder to source outside the USA. A great choice for ultralight rough-stuff touring.

REVOLUTION COUNTRY

'They say you want a Revolution ...'

At £399, Edinburgh Bicycle's Revolution Country is the cheapest fully-fledged touring bike on the market, yet it comes 'equipped, not stripped', as the car ads used to say. The aluminium frame has a steel fork and Rigida double-walled 700c 36-spoke wheels and 37mm (1.5") tyres, solid stuff and strong enough for mixed quality roads. The rest of the spec is similarly well-chosen and nothing is bargain-basement. You get mud-guards, toe clips, an aluminium rack as solid as Tortec's, combined brake and gear shifters with auxiliary levers on the classy anatomic-style drop bars – great for cruising around town – and mounting points for three bottle cages and a front rack.

The gear group is Shimano Sora with an 8-speed cassette and Suntour cranks and chainrings (the smallest is 28T). A plastic chainring guard is a nice touch that more expensive bikes don't bother with. You could spend a lot more than this upgrading an old bike and for the budget minded, this is the best value new tourer out there. Available online from 🖥 www.edinburghbicy cle.com or from shops in Aberdeen, Edinburgh and Newcastle.

DAWES GALAXY TWIN

A tandem version of Dawes's successful Galaxy tourer, the Twin is made of 7005 T6 aluminium alloy and shows how strong a tandem needs to be to carry two people and their gear. The extra lateral tubing for frame rigidity, the wider 145mm rear axle, the 48-spoke wheels and mechanical rear disc brake all give the Twin a solid feel, and with an XT rear mech it all adds up to a quality tour-ing tandem. A thoughtful feature for the rear-seated 'stoker' is a suspension seatpost, which should help keep the peace. There are cheaper tandems out there but they are designed for unloaded day rides. The stresses of touring massively increase weight and strength requirements and off-highway riding means that everything on a tandem needs to be that much stronger. The Galaxy Twin is an awesome bike for touring on sealed roads with the disc brake giving peace of mind on fast descents.

For a heavily loaded tandem tour in remote areas, you might have to con-sider a Thorn model which could set you back £2500 or more. The touring tan-dem market is about as specialized as it gets; bikes tend to be made to order,

BOB JACKSON 'WORLD TOUR 631'

Based in Leeds, England, Bob Jackson Cycles is a cycle shop offering hand built off-the-peg and custom frames. The World Tour 631 is their heavy tourer, though the bike illustrated is a custom example fitted with S&S couplings. These are toothed, stainless-steel lugs brazed into the top and down tubes which allow the frame to be taken apart for travel on planes or trains. I was able to use most of the components from my old bike on this new frame.

Frame

Bob Jackson offers frames in half inch increments from 18½" to 25½" with a wide range of colours, transfers and detailing options. The frame has a horizontal top tube which is more practical on tour as it gives you something to lean against while waiting at the tops of passes for your friends to catch up! The frame is lugged and brazed, beautifully built with many nice touches not found on mass-produced frames. Instead of large holes drilled through the seatstay and chainstay bridges, a bottle-cage boss has been brazed into each bridge for mudguard fixing. Cable guides are brazed onto the bottom bracket shell, rather than drilling it for a plastic guide. Reynolds 631 chromoly replaces 531 Super Tourist, the old standard for touring bikes. One of the differences with the new tubeset is wider seatstays which improve the rigidity of the rear triangle. The top eyes (where the seatstays are brazed into the seat cluster) have about three times the brazing area of my old frame, which significantly improves frame durability.

As can be seen from the picture, the handlebars are set at about the same height as the saddle, higher than on a normal road bike to give the maximum number of practical hand positions. The S&S couplings are

obviously very convenient but are undetectable when riding – they do not affect the rigidity of the frame.

Reservations are minor. This frame has only two sets of bottle-cage bosses rather than three; a compromise brought about by the S&S couplings. The frame has horizontal rather than the vertical dropouts as specified. These make wheel removal a bit awkward, but allow the rear wheel to be positioned further back in the frame to give clearance when using wider tyres.

Components

As illustrated, the bike is set up for expedition touring. The wheels are the handbuilt 700c; 40 spokes on the front wheel and 48 at the back, which has a Shimano seven-speed tandem freehub and Mavic T520 tandem rim. The spokes are laced four-cross with DT swaged stainless-steel spokes. The high spoke count, a 7-speed cassette to minimize wheel dish and tougher tandem rims make for an extremely strong set-up. The tyres are slick 35mm Michelins running at 90–100psi. I don't use mudguards on tour as they're just something else for baggage handlers to break but this bike is furnished with all the brazeons to fit them when required.

Steve Pells

raising the price but giving buyers a chance to hand pick the spec. Among the top tandem builders in the US, Co-Motion (🖥 www.co-motion.com) offer the Cappuccino Co-Pilot for around US$5500. As its name suggests, the Cappuccino provides a superbly smooth ride, featuring a Softride suspension beam for the stoker as well as two sets of S&S couplings. Other US tandem builders worth a look include Santana (🖥 www.santanatandem.com) and Burley (🖥 www.burley.com).

Buying a used mountain bike for touring

If you're on a tight budget, buying used will save a small fortune: bikes lose around half their value after three years or so. With a used bike, it's not such a disaster if the bike gets stolen or if you want to sell it while on the road. Furthermore, old mountain bikes from the 1990s make better touring bikes than most new MTBs owing to their more conservative designs and chromoly frames.

The benefits of an older mountain bike

- No suspension or disc brakes to worry about. (In any case, avoid early suspension systems).
- Most bikes were made of steel in the 1990s, so no worries about metal fatigue or field repairs.
- Longer wheelbases give a more stable ride. Look for good clearance for the rear tyre so you have enough room to carry panniers.
- Seven or 8-speed cassettes (gear clusters). Both are still easy to find and the wider chains wear better than today's 9-speeds. The cassette is also a little narrower meaning the wheel has less dish (see p.47) and so is stronger.
- Bar-top shifters. The older bikes had simple gear levers on top of the handlebars. Easy to use and fix, and they worked in 'friction' mode even if the 'auto-click' indexing broke. Gripshifters (twist-grip style gear changers) are also fine for touring – they work even when the indexing wears out.
- Threaded headsets. Not seen nowadays, but the advantage was the ease of adjusting handlebar heights compared with modern Aheadset systems.

Bear in mind the obvious downsides of buying an old bike: worn bearings, rims chains or gears could easily lead to the whole drivetrain requiring replacement. However, if you're setting off on a long tour, you'll want to start off with new components anyway. To check for a worn chain, lift the chain away from biggest front chainring; more than a centimetre gap means the chain is well past its best. The wheels should roll smoothly – take them out of the frame and spin them while holding the wheel by the axle. If it feels rough, it's probably time for a new hub and either a wheel re-build or replacement.

Some suitable mountain bikes

Two of the biggest manufacturers, Trek and Specialized made great chromoly mountain bikes, many of which are still on the road. Specialized's Hard Rock, Rockhopper and Stumpjumper are the ones to look for. The Hard Rock was the cheapest but was steadily upgraded through the 1990s at which point they switched to aluminium and the design changed completely. Trek manufactured similar bikes in aluminium and steel for years, with the steel bikes having 3-digit names like 'Trek 820' while the aluminium models had four digit numbering.

Marin and Giant also made good mid-range chromoly bikes. Mountain bike pioneer Gary Fisher was bought out by Trek, but continued to produce excellent bikes such as the Hoo-Koo-e-Koo and Montare in steel with 8-speed cassettes until 1998. Ridgeback is a good UK alternative. Their popular older bikes are 26" hybrids, with a slightly more upright riding position and narrower tyres, but otherwise suitable for hard roads or kerb-hopping.

Paul Woloshansky's 1993 Tech Pulse on tour in Vietnam.

ADAPTING OLD MTBs FOR TOURING

I hunted around for ages for an older bike with a large frame that I could use as a donor bike. The plan was to strip it completely and rebuild it with a more modern groupset and new wheels. After months of searching, I found a Giant Yukon with a 21.5" frame. I did some quick measurements and some bargaining and came out of the store with the bike for NZ$140 (about £50).

The Yukon was perfect: 4130 chromoly frame and fork, long wheelbase and chainstays and double rack eyelets (braze-ons) on both front and rear dropouts. The old 1" threaded headset could easily be adjusted for a comfy riding position. I noticed too that the down tube had been strengthened at the bottom bracket to increase stiffness in that area. The componentry was fairly basic, being mostly Acera-X and Alivio, but it all appeared to be in really good nick so over the winter I replaced all four bearings [headset, bottom bracket and both hubs), brake blocks, chain, tyres (Michelin Wildgripper City 26x1.5") and added front and rear racks.

I packed up the bike and headed over to Australia for a tour through the Grampians and the Great Ocean Road and back to Melbourne. I figured that if the bike was stolen or ruined, then I really hadn't lost a great deal of money.

The bike performed flawlessly, riding

nicely and handling predictably when fully loaded. The frame also felt solid and didn't flex while pedalling or even racing down hills. I found the old-fashioned gripshift 21 speed gearing perfect for my sedate style of touring. I found I only used a few gears on tour and they were low enough for grinding up the few steep bits, so I don't feel I was missing out by not having the full complement of 27 gears.

So, there you have it, I put together an ideal tourer from an old mountain bike by adding smooth tyres and racks, and all for about NZ$450 (£175). I would recommend upgrading parts if you're planning an extended tour, but the basics are just fine for starting out.

Roy Hoogenraad

Component considerations

Whether you're buying a new bike or fixing up the bike you already have, you're likely to be eyeing up the areas that will take the most wear and tear – gears, brakes and wheels. If you're on a tight schedule and only have a week or two for your trip, you won't want to be sitting around waiting for a new wheel to be built when the old one breaks, so don't take a chance on questionable components – have a bike mechanic check them out if you're unsure how long they will last. If you're headed for Europe, North America, Australia or New Zealand on a longer trip, there's no need to decide everything beforehand. As long as you can spare a day or two getting your bike fixed, you can afford a few mistakes as there are plenty of bike shops along the way. If you're heading for Africa, Asia and Latin America, though, you need either confidence gained from experience or bombproof kit as equipment failures are much harder to deal with.

GEARING SYSTEMS
There are two main types of gearing systems found on today's bicycles: the widely used front and rear derailleur, giving up to 27 speeds at the last count via three front chainrings and nine rear sprockets; and the much less common hub gear system, the classic Sturmey Archer units being best known. Both systems have been around almost as long as bicycles themselves and both have advantages and drawbacks for touring.

Derailleurs
Shimano dominates the market for bicycle gears more than ever these days, especially for bike touring where mountain bike derailleur gear groups are used. It's worth noting that new bikes come with components and gear ratios designed to work well together. Resist the urge to spec something different on a new bike, or radically change an old bike; the original groupset will probably work better than anything else. Certainly go for the highest quality groupsets you can afford; upgrading from Shimano Deore to LX or even XT cassettes is well worth it, along with a high quality chain. Riders splash out on XT components not to save weight, but because they last longer.

Shimano Deore XT 27-speed – the cream of rear shifters.

Gear range
What is a good gear range for touring? 'As wide as you can get' is most people's answer, but the truth is, you almost certainly don't need the massive range of gears found on most new

mountain bike gears, which includes a 22-tooth small chainring up front and a 9-speed, 11–34 tooth cassette on the back. These gears offer an excellent range and having 9 speeds at the back means a smooth progression, even if the very lowest gear will have you pedalling like mad but riding at less than walking speed. You may need these low gears should you find yourself climbing at over 4000m where the air is thin.

Older 8-speed cassettes don't have this range; with 13-30 teeth you may have to get off and push occasionally, but cyclists rode at altitude long before 9-speed cassettes came along. Avoid the temptation to upgrade from a 7-speed to an 8-speed cassette; an expensive move and not as easy as you might think.

Hub gears

The advantage of derailleurs, besides the high range of possible gearing, is that everything is external and easy to get at and usually to fix. Hub gears – a mind-bogglingly complex arrangement of cogs and rings fully enclosed in a hub – are not often seen on touring bikes. The most common kinds, Sturmey Archers or Shimano's Nexus come with no more than eight internal speeds and so don't give enough range for touring (although among others, Brompton folders – see p.30 –

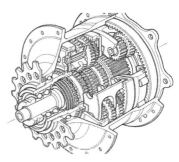

Inside a Rohloff 14-speed Speedhub – you wished you'd never looked.

get round this by combining derailleurs with hub gears). More importantly though, these brands of hub gears are more commonly fitted to city bikes and may not be strong enough for heavily loaded touring. However, one unit, the 14-speed Speedhub introduced by Rohloff in 1999, is making a name for itself among adventure touring bikers and is gaining popularity as bicycles are being designed and sold with the Speedhub installed. But at £625/€900, retro-fitting a Speedhub is expensive; far better to buy a bike designed for it such as the Thorn Raven reviewed on p.34. These bikes have dropouts designed to hold the Speedhub solidly in place and to maintain chain tension.

The genius of the Rohloff is that the gear ratios are evenly spaced with no overlap. A typical 27-speed derailleur will have several near-identical or unusable ratios. The Speedhub may not quite match the full range of a 27-speed derailleur, but the lowest ratio is almost as low as the lowest gear available on a derailleur: a 22T chainring turning a 34T sprocket; there is less than a single cog's difference in it and at the high end, the Rohloff matches all but the highest derailleur gears, the ones you can only use when barrelling downhill with a good tailwind.

Rohloff's advantages

- Extremely long life – Some Speedhubs have clocked up over 80,000km and are still running.
- Low maintenance – periodic chain tightening, an annual oil flushout and cable replacement are about it. No need to scrape grunge out of your gears anymore!

- Perfect shifting every time – the indexing is inside the hub and mis-shifting never happens.
- Because the chain always runs straight from the single front chainring to the single rear sprocket attached to the hub, a stronger chain can be used.
- The wheel is not dished on one side (see p.47), making it far stronger.
- Spoke breakages are very rare and are easier to fix if they do occur.
- You can change gear at a standstill or while freewheeling.

Drawbacks
- Speedhubs can be noisy in the lower gears, at least until they are broken in.
- Though the efficiency of the gears is high, it's not quite as high as a clean, correctly-adjusted, high-quality derailleur.
- Serious problems can only be fixed by returning the hub to the factory in Germany. Most problems, though, arise from riders not having replaced the control cables in good time.

For anyone with a big enough budget planning a long trip, the Rohloff eliminates a lot of uncertainties and provides excellent, reliable gear shifting but works much better as part of a new bike than retrofitted.

BRAKE CHOICES
Brakes are a much easier component to replace if you find yours don't give the stopping power you need – and remember your braking distances will increase when carrying a heavy touring load. Modern bicycle brake designs have resulted in much more powerful units over the years, even though the old cantilever styles are still fine for touring.

Today's V-brakes and the like are designed for mountain bikes with straight handlebars, and though adaptors such as the Travel Agent are available to make them work with dropped handlebar brakes, the result is never as good as it is with the handlebars that were designed for V-brakes. If your bike has dropped bars and the brakes are not up to snuff, consider fitting a Suntour SE self-energizing rear brake.

Disc brakes
Following suspension, disc brakes were the second major motorcycle-derived innovation to find its way onto bicycles. If today's rim brakes are so good, do tourers really need disc brakes? Bicycle touring is always based on tried and tested designs and it's almost certain that in a couple of years, disc brakes will become commonplace rather than a radical innovation. For the moment, most experienced tourers would say that disc brakes present problems of maintenance and repair in the field, and are not easy to fit on a bike that requires racks. The power of disc brakes, especially in wet conditions, or when compared to overheating and fast-wearing rim brakes on ultra-long descents is not contested. Here's what Philip Davis reported about his Hope Mono Mini disc brakes in North India:

'I was descending on the last stage of a trip from Leh to Manali in northern India with six other people all of whom had rim brakes. We hit torrential rain and sleet on

the 32km descent and the road was in very poor condition. Every other bike burned through at least one set of brake blocks on the descent – a very scary experience for the people involved, especially given the number of trucks coming up this very narrow road! With disc brakes I had no problems whatever, despite having clutched at the brake lever for over two hours. I would have felt quite smug if I hadn't been so cold and scared!'

Disc brakes on a bicycle, whatever next?! In fact, they're far superior to rim brakes.

So, disc brakes are stronger than any other brake, work well in the wet, don't wear out the wheel rim, work on out-of-true wheels and are generally reliable. But if you want to fit them to your bike you're better off starting out with new forks and wheels. Cable-actuated disc brakes are easier to maintain on tour than hydraulic disc brakes.

WHEELS

With additional information from Steve Pells

Bicycle wheels are designed to provide a blend of speed and strength while of course being built to a certain price. For a trip to the back of beyond, this means that, unless you're buying a high-end touring or expedition bike, your wheels won't be strong enough to be worry-free. Most new bike buyers tend to overlook wheels and instead look at the gear group (Deore, LX, etc) as an indication of overall quality. Knowing this, bike manufacturers save a little money and fit lighter but less robust wheels and tyres so a bike performs well on a test ride as light wheels give good acceleration. Furthermore, all but the best bikes from major manufacturers have machine-built wheels and this is one area where, interestingly, hand-built wheels are still regarded as the best.

Narrowing it down

There are several elements in building a wheel from scratch: the hub, spokes and rims can all be chosen separately. Because of this, smaller bike shops don't bother stocking made-up wheels but build them to order with a day or two's notice. A top quality wheel can easily cost £100 but it will be of 'expedition' quality, reliable under load and on the roughest roads many weeks from the nearest bike shop. A good set of wheels therefore gives peace of mind whether you're hitting kerbs on Clapham High Street or miles of washboard on the Great Divide.

A 700c wheel is about 2" taller than an MTB 26" rim.

Wheels do wear out in the normal course of things and though bearings, spokes and hubs can be replaced individually, it's better to replace all the component parts so they are well matched and equally strong. Wheels under heavy loads have a much shorter lifespan, especially the back wheel. And it's not just the weight, but the extra braking force on a loaded bike which literally grinds down the rims. Grit caught in the brake blocks gradually sands down a rim and so weakens the wheel, although cracks often appear first around the spoke holes.

If you're headed for somewhere like Africa or Asia, upgrade your wheels. If you can't afford handbuilt wheels or have just bought a new bike with machine-built wheels, you could either ask a good bike shop to check the spoke tension and stress-relieve the spokes, or take the bike on a shake-down tour. Leaving the UK across Europe on a new, heavily-loaded tourer with machine-built wheels, I lost six spokes on the back wheel before reaching Munich, only 1000km into the trip. After the rim cracked on a second major trip, I bought a new wheel with Sun Rhyno Lite rims handbuilt by a small shop in Northern California and haven't had to so much as true them after thousands more kilometres.

Wheel strength is vital; wheels take the brunt of the shock loads.

Choosing a new wheel

When specifying a new touring wheel you need to strike a balance between strength which usually means more weight, lightness which improves acceleration, and of course expense which rises exponentially as you near the cyclist's nirvana of both strength and lightness.

It won't be the same for all riders; body weight, payload, riding style, destination and the anticipated road surface are all factors in how far you need to go with custom wheels. This is what you need to know to avoid being baffled at the bike shop.

Hubs

Get the best hub you can afford. The easiest thing is to specify something like Shimano Deore, LX or XT as going for major brands simplifies things in terms of repair, replacement and compatibility. The advantage of a quality hub is simply a worry-free ride. Fit and forget: You'll have plenty more on your mind!

Rims

All good rims are double-walled and made of aluminium alloy. You can't see the inner wall, but it makes the rim substantially more rigid. A rim with eyelets around the spoke holes is a good sign. The eyelets spread the pulling force of the spokes and so reduce the possibility of cracks. A hard-anodized rim is not recommended for touring as it's more prone to cracks: go for a non-anodized 'silver' rim.

Number of spoke holes

The standard count for touring wheels is 36 holes although a strong 32-hole wheel, as is common on mountain bikes, may be good enough. Usually you'll find a shop only has the more common 32H Shimano hubs in stock so plan ahead. Any less than 32 (28 is the next lower possibility) is for racing; no good for touring. On tandems 40- and 48-holed rims are commonly found; it's generally more than you need even on an expedition bike but see p.39.

Spokes

Specify the heavier-gauge DT Swiss spokes, the most common high quality brand of spokes. A good spoke gauge to aim for is 13 or 14 (note that with spoke gauges, a lower number means a thicker spoke). Butted or swaged spokes are a little more expensive but well worth it. Butting means they are thicker at the ends – the place where spokes break – while weight is saved along the middle of the spoke, also enabling a little stretch or 'give' that helps avoid breakage.

Derailleurs are of course popular but among their drawbacks is that the angle of the spokes on the cassette side between the hub and the rims has to be relatively shallow to fit the cassette and hub between the frame drop-outs. This feature – the angle of the spokes against the flat rim – is called 'dishing'. The bigger the dishing angle the stronger the wheel; flat spoke angles add up to weaker wheels. You will find you break more spokes on the gear side of the rear wheel than anywhere else (see p.272 for the tool you need to carry to replace these gear side spokes).

Lacing pattern

Spokes are 'laced', that is, crossed over each other, to allow for the rotating torque on a rear wheel. Lacing the spokes also means that the tension on the hub flange works against a thicker section of the flange than if the spoke went straight out to the rim (a radial 'cart wheel' pattern as seen on the front of a Brompton folding bike; see p.30). Go for a 3-cross lacing pattern, the most common kind, for a simple reason: it works. There are some experienced tourers who argue that a 4-cross lacing pattern is stronger and springier than 3-cross, but the logic doesn't stand up, as 4-cross spokes are only fractionally longer.

You might find yourself in a situation where you build a new wheel out of old parts. You will probably fit your existing cassette onto the new hub rather than buy a new one. Don't be tempted to upgrade from a 7- to an 8-speed or from an 8- to 9-speed cassette, although this may be viable if you're changing hubs. In most cases your rear axle will not be wide enough, but remember too that bikes are designed to work with particular gear set-ups so stick with what you've got.

It's essential to put the spokes in the same position as they were on the old wheel, ie right or left side, leading or trailing, so that they are subject to the same stress as before, otherwise they will quickly fail. Lastly, when ordering a wheel, ask for several spare spokes of each length you need – front spokes, left and right rear spokes will all be different lengths and as explained above (dishing) you will need more of the right (cassette) side, which are more prone to breakage.

Tyre choice

Tyres change the way a bike feels and riding to work while planning your great escape is a good opportunity to try out different tyres and find out what suits you. City and hybrid bikes usually have tyres of around 1.5"/37mm width, strong enough to ride off kerbs but with a good turn of speed compared to 'fat' mountain bike tyres. This is a good tyre width to start with if you're carrying camping gear. The trick is not to buy more tyre than you need and remember the old cycling lore that an ounce on the wheels is like a pound on the frame – rotating weight feels heavier, because it affects acceleration.

One reason mountain bikes have become popular for touring is that fat tyres can compensate for cheap wheels. It's the most basic form of suspension. If you're going to run narrow tyres – and it makes pedalling a lot easier – you need either to carry less gear, get stronger wheels, or stick to good roads. Tyres in the 1-1.5" range are all you need for road touring around Europe, whereas for Asia 1.75-2" is a safer bet if you're carrying camping gear on medium quality wheels.

Many riders going out to the Far East start on fairly smooth 1.5-1.75" tyres and change to wider expedition tyres such as Schwalbe's Marathons at their first tyre change. Hopefully they have someone back home who can post the tyres to them to save carrying that 1.5kg for the first 5000km!

Unless you're riding an all off-road trail like the Great Divide along the American Rockies, don't buy knobbies. Even on that trail the ground is dry enough in summer to require only a shallow tread. Knobby tyres have too much rolling resistance for touring and are less puncture-resistant than tyres designed for roads.

Recommended brands

Schwalbe make a wide range of touring tyres – the Marathon XR is renowned among expedition tourers for use in Africa or the Himalaya. At 790g it's heavy but has thick sidewalls that protect against hits and scrapes on rocks as well as the stress and flex of carrying heavy loads. Expedition tyres like the Marathon XR have a good blend of road and off-road characteristics and work in practically all extreme bike touring situations you might find yourself in.

The Marathon Plus is a better choice for road–only trips, especially where thorns or broken glass are present (eg Baja California – see p.170) but it's a fraction heavier than the XR. A much lighter option for good roads is the Schwalbe Marathon Cross.

Vredestein is one of the largest European brands. They make mostly 700c road tyre sizes but also produce a very light (350g) folding 26" tyre at 1.3" width, good for road touring with a camping load

Continental has been producing touring tyres for a long time and, at 690g for the 26x1.75" size, the Top Touring 2000 model features an inverted tread pattern (ie much like a car

Schwalbe's Marathon XR tyre

tyre) designed for low rolling resistance and all-around strength. The thinner sidewalls flex more and so give a more comfortable and faster ride, at the cost of a shorter life as the sidewalls can fail while there is still plenty of tread left.

Panaracer makes high-quality lightweight tyres; the same 26x1.75" size as the Conti Top Touring weighs only 440g for the Panaracer Pasela. It's much more of a road tyre with thin sidewalls, but rides well. Avocet also make an inverted tread design, in fact, theirs was the first. Their long-established Cross tyre has a harder feel to it but is fast, lasts well and is suitable for road and hard-packed dirt. It's been around a long time and is still an excellent seller with a kevlar-belted version for added puncture resistance. The Cross is a favourite choice of tandem riders, and is available in both 26" and 700c sizes.

Ritchey's Tom Slick is available in 1" and 1.4" sizes, an excellent touring tyre often chosen by mountain bikers for commuting or touring. Specialized's 1.95" Hemisphere EX is another heavy tyre for road and hardpack trails. With good puncture resistance but a less lively ride, it also makes an excellent commuting tyre that seemingly lasts forever. A narrower and much faster tyre at 1.5" with similar levels of puncture resistance is the Specialized Nimbus Armadillo.

Spare tyres

Spare tyres are of course a good idea, especially for remote and rough destinations, but a conventional tyre is awkward to pack because its steel beading (the wire moulded into the two edges of the tyre) can get bent and damaged if folded or pressed on too harshly. Folding tyres get round this problem and so make ideal and compact spares to carry with you. It's easier to pack a folding tyre in your panniers, saving unnecessary exposure to the sun's UV which will shorten its lifespan.

Comfort – finding the sweet spot

There are three basic types of riding position. On traditional bikes the rider sits up straight with most of the weight on the saddle and almost none on the handlebars. This position is comfortable around town but for long rides it's unaerodynamic and your butt becomes sore. Racing and mountain bikes share most of the weight between the handlebars and pedals which can lead to wrist and neck problems over time. Touring bikes attempt to distribute your weight equally between saddle, handlebars and pedals. That's the position to go for (see illustration overleaf).

Choosing a saddle

Touring saddles are the opposite of what you might expect. Soft saddles which work on short rides around town and mountain bike rides are usually disastrous on longer rides. This is because your body sinks into the foam or gel, and the delicate tissue in your nether regions, whether you're male or female, is now in contact with the saddle base. Touring saddles are fairly firm, like racing saddles, but with a larger surface area to spread the load. The idea is that

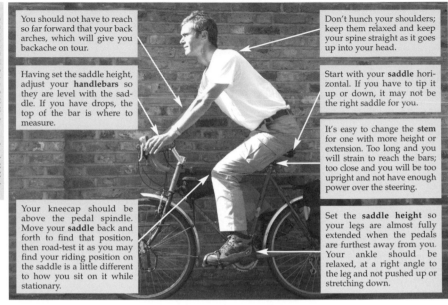

You should not have to reach so far forward that your back arches, which will give you backache on tour.

Having set the saddle height, adjust your **handlebars** so they are level with the saddle. If you have drops, the top of the bar is where to measure.

Your kneecap should be above the pedal spindle. Move your **saddle** back and forth to find that position, then road-test it as you may find your riding position on the saddle is a little different to how you sit on it while stationary.

Don't hunch your shoulders; keep them relaxed and keep your spine straight as it goes up into your head.

Start with your **saddle** horizontal. If you have to tip it up or down, it may not be the right saddle for you.

It's easy to change the **stem** for one with more height or extension. Too long and you will strain to reach the bars; too close and you will be too upright and not have enough power over the steering.

Set the **saddle height** so your legs are almost fully extended when the pedals are furthest away from you. Your ankle should be relaxed, at a right angle to the leg and not pushed up or stretching down.

your sit bones – the bony bits that you will feel if you sit on a wooden chair and raise your knees – support your weight, not the soft tissue in between. Look for something a little longer than a mountain bike saddle, with a firm top, reasonably wide at the back and made with high quality materials, firm to the touch. They generally aren't cheap, but let comfort be your guide.

There are two quite different saddle types that aim to spare your privates from pain. The oldest style, unchanged after over 80 years, is a Brooks saddle where hard leather supports the sit bones, giving a little over time to conform around your particular shape.

The other approach is the cutaway style where there is a central channel or hole cut out and firm support either side. The Terry Liberator saddle for women was the first such saddle and is still a good choice; there are now men's versions available. Another popular saddle is the V-shaped Specialized Body Geometry with a long channel down the middle. Touring saddles are fairly long, giving you a little room to move around and find a more comfort-

A Brooks Conquest saddle – the cheapest suspension system

able spot as it's normal to get sore from hours of pedalling in the same position. Long saddles have more room to set them further back if you find you want to sit a little further back.

Brooks are well worth a look. They create a certain controversy because they aren't the right prescription for every saddle problem and some riders need a couple of hundred miles on the saddle before it – or they – are broken in. But for many Brooks riders, they work fine straight out of the box and continue to get better and better throughout their long lives. No other saddle lasts a fraction as long as a Brooks. Lucky for us the least expensive Brooks saddle, the B17 model, is also the best for touring. It comes in a fairly wide 'standard' and a 'narrow' width, which looks wide enough. The leather is thinner than some of the Brooks saddles and so easier to break in. One place to learn about Brooks saddles is 💻 www.wallbike.com, the website of Wallingford Bike Parts in the USA. It's not only a more informative site than Brooks' own website, it's also perhaps the best place to buy a Brooks if you live in the US because they offer a returns policy if you can't live with your saddle. That's hard to find anywhere in the world.

You might get lucky and have no problems with a cheap saddle, or transfer a saddle you like from an old bike. If you can't find something you like, you'll have to go through the catalogues or internet to find one that suits you, or find a professional bike fitter to study your riding position and adjust your bike. Good saddles are not cheap but they should be hard-wearing to support you through a long trip.

Handlebar choice

You may not yet have chosen your bike and are unsure what the merits are of different handlebars. Drops and flat, straight, or mountain bike bars evolved with very different purposes in mind and it's surprising that mountain bike bars are now frequently seen on touring rigs – in fact, probably slightly more commonly than traditional dropped bars. The advantages of each type are:

Straight / MTB-style bars
- Gear and brake controls at your fingertips
- More powerful brakes
- Greater control over steering

Dropped handlebars
- Greater comfort – less wrist troubles
- Optional low hand position

That's the dilemma you face. Straight bars have improved a lot over the last few years, and riders who don't find them particularly uncomfortable are likely to prefer that style for these advantages of convenience. It's a slightly easi-

---

THE DREADED 'ED'

Both men and women can find themselves numb in the groin after a long ride or a mountain bike trip. There was some alarm after a study by Dr. Irwin Goldstein reported that many sufferers from Erectile Dysfunction, or 'ED' were cyclists. This spurred moves by saddle makers to produce channelled and cutaway designs for men – it was certainly a convincing marketing pitch to anxious male cyclists! In fact the connection was overstated, as ED sufferers were 'self-reporting' that their troubles were caused by cycling. In fact, though numbness can lead to nerve damage if ignored, nerves will regenerate and ED comes from either the head or hormones, not cycling. Don't ignore numbness, though. Take breaks, raise your handlebars, check the saddle angle, change saddles, wear padded bike shorts, but whatever you do, don't put up with pain or numbness.

er setup for routing cables and changing things around. Adding bar-ends gives you more places to rest your hands, on the corners or on the bar-ends themselves, and that variety may save you from wrist troubles on a long ride. Alternatively, change your handlebar for something suited for touring and not racing. Getting a bar with some rise and sweep will bring your riding position up and back just a touch, and angle the grips inward to a more natural position for your wrists. Thorn's Comfort bar (🖥 www.sjscycles.com) does exactly this and has become a popular alternative to dropped handlebars on their own bikes. A handlebar that is already swept won't work as well with bar-ends but it is much less likely to need them.

Avoid the temptation to change your bike's bars from dropped to straight or vice-versa. Yes, it can be done and people will boast about how they did it, but it is neither simple nor cheap, involving changing brake levers, cables, stem and probably the brakes themselves. Most of all, it's against the philosophy of this book, which is to go with the reliable, tried and tested principles that work! Save the money and put it into your Next Bike Fund. Only a few bikes, Thorns among them, are designed with frames that work well with either style of bar.

You might also be tempted by multi-position bars, most commonly 'butterfly' or 'pretzel' bars and you will see a lot of them on the continent. Generally they work better with an upright riding position and are not always strong enough or comfortable enough to take a touring rider's weight in a slightly more leaning position. In my experience they promise a lot, but deliver little. Wearing padded gloves helps a lot with wrist and hand complaints, or alternatively, pad the bar itself. I've used double or even triple layers of tape on drops and use foam grips on bar-ends as I like to cycle with bare hands.

Carrying your gear

Ortlieb OMM panniers on Cold Spring racks

Now you've got your bike set up, it's time to pile on all the worldly goods you intend to carry around the planet. At first glance, it looks as though you can get a lot of stuff on a bike and though many people do so for a living this is your big trip and your bike ought to be fun to ride, even when it's loaded. Ask yourself: do you really need all that gear? The answer that many tourers learn after a few weeks on the road is usually 'no', but that's for you to decide.

A typical set of panniers has a capacity of around 65 litres, with additional space available from a handlebar bag and on top of the rear rack. That adds up to about the same capacity as a normal backpack for camping. To carry more than that – as many people do for year-long, trans-continental tours – you will probably lash a large holdall to the rear panniers, adding another 30-50 litres. It's not pretty and it's less fun to ride, but you could push your total capacity up to around 100-130 litres – far beyond a normal backpacking load. Useful if you need to carry a month's supply of food and water to last a couple of days, but if you are not on an expedition and you expect to be able to stock up on food every couple of days, rethink whether you need all that capacity.

RACKS OR TRAILERS?

There is some debate about whether a trailer isn't better for carrying gear than the more traditional way of using racks and panniers, but mostly that's because the few happy trailer users tend to be very vocal about their choice. Trailers are a good choice for rides such as the Great Divide in the Rocky Mountains, where most riders are on mountain bikes – often with rear suspension – and cannot easily fit racks. A bike with this complex setup is inviting trouble and is not recommended for general touring.

BOB Yaking along the Continental Divide in the US. © Scott Morris

Trailers may cause a number of problems, including broken rear spokes, bent axles or dropouts. Most bikes, even mountain bikes, were never designed to deal with the sorts of stresses that trailers create. You must also consider the additional weight (around 6kg) and complexity as well as the greater drag from the trailer wheel. And a trailer is an additional hassle if transporting your bike by air.

If your bike or your intended ride forces you to consider a trailer, the BOB Yak is the best choice. Strong enough for off-road riding, the single wheel is as efficient as you'll get but even then a trailer definitely needs a shake-down tour before heading on a long trip.

Rear racks

With careful gear and clothing choices, you can get away with just a rear rack and still carry camping gear, as Kym McConnell (author of *Tibet Overland*, see p.287) did when he rode from Lhasa to Kathmandu. Set up like this, your bike's steering will remain light and responsive but be careful not to overload or your bike will wobble dangerously when going downhill. Taking only a rear rack and panniers implies a commitment to optimizing your gear, not trying to squeeze four panniers' worth of gear into two!

Rack failure on the road is something you cannot afford to happen,

Tubus Cargo – the chromoly classic.

especially when well away from bicycle shops, as field repairs will last only a short time. It's possible to choose your rack carefully and save some weight, but don't skimp on quality as you want your racks to be like your touring wheels: something you can fit and forget. The following racks are all strong enough to cope with a normal load of two full panniers plus a tent, the stronger ones being good enough for that extra bag on top if you need it.

Blackburn racks have been around for years and are strong for their weight. However, these days either tourers are carrying more or they're riding more off-road, so Blackburn's top of the line Expedition rack at 570g (and good for hauling 25kg) is the lightest rack most riders would consider for long tours. UK manufacturer TorTec makes good value expedition-quality racks, either in stainless steel or aluminium, the latter being cheaper and lighter but extremely rugged, made of 10mm tubing and weighing 900g. It costs £30 and is rated for 35kg; the steel version costs £50 and is good for 40kg of luggage. A light packer can save almost half a kilo by sticking with Blackburn, but if you want a bombproof setup for a good price, the stainless steel Tortec Expedition rack can't be beaten.

The Tortec looks like a cheaper version of the Tubus Logo. Tubus is the world leader for high-end bicycle racks and was responsible for the resurgence of interest in chromoly steel as a material for heavy-duty racks. The Logo is priced at £80 in the UK (though it retails for around €80 on the continent) and is about 200g lighter than the Tortec. A key advantage of both racks is that the panniers are hung below the top rack, making it much easier to strap on a tent or bag to the top of the rack. They are also designed to allow positioning the panniers further away from your heels. If your bike doesn't have braze-ons on the rear dropouts (as some mountain bikes don't) Tubus makes accessory mounts to fit the Logo rack that push the rack even further back.

The Tubus Cargo is the classic that made Tubus' name and is still probably the most common expedition rack you'll see on the road. It carries the same 40kg but weighs only 610g, very light for solid 10mm chromoly tubing.

Finding racks to fit mountain bikes has become harder over the last decade or so as first, front shocks and then disc brakes came along and made it difficult to fit racks on the forks. Old Man Mountain racks solve both problems. Extending out from the axle using their own extra long skewers, OMMs

fit around disc brakes and so have a wide base to support their load and provide great lateral stiffness. They are expensive racks in the USA, on a par with Tubus and available direct from the maker in Santa Barbara or in the UK through Carradice. OMM rates their strongest racks as good for 25kg, but these are conservative figures as the racks are designed and tested for extreme mountain biking use. OMMs are in the top tier for strength.

Old Man Mountain, that Old Man Mountain ...

The UK's Thorn makes chromoly racks as strong as any and designed for their own bikes. They also make the strongest tandem rack available. It's important to bear in mind that load capacity ratings come from the makers themselves and are only indicative. Don't worry too much about them, just make sure your own load is less than 50% of the recommended limit and the rack will never break in use.

Front racks

Carrying camping gear generally involves fitting front racks to help distribute the extra weight across the bike. Although the steering becomes heavier and less responsive, the ride will be more predictable and stable. More important from a safety point of view, the bike's frame is less likely to flex and cause unnerving wobbling, something that is especially noticeable as you build up speed going downhill. Solid racks on a solid frame make

... he just keeps rollin' along.

downhills a breeze, and that's how a well set-up touring bike should perform.

Having front racks and panniers make it easier to pack the bike too as you aren't struggling to bungee things on top of your panniers or trying to find things at the bottom of your bags. You will need – and develop – a little more arm muscle riding a bike with a load over the front wheels and may find that wide straight bars make steering easier. But whichever bars you use, be cautious on your first long downhills as you get used to handling a loaded bike. An unexpected tightening of a bend while you are cornering downhill will force you to lean more to keep in your lane. Hitting a pothole at this point can be disastrous so don't let your bike run away with you.

High vs low-rider front racks

Low-rider racks place the panniers either side of the axle for a low centre of gravity and are the best choice for most bike tourers. It's much easier to handle the bike when trying to park it somewhere if the weight is low – set up like this it's far less likely to topple over than if it has high-mounted racks. High racks place the panniers either side of the top of the wheel and are designed for extreme off-road situations, but the clearance on nearly all low-rider panniers is sufficient for most trails, even rocky ones.

The best feature of high-mounted front racks is the platform on top for carrying stuff over the front wheel itself. You don't have to use it all the time, but it's there for exceptional situations such as the occasional need for carrying extra water. A high rack works best with panniers that don't, like those in the photo on p.52, sit high themselves, and with straight bars rather than dropped.

Some recommended racks

Blackburn's low-rider front rack was for years the champ and the FL1 with the hoop over the wheel is still among the top choices, unless you are using Ortlieb panniers as the U-bolts and the reinforcing plate get in the way of

Ortlieb's mounting clips. U-bolts are provided to attach the rack to your forks, arguably a more secure mounting than using rack eyelets, as two bolts share the load. A bolt sheering off in the braze-on (a common complaint) is bad news – but see below. Blackburn also makes a good high-mounted front rack, suitable for hard mountain bike use.

Tubus makes four different chromoly front racks and one of them will suit your bike no matter what forks you have. They also produce all the mounting clips you might need for a secure fit. The long-running hoop design – either the Tara or Ergo – is the best, as front racks without a supporting hoop have to be that much stronger just to maintain rigidity. And more rigidity means less stress on the forks.

Even if your bike does not have rack eyelets drilled into the fork ends (some manufacturers like Thorn prefer a brazed-on eyelet rather than weakening the forks by drilling holes in them), Tubus has the parts to make them fit. Tubus also make the Swing, a very simple rack to fit most suspension forks and disc brakes, but take your bike to the shop to be sure it fits yours. A Swing sits high and is attached to the fork crown but hasn't really caught on, perhaps because the panniers don't hang vertically but lean inwards.

Old Man Mountain racks are the easiest solution for bikes with shock forks and/or disc brakes. They come off fairly easily when you need to pack the bike for flying, and come with a shelf on top – always handy. OMM makes a great low rider rack too. You can mount the bags high or low and if you choose 'low', there's space to strap on other small items if need be. A short hoop over the wheel ensures rigidity.

Whichever racks you buy, make sure you carry a few spare bolts and washers. Hose clamps (aka: jubilee clips) make great general purpose repairs on racks. An old inner tube should be part of your repair kit too (see p.75): cut off pieces of rubber to line a hose clamp or U-bolt repair to prevent slippage and frame damage. Rack bolts should be made of stainless steel only. Get slightly longer bolts than you need so you can add a nut on the end of the bolt to reduce the changes of loosening. Also, if the bolt shears on you while touring, at least you'll have some remaining steel sticking out of the braze-on or eyelet to help remove the broken piece. Bolts that need a spanner or wrench have a slight edge over bolts that require Allen keys as they are slightly easier to reach in tight places, and harder to damage.

PANNIERS

As with so much equipment for touring, it's not worth skimping on panniers; they take more of a beating than you might think, and economies in zip quality, stitching or bag design soon show up in leaks, tears, or the pannier flapping into your wheels. Even if you have never been touring, you can't avoid seeing all those Ortlieb panniers on commuting bikes around town. Shoppers use them, students use them, I've used them myself for decorating and home maintenance jobs; Ortliebs are the top brand of panniers for all sorts of reasons. They are very adaptable and fit all sorts of racks and if you find your Ortliebs won't fit your rack (it generally only happens with front racks), you'd be more likely to want to change your racks than your Ortliebs.

PART 1 – PRACTICALITIES

GOING ULTRALIGHT

Each to his own obviously but when I see someone slogging up an alpine pass at 5kph on a knobbly-tyred MTB loaded with four panniers, I do wonder. After all, you won't feel the wind in your hair if the bike can't exceed 10kph. There is an alternative. Ride a bike light enough to climb with the local racers on their Saturday ride, agile enough to hit 80kph on a mountain descent, with wheels strong enough to go off road but fast and efficient when on it, and just enough kit to be independent rather than encumbered: go ultralight.

Lightweight strategies include limiting your luggage to under 10kg and riding a road or touring bike with high-pressure 25-28 mm tyres and 36-spoke hand-built wheels. A light bike tackles trails confidently, without the need to slow down or walk. Fording rivers, portaging landslides and the like are all much easier without panniers. Yet on the road, speeds as high as unladen day rides at home are typical.

Try to avoid camping: in practice there is always somewhere to stay. As the bike is light and fast it is easy to make it to the next village. If you're not camping, minimal tools, cycle clothing, one set of 'civilian' clothing and wash kit are all that is required to travel indefinitely. Just take the tools you need to keep the bike on the road. This is typically three or four Allen keys, an adjustable spanner, cassette removal tool, puncture repair kit, pump, tyre levers, spoke key, chain tool and penknife. Shower gel is good for washing clothes to dry overnight. A sleeping bag liner will do for hostels. Trim your guidebook down to the section you actually need.

For ultralight luggage nothing beats a saddlebag. It puts the weight close to the centre of gravity where it has a minimal effect on handling; much less noticeable than panniers. I use a waterproof canvas Carradice saddlebag; just sling it on at the last minute, cancel the milk and hit the road.

I recommend *Journey to the Centre of the Earth* by Richard and Nicholas Crane (read on the web at 💻 www.koopmann.light up.net/crane) for a remarkable account of this style of travel. On the lighter side, read Tim Moore's *French Revolutions*. Igor Kovse's tour of Kyrgyzstan on p.243 was accomplished on a similarly light bike.

Steve Pells

The waterproof material is heat welded, not stitched and is the strongest fabric used for any pannier, whether you pick the lighter cordura or the original polyester/PVC. If you're cycling in places where waterproofing doesn't matter, you'll still appreciate these bags for keeping dust out. If you don't like Ortlieb's dry-bag style roll-top closure, you can get them with a drawstring and clips. Ortliebs cost no more than other good quality panniers and the cheaper 'basic' or 'classic' bags work as well as the more expensive models.

Ortliebs have a capacity of 40 litres per pair at the rear, more than enough for most needs. A bike hauling more than this won't be such a treat to ride, but if you need larger panniers, UK manufacturer Altura makes the Orkney 56 rear panniers and Orkney 34 for the front. These bags will

Keeping weight low: water bags below panniers © Mark McLean

give you fifty percent more capacity than Ortliebs and have a waterproof main compartment and a couple of pockets, which Ortliebs lack. The clip attachments are German Rixen and Kaul Klickfix, on a par with Ortlieb for a solid attachment that won't easily fly off.

Jandd makes the largest panniers available, the Mountain Expedition panniers with a capacity of up to 163 litres per pair – strictly for tandems or child smuggling, as are their Large Mountain panniers at a lesser 109 litres per pair. Better to consider the Mountain or Mini-Mountain models, both of which expand up to either 67 or 42 litres. They feature lots of zips and pockets, a rugged construction and you get to customize the simple hook fittings to your rack.

North American designs tend to favour zips and pockets – Canadian maker Arkel is the top of the line with pockets galore and a metal frame to resist flexing and so ensure a secure fitting but all these features add up to 2.6kg for a pair of 42 litre Touring panniers. Stitched and zippered designs are far less rain-resistant than the simple Ortlieb bag and there is far more to go wrong on them. Lastly, zips can be a temptation to dishonest baggage handlers or while you leave your bike to nip into a shop, whereas a large single compartment with less familiar-looking openings is far less tempting.

Handlebar bags

Handlebar bags, handy for keeping valuables and route maps in view.

Handlebar bags complete your bike's touring rig perfectly because here is a single place for your camera, valuables and those must-have electronic goodies you've brought along. A bag like Ortlieb's 6-litre bag is perfect: its waterproof material means you don't need to wrap everything inside and it unclips from the bike quickly to be carried on your shoulder when you leave the bike. It comes with a map holder and padded camera inserts are available. There is a larger, 8.5-litre size but you might have trouble fitting it to a bike with STI gears because of the gear cables, as shown in the picture above.

Bringing along a backpack

Don't even think of riding with a backpack on; that's giving up the great advantage of being on a bike – having your bike carry the gear. At most, wear a Camelbak, and then only for extreme heat or mountain bike riding. But taking a small backpack on your trip is useful off the bike. A super-light pack like the GoLite Breeze (🖥 www.golite.com) weighs only 400g but can hold 47 litres. Use it to carry your tent on the bike. Alternatively, there are a number of bumbags/lumbar packs that have a foldaway day pack, or adventure racing packs which work much better than hauling a pannier on your shoulder.

Transporting your bike by air

Regulations for checking bikes onto planes are confusing to say the least, varying between airlines and airports, but seemingly also depending on who checks you in and what mood they're in. The post-9/11 situation has only worsened things. George Farnsworth's excellent website, Travel with Bicycles (⌨ www.bikeaccess.net) is based on travellers' reports and is one place to start your enquiries. Forewarned is forearmed, and calling around the airlines before you book and again before you fly for airport-specific information is wise. Even then, telephone staff may not know the situation at the airport you are flying from. Are bike boxes available? Will they take an unboxed bike? Even if you get a clear answer, you can never be sure what will happen at check-in.

For flights and airports you're unfamiliar with, the prudent thing is to box the bike yourself before setting out for the airport on public transport. That way, you won't be dependent on the check-in staff's mercy to get your bike on the plane. It may also be easier to take public transport away from the airport when you land, rather than try cycling after a long flight or perhaps at night. A boxed bike makes this an option whereas a fully assembled bike may not be allowed on a bus or fit in or taxi. The key issues you need to think about are:

One bike-in-a-bag, a couple of cats and a packet of crisps, please.

Weight limits

Usually 20-23kg on short haul and two items of up to 32kg each for trans-oceanic flights. US airlines may charge for bikes even though they are within the weight limit because of 'special handling' – and you can guess what kind of handling they have in mind while signing the baggage waivers that let them off the hook for damage. For European flights you should be allowed an extra 7kg or so for 'sporting goods', giving you up to 30kg in total. Major airlines like to charge for excess baggage by the kilo, but some budget online carriers now have a flat charge for a bike, though they ask that you do not pack extra items with the bike.

Be prepared to argue if your flight has several legs and the airline tries to charge you for excess baggage on the shorter hop. Get your bike checked all the way to your final destination, and even if there are days or months between flights, make sure (or simply bluff and bluster) that you're entitled to the larger allowance for *all* flight segments, as you cannot be expected to shrink your bags for some flights when they were all booked together, as is the case with a RTW ticket.

Bike boxes

Will they have them at the airport check-in and can you reserve one on booking? They may say yes over the phone but personally I've never believed it. Out of interest I've often asked at check-in but have yet to get anything other than an uncomprehending stare in response. Ask if your bike must be boxed at all – some airlines will happily seal the bike in a polythene bag.

Camping stoves

Obviously flying with fuel of any kind is out of the question, but apart from that, the less said the better when it comes to stoves. Policy in the USA appears to be a big 'NO' these days – follow this topic through George Farnsworth's site. Of the 'remote fuel reservoir' types of stoves recommended on p.74, you may get away with the stove head if thoroughly vented and not smelling of fuel, but used fuel bottles, no matter how fragrant, will probably not be allowed. In the US don't argue, just buy a new bottle later. Trangias running on meths should be OK as they're not pressurized stoves and their plastic fuel bottles may not show up on X-ray machines. The only clear guidance at the moment is that the USA is the trouble spot; elsewhere, check-in staff should use their common sense.

Boxing the bike

To avoid additional stress at the airport, box your bike at home, or have your local bike shop do it, as is common in the USA. Bike shops usually do a nice job in boxing your bike for a small fee and are helpful in providing boxes – just give them a few days notice as they don't keep them on hand. If you're flying within the US, the bike shop can box and send your bike via UPS, though it might cost almost as much as the airline would charge and may take up to five days to arrive by surface freight. Ask the shop to leave the box open so you can add extra luggage before flying.

Coming back – DIY bike boxing

On the return journey from somewhere exotic you'll more than likely have to box the bike yourself. It can be hard to find a good box, but you will find all sorts of packing materials in local markets. It takes about an hour per bike to wrap or box it. I usually cut the box down to the size of the bike so it's easier to get in a taxi or bus. I have always boxed my bikes myself and never had damage or trouble in dozens of flights.

To prepare the bike for flight, you need to make it into a dense, tightly packed shape so that all components together reinforce each other and all vulnerable parts are inside this mass. The smaller the package, the stronger.

1. Remove the pedals. You'll need a 15mm wrench, though on some pedals you need an Allen (hex) key. Note that the left pedal is reverse-threaded and loosens by turning *clockwise* – most important! Never just throw pedals (or anything else) in your bike box, they will surely damage the paintwork and may fall out of any holes in the box. Duct tape or zip tie them to the frame or racks.

2. Remove or lower the saddle all the way down depending on whether you want to protect the saddle by taping it down somewhere in the middle triangle of the frame, or use it to provide padding for the bike. Usually, lowering it is best as the seat post is safely in the seat tube and the package will have some soft padding.

3. Disconnect the brakes and release the wheel. Unless you have a lot of slack cable, unscrew the brake cable from the caliper and pull it out so that there is plenty of play in the brake cable and no chance of it getting kinked. Kinked cables, especially gear cables, are as good as junk. Your brake

A compact package means less chance of damage though a block of wood between the fork and chain stays is a good idea.

calipers will spring outwards and are safer if taped tightly together, with tape going round the forks. If you have disc brakes, don't forget to tape a wedge between the brake calipers to prevent the brake levers closing.

4. Wheels and tyres. Remove the quick-release skewers from the wheel axles and tape them somewhere safe. Place the wheels either side of the bike and tape or bind tightly together (as in the photo above). You may wish to put some cardboard in between wheel and frame. Partially deflate the tyres, although these days check-in staff ask you to deflate tyres entirely. Aircraft holds are only partially pressurized, so there is the possibility that if your tyres were at maximum pressure at ground level, reduced pressure while flying could cause them to burst. It's a very slight risk but a waste of time to argue physics when you need the goodwill of the flight agents. Try to keep some air in the tyres to protect the rims.

5. Unscrew the derailleur where is bolted to the dropout. This way, you don't have to disconnect the cable. Just ensure it is loose enough by pulling it out of the brazed-on frame guides on the chain stays so it will not get kinked anywhere. Wrap the derailleur in a rag or bubblewrap and tape it to the bike frame inside the rear triangle. Wrap up as much of the chain as you can in rags or newspaper and tape that to the frame.

6. Remove the handlebars. You should have enough slack in the cables to do this. Disconnect cables entirely if you think they may get tight in transit; it could kink and so ruin the cables. It's best to tape the handlebars to the frame in the most space-saving place. Your wheels may be far forward enough to position flat handlebars in between them. You have a lot of important and fragile gear on those handlebars, so place the handlebars where they are protected, or allow for some looseness so that if bar-end shifters take a hit, they are not fixed in place but can roll with the punches.

7. Mudguards. The rear mudguard has to come off and is quite well protected if simply wrapped around the rear wheel. The front mudguard may be OK on the bike if it is flexible as the best SKS mudguards are. Racks really depend on

A DIY box need not cover the entire machine – indeed there is something to be said for letting it be seen as being a bike.

your bike and the box and how small you need the package to be. Left on they are at greater risk but if you have a sturdy bike box and plan on riding away from the airport, leave them on. Taking them off leaves you a smaller package, which is important if you have to take a cab at the other end or need to carry it on the airport bus.

8. Some finishing touches. Screw rack and mudguard bolts back on the bike, all the way in – safe and easy to find later. Consider some extra padding around the rear stays and especially the derailleur hanger. Removing the largest chainring removes one very sharp edge and makes the package easier to stand up. Extra cardboard around the chainrings helps protect them. Fitting plastic supports or a block of wood in between the rear stays and the forks gives a huge amount of protection. Bike shops will give you these plastic blocks and they're worth carrying with you to use on your return trip. I put fragile items such as a helmet in the middle of the rear triangle or inside the main triangle, and tape them in. The tent often goes under the rear stays. Make sure that no small parts are loose in the box, as they will fall out of the inevitable holes that have appeared in the box since check-in.

Bike bags

Bike bags are nylon zipped bags designed for bikes – no surprise there! They typically have sleeves to hold the wheels either side of the bike, giving some protection from scratching. One of the best around is New Zealand's Ground Effect Tardis bag, with all the right pockets, sleeves and padding to protect your pride and joy. The Tardis costs around €100 in Europe and weighs 1.45Kg. For a day trip involving trains to a week or two's touring, bike bags are a brilliant idea, though on a longer trip, the bag becomes dead weight. If you're in Japan, bike bags can be found in Tokyu Hands stores under the catchy brand name 'The Big Bicycling'. These are the lightest bags around.

Ground Effect's excellent Tardis bike bag.
© Roy Hoogenraad

Another option is to buy a bike with S&S Couplings. These are high quality couplings built into the frame (best specified when ordering the bike) so it can be broken into two sections. This is very useful for tandems, which often have difficulties getting checked onto planes or into trains.

A third option, though not a very flexible one, is to buy a hard case for your bike. You would have to stash it somewhere while you make the trip, and return to the same place to return with it, but it works well if you want to fly to one airport for a circular trip of a couple of weeks. And your bike will remain in pristine condition. Bike Fridays (see p.31) are designed to fit in a Samsonite-style suitcase that can be towed behind or left at a hotel until your return flight.

The unpackaged alternative

There is a large minority opinion that you are better off not boxing the bike at all, but trying to check it in 'as is', on the grounds that if it looks like a bike, they'll treat it like a bike. Sounds good, but is it? Bikers have reported seeing their boxed bike arriving in a crumpled mess while seeing other people wheeling away ready-assembled bikes. Others have reported airlines using huge plastic bags to wrap the bike and check it in without a fuss. Supposedly pedal removal and handlebar turning is all that is required.

The trouble is, these are all anecdotal stories, and with thousands of airports and situations out there, what works on one airline or flight may not work on another. Stories have appeared of wheeled-on bikes being squashed under everyone else's bags, which evens it up a bit for the pro-boxing side. I think the non-boxing idea is a little optimistic and that boxing your bike, overall, has a lot more advantages in getting to and from the airport.

Clothing

With thoughts and inspiration from Cass Gilbert

Every trip you take will call for its own choice of clothing, depending on the climate, seasons and type of ride you're doing. A fast ride around France for a few weeks in summer will call for very different clothing from an overland trip to Australia. Short trips where it's all about the riding make cycling-specific clothing the best choice, as for sheer efficiency it cannot be beaten. On the other hand, cyclists on longer trips get tired of dressing in bikers' gear for months on end and tend to adopt cheap local clothes after their original kit has worn out (read how Edward Genochio ended up wearing Russian army surplus on p.215).

If you're going round the world, don't expect to be able to carry clothing for every eventuality. Just buy what you need as you go and send home or send on what you don't need.

Cycling shorts

If you've never tried, try riding in proper skin-tight lycra cycling shorts and you'll soon realize why most cyclists prefer them. The reason they work is partly the padding of course, but also because they become a slippery second skin that slides over – rather than snags – on the saddle and so reduces friction and consequent soreness. Not all men like to walk around with their family jewels exposed in such an acutely sculpted profile (and in some Moslem countries close fitting clothing of any type is bad form) and so riders often wear baggy shorts on top.

No one ever tells you to wear bike shorts without underwear (also known as 'going commando'), but that is the most comfortable way to do it for both men and women as the rubbing seams of your underwear are what you're trying to avoid. It's hard to find real chamois leather linings in bike shorts, except in the most expensive ones, but they're not that suitable for touring anyway. There is nothing like pulling up a pair of cold, damp chamois-lined cycling shorts to wake you up in the morning! Even synthetic bike shorts take so long to dry that you really need two pairs for touring if you want to wear them every day. Other riders find that they can alternate between bike shorts and ordinary clothes to keep sores at bay.

LAYERING

Layering is generally accepted as the best way to regulate body temperature. Layers keep you warmer by trapping air and can be added or taken off as you ride, depending on how you feel. The layering system extends from your thermal underwear to the waterproof mitts over your gloves. Performance clothing

is generally broken down into three levels: base, insulating (or mid-layer) and shell (or outer-layer). Natural materials may work best for your base layer on a long ride. Some people find their synthetic base layers smell after a few hours, others have no complaints after a few days.

Synthetics

Synthetic materials can also cause or exacerbate allergies. Personally, I would not look forward to a long tour if I had to spend months wearing synthetic materials next to my skin, especially close-fitting cycling clothes. On a short ultralight tour though, it's the efficient way to go. One synthetic fabric that many people have found to be comfortable and odour free is Lowe-Alpine's Dri-Flo.

Layering works well anywhere, particularly in a Yukon summer.

New synthetic fabrics that use silver filaments woven into the material are lightweight, dry quickly and are highly efficient in wicking and odour control.

Tights in particular may induce 'crotch rot', a fungal infection around the groin caused by excessive bacterial growth. Synthetics are easily washable and should be changed daily, but that's not always easy done in a cold climate (admittedly it's even harder to get wool clothing to dry in the cold). If you come down with crotch rot, regular washing, using talc and wearing airy shorts is the simplest cure. If this doesn't work buy some anti-fungal ointment.

Natural fabrics

The recent revolution in technical clothing has seen a counter-attack from natural fabrics in the form of merino wool, led by New Zealand companies (eg Icebreaker), where much of the merino wool comes from. These clothes are supremely comfortable across a wide temperature range and thus make ideal

(**Opposite**): The more gadgets you have, the more interest you'll attract! (Photo © Cass Gilbert).

base layers. Drawbacks with wool include the price, maintenance and slow drying when soaked. And moths consider it a delicacy. Wool is a touch heavier than equivalent fleece middle layers, but on a long tour, you will crave 'normal' clothes that feel comfortable, and merino wool has a luxurious texture.

You may also tire of close-fitting technical clothes. Certainly they're more efficient, but most travel is not a matter of life and death and you want

Loose-fitting, untechnical clothes in Morocco.
© Raf Verbeelen

to look and feel cool too. The best solution for planning your layers is to have a combination of fabrics to maximize flexibility for all conditions. Perhaps a thin wool or silk skin layer, then a micro-fleece on top.

Technical skin layers can often be covered up with local clothes. Underwear and socks are cheap enough to buy, wear out and discard en route. T-shirts are usually cheap everywhere and also make good souvenirs. Tailor-made clothes may seem like a luxury in the West but are great value in Asia and Africa. Having a long sleeved top made in local cotton can be the best option for cycling in India.

FEET, HANDS AND HELMETS

While cycling easily generates heat to warm the body core, the wind chill means it's not so easy to keep your hands and feet warm, unlike when walking and running where circulation gets down to all extremities. If you're travelling in bike-specific shoes rather than trekking boots, a pair of neoprene booties or Gore-Tex overshoes can make all the difference. Layering applies to the hands too. A pair of fleece gloves is ideal for cold mornings and evenings. Throw a waterproof shell over the top and you're ready to take on more severe conditions.

Heads also feel the cold. 80% of body heat is lost through the head and the ears are real superconductors. Convertible neck gaiters are light and versatile, as they can be cinched up for a hat or used as a scarf. Leggings and sleeves are another good way to keep warm while riding and take up next to no space in panniers.

There's no doubt helmets are gaining in popularity among adventure tourers and seem to be worn just as much on the Friendship Highway between Lhasa and Kathmandu as they are on your local commute. It's a hassle to bring one along; another bulky item that has to be treated with care. But how else are you going to be able to lay your hands on your hard hat for a hairy mountain descent when you most need it? Finding a good helmet while you're on the road is almost impossible: you've left it too late. Far better to bring it along, even if you only wear it half the time. Also bear in mind there are a few countries out there, Australia and Spain being two of them, where helmets are compulsory.

(Opposite): Climatic extremes in Africa, a continent where you might expect just high temperatures and humidity. **Top:** Snow in Lesotho. (Photo © Kenichi Kuroe). **Bottom:** Desert heat on the edge of the Sahara. (Photo © Cass Gilbert).

It may help with a tan but dressed like this in desert heat will double your water consumption and lead to sunstroke.
© Kenichi Kuroe

Hot climates

For most people, cotton is the best material for hot climates. It feels cool to the touch, especially when wet and absorbs sweat. In extremely hot climates, however, cotton can become blocked with sweat so that the salt clogs up the fabric and will start to sting. In these situations, 'silk-weight' polyesters such as those made by Patagonia or Lowe-Alpine may be more comfortable. You can't expect miracles from technical fabrics as there's a limit to how comfortable you can be in extreme heat if you're exerting yourself, but it's worth a try. Above all, always wear a hat, one that can be soaked in water, so that your head can be cooled by evaporation. On the road the biggest enemy is sunburn and here a broad-rimmed but collapsible hat such as the Tilley works well. In extreme sun a lightweight long-sleeve top is recommended over short sleeves and saves on sun cream.

Long-distance cyclists rarely get any shade and need the strongest levels of sun protection possible. Melanomas don't necessarily wait fifty years before erupting and fair-skinned tourers from the northern hemisphere facing prolonged exposure to the sun are likely victims unless they cover up.

When the heat is on common sense suggests reducing your daily mileage, cycling more slowly for fewer hours and where possible staying out of the sun during the hottest part of the day. Cotton and silk are also comfortable fabrics for sleeping in and are sure to be much cheaper and better suited to the country you're in if bought locally. There is a lot to be said for doing as the locals do, especially in the heat.

Cold climates

Cycling in cold climates requires more planning. Although local wools and even animal skins can be bought at the nearest market, technical apparel, with its low bulk and low weight, is much more suitable and quick drying.

Keeping warm by pushing through deep snow in China. © Janne Corax

Regulating body temperature is hard when you cycle – it's easy to be sweating up a sunny incline one minute and then turning numb with the cold as you freewheel down a shady descent. Layers work well as they can be shed quickly as you heat up and put back on when you stop for a break or freewheel. Look for highly breathable fabrics to keep your body well ventilated and avoid a build-up of sweat.

Outdoor gear makers and shops sometimes give the impression that technical clothing can help regulate your body temperature so well that you won't actually sweat. Cycling with a load will make your body sweat and you need to feel comfortable by managing that heat. Ideally, synthetic fabrics expel moisture but retain heat. The worst clothing to wear in the cold, cotton, will do the opposite – release the heat and keep the moisture next to your skin. Help your fabrics do the magic moisture transfer in the cold by keeping an even effort so you don't work up a sweat.

Windproof fabrics are usually a poor choice because they don't allow excess heat to escape quickly enough. These garments also tend to be bulky and expensive so you don't get a lot of bang for the buck in terms of cost, weight or pannier space taken up. Putting on your shell jacket is a lighter and easier way to block wind when you're taking a break or facing a blizzard up in the Andes.

Down jackets

Winter and cold weather tours will require all three layers, including thermal underwear, a warm fleece and waterproof tops and bottoms. Of course, much will depend on your own personal comfort level – women tend to feel the cold more than men. Thin layer garments work well while cycling, but the moment you stop, your body cools down and those layers may not be adequate. Carrying a thin down jacket on all cold-weather trips packs a lot of loft into a small package, probably no thicker than a fleece jacket when packed but a lot warmer. They make great pillows too if you're carrying a pillowcase (also useful as a laundry bag) or you can put it in a T-shirt. A lightweight down jacket is also good insurance for really cold nights when you can wear it in your sleeping bag. Don't feel you have to buy a top of the line North Face Nuptse; a cheap down jacket picked up locally can do the trick and be given away when the seasons or altitudes change.

Waterproofs

Rain on a long tour can be a refreshing change – even a great way to cool off in the tropics. However, there is nothing more depressing than a week-long forecast of downpours, particularly in colder climates or on camping tours. Investing in a good set of waterproofs is important and while these may seem unnecessarily expensive, more often than not, price reflects quality and durability. The best waterproofs will keep you bone dry even in a downpour and are breathable enough so you don't soak in your own sweat. While Gore-Tex is the industry standard, there are many other materials with similar properties under different badges – beware the Gore-Tex premium, that's all it is. Waterproof trousers are also a good idea, and can be used as an extra layer in cold climates.

Improvising with a £3-PVC poncho before a typhoon rolls in off the Japan Sea.

Despite what is claimed, breathable waterproof fabrics cannot achieve the impossible. If you're pedalling hard in the rain, it's impossible to stay as dry as you would if you stood still, yet this is how the waterproof tests are usually conducted. Riding creates heat and moisture from the rider and waterproof breathable jackets can only vent moisture slowly, particularly when it is raining. The answer is to ride more slowly in the rain so that your body generates less heat.

Your clothing should enable you to feel comfortably warm in the rain. If you're on a short summer ride, you'll not need a three-season rainjacket and can save around 400g by choosing a lightweight two-layer jacket. They're not quite as effective in a full day's downpour, but should hold out for several hours, long enough for you to find shelter. For a year-long trip involving wet, high or cold places as well as warm ones, it may be worth investing in a top quality jacket.

Cycle-specific waterproof jackets generally include a longer back and sleeves to allow for reach, a more fitted torso for wind resistance and features like pit zips, map pockets and reflective piping. Trousers are also cut for cycling, with zipped ankles to fit over shoes, a bend in the knees and Velcro closures to stop cuffs catching in the chain. Whether the increased utility of these clothes on the bike compensates for their lesser suitability off the bike is your decision; you might prefer an all-round jacket for trekking as well as cycling.

Footwear

No one denies the greater efficiency of stiff-soled cycling shoes over conventional sports trainers or sandals. Nowadays there is a huge range of cycle-specific footwear on the market, ranging from sandals to light hiking boots (eg Shimano's MT90 boot), most with a recessed Shimano SPD cleat built into the sole of the shoe. Many bike tourers choose combination pedals that have an SPD fitting on one side and a platform on the other, so they can ride the bike with ordinary shoes as well as their bike shoes.

Opinions differ as to how good these shoes are for walking in, especially for long walks, and there are those who cannot find a cycling shoe wide enough for their foot or just to their liking. On ultra-long rides, it's relatively common to find cyclists wearing trainers or sandals or even hiking boots. Over long trips of many months, there's no telling what problems may develop from wearing sandals all day, or from wearing cycling shoes that give a limited range of movement for your feet and that's why it's difficult to tell what will work for you over the long term. I've seen people happy with their san-

dals even though they appear to have developed flat feet like rickshaw drivers from pressing their feet into pedals all day. My own very thick sandals split after a few months cycling. Since then, real hiking boots have been the solution for me – stiff, comfortable, waterproof, warm – and great for walking in.

Footwear is an individual thing and, though you may be giving up some efficiency, on a long trip you have to have happy feet!

Light hiking boots are very versatile yet comfortable on a long tour.

Camping gear

Knowing that your carrying capacity is about the same as a backpacker's, take a leaf out of their book and get some good quality, light and compact equipment. These are some of the classic bike-touring choices for camping – tough tents, tiny stoves, snug sleeping bags, compact water filters and a few other bits and pieces you will come to rely on.

TENTS

Assuming you need one at all your choice of tent is one of the most important equipment decisions you have to make. A strong tent will stand you in good stead but be prepared to pay upwards of £200 in the UK or about $300 in the USA. Choose a two-person tent even if you're travelling solo; you're going to spend a lot of time in your tent and you'll need space as well the comfort. And who knows, you might have guests!

Macpac Minaret – a tough but cosy tunnel tent.

If you're travelling as a couple aim for a spacious 2-3 person model and make sure the tent has a large vestibule for storing gear as well as to cook in. Too little space and you'll end up fighting all the sooner, though two doors may help keep the peace. Expect the weight to be 2.5-3kg. It's not worth paying extra or giving up space or strength for the sub-two kilo tent; leave these to hard-core backpackers. If you're ordering a tent from the internet, check the weight figures carefully first; manufacturer's figures are often quoted by mail-order shops without checking and needless to say, manufacturers are often optimistic, especially American ones. You may learn a lot more from a visit to a specialist shop, fishing scales in hand to weigh up the choices.

PEGGING DOWN YOUR PREFERENCE

Think about where you want to go on this and future trips. If you're definitely headed for mountains, consider a 4-season tent; otherwise 3-season tents are fine for the job and the better ones have been used many times by bikers going through the Himalayas. As a rule, tents tend to be designed for the weather in the countries where they are made. European tents generally work well in the rain and cold weather, American tents ventilate well in hot weather and often perform well in strong winds. The better tents from New Zealand have excellent rain protection and are good mountain tents. Four-season tents usually have steep roofs to shed snow and often have four poles to support a snowfall. Good ones have two doors to facilitate escape if you wake up to your front door covered by a snowdrift; and aluminium poles are the standard.

If this sounds like overkill for your type of travel, look at the stronger 3-season models, which may be more comfortable in terms of a high-volume shape and larger doors. Choose a drab, natural-coloured tent that will draw less attention than a bright-coloured tent.

Avoid expensive ultra-light tents, as they lose out on strength and long-term durability. A recent long-term tent test against ultraviolet light revealed that some of the most expensive and lightest tents fared worst. Polyester flysheets generally held up better against UV damage but it was clear that the thicker flysheets did best of all and this underlines the need to ask yourself if you really must minimize weight or if you should get something a bit more durable, especially if you're a long-haul traveller who can expect to leave the tent up in the sun day after day.

Always use an extra groundsheet underneath the sewn-in tent floor. It keeps mud off your tent (remember New Zealand and Australian immigration officials don't like foreign mud!) and takes the beating your tent would otherwise receive. It reduces condensation under the tent floor so that when you pack up, your tent will be fairly dry. It's not necessary to buy the custom-fitted groundsheet made by the tent maker, they are expensive for what they are; blue polythene tarps serve just as well, are far cheaper and make a handy rain cape or shade cloth.

Freestanding or tunnel tents?

Tunnel tents are popular among bikers because the poles are shorter and fewer, so you get a lot of space for the weight. If you pitch them into the wind, they are pretty aerodynamic and you won't have a problem, but if the wind should shift, a weaker tent would be in trouble. Most of Swedish tentmaker Hilleberg's designs are tunnel tents and come with plenty of pegs and guy lines to cope with changing conditions. Tunnel tents also go up and down very quickly and safely, often with the flysheet already attached. The main source of irritation with these tents is on hard ground, where it's hard to get the pegs in. Stake out all your guy lines before going to bed or you'll be in trouble if a key guy line comes loose in the middle of a night of howling winds.

Freestanding tents offer the convenience of not needing pegs to stand up, but you'd be wise to stake out the tent anyway in the mountains or chuck something inside before fully erecting them. In a fierce storm, you will probably have less anxiety in a pegged and weighted freestanding tent but if your pegs are secure, a good tunnel tent will survive. Freestanding tents usually are a little better ventilated and the designers offer a lot more freedom in creating a useful shape.

Some brands to look out for

Top names from the USA are The North Face, Sierra Designs, Marmot, and Mountain Hardwear. They all make some excellent 4-season and 3+ season tents with three or four poles. The North Face tents probably have the edge for bikers; a touch lighter than the heavier duty Mountain Hardwear or Marmot tents.

High quality European names include Vaude and Salewa of Germany, very expensive Hilleberg of Sweden, and Terra-Nova of the UK. Terra-Nova's

Voyager is a classic: its virtues are extreme strength and wind-resistance, and a good vestibule for cooking. Terra-Nova's Laserlarge tents are worth a look too, but may be a little delicate for a long trip. Vaude tents are affordable, good all-rounders which come in a natural shade of green. Salewa makes some classic mountain tents, strong and compact in design. Hilleberg's Nallo GT, for light weight and a large vestibule has been mentioned by numerous cycletourers, though it costs about fifty percent more than the competition. Either the Nallo GT or Terra Nova Voyager would probably win in a European bike tourers opinion poll for best tent. New Zealand's MacPac makes some of the best tents: thick groundsheets, quick to set up or take down, good in high winds and the polyester flysheets don't sag when they get wet. Their Minaret tent is a classic two-person mountain tent, though a bike-touring couple ought to go for the larger Olympus, which would handle a side wind better.

There are a couple of tents designed with vestibules big enough to store a bike or two – Vaude's Monolith, the MSR Velo and Terra-Nova's LaserLarge. It's a nice thought, but a luxury you don't need. Make your bike suffer outside the tent.

If all this sounds like too much expense, go with what you already have, but if you're using a cheap tent, be more cautious choosing a campsite, avoiding open spaces, hills and beaches and stick to campgrounds or woods where you can find a sheltered spot. You will meet many travellers with cheap and cheerful tents – we met a Japanese biker travelling down the US Pacific Coast on a $20-bike and a 75 cent-tent! It had no poles, so he had to find trees to tie the guy lines to, but most important of all, it did not stop him making his trip. On another occasion a German biker in New Zealand was using a cheap one-pole tent, basically waterproof but he had to accept the odd blow-down every now and then and sometimes had to spend a few hours drying things out. He told us he never worried, because he only spent the equivalent of €100 on the tent and felt he had nothing to lose.

Tent repairs

Be sure to carry some SeamGrip in your repair kit. This urethane-based glue is excellent for sealing seams on your tent and great for repairs, used alone or with a repair kit full of circular patches – the Thermarest repair kit works great for tents. Also look out for aluminium collars of 9-10mm width sold as a repair sleeve for a broken tent pole. Some tents come with them and they beat the alternative, which is to use a tent peg as a splint bound with duct tape.

Tent pegs

Commonly overlooked because they come with your tent, pegs are what holds your tent up in a storm and for a long trip; it's worth getting good ones. In the picture on p72 the choice of tent pegs covers the cheapest on the left to the best pegs on the market on the right. If your tent came with pegs like the **example on the far left**, throw them in your recycling bin and give some thought to whether the tent itself is good enough for extended touring. The **second** and **third pegs** along are made from steel and aluminium respectively. They are both light, good for general use and the easiest to put in and take out by hand, but will bend in hard ground and on a long trip you may have to straighten them once a week by bashing them on a flat stone.

The **peg in the middle** is made of tent pole aluminium and is the most expensive. It's excellent in soft or hard ground, but not quite as strong as it looks (notice the bend in this one). Hit this peg hard off-centre and it can snap. The **big plastic peg** is very good for soft ground, sand or snow. If they are damaged, they can be sharpened or filed back into shape. The **large aluminium peg** to the right is reasonably

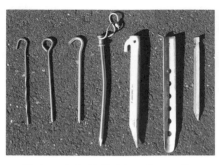

Tent peg tech. Quite interesting, really.

light for its size and is designed for sand or snow. Its blunt tip makes it a poor performer on hard ground.

The hard-core camper's choice

The **peg on the far right** is by far the strongest peg I've used. It's not hand-friendly and needs pushing in with a boot sole or stone and pulling out with another tent peg or a loop of nylon, but it will not bend or break and is excellent in hard and soft ground. The 'V' shape provides rigidity and gives it a lot of stickiness in soft ground. This is the only type of peg I use on most trips.

SLEEPING BAGS

Your sleeping bag is both delicate and vital, so if possible keep it in your panniers for extra protection against rain, dust or any damage. Choose a down sleeping bag to get the maximum warmth for volume and weight. Down must be kept dry as it's useless when wet and dries very slowly, so besides consid-

---

TIPS FOR A HAPPY MARRIED LIFE IN THE TENT

If you're a camping couple, see if you can find semi-rectangular sleeping bags rather than mummy bags so that when zipped together, the zips are at the side of the bag and not at the centre as they are with mummy-style bags. Zips at the side mean the warmer person can cool off a bit without freezing the cooler person. You have a lot more room to move around when two semi-rectangular bags are zipped together. The sleeping bags we use (⌨ www.zwerfkei.nl) weigh less than 1kg and are rated down to –7°C. A similar bag in the USA is LL Bean's Katahdin 20 degree (ie: 20 degrees Fahrenheit) rectangular bag, though the temperature rating on this bag may be a bit optimistic.

Our next tip to foster togetherness is to prevent Thermarest-type mats from slipping apart: a possible cause of marital disharmony. We use the backrest conversion kits on

our Thermarests and leave them on the mats even when not using them to sit up in. We stitched Velcro on the front and backs of the side straps on the backrests and Velcro the two Thermarests together so they do not slip apart. Seems to work for us as Heleen became pregnant towards the end of the trip and has just given birth to our first baby!

Robin and Heleen Wielders-Boerman

ering waterproof panniers or reliable liner bags, you should store your bag in a lightweight dry bag such as kayakers and canoeists use, with a roll-top closure. These bags are very airtight, you can squeeze a lot of air out of the sleeping bag when you roll down the dry bag, compressing it in the process.

Buying the best quality bag you can afford will save more weight and volume. Don't worry too much about whether the down is Hungarian, Polish or Chinese, just compare by looking at the fill-power of the down. This is a standardized measure between all manufacturers, though US makers use a slightly different way of measuring and their numbers come out a little higher. Cheap down is usually rated at around 550 fill-power, and the best is around 775. To get those last few feathers out of the down takes human hands and hence a higher cost for the best down.

Always be sceptical about manufacturers' temperature ratings – there is no independent standard for these. Get a bag suited to where you're going because there is such a thing as having too warm a sleeping bag. There are very few quality bags made with zips that go all the way round the foot, but this type of bag can be opened up to lay out flat, which is great in warm weather. Western Mountaineering in the US manufacture several such bags.

Plan on sleeping with all your clothes and a hat on in the coldest weather, or if you're a couple, buy matching bags to zip together on the coldest nights. This saves a lot of heat. Try to select a bag that will be warm enough 95 percent of the time rather than a bag that will cope with every imaginable cold night but be too warm 95 percent of the time. Obviously if you're going to Tibet in winter, where you're likely to be in –30°C weather for weeks on end, take no chances; splash out a –30°C bag or seek out local instruction on meditation and mind control.

Sleeping pads and air mattresses

To save space most bikers choose a Thermarest inflatable mat, generally picking the very lightest models. Even these are at least twice as thick (1"/2.5cm) as a closed-cell foam mat for less than half the packed volume. The thinnest Thermarests, however, are also the most delicate. If you ever use them outside the tent, you're risking a puncture. Repairing them is much like repairing a bike tyre puncture, only a patch is normally not necessary.

Urethane glues such as SeamGrip will fix a puncture but need four to six hours to set, so it's bad luck if you discover your puncture in the evening – set to work immediately, use only a drop of glue and go to bed as late as you can. Duct tape might work in a pinch, but clean it all off in the morning and then glue the hole, riding with the repair exposed to the air if you have to ride that day.

The thin Thermarests – those with holes cut into the foam rather than solid foam – are also vulnerable to delamination due to grease migrating through the nylon. It's vital to keep this type of mat as clean as you can, washing off any dirt or sweat regularly. The short length is fine, but in cold weather you need to put clothing under your legs for insulation against ground cold.

The reliable, indeed almost indestructible alternative is a closed-cell foam mat. These are bulkier, less thick and less comfortable but are slightly lighter than air mattresses. The cheap generic kinds are less than a centimetre thick and take some getting used to – it's well worth getting something more comfortable and warmer on cold ground. If you do not want the risk of punctures and enjoy lying on your mat outside your tent, look at high quality closed cell foam mats. The best ones, again, are made by Thermarest. Climbers have long favoured their Ridge-Rest model. It's 1.5cm thick, rolls up into a fairly bulky package but is very strong and works well on sloping ground – you will not slip off it easily. At 1.9cm the Z-rest is thicker and more comfortable and folds into a more compact box shape but it's easily damaged by being tightly strapped on a bike rack. Hard-core types often go with the Ridge-Rest while those who want a full night's sleep go with an air mattress but suffer the anxiety that it might delaminate on the road.

A farewell British dinner of potatoes, sausage and leeks cooked on the road by Mark and Juliette McLean before leaving the country for two years.

STOVES

If you're not going far afield, it's easy to find a stove that uses fuel widely available in your own country. On short trips, for instance, I often take a butane gas stove because one canister might last the entire trip and these types of stove are far and away the most convenient to use. You will find the old style Camping Gaz '206' puncture-type canisters all over Europe, including Eastern Europe, where the newer resealable canisters of any brand are almost impossible to find. The '206' size is found in many different brands throughout much of Europe and so is much cheaper than the larger resealing type made only by Camping Gaz. However, on a longer trip, the cost of those canisters adds up and once you leave Europe, the chances of finding them become slimmer. You need a multi-fuel stove.

There's a wide choice of lightweight stoves. MSR's WhisperLite Internationale lives up to its name and burns unleaded petrol (gasoline) and kerosene (paraffin) as well as more refined Coleman fuel/white gas. MSR's Dragonfly is noisier and bulkier but has the ability to simmer and so is the cook's choice. Mountaineers go for MSR's XGK II. No frills and made for boiling noodles at altitude. The XGK burns anything, it ain't fussy.

Swedish brands Primus and Optimus also make very good stoves. The Primus multifuel stoves have a wide base and pot supports – an important consideration as watching your dinner tip into the sand can really ruin your day. Primuses are a touch heavier but solid. The best model, the Omnifuel, has a simmering control but, with all these stoves, that extra valve is one more thing to go wrong. With a bit of experience, you won't need it – to regulate the flame just partially cover it with a tin can top or similar. A rugged stove weighing a few extra grams is worth it. I've owned fourteen stoves and broken eight

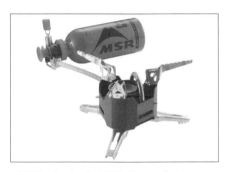

MSR's classic, the XGK. Known for its roar but then as Janne Corax says, 'I love that sound. It means dinner is coming!'

While backpackers make do with single-shot espresso pots cyclists can carry a six-shot model like this for multiple caffeine hits.

of them, though that includes driving over one. I've yet to break my Primus Omnifuel. The Optimus Nova folds up into a very compact bundle and appears a little more delicate than the others, but has a novel jet-cleaning trick enabling you to clean soot out while the stove is going.

With all these stoves, get the maintenance kit with the necessary spare parts. There's a certain campers' lore about the regular need to dismantle and clean these types of stoves but most of these problems have to do with using low-quality fuel rather than any fault in design. Lastly, buy and use MSR's foil windshield, which wraps around the stove and pot. Even if it's not windy, using a windshield saves fuel and helps spread heat around the pot.

CARRYING FUEL

Liquid fuel bottles need to be packed well away from food and many riders take no chances of a messy leak inside their panniers by carrying their fuel on the bike frame itself. A fuel bottle which has the fuel pump screwed into it is more likely to leak than bottles sealed with the screw-in stopper, so that's the best one to carry externally. In places like India which are notorious for inquisitive young hands fiddling with everything on your bike, better to double wrap your fuel bottle in plastic and keep it with your stove rather than near food or clothing.

Only the small 600ml fuel bottles such as those made by Sigg (shown here) fit standard bike bottle cages, but it is this size which manufacturers like Primus and Optimus supply with their stoves and which work best with those stoves. (MSR recommends no particular size fuel bottle for its stoves). For carrying larger fuel bottles (a one litre bottle for storage plus a 600ml bottle as the fuel tank should give a week's cooking for two), consider buying a bottle

Bikebuddy

600ml Sigg

cage such as the Bikebuddy (🖳 www.bike buddy.co.uk), also shown here. The Bikebuddy fits any frame and will hold a bottle up to 2 litres very securely.

When carrying a fuel bottle, wrapping the bottle in an old inner tube (as shown above) will prevent it from coming loose from the bottle cage or flying off the bike. For off-road trips or long downhills on rough roads, extra precautions to tie your bottles on to your bike are a good idea – elastic bands made from old inner tubes work well.

PART 1 – PRACTICALITIES

GSI's hard-anodized aluminium pots.

KITCHEN ESSENTIALS

There are pots and pans to suit every style nowadays; camp cooking is no longer a matter of boiling noodles and blackening the pot just because your stove cannot simmer. Mountaineers using a stove like MSR's classic XGK are perhaps mainly interested in a rapid boil, but on a long trip you might want to refine your cooking skills and make pancakes or omelettes. A Teflon-coated pot will be much easier to clean, though you cannot use the old technique of scouring it with wet sand or river grit the way you can with stainless steel. I've found the best pots on the market to be hard-anodized aluminium jobbies made by GSI and Optimus – tough as stainless steel but with better heat dispersion and a more hard-wearing Teflon coating. MSR pots are also good but you can't use the lid as a frying pan. If you can afford titanium, you will surely appreciate its light weight for your entire trip. There is no coating to worry about but hot spots are not as bad as with stainless steel.

For plates or bowls GSI has everything you could possibly want as long as you like Lexan, the practically indestructible plastic from which Oakley cycling shades and now Nalgene bottles are made. I go for a large, deep bowl that holds cyclist-sized portions, keeps the wind out, and works for cereals, soups and anything else. Having tried out (and broken) many different mugs of all materials, I have been using a Lexan 500ml mug for several years; it retains heat almost as well as a double-walled mug but is lighter and hasn't melted on the espresso pot yet, unlike other plastics. Steel mugs impart a taste to drinks (as does polythene) and weigh more, all of which brings us back to Lexan as the material that will outlast us all. The large mugs may fit around bottles or at the least can be stuffed with teacloths or teabags in your panniers.

Ordinary spoons and forks, which is to say any old, used or cheap supermarket pressed or stamped steel spoon or fork are better than trying to find something flash in a camping shop to do the same job at twice the price. Avoid expensive stuff, especially obvious junk such as folding spoon sets or telescoping chopsticks. Cheap cutlery works best and costs next to nothing. Chopsticks are indeed useful, but get the real kind which work well for all sorts of things, including picking pasta out of the pot for testing, or carrying in your pocket to a street restaurant where you're unsure of the cleanliness of their chopsticks.

Ortlieb's folding sink. No draining board...

If you're going to carry the kitchen sink, make it Ortlieb's folding version. There are other kinds, but even though it lacks taps and a draining board, Ortlieb's is far and away the best. Available in 5L and 10L sizes, the 5L is what you need for a bike trip. It will hold all your pots and plates for washing up and can be used for a footbath or even an al fresco shower stand where you don't want to get mud on your feet. The Ortlieb sink isn't bad as a shopping basket either and is great for a fishing trip or beachcombing.

Go for the Lexan Nalgene bottles, as they don't spoil the taste and can be boiled, which you will occasionally want to do for hygiene. Putting anything other than water in your bottles makes them a bacterial breeding ground. One piece of camping gear that works great is Sigg's aluminium box, available in two sizes. It's strong and excellent for food use and would work well for carrying a cooked lunch. Another cunning tip pinched from Kym McConnell's *Tibet Overland* book is to order two lunches in a restaurant; eat one and take away the other to reheat later.

HEADTORCHES

It's no longer a torch or a flashlight that you want, it's a headtorch – and one with an LED beam, as these last the longest and consume least power. Keep an eye out in the shops as the latest LED headtorches get better and better, though one of the originals, the tiny Petzl Tikka is still one of the best. Better versions are bright enough to use while cycling, and though there are more powerful headlights on the market, you may not want to have batteries behind your head – it makes

Petzl Tikka. Won't burn the night down but it won't overload your spokes either

reading in bed uncomfortable if you lie on your back. Battery life is incredible with these modern LED lights, but the figures they give are always for tests at around 20°C, unrealistically warm for real-life use. Battery life is much shorter in cold temperatures, something to consider when stocking up for a long trip in the wilds outside of summer.

WATER FILTERS

If you're travelling only in developed countries or densely populated India or South-east Asia, where you may never camp or cook by yourself, you're probably better off buying bottled water or treating it with chlorine or iodine pills as circumstances demand (though check the cap seals). Off the beaten track, being able to filter river or lake water will save money and the environment from a lot of empty plastic bottles. Don't filter tap water just to save money or plastic, as tap water tastes awful in many tropical countries – better to buy drinking water like everyone else.

Filtering water is not a perfect solution and most water filter manufacturers no longer claim they are 'purifiers' after it was established that pumping water through an iodine resin layer in a filter was too fast a process to reliably kill all viruses. What you're doing is drastically improving the odds, not eliminating all risk. Iodine takes about half an hour to do its work, which is why

Katadyn's Hiker water filter

you have to wait after putting iodine pills or drops in your water bottles. Iodine has the drawbacks of bad taste, the possibility of overdosing and the fact that it's not advised for long-term use, but travellers still use it because it kills all bacteria and viruses and the pills or drops are so compact. Bear in mind that iodine takes longer to kill viruses in cold water.

Water filters do not kill viruses as these are far too small to filter out, but you can make a reasonable assessment as to how likely it is that viruses are present in the water: tropical areas, known cholera country and high concentrations of population are all high-risk places for viruses, though you'll probably want to steer clear of river water in all densely populated areas or farmland (beware of agricultural run-off including pesticides in streams). It's in the high country or rural areas where you're wild camping that your filter will be useful. There are few places left in the world safe from pathogens such as giardia (it is found even in Tibet) and you would be wise to treat all water when wild-camping, no matter how remote your location.

Swiss-made Katadyn filters have been around the longest and a few years ago Katadyn acquired the largest US filter manufacturer, Pur. Katadyn's own filters are the best in terms of quality and strength but are the most expensive too – about US$200, or £190 in the UK for the Pocket model. These ceramic core filters are good for 50,000 litres, which should last a group of riders several years of heavy use.

The UK's own Pre-mac filters are well regarded but the filter is good for only 200 litres. Don't bother with the tiny filters that fit into a water bottle. These are only good for day rides on your bike and will not last long enough for a bike tour. Katadyn makes the biggest seller in the US, the Hiker filter, which is good for 200 gallons and pumps faster than any of them because the filter is made of pleated fibreglass, not ceramic. Needing less pressure to pump makes it less likely to break. Most filters can be maintained in the field, which can mean unclogging some of the innards with a toothbrush once the flow-rate starts to dwindle.

First Need of the USA makes the only water purifier which meets the standard set by the US Environmental Protection Agency for non-chemical purifying of water, ie: removing all bacteria, cysts and viruses. This model, the Deluxe, uses an electrostatic charge to remove viruses and filters out bacteria. Cartridges are good for 470 litres of water and the whole unit weighs just 425g. If you can find the First Need model, it will give total peace of mind, but water-borne viruses are extremely rare in the remote areas where you would think of filtering water. Filtered water will taste much better than water treated with pills and it will be immediately drinkable; handy to have on a long trip.

GPS

Luke Skinner

Since the technology has become cheaper and handsets smaller over the last ten years or so, the GPS (Global Positioning System) has become an invaluable navigational aid and one which many cycle tourists find useful.

GPS receivers work by calculating the time taken for a signal to reach the user from satellites orbiting the Earth. Since the signal travels at constant speed, the time can be used to calculate distance, and with three signals, the unit can give latitude and longi-

Garmin Etrex – a navigation *aid*, not an alternative.

tude. A fourth signal is needed to give an accurate altitude. There's a total of 24 satellites in orbit, of which 12 are visible from anywhere at any time. Most modern receivers have 12 channels, meaning that they can receive signals from all of these satellites at any one time. The signals do require a clear line of sight, so it is very rare to find all 12 available, although most receivers rarely have trouble locating the necessary four (except when indoors, under overhanging cliffs or in very dense forest).

Since the US government turned off 'Selective Availability' (the deliberate degradation of the signal for civilian use) in 2000, it has been possible to pinpoint your location with an error of less than 5m anywhere in the world. This is obviously very, very accurate, but it must be remembered that the position given is only useful when you have something to compare it with. In most parts of the world, maps (even when they are available at a scale which would make such small measurements meaningful) are nowhere near accurate enough for a position found by GPS to be helpful. When testing out our unit in the Western Sahara, we found that the position given, when plotted on our map, often put us many kilometers to one side or other of the road we were standing on! Other users have found that their GPS showed that important features on their maps were displaced by several kilometres. All this serves to emphasize the point that GPS can only really be as accurate as the maps you use it with.

It's worth thinking carefully about what maps are needed to complement a GPS. In many European countries, a grid exists similar to the Ordnance Survey grid in Britain, and most GPS units will be able to provide a grid reference in place of a latitude/longitude (lat/long) position. However, in less well-mapped areas, you'll be relying on plotting lat/long on the map, so something with grid lines is essential. Bear in mind that if the grid is too widely spaced you can fill in the gaps with a ruler and sharp pencil, but on most projections the lines of longitude are very slightly curved. If your map is of a small scale then drawing straight lines to interpolate can be a significant source of error. In terms of scale, you need a scale of 1:250,000 or at the very least 1:500,000 to really take advantage of the accuracy offered – anyone trying to navigate in an area remote enough to make GPS worthwhile would be well advised to get hold of the most detailed maps available.

One situation where GPS is extremely helpful is when you have known waypoints for important landmarks. Obviously, if these are taken from maps suffering from the inaccuracies mentioned above, GPS can do little more than point out these errors. However, if the waypoints are known to be correct, GPS can be used to point the way with incredible accuracy and reliability. GPS waypoints are becoming more and more widely available on the internet and in guidebooks, particularly for popular overland routes. Arriving as the sun went down at a ruined French fort in southern Morocco, after a gruelling day on atrocious tracks, we were relieved when a previously stored waypoint helped us find the nearby auberge. Our guidebook simply told us it was near the fort – when in fact it was out of sight of the fort itself, over a small rise. Without the GPS we could have spent hours searching the area as darkness fell. However, a warning against relying totally on someone else's waypoints in a remote environment hardly needs to be given.

Bearing all this in mind, if you decide to add a GPS to your navigational toolset then the next obvious question is: which unit? There is a bewildering range available, varying in size, complexity and price but for cycle-touring the smaller, simpler units are the obvious choice. Anything allowing you to upload digital maps will be of little use outside Europe and North America, and the size and power requirements of these units makes them unsuited to use outside a vehicle anyway. A relatively basic model, such as Garmin's excellent Etrex range, will do everything you could ask for and more and could be had for less than £150. A handlebar mount is extremely useful, enabling virtually hands-free operation, although bear in mind that if using a wireless bike computer interference is possible which can give some interesting distance readings at the end of the day! In theory it ought to be possible to do away with bike computers altogether and use the GPS to give (far more accurate) readings for distance, speed, etc, although until battery life improves significantly it is not really feasible to leave most units on all day – my Etrex Summit, admittedly a few years old, goes through a pair of AA batteries about every 15 hours if used this way.

GPS definitely has its place on a cycling expedition in the more far-flung parts of the world but it should be seen as a useful aid to navigation rather than a magic wand. It would be extremely unwise to set out into a remote area without the best map you can get, a compass, and the knowledge to use them – apart from anything else, you never know when the electronics might fail or the batteries unexpectedly go flat!

PART 2: ROUTE OUTLINES

The world's your oyster – but you don't have to try and swallow it in one go. This section gives a broad overview of some of the best adventure cycling opportunities out there on the basis that prospective cycle-tourers like ideas and inspiration, but don't necessarily want a route map telling them exactly where to go. If you want that kind of detail, there are guidebooks and websites aplenty, but a lot of riders looking for a bit of adventure want to keep their options open and choose a route as their trip unfolds.

Many riders are drawn to the idea of an epic RTW or transcontinental ride; it's a lifetime's dream and drawing a line across the map is easy, but don't feel you have to stick to an ambitious plan once you're on the road. You may well find greater rewards from exploring one region intimately rather than having a series of distant destinations in mind. And you may find that some parts of the route are just too tough, too dangerous or too boring to ride.

Some world travellers vow never to hitch a lift or put their bike on a bus. We doesn't subscribe to that view. Travelling is at the core of this book, principally on a bicycle of course, but there's no need to slog every single miserable mile. Using other transportation you'll meet the locals, rest, and save time to enjoy something better later. Cherry pick the best bits because there are many parts of the world that are well worth missing – especially on a bike. Much of the West has become a no-go area for bikers or lacks the challenge of wilder, exotic places. That's why this section of this book really gets stuck in where the bike lanes stop – beyond Western Europe.

© TRACEY MAUND

TRIP REPORT
TURKEY TO KYRGYZSTAN

Name	Cass Gilbert
Year of birth	1974
Occupation	I run bike trips – www.out-there-biking.com
Nationality	British
Other bike travels	Sydney to London

This trip	Turkey to Kyrgyzstan
Trip duration	Four months
Number in group	Two
Total distance	5000km (3125 miles)
Cost of trip	£800 each plus £600 for flights and loads for visas

Longest day	190km
Best day	Reaching Buchara, Uzbekistan, and eating ice cream after the long traverse of the desert
Worst day	Killer headwinds, soft tarmac and 50°C in the Karakum Desert: a lethal combination
Favourite ride	Circling round the pastures of Son Kol Lake, Kyrgyzstan, amongst the yurts and wild horses
Biggest headache	Finding decent tandem tyres in Bishkek market
Biggest mistake	Not bringing Marathon XR tyres
Couldn't do without	Rosal, my tandem companion
Pleasant surprise	The incredible reception we always received; in Iran the police had to funnel a path for us through the crowds!
Any illness	None

Bike model	Thorn Adventure tandem
New/used	New
Modifications	Roller brake; upgraded XT drivetrain and Sun rims
Wish you'd fitted	Suspension seat post for the stoker, spare (extra long) cable for drag brake
Tyres used	Vredestein Spyders for mixed conditions (rubbish), Panaracer Pasela Tourguards for smooth (excellent)
Baggage Setup	Four panniers, roll top bag, bar bag; lots bungied on
Wish you'd brought	More pictures from home – a great ice breaker
Wish you hadn't brought	Nothing: you have to be more selective with a tandem

Bike problems	None mechanical thanks to rock-solid frame & wheels
Accidents	Pile-up in Iran when someone was ogling the tandem
Same bike again	My tandem days are over now!
Recommendations	See www.tandemtoturkestan.com
General tip	A tandem trip is very social way of travelling as long as you're getting on well
Road philosophy	(1) Allow lots of time off the saddle, too, to take a break, recharge and explore. (2) A bit of discomfort here and there helps reawaken the senses!

Europe

Europe: So many bike roads, so little sunshine. © Jon Housego.

Many first biking adventures start in Europe, as do many round-the-world trips – think of the old Magic Bus route from London to Kathmandu – cross the channel and your adventure has begun. Europe is made for bike touring and is also a great place to give you and your bike a shakedown while building strength for more challenging riding and destinations later on.

While it might not sound the most adventurous place in the world to ride, Europe has so many advantages and so much variety that it can't be overlooked. You don't need a guidebook for a bike trip in Europe – it's easy to find campgrounds by using a map and easy to get around on minor roads. If you have mechanical troubles, it's not too difficult to find parts or get your bike repaired.

Getting there is also a piece of cake. If travelling from the British Isles, you have plenty of ferry options and a dedicated bus service (💻 www.bike-express.co.uk) from the UK to four destinations in France, Spain and Italy which will carry your bike fully assembled. You can bring your bike with you on the Eurostar train to Paris, Lille or Brussels, though it has to be booked in advance and bagged. Those who have flown with their bikes to Europe frequently suggest using Europe's smaller airports if you plan on riding away from the airport. On the other hand, long-haul travellers say that Amsterdam's Schiphol Airport is one of the best: it even has a bike path leading to the city or nearby campgrounds.

PART 2 – ROUTE OUTLINES

READY-MADE ROUTES

As governments have developed national cycling routes, so the EU is taking an interest in trans-European routes (though has yet to throw in some funding). The planning is being done by national cycling federations and groups like the UK's Sustrans organization (💻 www.sustrans.org.uk). Following a signposted route obviously makes navigating easier – as long as the signposts are easy to find and follow – and the routes keep you off busy roads and tend to avoid steep hills.

A look at the Eurovelo map shows what will be on offer in a couple of years – many of these routes are already completed, and of course you don't have to wait before the signposts are in place to ride them. Sustrans already has books and maps available for routes such as the North Sea coast route (see box, p.86). The Danube route has been going for ages with plans to extend it to run from the Atlantic to the Black Sea. Many of the other Eurovelo routes have some historical theme to them, though some will mostly follow existing roads.

WESTERN EUROPE

France has the best road network in the world for bikes. A look at a map shows you a disproportionately high number of small roads (look for 'D' roads on French road maps) which have very little traffic on them – far more than any other country. It's so good for cycling that France hardly bothers with bicycle routes because these roads are so biker-friendly. You won't see many locals bike-touring until you hit Germany, but biking in all forms is well established in France. The camping scene is the best, with good campgrounds in almost every town and many villages too. Go for the municipal two-star camp-grounds – these are generally the best value, having the necessaries but no frills and fewer caravans. There's an excellent hostel network and also the pri-vate gîtes d'étape for cheap overnight accommodation with meals.

Your bike travels with you on most regional trains and will not need to be bagged. Bikes are now allowed on many TGVs (high speed trains) too, though they must be dismantled and bagged; your bike normally travels on the same train as you but this is not guaranteed. Sheldon Brown (🖳 www.sheldon-brown.com) has a number of interesting pages on France, including a useful French-English bicycle dictionary. France is more a nation of cycling spectators than participants these days, and though you will be able to get repairs done easily enough, it is harder than you might expect to find specialist touring gear in France. Wait till you're in Germany for that.

Spain is less oriented than France to cycle touring but that only makes a cycle-tourist an exotic visitor. Few tourists stray more than a few miles inland from the Mediterranean coast but this is the real rural Spain, far from the 'costas' and where you'll hear little English spoken. If you're headed for Africa, consider riding there through Spain and taking the ferry from Algeciras in southern Spain to Morocco. The ferry to the tiny Spanish enclave of Ceuta is the preferred ferry as it takes bikes for free and the Spanish-Moroccan border at Ceuta is relatively quiet compared to the hustle of Tangiers.

Mountain biking is a popular recreational activity here and there are many signposted MTB routes in the Pyrenees and elsewhere, besides the

Viva la Via Verde. © Luke Skinner.

Vias Verdes, the network of disused railway lines. Hopefully one day these routes will be combined to make one long off-highway route across Spain but until then the ancient pilgrimage route from Seville to Santiago, the Via de la Plata, is the closest thing. Running along on a former Roman road (forward thinking Romans – it's well suited to cycling), this 1000km trail runs through fairly remote country. Accommodation is in small hotels and hostels as well as pilgrim refuges and the occasional monastery. It's a simple, spartan trip.

The better known Camino de Santiago is set to become a recognized long-distance cycle route, but bikes don't follow the often steep and difficult walk-ing path exactly, and pedestrian pilgrims take priority over cyclists for beds in the refuges, but a biker has the luxury of carrying camping gear, and a night in the tent beats a night with a hundred snoring pilgrims keen to get up at 5.30am.

Bike paths abound in Germany, Austria and Switzerland and are often easily found on approaches to cities. Germany is a federal state and bike trails are organized regionally, making planning a trip the length of the country a little tricky. Start at Germany's government tourism website (💻 www.germany-tourism.de/biking takes you to their interactive map) and you will see a network of regional routes – combine these and you have a ready-made route across Germany. Scenically, it can be mundane, but the routes are away from traffic, offer much to see and have amenities for cyclists along the way. Your

---

WILD CAMPING IN EUROPE

The subject that hardly dares speak its name, wild camping is something we never imagine exists in Europe outside of the national parks. Only as a very last resort might one be forced to camp wild without permission, as it is usually easy to find a proper campground or hostel. But there are many long-distance travellers who choose to camp wild, even in Europe, either for budgetary reasons or for the challenge – asserting ancient rights to camp on land that was once owned by no-one!

The late Ken Kifer (💻 www.kenkifer.com) was one bike tourer who preferred camping in the wilds. He wrote: From my very first tour, I have been another kind of traveller, one who is as independent of public facilities as I am of the gas pump. I don't camp back in the woods because I'm poor, because I can't make friends with people, or because I can't reach my destination. I camp because it's the greatest experience on Earth. I don't camp out to travel nearly as much as I travel to camp out.

Though it's illegal, bikers have reported good wild-camping prospects in Spain and they're not bad in France due to low population density and fairly common patches of dense woodlands. The French no doubt don't enjoy discovering anyone wild camping on their early-morning mushroom hunts and free-campers will likely be asked to move on if discovered. Most land is earmarked for one activity or another, such as hunting, and a footpath suggests regular visits by people, so be discreet.

Eastern Europe and the poorer countries to the south are less territorial and if you ask, people will probably suggest somewhere to camp for free. Numerous bikers have been invited to camp in people's gardens in the Balkan countries. Greece is a great free-camping country (especially along the coast) where people tend to interpret the law in their own favour.

The Scandinavian countries have 'Jedermannsrechte' laws which enshrine Everyman's right to camp freely on public land and in certain cases on private land, subject to restrictions, principally that the right to camp is for one night only and generally only when nothing else is available. Scotland now has a similar law. Germany has no such law but Sebastian Eissing (see his Africa report on p.193) recommends Germany for having clean rivers and municipal sports centres for showers. Another biker, 'Catskill', wrote in Lonely Planet's Thorn Tree forum that 'Germany was very easy. Sometimes I would push the bike down a trail – the first fifty yards might have toilet paper. The next fifty yards might have some spent condoms. Then it was camping time.' A pleasant thought.

Camping in Serbia. © Luka Romih.

THE NORTH SEA CYCLE ROUTE

Said to be the longest signposted cycle trail in the world and passing through seven countries, this 6000km-route follows the North Sea coast, mostly on protected cycle paths or minor roads.

Expect wind and rain to be the biggest headaches and to have to camp for at least half the time. Ferries – of which 28 are needed for the whole circuit – link the British Isles with the continent and would also allow a shorter circuit, using the ferry from Newcastle in north-eastern England to Gothenburg – one of the route's highlights.

In Norway you can expect to see very little traffic except on occasional short stretches of main road. Major cities passed through are Newcastle, Aberdeen, Edinburgh, Bergen, Gothenburg, The Hague and Hamburg. It's a short season as ferry services are less frequent by mid-August and the Bergen (Norway) to Lerwick (Shetland Islands) service runs only once a week even in summer. It can be cycled in either direction but most maps, the UK's excellent Sustrans maps being an exception, assume you will cycle it anti-clockwise.

only distractions are food, beer, villages, old churches, museums and changing scenery along the way. To me, it's heaven and when on a world tour you encounter thundering traffic, potholes and no shade for miles on end, you'll remember it fondly.

The River Danube route attracts lots of cyclists – not just long-distance tourers but day-trippers and commuters so it can be crowded at weekends. Until it's extended you're likely to lose the trail soon after leaving Vienna as it doesn't go further than Bratislava.

The most popular section is that between Ingolstadt and Vienna, but the far western section from the very beginnings of the river at Donaueschingen in the Black Forest is the quietest and most beautiful. There are campgrounds, but you can also ask at boat clubs if you can camp on their lawns – I was never refused. Far less well-known but equally interesting and useful as a route through Germany is the path along the River Elbe, which runs as far as the Czech Republic and could be easily be combined with the Prague-Vienna Greenway (⌨ www.pragueviennagreenways.org).

EASTERN EUROPE AND THE BALKANS

Travelling east puts some of the excitement back into border crossings, where they still exist. The EU now extends considerably further east and the most recent EU member states will use the Euro from 2007 at the earliest, starting with Slovenia. Countries like Poland, Hungary and Slovenia are now relatively Westernized in the cities but the countryside remains slow-paced and far cheaper than the West, while the economies have grown so fast that major roads are now too busy for cyclists.

Slovenia is a great touring destination; Ljubljana city is a manageable size with an excellent campground on its northern side. The Julian Alps which border Italy and Austria are recommended. Road passes reach as high as 2100m and there are good free-camping possibilities everywhere except Triglav National Park. In the park itself there are more quality campsites per kilometre than anywhere else in the country. A circuit of the north-west takes you through Soca, good for hiking, kayaking and rafting trips as well as cycling. To the south, the karst formations of the Kras region offer laidback villages, forests good for camping, vineyards and rolling hills. And in the far south of

SLAVS REUNITED

Even though Serbia used to be a part of our own country – the old Yugoslavia, that is – we'd never been there. We found ourselves cycling through the northern part of Croatia and wondered what it would be like in Serbia. After hearing so much about how friendly they are and the recent Serbian-Croatian-Bosnian war, we really had no idea what to expect.

Vojvodina, the northern part of Serbia, is almost completely flat and is home to some two dozen nationalities or ethnic groups, though only the major ones are represented by a number larger than that of a small village. This makes the whole province a fascinating place if you're interested in people though the landscape appeals only to those who are not looking for obstacles to cross.

Straight after our arrival in Serbia we noticed a radical change from Croatia; everybody was a lot more relaxed, easy-going, always thinking (as we say) the Balkan way: no worries! Yet they have a lot to worry about: the country's economy is devastated, people are lucky to have a job and even if they do, they can make only a part of what they need to see them through a month. Everyone has to make some extra effort to make enough money and they laugh sadly when they tell you 'funny' stories about the regime's godfathers and their way of doing business.

We were continually surprised by the hospitality we received in Serbia. Though we had problems finding a secure place to pitch a tent in Croatia, we never had that problem in Serbia. In Croatia, people warned us about warmongering lunatics wandering around and how dangerous it might be to camp freely. Instead, everyone in Serbia reassured us that the worst we would encounter even if we slept in the middle of a village would be noisy and curious drunks coming home in the middle of the night.

As Slovenians, we could speak the language and were welcomed as former brothers from Yugoslavian times, but we're not sure how much of that hospitality would be extended to a stranger who couldn't communicate with the locals. Then again, Serbia was once part of a prosperous country, so the people don't see you as a Space Viking coming from another planet, as is often the case in parts of Asia. On the other hand, they are often quite angry with English-speaking people because they see them as part of the 'willing coalition' of countries that supported the USA during their bombing of Serbia. So some caution when expressing one's view of world politics is quite important. As with all Mediterranean people, you're either their friend or their enemy.

For scenery, Serbia south of the Danube (and especially the Djerdap Canyon through which the Danube flows) is much more interesting. Hills and mountains and forests are abundant all the way through southern Bulgaria and would be a real shame to miss.

We found the people in Bulgaria much more reserved than those in Serbia. They rarely approached us even when we waited to see if anyone would ask us if we needed help with something. In the end, we gave up and had to make an effort to find someone who would be willing to do so. On the contrary, when we came to the first Turkish settlements (there are about 600,000 Turkish people living in Bulgaria since Ottoman times) we found the people much more open and approachable. We could recognize each Turkish village by its mosque, whose minarets were positioned to be seen from a distance. We were really happy to find such villages at camping time; after a day in the saddle Bulgarian kebabs were much more delicious than the 'original' Turkish variety and came with chips.

Rila monastery in Bulgaria. © Luka Romih.

Luka Romih and **Manca Ravnikar**

TRIP REPORT
EUROPE TO SOUTH-EAST ASIA

Name Cameron Smith
Year of birth 1979
Occupation Puppeteer
Nationality Australian
Other bike travels New Zealand's North and South islands

This trip Netherlands, Germany, Austria, Slovakia, Hungary, Romania, Bulgaria, Turkey, Iran, Pakistan, China Tibet, Nepal, Thailand, Laos
Trip duration 10 months
Number in group Two
Total distance 15,000km (9400 miles)
Cost of trip US$6000 total

Longest day 200km
Best day Arriving in Lhasa to see the Potala
Worst day Swelteringly hot day in Iran
Favourite ride Romania is a gem of a place for a cycle tour
Biggest headache Quite literally – in Tibet from the altitude
Biggest mistake Not taking Mum along: had to cook my own meals
Any illness Mostly stomach problems from the water or food

Bike model Mongoose Randonneur
New/used One year old
Modifications Front and rear racks; high rise stem; lower gearing; changed drop bars to wide flat bars and bar ends for comfort
Tyres used Schwalbe Marathon XR tyres: 700c by 35mm Still using original front tyre: wouldn't use any other tyre for touring
Baggage Setup Two panniers on front lowrider; two on rear
Wish you'd brought I would use a free standing tent next time.

Bike problems Pedals and headset had to be replaced
Accidents One
Punctures Two: both rear
Same bike again For sure. It's comfortable and reliable.
Recommendations The Rhine and Donau rivers in Europe have bike paths that are great to introduce yourself to cycle touring. Easy and enjoyable for beginners.

Road philosophy Travel light. Your bike and your body will thank you.

the country you have Slovenia's small but attractive coastline, while the southeast has rolling hills with spas, campsites on farms and easier riding.

Travellers in a hurry to make tracks east or down the Dalmatian coast of Croatia may well avoid the Istrian Peninsula, but it would be a pity, for this area is full of towns built in the Venetian style during the Middle Ages. It's a popular holiday area, not particularly cheap although there are campgrounds, mostly built in the communist era on a grand scale. Some are now for nudists only; a revealing experience for a night or two. As a cyclist you will probably be in better shape than anyone else there!

You could take a ferry from Pula on the Istrian Peninsula to Losinj, one of the chains of islands off the Croatian coast. Going this way via the islands you avoid the traffic on the busy but beautiful coastal road. If you're riding down the coast to the historic Croatian city of Dubrovnik you'll ride through a 20km stretch of Bosnian territory though you won't have to undergo any entry formalities. EU citizens get a three-month visa for Croatia or Bosnia-Herzegovina at the border. Travel south of Dubrovnik is either by ferry to Italy, and then again to Greece, or by cycling through Albania. Mostly Muslim but a secular state, Albania is considered a safe but certainly an adventurous destination, though gun ownership is widespread and organized crime and corruption are still major problems.

Serbia and Montenegro also have much to offer bikers. The hilly areas of the south are free of tourists, with quiet villages where traditional farming techniques are still practised, though the country is not as cheap as it should be owing to the controlled exchange rate. Luka Romih (see p87) found local people very hospitable, offering food and places to stay. This was also the case in Bulgaria and Romania.

Bulgaria and Romania are less expensive than Serbia but with little traffic and offer superb touring. Horse-drawn carts are still more common than any other form of transport across much of the countryside. The range of food in these countries is relatively meagre but there is an abundance of home-grown produce that villagers or farmers will happily sell to you. Accommodation is often in private rooms (around €6 per room), people's gardens, farmland (farmers are easily found, so ask permission) or even in churches. Hot springs may cost only €0.50.

Russia

Edward Genochio

Russia covers an immense territory but much of it is devoid of roads and inaccessible to cyclists. The road network in European Russia (west of the Urals) is relatively well developed, leaving you plenty of choice for touring, but in Siberia (east of the Urals), roads are few and far between: if you're planning to ride to Vladivostok on the Pacific coast, there's basically just one east-west road, the Trans-Siberian highway although there are unsealed chunks between Chita and Blagoveschensk (halfway to Vladivostok). In theory the whole route

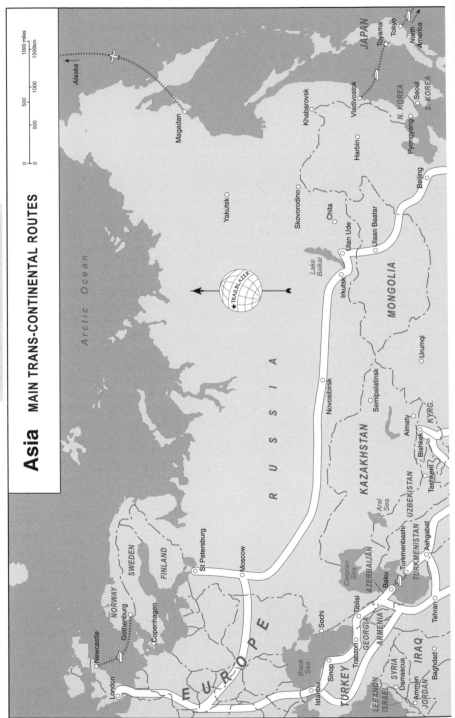

Asia MAIN TRANS-CONTINENTAL ROUTES

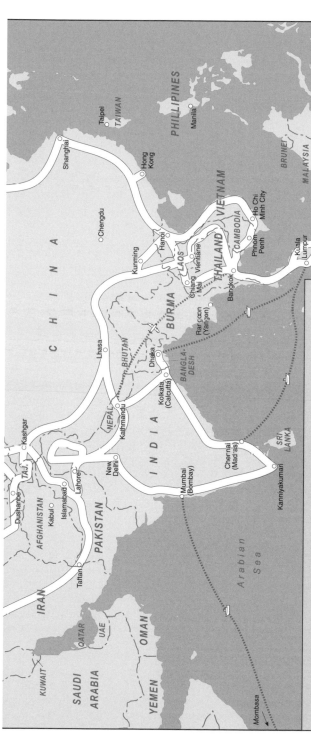

ROUTE RESTRICTIONS

Two Central Asian countries, Turkmenistan and Kazakhstan, offer only short visas making it a race against time for bikers determined to cycle every mile across Asia. Iran can also be difficult for Brits and Americans to get visas. Afghanistan is a country to watch over the next few years but, for now, watch it from nearby Tajikistan. The Altay/Tuva region of Russia is of great interest to adventure riders and it is hoped that a land crossing may be permitted from Altay to Mongolia in the near future. To the south, Myanmar (Burma) remains a barrier to trans-continental riders, though you can fly in and ride around the country but you must fly out. Bikes can enter Tibet from Nepal only on short, group visas

On the dirt in Russia. © Mark McLean.

should be paved within the next few years but don't count on it.

Russian road maps

Decent road maps suitable for cycle touring are hard to come by outside Russia (though specialist maps shops can help), but once you're in the country you should be able to pick up a comprehensive atlas. A good one to look out for is *Atlas Avtodorog Rossii* (Atlas of Russian Roads), jointly published by Astrel and AST. This covers the whole of Russia in 150 pages but it's lightweight and easily portable, with the area around Moscow shown at 1:500,000, the rest of European Russia at 1:1m and Siberia at 1:2.5m Since there are so few roads in Siberia anyway, that scale is adequate for all touring unless you plan to follow hunters' trails in the back-country, in which case you might be able to pick up maps locally.

In fact, virtually all mapping of Russia is based on the same cartographic style so whichever atlas you have the mapping will be the same. If your tour is limited to a small part of Russia, smaller atlases are also available, extracting the same mapping for a particular region.

In the atlas referred to above and on most other road maps 'federal roads' are shown in red; they should be sealed and of reasonable quality. Many red roads are designated 'M' roads, for example the M53 from Krasnoyarsk to Irkutsk; though technically motorways, there's no restriction stopping bikes being ridden on them. Federal roads are now quite well signposted but this is not so on other roads, so trust your map, compass and judgement, or ask a local.

All other roads shown on the map are unpredictable and occasionally don't exist at all. Roads shown in yellow with black edges should be sealed, but you can't always count on this, especially in Siberia. Sometimes 'yellow' roads are very good though; ask locally. Roads shown in green on the map are never sealed, though in dry weather they can be fine to ride and will have very little traffic. If it's been raining, green roads are a write-off – just one passing tractor will turn them into quagmires.

Visa registration

A headache for cycle tourists in Russia is the system of visa registration. In theory you are supposed to have your visa 'registered', either at an official tourist hotel or at an OVIR office (effectively a branch of the police – the police can always direct you there) within 72 hours of arrival. That is fine for tourists on package tours of Moscow but causes problems for cyclists who may not even reach a town big enough to have a tourist hotel or OVIR office for several days after entering the country.

The rules about visa registration are subject to local interpretation and this 'flexibility' can either work for you or against you. The safest and simplest option is to try to spend one night in a tourist hotel (you'll need to find a decent-sized town) as soon as feasibly possible after entering the country. Registering directly at OVIR is usually more of a hassle.

Camping and other accommodation

Camping is possible virtually everywhere in Russia outside the big cities. You'll not find organized campsites except in very touristy areas like Lake Baikal, but there's plenty of space for your tent everywhere you go and nobody will mind so long as you're not trampling their tomato plants.

If you're really out in the wilds of Siberia, you should be careful about bears – seek local advice – though local people on the Trans-Siberian highway claim that bears don't wander near the main road anyway. In Ussuriya, in the Russian Far East, there is a theoretical risk from tigers but you'd be very lucky to see one. The real threats come from smaller creatures. Mosquitoes and horseflies will drive you to distraction but are not serious hazards; ticks, on the other hand, are and they are widespread across much of Russia. They carry serious diseases including tick-borne encephalitis and Lyme disease, so make sure you are inoculated in advance and take precautions against tick bites. Wear long trousers tucked into your socks when walking in the woods or in long grass; locals recommend wearing a hat as well. Check your clothing before getting into your tent. Show no mercy to any ticks that you find – they look like little spiders but have hard bodies and are very difficult to crush. Fancifully painted signs by the roadside warn you of the tick danger and what the local species look like.

On major trucking routes you will find motel-type accommodation for around US$10 per night – but it's not always at conveniently spaced day-ride intervals. In most of Russia you really do need to carry a tent or at least a bivvy bag. If you chat to locals in towns and villages you will often find yourself invited to stay the night but you can't count on that every night.

Shops and provisions

You can ride a long way in Russia without going near a town but even in Siberia you'll probably pass through or close by a village at least once a day. Almost all villages have a shop that will sell a few basic provisions, though the shop is not always easily recognized – it may be in someone's front room. Ask around for *magazin* and you'll quickly be pointed to the right house. In the morning you'll probably get bread, and there's always pasta in various guises (all called 'macaroni'), rice, biscuits, and tins of fish and meat. You'll often find a few oranges, apples or bananas, too.

For fresh local produce, you're better off asking at private houses. Most village people cultivate a vegetable plot and are usually more than happy to sell you whatever is in season. Potatoes are ubiquitous, and you'll also find cabbages, cucumbers, carrots and tomatoes. Eggs, and fresh-from-the-cow milk are available too, just ask around the village for *moloko* (milk) and *yaiytsy* (eggs). Meat can be harder to find, though shops will often sell a variety of salamis (*kolbasa*). Where there's reliable electricity, many shops will sell ice-creams which are cheap, tasty and morale-boosting. Several varieties of refreshing yoghurts are sometimes available too, along with cheese and choco-late-flavoured butter.

Every village will have a pump or well from which you can draw water. Generally it is OK to drink, though in some places it can be rather salty. Residents will quickly tell you if the local water is contaminated. Finding the village pump-house or well is not always easy – they come in a variety of

GIVING YOURSELF A DAMN GOOD THRASHING

If you're riding in Russia, there's a good chance that someone will invite you in for a *banya* – a traditional Russian sauna. Never mind that at home you might think twice before accepting an offer to work up a sweat over a few beers and a spot of light sado-masochism with a burly Russian woodcutter, out here you should not turn down a *banya* invitation. These things have magical restorative properties.

I had been flogging into the wind all day somewhere in the southern Urals. Eight hours in the saddle and I was all but spent, ready to find a camp-spot and call it a day. I stopped in a village seeking bananas for a quick carb' fix, too tired to contemplate cooking dinner. Instead I found Aleksey, who insisted that he fire up his banya for me. An hour later when I emerged, I'd sweated out all the day's tiredness and aches and felt ready to ride another eight hours. It was like getting two days for the price of one!

It's standard practice in a Russian *banya* to give your fellow bathers vigorous beatings with bundles of birch branches. This is supposed to encourage the pores to open and ensure a deeper cleansing. It's also fun, some people think.

Siberians, though, who enjoy living up to their reputation as Russia's hard men, think birch branches are for wimps. Real men – or real Siberians, anyway – like to be beaten with giant Siberian stinging nettles. The odd thing is that it feels so good. The nettles do their stinging stuff, but within a few minutes the pain soothes into an all-over body tingling that lasts for several days. I'll never go back to boring old birch.

Of course, if you visit Siberia in winter, there may not be any stinging nettles available. Real men just have to make do with a dip in Lake Baikal instead – hopping into swimming holes cut through the ice.

Edward Genochio

well-camouflaged guises. Ask around for the *kolonka* (water-pump) or *kolodyets* (well).

If you prefer someone else to do the cooking, you'll find regular truck-stop cafés along major routes where you can eat hearty though repetitive fare for a few dollars. Expect to slurp your way through a lot of borsch (beetroot consommé), mashed potato and goulash. Off the main routes, you may struggle to find eateries, though it's worth asking in villages for the *stolovaya*, or canteen. Set up to feed workers on the collective farms, many have now closed and not all will serve 'outsiders', but it's worth asking: sometimes you'll get lucky and score a hearty meal for a bargain price.

Police, the 'GAI', and bureaucracy

Russian drivers love to complain about the cops, who have a bad reputation for shaking down motorists for trivial or fabricated offences. Still widely known by their Soviet-era acronym of GAI, the armed traffic police are now formally known as the DPS. Their regular checkpoints can look intimidating but in fact they rarely cause trouble for cyclists.

Beware of roads near borders – particularly the borders with former Soviet republics which until recently were pretty porous. There is a 'restricted zone' stretching several miles inland from most Russian borders, though these are not always clearly marked. If you stray into such a zone you run the risk of being picked up by the local border guards and potentially subject to a fine. If you are planning to cross the border legitimately via a recognized route, you should have no trouble; problems arise on small local roads that run parallel to the border. I was arrested on one such road near the Kazakh border and held and interrogated for 24 hours (see p.215).

ROADS AND ROUTES IN RUSSIA

If you're heading east on a Trans-Siberian route, you have a few choices as far as Omsk. Thereafter, there is only one road, though there are a few side-trips to the north and south that you could consider along the way. Many people enter the country in the north around St Petersburg but this means that you have to get through or around Moscow before heading further east, so consider entering from further south, between Kursk and Rostov-on-Don – traffic in the south, away from Moscow and the main roads to Europe, is generally lighter.

If you're riding through European Russia, you'll cover a lot of very flat miles, so reaching the Urals may come as something of a relief. Don't expect towering peaks, though – the Urals are more rolling hills than serious mountains.

Many people assume that Siberia is a frozen wasteland but in fact its southern half enjoys a warm if short summer, from late May to September, during which you're more likely to feel too hot rather than too cold. (In spite of this, Siberians, with their characteristic dark humour, enjoy saying that 'In June summer hasn't quite started, but by July it's already over'.) Once you've encountered Siberia's insect life, though, you may seriously want to consider Arctic conditions. Between Chelyabinsk and Novosibirsk, in particular, you're basically riding through an uninterrupted swamp inhabited by a few unfortunate people and a vast number of extremely hungry mosquitoes and giant horseflies. Repellent (available locally, or try vodka – drinking it, that is) helps a bit against the mozzies, but the horseflies seem impervious. These guys are big, and when they bite it hurts (they've got teeth). There's not much you can do to escape – they'll be with you all day, and they have no difficulty maintaining a touring bike's pace. Take comfort from the fact that the worst of it lasts only about 2000 km; once you're past Novosibirsk the swamp gives way to hillier terrain and the flying tormentors become fewer.

Heading east, you can break the monotony of the Trans-Siberian route by branching off south of the highway. Good options include:

● **The M52 south from Novosibirsk.** This will take you down to the Altay Republic, with some fine scenery and a back-door route into western Mongolia via Tashanta (see p.134). An alternative, adventurous option is to ride the track from Kosh-Agach north-west into Tuva, rejoining a decent road at Ak-Dovurak. Seek local advice about this route. You'll need to take food for several days, be prepared to ford some sizeable rivers and carry good local maps and a compass.

River crossing in Tuva. © Mark McLean.

● **Turn south at Achinsk** (west of Krasnoyarsk) and head for Abakan. From there you can ride the 1200-km 'Sayan Loop' through the Sayan Mountains. Take the M54 south-east to Kyzyl in Tuva, then turn west to Ak-Dovurak. From there you can attempt the track crossing to Altay Republic (see the route above), or complete the loop by turning north back towards Abakan, through more spectacular scenery on the border between Tuva and Khakasia. This loop route includes a few sections of unpaved road and a couple of serious passes. A variant would be to turn south halfway between Kyzyl and Ak-Dovurak and head for the Mongolian border at Khandagayty. There is a Mongolian consulate in Kyzyl that will issue tourist visas (see also p.134).

● **To the Mongolian border** From the south-western tip of Lake Baikal, the A164 heads west along a broad valley towards the Mongolian border at Mondy. It's a scenic route with a couple of short side-spurs on the northern side of the valley that you can explore. One day they may open the border, creating a fantastic route linking Baikal and Lake Hovsgol in Mongolia, but at present that border is firmly shut.

Turkey

Turkey is an exciting milestone to pass on the road east: crossing the Bosphorus Straits into Asia Minor is a momentous event for anyone. A word of warning: although there are minor roads approaching Istanbul, many cyclists choose to take a cab or minibus for the last 20km or so into the city where it seems the whole of Europe is funnelling into the bottleneck crossing into Asia. The minor road No 020 will take you into Istanbul rather more peacefully but there are plenty of short hills on that route. Commuter trains may be another option outside rush hour.

Istanbul itself is an ordeal for cyclists. Similarly on the way out east, many take a long-distance bus just to get out of Istanbul. Trains also run east from Istanbul and the long-distance bus service is cheap and efficient. Alternatively, taking your bike on the ferry from Istanbul, perhaps down to Izmir, would put you a little further west than Istanbul but in a good position to ride through the centre of the country or round the Antalyan coast, though the latter is going to be much more built-up and busy than any other route.

Coastal routes around Turkey look appealing compared to the mountainous interior but are no flatter, though they don't reach the altitudes or extreme temperatures (both high and low) of the interior. It's a rocky coastline and though beautiful, involves steeper hills than going inland. The Black Sea route is dramatic but can be cold and rainy. By all accounts it is not a route you would regret, though it's perhaps not the Turkey most people come to see. It's relatively unspoiled and with plenty to offer in terms of history. Trabzon, the largest city, has ancient origins and plenty of Byzantine architecture. You should be able to get a visa for Georgia here. The monastery built into the rock face at Sumela is a 'must-see' side trip.

Turkey is twice the size of Germany and the ride across it is around 1100 miles (1800km), or three solid weeks of riding, but it is far better to allow for plenty of rest and time to visit spectacular sights such as Göreme and the caves of Cappadocia, which make an excellent rest stop halfway across the country.

(Opposite): Pakistan (see p.109). Superb mountain views from the Karakoram Hwy, a classic route.
(Overleaf): High point on the Silk Route: The Registan, Samarkand, Uzbekistan. (Photos © Cass Gilbert).

Turkish hospitality is renowned the world over as being incredibly warm and genuine, particularly in small villages, and you need to plan your daily distances to factor in inevitabilities such as meeting people and sharing meals with them – it's a great shame to have to tell people you don't have time to stop and drink tea.

A trip through the centre of Turkey will find the warmth of the welcome increasing as the population density decreases. The dogs of central

Approaching Istanbul – the wrong sort of adventure cycling. © Luka Romih

and eastern Turkey, however, have a very different welcome in mind for you. These are vicious, lawless dogs known for attacking vehicles and cyclists. And then there are the sheepdogs trained to defend their flocks against wild dogs and wolves. These beasts are professionals and wear studded collars. You may need to set your Dog Dazer on a higher level than 'stun' for all dogs in rural Turkey and forget the diplomatic niceties suggested on p.24.

Erzerum is a great travellers' hangout in eastern Turkey (for travellers headed for Armenia or Georgia as well as those going on to Iran) and the road to Dogubayazit, (aka 'Dog biscuit' to travellers) is a classic route into Iran. It is possible to camp next to the famous mosque, Ishak Pasha, up on the hill above the town. Tim Mulliner of New Zealand adds that, unbeknown to most travellers, there are two official border crossings between Iran and Turkey. As well as the main crossing point due east of Dogubayazit in Turkey, the Esendere/Sero crossing 200km south is open to foreigners too. The scenery on both sides of the border is fantastic. From Van (east of Lake Van; a ferry crosses the lake for about US$0.50) on the Turkish side the road climbs high mountain passes of the Hakkari range and weaves through raging gorges. It may be 40°C as you enter Iran; the altitudes in the mountains are over 2000m. The road also passes many historic relics including the magnificent Hoşap Castle at Güzelsu. The Iranian side is less dramatic but it is a lovely ride over beautifully green rolling hills to Lake Orumiyeh.

THE DOGS OF EASTERN TURKEY

Aggressive dogs chase us every day but they have never bitten me or my bike, so far. Today we cycle on a remote road near Tuz Lake (Salt Lake). In a small village we see four dogs running at full speed straight at us. We're doing 25km/h (15mph), so they catch up with us in a few seconds. Henk is ahead of me and gets away. The dogs are now close to my legs and look ready to attack so I draw my legs up on top of the frame. Then the bike stops, and I

hear something snap behind me. The most aggressive dog has gripped my bag on the rear rack. He's managed to stop me and the bike. The force was too much for the elastic strap that held the bag. A young woman comes out to chase the dog away by throwing rocks. It takes quite a few rocks to make the beast walk away. I get my bag back and move on. Pray that you never meet this dog or its descendants. **Tom Hermansson Snickars**

(Opposite) Top: Bike repairs beside a yurt on the steppes of Kazakhstan. (Photo © Cass Gilbert).
Bottom: Signage is entertainingly comprehensive in the hilly regions of India. (Photo © Laura Stone).

PART 2 – ROUTE OUTLINES

TRIP REPORT
EUROPE AND NORTH AFRICA

Name	Heleen Wielders-Boerman
Year of birth	1971
Occupation	Social worker
Nationality	Netherlands
Other bike travels	Eastern Europe

This trip	From Holland through Eastern Europe (including Ukraine) to Middle East, Egypt, Morocco and back via Spain and France
Trip duration	One year
Number in group	Two
Total distance	10,000km (6250 miles)
Cost of trip	About €10 per day each

Longest day	130km
Best day	Cycling the King's Highway, Jordan, through the Wadi Mujib: very steep and beautiful
Worst day	Madaba (Jordan): kids throwing stones, blocking the road and spitting
Favourite ride	King's Highway, Jordan
Biggest headache	After vodka in Ukraine – they drink it like water!
Biggest mistake	None – all things that might go wrong are part of it
Couldn't do without	Robin and my bike (with rearview-mirror)
Pleasant surprise	Ukrainians though so poor were most generous, inviting you to eat with them or stay at their houses
Any illness	Usual stomach and bowel problems

Bike model	Vittorio (www.vittorio.nl)
New/used	New
Modifications	None
Wish you'd fitted	Nothing
Tyres used	Continental Top Touring 2000
Baggage Setup	Old Karrimors and new Ortliebs
Wish you'd brought	Strong sunscreen lotion
Wish you hadn't brought	Nothing

Bike problems	Broken saddle
Accidents	None
Punctures	Three
Same bike again	Definitely!
Recommendations	Do not plan the whole trip, so you're free to go whenever and wherever you want to go

General tip	Just do it!

Things are considerably more relaxed than they were just a few years ago now that Turkey has begun to resolve its problems with the Kurdish people in this region.

Lebanon, Syria and Jordan

Philip Davis

With its easy accessibility from Europe, wonderful climate, amazing archaeological ruins and beautiful scenery, why isn't this part of the world thronged with tourists? Politics and history are two obvious answers. But these issues aside, it's a fine region to cycle in, even for the novice (it was my first solo tour). The people are immensely friendly, the roads are good for cycling and the food is great. What more could you want?!

Visas and practicalities

Only Syria requires visas in advance of arrival for those nationals whose country has a Syrian embassy, though many travellers report getting visas on arrival even though their countries have Syrian representation. Entry is at the whim of border guards who may act like bouncers at a night club – not everyone gets in. Neither Lebanon nor Syria allows people who have visited Israel to enter their countries and you may still be denied entry at the border even though you have a Syrian visa. Jordan and Lebanon issue visas at the border.

Most basics can be bought in the region but it's hard to get parts for modern bikes, so bring a basic toolkit and spare spokes, chain links, etc. Note that the inland areas of Syria are largely desert and there can be long stretches without villages or shops: on the route to Palmyra, for example. Although primarily Islamic countries, Jordan, Syria and the Lebanon are quite liberal and cosmopolitan so there is no great problem with wearing shorts and T-shirts on the bike but you will need to cover yourself when visiting holy places. You should try to bring a respectable clean set of clothes for visiting people's homes.

Camping is possible in some parts of the region, especially in the grounds of some hotels, but not a really suitable option in many areas. As this region is not on the backpacker trail there can be a shortage of good-quality budget accommodation. Most towns will have a hotel but expect to have to bargain to get a room at a reasonable price. As wealthier local people like to holiday in the cooler uplands, there are many attractive hotels and small resorts in the mountain areas of all three countries. These can be very reasonably priced out of season.

Safety

All three countries are relatively safe with low crime rates. There is a low hassle factor in comparison with some other countries in the region. Local people can be immensely friendly and helpful, although they will usually be puzzled as to why anyone would choose a bike as a means of travel (especially in Lebanon). People will cheerily invite you to join them for a meal or a hubbly-bubbly, or casually offer to lead you to wherever you want to go. A driver in Beirut led me to my hotel by allowing me to slipstream behind him! Many women travel the area solo with few problems.

SOME ROUTES

From Amman, there is a road north to the border and Damascus. This road is busy but has a generous hard shoulder which is perfect for cycling. An unmissable stop one day's ride north of Amman is the Roman City of Jerash. This is one of those places that make the region special – an ancient site that would be thronged with tourists all year round if located in Europe. But here you can explore it in relative isolation. There are some guesthouses around but a good bet is to cycle up into the hills to the west to the peaceful Olive Branch Resort, which has good deals out of season and camping is allowed in its grounds. It is an excellent base to explore the area.

From Jerash you can cycle direct to the border, but it's much better to bear north-west into the uplands towards the university city of Irbid, a town with no shortage of fast food outlets to satisfy the hunger that will hit you after tackling your first big climbs. Around Irbid there are rarely-visited Roman remains and beautiful countryside. The roads are generally in very good condition with light traffic but gradients are steep.

It's a nice, flat day ride from Irbid to the Syrian border town of Deraa, best known as the place where T.E. Lawrence had a painful encounter with a Turkish police officer. It's a dull place but train buffs will find the local rail yard fascinating, with its collection of ancient steam engines rotting away on sidings. There are also some very interesting Roman remains in the area.

Then from Deraa it's a straight, 100km ride to Damascus. But be careful to take the old Damascus road, not the new motorway! It's an easy ride that will be a perfect introduction to this region.

South of Amman in Jordan is very cyclable and includes some memorable destinations, most famously the desert landscapes of Wadi Rum and the magnificent ruins at Petra. The Kings Highway runs through the heart of the country linking these sites and others. These two areas are somewhat touristy so be careful of your belongings. Note that central and south Jordan is very hot in the summer months with temperatures often reaching 40°C. The Dead Sea features many attractive resorts but don't forget it's well below sea level so expect a long, hard slog to get out of there.

Desert camp in Jordan. © Robin Wielders

Damascus

Entering Damascus is a little bewildering but no more difficult than any other large city. Don't be surprised if a local cyclist (and there are many on the road using big old bikes, locally called 'donkeys') comes up to you and offers to lead you to where you are going. This is typical of the casual generosity of Syrians. Most tourist and backpacker accommodation is in the central Martyrs Square area but note that as it isn't a major tourist destination, there isn't a huge range of options. It's well worth staying in the city for a few days; it's safe, easy to walk and cycle around and almost hassle free and the Old City (the oldest continually inhabited site in the world) in particular is fascinating.

Lebanon and northern Syria

It takes just a day to get into Lebanon from Damascus, and a lovely day's cycling it is. There are longer routes on minor roads to the north, but the border crossings can't be guaranteed. The main road leading to the Bekaa Valley is relatively quiet and despite its name it's more of an upland plain, penned in by two parallel mountain ridges. After cycling through barren, desert areas your eyes will be dazzled by the iridescent irrigated fields of wheat that carpet the ground in spring.

The northern part of the Bekaa is primarily Shi'ite so don't be too surprised to find yourself at a Hizbollah checkpoint. But don't worry, they are welcoming of the occasional tourist who braves it this far north. The biggest attraction by far is the amazing Roman temple complex at Baalbek. The scale of these ruins has to be seen to be believed, dwarfing even the finest temples of Italy and Greece.

The south of the Bekaa features some less impressive ruins, but offers pleasant cycling. It gradually gives way to the hilly countryside of south Lebanon. This area is under the control of the UN but it's a relatively safe area in which to travel.

Beirut and the coast of Lebanon are a hostile environment for cyclists. Traffic is thunderous and there are few refuges. Nobody cycles. Take the bus north to Tripoli, then continue into Syria. The road is along a beach, which sadly is also a huge Palestinian refugee camp. It's safe, but a grim reminder of the history of the region.

North of Lebanon, it's easy to get into the north-western highlands of Syria. This is a great place for cycling with good quiet roads. The rolling hills, olive groves and upland forests of the area are reminiscent of the south of France or northern Italy yet it is almost totally unexplored by tourists.

Culturally it is very distinctive, inhabited by a mixture of Orthodox Christians and Alawis (a somewhat mysterious offshoot of Shi'ite Islam with many Christian and even pagan elements). And most of all, it has one of the true wonders of the world, the Krak de Chevaliers (signposted as 'Citadel'), probably the finest intact mediaeval castle in the world. Although by Syrian standards it's a major attraction, it is quiet for much of the day. And it's not the only castle in the area – the whole region is dotted with crusader remains, sometimes in spectacular locations.

PART 2 – ROUTE OUTLINES

Georgia, Armenia and Azerbaijan

Mark Elliott

The fascinating Caucasus is a cradle of human civilization. Arguably the historical location of the Biblical Garden of Eden, nowhere in the world has so much history, scenic variety, passion and political complexity crammed into such a tiny area. Officially there are three independent countries in the south Caucasus: Georgia and Armenia (ancient, Christian nations recovering from years of turmoil) and Azerbaijan (a low-key Islamic-Turkic country with oil-wealth potential) whose Nakhchivan enclave is a totally disconnected lozenge west of Armenia.

Since Armenia and Azerbaijan fought an officially unresolved war in the 1990s the borders between their territories have been firmly closed. The Armenian puppet state of Nagorno Karabagh still occupies over 15% of Azerbaijan's land and is a de facto country of its own (pick up visas from Yerevan). Landmines and ruined cities fill the no-man's land between Armenia/Nagorno-Karabagh and Azerbaijan so there's no earthly way to cycle across the borders whatever a map may suggest.

Georgia

Glorious Georgia, with its fabulous castles, Caucasian mountain tower villages and passion for wine (that many claim originated in Georgia 5000 years ago) is the obvious starting point when cycling east from Turkey. Since the Rose Revolution that brought Mikhail Saakashvili to power in November 2003, many of Georgia's corruption and insecurity problems have been solved and the cost of visas has dropped to a token US$10. Theoretically you can get visas at the borders but in reality it's wise to get them in advance, most easily in Trabzon, Turkey (upstairs at 20 Gazifasha St) where they're issued on the spot.

Tbilisi, Georgia's delightful capital, is one of the most appealing cities in Eastern Europe and well worth a few days' exploration. However, Georgia does retain plenty of scars from the civil wars of the 1990s and from the years of corrupt governance under Sheverdnadze (Gorbachev's former henchman who was Georgia's much-hated president 1992-2003). The border with Russia remains closed (Georgia was accused of helping the Chechens), Abkhazia (the beautiful north-western beach area) has declared independence and remains inaccessible, while highly autonomous South Ossetia remains very unstable. None of these factors need deter you from a trip as each requires a detour, but it's worth being aware of the issues.

Azerbaijan

Crossing from Georgia to Azerbaijan is straightforward though you'll need an Azerbaijani visa in advance (get it easily in Istanbul or Tbilisi). There are two road options but by far the nicer is in Georgia's wine-paradise region (Kaheti).

You cross between Lagodeghi and Balakan then continue along a most beautiful – yet quiet – asphalted road along the base of Azerbaijan's stunning high Caucasus foothills. There are oak avenues and appealing side trips, with a must-see stop in Sheki where there's a delightful old town, a renovated khan's palace and a cheap hotel in a superbly atmospheric old caravanserai.

As you cross Azerbaijan the landscapes evolve from thick deciduous forests via rolling grasslands to deserts outside the cosmopolitan capital Baku. With great cheap restaurants plus a plethora of expensive expat bars and Anglo-Irish pubs (for the oil execs), Baku is a great place to recharge the batteries. With the Azerbaijan-Russia border closed, you have two main options from here. The best choice is to cycle south into Iran along an attractive but often busy and very rainy route through Iran's lush, rice-growing Caspian provinces. Visas for Iran are now possible to arrange in Baku though they'll take a couple of weeks so it's better to come pre-prepared. This is the route followed by Cass Gilbert in his Tandem to Turkestan ride (🖥 www.tandemto turkestan.com).

The alternative is to cross the Caspian Sea by ferry to Central Asia. Ferries are actually glorified ro-ro (roll-on roll-off) cargo ships that take passengers for around US$50 per person to either Aktau (Kazakhstan) or Turkmenbashi (Turkmenistan). Departures on either are hit and miss (schedules are entirely ignored) but the latter route generally leaves several times per week while to get to Aktau you may be waiting for days or weeks while the ship awaits a little more cargo to justify the trip.

Getting to Central Asia

Whether from Aktau or Turkmenbashi, cycling onwards will not be too exciting: there's endless dull steppe (treeless plains) or the raging Karakum Desert to cross. However, both cities are railheads so you could zip across to more appealing parts of Central Asia fairly conveniently if you are not fixated on a punishing long-distance slog. The added complication is the annoying visa details: Kazakhstan visas tend to have fixed starting dates. Given the uncertainty of the ferry schedules you are quite likely to end up wasting a fair amount of your valuable visa validity waiting around and westbound you could end up overstaying (which would be very unpleasant indeed). There's a similar problem for Turkmenistan compounded by the fact that Turkmen transit visas are already very short for anyone planning to cycle. Neither is easily available in Baku.

There are two variants to those discussed above. One is to cross Turkey-Georgia-Armenia-Iran which is fairly straightforward with some high mountain roads en route. Armenian visas are available on both the Georgian and Iranian borders and Armenia is relatively accustomed to foreign visitors (see 🖥 www.cilicia.com for oodles of travel advice).

A second alternative is to swing past Agri Dag (Mount Ararat) in eastern Turkey, cross into Nakhchivan (Azerbaijan's disconnected territory) and continue into Iran from Culfa/Jolfa. For that you'd need an Azerbaijan visa (easily available in Istanbul) but you may find that there are some problems with officials who are notoriously corrupt at the Nakhchivan-Turkish border and, having rarely if ever encountered a foreign traveller, can be very suspicious, notably around Culfa.

TRIP REPORT
SWITZERLAND TO CHINA

Name Beat Heim
Year of birth 1966
Occupation Software Engineer
Nationality Swiss
Other bike travels China, Pakistan, India, Tibet and Nepal

This trip Switzerland, Italy, Slovenia, Croatia, Serbia, Bosnia, Bulgaria, Greece, Turkey, Georgia, Azerbaijan, Iran, Turkmenistan, Uzbekistan, Tajikistan, Kyrgyzstan, Tibet & China
Trip duration 13 months
Number in group One
Total distance 22,750km (14,220 miles)
Cost of trip About €8000

Longest day 161km, or 2350 vertical metres
Best day Reaching Kailash in west Tibet
Worst day Truck drove over my bike near Everest Base Camp
Favourite ride Western Tibet, Changtang
Biggest headache Visas
Pleasant surprise Friendliness of people everywhere!
Any illness Had an operation on my intestine at the end of the trip in China; probably nothing to do with the trip

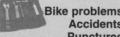

Bike model MTB – Cycletech Papalagi
New/used Five years old
Modifications Everything modified – got only the frame and made all the rest myself.
Wish you'd fitted Truck horn
Tyres used Schwalbe marathon XR, two sets in 23,000km

Baggage Setup 2 panniers in front, 2 in the back, one waterproof bag in the back, handlebar bag for camera.
Wish you'd brought Swiss cheese and bread
Wish you hadn't brought Nothing

Bike problems None, apart from accident: truck drove over bike
Accidents Back wheel and frame totally bent
Punctures 5 in 23,000 km
Recommendations Maybe this is not the sort of trip (particularly Western Tibet) to do if you are a first timer!

General tip Go for simple, rugged gear. The less exotic your bike and components are compared to what you will find in the countries you visit, the more likely you can find help when there is trouble.

Central Asia

These five closely related countries have gone their separate ways since the collapse of the Soviet Union. A summary of each helps distinguish them.

Turkmenistan

The most westerly of the five nations, Turkmenistan is dominated by the personality cult of its leader, President Niyazov. Getting a visa for more than seven days is almost impossible. Ashgabat, the capital, is worth a visit and the statues and billboards promoting the cult of Niyazov are a fascinating anachronism in today's largely post-Communist world.

Uzbekistan

Also dominated by its ruler, the altogether more hardline Islam Karimov, Uzbekistan is becoming a more difficult country to visit for independent travellers, which is unfortunate because it has the famous Silk Road cities of Khiva, Bukhara and Samarkand in the west of the country. To the south, US military bases were allowed as part of the Afghanistan war so Americans find it easier to get a visa. There are problems with Islamic fundamentalism and terrorist incursions from the Afghan side. The Fergana Valley which protrudes into Kyrgyzstan is a trouble spot owing to Islamic resistance to Karimov and the borders here are rigorously policed, making this a difficult area to pass through – a look at the map shows roads cutting through the jigsaw shape of borders in this area. Now that the borders are more rigorously policed, your already difficult visa situation is further complicated.

Tajikistan

The poorest of the 'stans, Tajikistan nevertheless has its highlights. The Ismaili Muslim Pamir region (see Pamir Highway, p.108), in particular, is of great interest. Development funds from the Aga Khan are invested here. The border with Afghanistan attracts travellers but there is inevitably heightened security and risks in travelling through this region. A border with China might open soon but may be for locals only.

Kazakhstan

By far the largest and least-visited country, Kazakhstan is known for vast deserts, arid steppes and severe environmental pollution from nuclear tests, rocket launches and chemical plants. A trip to Ashgabat or Almaty is enough for most travellers. It's not easy to get a tourist visa but riders passing through the region can avoid Kazakhstan.

Kyrgyzstan

Kyrgyzstan is the most relaxed of the 'stans and has the easiest visa system, though you must register with OVIR on arrival. It has lots to interest the traveller, from the Tien Shan Mountains to the Issy-Kul lake region with two border crossings into western China. A friendly place but poverty, alcoholism and a rising crime rate are travellers' concerns. The revolution in May 2005 may break out of the pattern of liberalization followed by crackdowns, but check for up-to-date news on the country and its regions before planning a trip.

RIDING IN CENTRAL ASIA

Cass Gilbert

Entrenched in a rich and turbulent past, conquered by Turkic tribes and Mongols, Central Asia has long been home to marauding bandits and nomadic groups. After falling to Russian Imperialism at the turn of the last century, the Central Asia of today is emerging into independence under the shadow of the fall of communism, the latest chapter in its assorted history of takeovers and skirmishes. Its breathtaking geography matches its cultural diversity. From the oil-rich Caspian Sea in the west to the fringes of the searing Taklamakan Desert in the east, there is an abundance of high pastures and spectacular lakes, stunning glacial views and rugged wilderness. Boasting some of the region's finest Islamic architecture, few parts of the world can offer such a jaw-dropping range of unspoiled mountainscape.

The distance between the Iranian border with Turkmenistan and the Torugart Pass, the gateway to western China, is only some 1500km. While the route is fairly direct between Turkmenistan and Uzbekistan, Kyrgyzstan offers the most possibilities for side trips, with its network of jeep tracks that cross the country. Aim for a ten-day visa for Turkmenistan (you may get longer if you go through an agency, less if you try for a transit visa from an embassy en route; try 🖳 www.stantours.com), unless you enjoy racing across the desert. One cunning traveller (Alastair Humphreys, see p103) gave himself a couple of extra days by changing the '7 '(days) on his visa into a '9'.

A few weeks in Uzbekistan should be enough to enjoy the magnificent Silk Road cities of Bukhara and Samarkand without rushing. A month allows plenty of interesting routes to be discovered in Kyrgyzstan. Options include heading south via the Torugart Pass to Kashgar, or crossing the Kazakh border to Almaty, before looping around to Urumqi.

When to travel

With such a wide spectrum of topography – deserts to steppe to mountains – broadly speaking the cycling season in Central Asia lies between April and October. To avoid being flash-fried in this land of extremes, visit in the spring and autumn when the deserts and plains are at their most bearable. However, for those coming from Europe, it might well be early summer by the time you make it – we had temperatures pushing 50°C in the Karakum Desert, though the plains of Uzbekistan were far more bearable.

On the plus side the warm weather brings with it the watermelon season, when the bazaars and roadside stalls are overloaded with fresh fruit. By then you will be yearning for the mountains. The Tien Shan mountains are best visited from June to September, when there is the least likelihood of snow and rain – though the 4000m passes can always unleash unexpected snowstorms. If you are there earlier, the rains at the beginning of spring (April/May) can bring a burst of colour to the green pastures, as miniature tulips and other wild flowers coat the steppe, though the higher passes will still be snow-bound. Later in the season, from August to September, is also a good time for riding. Conditions are cooler, there is plenty of fresh fruit and the weather is still clear before the onset of an incredibly harsh winter.

Visas

Cycling in Central Asia should be approached with strategic determination. The post-Communist era has not seen a significant relaxation of awkward visa regulations; in fact, now that these nations are truly independent, some crossings have become more difficult, especially where Uzbekistan is involved. In general the region is still renowned for complicated and expensive visa regulations. Vague at the best of times, rules can bend at the whim of a particular embassy or border, so for a fuss-free visit, organize as much as possible in advance. This may entail keeping to a tighter schedule than you'd like but it will avoid endless hassles en route. In any case, entry/exit dates and exact border crossings have to be stipulated for some visas, tying you in to planning your route ahead.

Even if you can get your head around the latest changes, applying through a visa specialist is the only effective way of tackling wily Central Asian bureaucracy, particularly for Uzbekistan, Tajikistan, Turkmenistan and Kazakhstan, which may require 'letters of recommendation'. This mythical piece of paper – which you will probably never see – can be faxed ahead to embassies en route, ready for your arrival, for a charge of around US$30-60. Still, it pays to allow yourself as much time as possible and factor in delays or you'll find yourself throwing your bike on a bus to make it to the next border on time. A welcome exception is laidback Kyrgyzstan with visas that you can apply for yourself. As a result it's by far the most trouble-free 'stan to visit, with a cheap and easily extendable one-month visa delivered quickly – and even courteously. Remember to bring US dollars for visa applications en route.

Visa regulations change and the best way to stay up to date is by checking in with recent travellers or by visiting Lonely Planet's excellent Central Asia branch on the Thorn Tree forum, whose contributors are sometimes the same people you will run into on the road. Alternatively, sources like 🖥 www.traveltajikistan.com, though ultimately travel agents, will provide fairly up-to-date information. Many people end up in the hands of visa agents in any case and often claim the fees paid are worth it in terms of time and stress saved.

CHILLING IN CENTRAL ASIA

The really wonderful thing about Central Asia is that it is still largely untouched by Western tourists. There are no Khao San Roads here and for cyclists who travel less well-worn paths, you will find a people who are still interested in travellers for a cultural exchange rather than just a quick buck. One night, far from anywhere, a shepherd with one eye and a wooden leg wandered by and decided to join us as we relaxed at the end of another day. He spoke no English, and we not enough Kyrgyz, but we sat together, shared some tea, and had one of those moments that travel is supposed to be about, laughing at scurrying insects and other inanities.

Mark Eskdale

Rusty Japikse crossing a river in Kyrgyzstan. 'It would have been more fun if all the wood hadn't been nicked', he noted.

Maps of Central Asia

If you really want to get off the beaten track, try to buy a local map, which can offer a surprising level of detail – a throwback to Soviet times. They're available cheaply in Russian or English at Geodesiya on Atabeyera, a block past the UN building in Ashgabat.

A goldmine for mountain bikers, the Kyrgyz Cartographic Institute in Bishkek houses a wonderful selection of detailed 1:200,000-scale sheet maps covering most areas of the country. These declassified Soviet military maps include jeep trails and minor roads, opening up the country to fantastic off-road touring potential. Contours, passes and altitudes are marked. The office is at Kiev St 107, 3rd floor, room 4 (above DHL, next to a computer shop).

Entering the 'stans from the west

There are a couple of possible crossings from Iran. If your time in Turkmenistan is short, you will probably need to travel via Mashad directly onto the fringes of the Karakum Desert, a ride of around five days over the Uzbek border to Bukhara. Well worth the detour if you can get more than a transit visa, Ashgabat is Central Asia's most bizarre city, an immaculate metropolis of pres-

TAJIKISTAN'S PAMIR HIGHWAY

I rode the Pamir Highway in 2000 and thought it more beautiful than the Manali-Leh road in India and more impressive than Pakistan's famous Karakoram Highway. As the Russian influence wanes, nomadic ways are returning in the form of new yurts. Expect to have to entertain bored soldiers at checkpoints.

Built by the Russians during their occupation of Afghanistan in the 1980s, the Pamir Highway is about 450km in length, though riders going from Dushanbe all the way through to Osh in Kyrgyzstan will travel some 1100km. The road passes through some spectacular scenery and is above 3500m in altitude for more than 400km of its length. Following the Panj River, there is little food to be found between Khorog and Murghab and travellers need to be self-sufficient, though they may well find hospitality along the way from the predominantly Ismaili Muslim villagers.

Tajikistan is the poorest of the 'stans and this region was the losing side in the civil war which erupted after the fall of the Soviet Union and lasted until 1997. Expect checkpoints, some still manned by Russian soldiers, and be ready to show your permit for the area, known as GBAO (Gorno-Badakshan Autonomous Oblast), though it is just as likely that it will not be called for at all. The GBAO permit is best obtained when you apply for your Tajikistan visa and can be picked up when registering with OVIR in Dushanbe or offices in Khorog or Murghab. Watch out for scams such as the local KGB telling you that foreigners can travel only in a group with a local escort. They are in league with a travel agent in Khorog who offers guiding services and who also reports foreign travellers to the KGB. Stand firm and resist these ploys: you have the permit and that is all you need. There were reports of bandits and militia in this area following the civil war but nothing in recent years. The area has also experienced droughts for several years in a row – as usual, research this before setting out on the Pamir Highway.

Mark Eskdale

idential billboards, neo-Roman/Islamic architecture and dozens of fountains that stand defiant amidst a desert background, with a weekend market that matches the better known one at Kashgar in western China.

Food and drink

Central Asians like their meat – or rather, their fat. Main staples include shashlyk, skewers of kebab chequered with lumps of grisly fat. Plovs are a buttery rice served with chopped carrot, sultanas and chunks of mutton, soaked in the fat of the sheep's tail. Lagman is another popular dish: fresh fat noodles in a meat and vegetable soup, dunked with frisbee-shaped bread and washed down with green tea. Bazaars sell an abundance of pastries, Korean salads, white cheese and fresh fruit – plums, apricots, cherries, figs, the lot!

Ice-cream is available on every street corner, as are bowling-ball sized watermelons that make great thirst quenchers. *Gazli su* is carbonated local tap water, sweetened with shots of syrup to mask the rust. Beverages with more of a kick (in the stomach, and often out the other end) are camel and horse milk – a powerful and pungent alcoholic brew, drunk for strength and virility.

KARAKORAM HIGHWAY (KKH)

The first of the modern roads to be built through the Himalaya, the Karakoram Highway (KKH) was a joint project of China and Pakistan, linking Kashgar in western China with the Pakistani capital, Islamabad. It's 1300km (800 miles) long and it took 20 years and some 400 lives to build, cutting through extremely steep valleys in an area of highly unstable geology – witness the major earthquake in the region in October 2005. An enormous achievement, the road is entirely paved and runs at gentle gradients – ideal for cyclists.

The route

Many cyclists fly or take a bus from Islamabad to Gilgit to avoid the extreme heat of a Pakistani summer or catch the highlight of the KKH, the Hunza valley with its sheer walls and views of 8000m peaks such as Nanga Parbat. Gilgit, at 1454m is a good base for exploring the area too, taking either the rugged Shandur Pass route west to Chitral near the Afghanistan border, or Skardu to the east in the Karakoram range. The ride to Chitral is extremely challenging and easier from the Gilgit side of the 3800m Shandur pass. It's a jeep road, with plenty of landslides, rocks on the road and river crossings along the way. Allow up to 10 days to reach Chitral, famous for its fort and spectacular mosque. Roads to the south lead to Peshawar but may not be open to foreigners – remember, this region is right on the Afghan border and is notoriously lawless.

North of Gilgit, the Hunza valley offers some of the best camping anywhere, with stunning alpine scenery up to the 4800m Khunjerab Pass. A disappointment for cyclists is that the Chinese authorities no longer allow them to ride from the Chinese border into Xinjiang. Bikers are bussed past the sensitive Afghanistan border to Tashkurgan. It's only a 120km stretch, but a smooth paved descent of around 1500m is missed and for bikers planning to ride every inch of the way, it's reason enough to take the Central Asian route into China (see p.120).

Hazards

The region has a noticeable police presence and occasional civil unrest or crime will cause roads to be closed, particularly to foreigners. It's nonetheless a very friendly region peopled mostly by Ismaili Muslims, though the drugs 'n' guns town of Peshawar is probably best avoided. Landslides are another, more common, hazard but bikers can usually carry their bikes over minor rockfalls which can block all motorized traffic for days. And then there are reports of rock-throwing kids amusing themselves from safe perches high above the road – it's definitely helmet country!

When to go

The KKH has a fairly short summer season for travellers and the Khunjerab pass itself is open only from the end of April until December. September and October (some of the driest months) are popular times to go.

Last but not least, thanks to the Russians, vodka is every Central Asian's favourite tipple. Combining Islamic hospitality and a Russian fondness for alcohol can have lethal results for inexperienced bikers who have been 'on the wagon' in Iran before arriving in the 'stans. Forced invitations are plentiful, as are celebratory shots of vodka. Don't expect Absolut or Smirnoff – we're talking paint stripper if you're lucky, engine degreaser if you're not! On a good day you might get away with a couple of beers or something a little more 'organic'.

India

Simon Hill

India is a fascinating country. The people are friendly, the sights are amazing and it's about as inexpensive as anywhere to tour in. Contrary to popular belief, the road system is pretty good and if care is taken choosing the route, these roads can be relatively traffic-free and enjoyable. Unfortunately, many people will never consider cycling in India because it's seen as a dangerous, dirty and unpleasant place to cycle.

There are several reasons why India has a bad reputation as a place to cycle in. First, most people begin their trip in Delhi or Mumbai which are probably the two most polluted and overcrowded cities this side of Alpha Centauri. They then schlep off to the 'must-do' tourist sights in Agra, Jaipur, Varanasi and so on. These places certainly have worthwhile sights but they're not good places for cycling, particularly if it's your first trip here. They're crowded, bedevilled by tourist touts and beggars and the roads are polluted torrents of clashing steel, rubber and holy cows.

Also, many people's first experience of travel in India is on a bus or train which could give them the impression that travel by bike must be a horrendous experience. However, once you're pedalling out in the country, it's nothing like that! On a bus you have constant noise from the moment you leave the terminal to the moment you arrive at your destination. On a bike, you hear the bus horn a few minutes before it gets to you. The sound gets more insistent as the bus approaches and at the last second you can pull off the road and just let

it roar past. So the cyclist has a few seconds of noise and dust, whereas the miserable bus passenger has it 24/7 till the final destination is reached. There is no comparison!

The careful selection of routes and places to visit is obviously very important. If you're new to India, I'd recommend the south. Generally the south is less crowded than the north, the food is better, it is more affluent and there is plenty to see and do. For example, the

Hell on two wheels? Not here matey.

state of Tamil Nadu has many interesting temple and fort towns, so apart from the cycling, there is plenty of historical and cultural sightseeing. If you're more into scenery and hills, then the Western Ghats take some beating, as do the rural backwaters of Kerala. If you want beaches, try Goa, Karnataka and Kerala. A good guidebook is useful to locate the better-known sights and help plan the route but one of the delights of cycle touring is that you will come across many amazing sights that are not in any book.

Although many of the roads, particularly around the large towns and cities, are extremely busy and polluted, as in most countries if you get off the main highways you may find yourself in a quiet rural idyll. For example, on a recent trip I was cycling from Kanyakumari at the southern tip of India to the fascinating temple town of Madurai. There is a national highway that runs straight between the two towns but instead I found a route following state highways to the west in the shadow of the Ghats, which gave great mountain views. These roads were very quiet with only local traffic and they passed through many villages and small, interesting, un-touristy towns. It was a bit longer than the main route but was well worth it. So, where possible, go by state highway instead of the national one. The Nelles maps of India are good enough to enable you to do this.

Accommodation and food
As India develops, so do the hotels and most sizeable towns will have at least one 'business' hotel. These are normally of a good standard and cost from Rs200 to Rs300 (£2.50-£3.80) a double per night. Sometimes there are only cheaper hotels available but they will almost always have rooms with attached bathrooms. It is, of course, possible to go really cheap but after a day in the saddle you'll probably want a bit of comfort and, more importantly, privacy. Your room is often your only place away from constant attention. We almost always kept our bikes in our hotel room, which meant that they were safe. Once, we even rented a small room for our bikes for a night when we went off to Calcutta by train. On two occasions we weren't allowed to take the bikes into the rooms but we were allowed to leave them in the hotel's secure underground car park. In one, when I told the car-park wallah that I was worried that the gear levers might be fiddled with, he gave us large pieces of cardboard to cover the handlebars. Sometimes I'm overwhelmed and embarrassed by the respect and helpfulness I get from people in India.

Another delight of cycling in India is the numerous food stops. A cheap curry or cup of chai (tea) can usually be found every few kilometres. This makes touring a dream and means that you don't have to carry supplies. Bottled water is available in all large towns and at many roadside establishments. A small water filter could be useful in emergencies or if you're going off the beaten track. I don't drink the water from the taps or as served up in restaurants. Toilets are virtually non-existent on the road, so you can do what everyone else does and go (within reason) anywhere – a very liberating experience as you'll always find somewhere to go!

Security and traffic madness
As far as security, I have only ever once been mildly worried in nine months of touring the subcontinent. Nothing actually happened, I just felt a bit uneasy in one particular town. Away from the tourist areas the people are incredibly

friendly and honest. No beggars, only curiosity – if you don't like people staring at you or asking you questions then India probably isn't for you. One slight problem is that Indians love to touch things; they often do this unconsciously, flicking a brake or gear lever as they talk to you. I call them 'twiddlers'. There is no malice and a polite 'please don't do that' is usually enough.

The traffic rules are very simple. On a bike you are at the bottom of the pile (nothing new there, then) and you know that every other road user will treat you accordingly. Although many Westerners find this very annoying, in some way it is actually safer than in the UK where most vehicles observe the road rules but it is the 1% who don't who will kill you. In India you know the rules (or lack of them) and you cycle accordingly.

India is a great place for festivals and I've experienced many just by chance. If you're in a non-tourist town when a festival is under way you'll almost certainly be expected to join in or at least watch. Of course India is crowded but there's always something going on. This is definitely not somewhere where you'll get bored cycling – dive in and experience it!

CYCLING THE INDIAN HIMALAYA

Laura Stone

Soaring thousands of metres above the rush, heat and chaos of India's plains, the Indian Himalaya are a world apart. Prayer flags snap in the wind on high passes, immense yaks thresh the barley at harvest time and colourful Tata trucks crawl up the hairpins like ants. The people, especially in Buddhist Ladakh, are cheerful, honest and gentle. The landscape is a reflection of their religion – white chortens line the roads and approaches to villages like pawns from a giant's game of chess, burgundy-clad monks hitch lifts at the side of the road, gompas perch on spectacular crags and everywhere the air is alive with the flutter of prayer flags. Here you'll find some of the most starkly spectacular mountain scenery anywhere in the world.

Cycling allows you to travel at the pace that life has been lived at here for thousands of years. Even today, the evening rush-hour of wild-eyed goats blocks the roads and backstreets of small towns. At dawn on the high-altitude grasslands, silhouetted nomads canter past the tent on horseback, stopping their singing to call out 'Jullay!'. The riding is challenging, but road conditions are generally good and gradients forgiving to heavily loaded touring bikes.

The bicycle thieves of Zanskar – if they reach a downhill you're buggered! © Laura Stone

That is unless you head off-road onto one of the many fantastic trails, where the going will be much tougher but you'll have only glaciers, snow-capped mountains and an intense high-altitude sky around you.

A flight to Delhi and an overnight bus ride will bring you and your bike to the foothills of Rohtang La – gateway to the Indian Himalaya. Isolated for up to eight months of the year by snowfall, the valleys beyond the pass are spectacularly beautiful, diverse and a fascinating meld of Hindu, Buddhist and Muslim cultures extending as far east as Tibet, north to China and west to Kashmir and Pakistan.

Classic rides such as the Manali-Leh Highway strike out across this extreme landscape – where over half the journey is above 4000m and rises from the Hindu temples and pine trees of the Kullu Valley to the arid moonscape of Ladakh and the ancient civilization of the Indus Valley, in the shadow of the Karakorams.

Visas and permits

The paperwork is almost painless. Tourist visas are valid for six months but don't get caught out: visas are valid from the date of issue not arrival and cannot be extended. Unless you fancy nipping across to Nepal or Sri Lanka, get it as late as possible if you're staying a while. Indian visas are generally easier to get in your home country and are tedious and expensive to obtain in Nepal.

Once in India, the only other red tape you'll encounter is when applying for Inner Line Permits, obtainable in Leh. These may be scrapped in the next few years but at present you'll need one to travel near India's sensitive borders with China, Tibet and Pakistan – ie in eastern Spiti and northern Ladakh. These permits are valid only for seven days.

When to go

The Manali-Leh Highway opens in mid-June, as summer arrives in Ladakh and the snow lingering on the high passes melts away. Summer in Ladakh is brief: the Highway officially closes in mid-September, though private jeeps and buses continue running until early October. By late October, snow blocks the passes once more and the mercury heads down to zero, above which it won't often rise until April. Spiti is equally isolated by the extreme climate and is only accessible from July to the end of October, after which snowfall makes the Kunzum La impassable. Lahaul, lying as it does between Kunzum La to the east and Baralacha La to the north, is open as long as Rohtang La is passable, as late as mid-November. Kinnaur, Kullu and Shimla can be reached by road year-round (landslides permitting). By late September, Ladakh is almost empty of tourists and chilly at night; by late October, Manali's cafés are used as haybarns and it reverts to being a village.

The monsoon is also a consideration when planning your trip: it sweeps up from southern India during June, and douses the southern reaches of the Himalaya, ie Shimla, Manali and the Kullu Valley, until mid-September. North of the Rohtang La, Lahaul and Spiti get some scattered monsoon rain; north of the Baralacha La, Ladakh's high-altitude desert sees almost none.

Riding conditions

These depend on the military significance of the road. Cyclists on the Leh-Srinigar Highway will glide along on glossy tarmac, while cyclists in eastern Lahaul will bump and grind along boulders and riverbeds. Between

Letting the mules take the strain on the 5000m Shingo La pass. © Laura Stone.

these two extremes, the Manali-Leh Highway is about 75% tarmac, the remaining 25% consisting of packed mud, rocks and potholes. Everywhere in the Himalaya, the gradients are gentle, to allow the diesel-belching Tata trucks a chance to make it to the top. A familiar sight in the Himalaya are the beleaguered and blackened road crews, workers from Bihar, Nepal and Tibet, who day by day inch their way along these remote routes, accompanied by barrels of boiling tar and, often, their small children. During monsoon season, their work is made infinitely more hazardous by frequent 'cloudbursts' and landslides, especially on the Hindustan-Tibet Highway, which runs through Kinnaur. When these occur in tandem, entire valleys can be cut off for weeks.

If the exception proves the rule, cyclists might appreciate the road sign outside Leh which states categorically: 'You are now travelling on a pot-hole free road'.

Safety

The Indian Himalaya is generally a very safe region to travel in, where violent crime is extremely rare and local culture esteems hospitality and honesty. That said, certain precautions are always worth taking – lock the bike and keep your luggage in sight when you're not in the saddle. Nearly all hotels, guesthouses and family houses will find you a safe place to leave your bike overnight, or else you can keep it with you in the room. India has something of a love affair with 'sykels', and any foreign bike will be surrounded by curious men in seconds, particularly if it's boasting gears, a bell or anything as weird as a BOB trailer. Your gears will be fondled until the chain falls off, the bell will be flicked and the brakes will be squeezed knowingly but most people wouldn't dream of actually taking anything. Any dangers usually come from involvement in the shadier side of Himalayan horticulture, specifically the lucrative charas (marijuana) production in the Kullu and Parvati valleys, both of which are occasionally featured in the Western press when another backpacker goes missing.

Women in particular will notice that the harassment levels are much lower in the mountains than on the plains – usually the most hassle either sex will receive is from Kashmiri carpet sellers. The political situation in Kashmir is another consideration when planning routes through the region – is it safe to visit? Despite the legions of Kashmiri 'travel agents' in Delhi, Manali and Leh

---

NO MORE ROAD

Don't know that we're the first pushies to get to Srinigar for a while but we're definitely the first pushies ever to pedal the Wari La from Pangong Tso into the Nubra Valley. Three 5300m passes in three days, and just under 6000m of vertical ascent. Level roads just don't do it for me anymore.

All day hundreds of marmots thumped across the 'road' before it turned into river. It's still being constructed and Indian directions are as unreliable as ever. Forty five kms into the day a road worker set down his spade to tell us there was no more road, no village for six hours and no water. Thankfully, when he added 'why don't you stay here with us ...' we got the message and decided to push on.

He was right though, there wasn't really a road, but it was good enough for us; there wasn't a village either, well not for 87km but at least we didn't have to stay with him and his drooling, crotch-scratching friends.

Laura Stone

who'll swear blind that there's no risk at all, the fact that a million Indian troops are posted along the border will either make you feel safer or even more circumspect.

Language and culture

English is widely spoken throughout the Himalaya, and signposts on major routes are frequently in Roman script. Minor roads and junctions are signposted too, albeit in Hindi, so consider photocopying the alphabet page of a Hindi grammar for when there's no-one from whom to ask directions. Hindi directions take on a life of their own when translated into English – houses acquire 'backsides', roads have 'downsides', and lefting and righting are a matter of course. As always, once off into the villages people will appreciate your attempts at Hindi/Ladakhi – even if they also find them hilarious.

The Indian Himalaya is a patchwork of three of the world's greatest religions – Islam in western Ladakh and Kashmir, Buddhism in Ladakh and Spiti, and Hinduism in most of Himachal Pradesh. In places these cultures have fused – in Buddhist Leh travellers will find themselves waking at 4.30am to the plaintive cry of the Muslim muezzin's call to prayer, and in Kinnaur Hindu and Buddhist gods stand side by side in the temples and gompas. Within these regions, smaller pockets of unique cultures exist – such as the Balti Dards of Dha-Hanu and the Khampa nomads of the Chang-Tang plateau. Muslim girls in Leh have greater freedoms than their sisters in Kashmir, who are secluded and, when seen on the street, are always covered up. In contrast, Ladakhi women enjoy equal status to their men, are totally self-assured and seem to do all the work.

Hike and bike

If you've ridden through Lahaul and Spiti and still have a thirst for riding over boulders, river and yak tracks, a fantastic network of ancient trading trails leads all over the Himalaya. Still the lifeline for many small villages tucked up side valleys, these trails lead over windy passes, spectacular gorges and high-altitude pastures – days from the nearest road. In Leh, mountain bikers can pore over *Trekking in Ladakh* by Charlie Loram (also from Trailblazer, see p.286) and Sonam Tsetan's *Trekking Map of Ladakh* for inspiration. If you don't fancy carrying your bike over the trickiest sections, then hire a horse to put your bike and panniers on while you trek on foot. The hike & bike option is particularly attractive as a way of returning overland from Ladakh to Manali without cycling back down the highway (or vice versa). From Kargil, it takes four days to cycle to Padum, at the head of the Suru Valley. From here it's an eight- to ten-day trek across the famously stunning Zanskar landscape to Darcha, two days' cycling from Manali. A horseman and his horse cost from $5 a day.

The Manali–Leh Highway

This is the classic ride of the Indian Himalaya. The second highest road in the world winds from the pine-clad Kullu Valley through breathtakingly raw, high-altitude scenery to the stark moonscape of Ladakh, 475km later. Over half of the route traverses a landscape so high and so barren that there's no human habitation at all – only marmots, wild donkeys and birds of prey. Weird, wind-eroded landforms loom out of the surrounding mountains – arches, turrets and antennae in pinks, greens and oranges. The five passes, two of which cross 5000m, drop down to grassland plateaux sliced by canyons, or deep red gorges.

● **Duration** 7–10 days.

● **Best time** June–October. The road is guaranteed open each year from 15 June to 15 September.

● **What to take** For speedy cycling, you can leave the tent and stove behind. Dhabas, guesthouses and parachute tents en route can rustle up a rug and hot meal but only if you can do days long enough to reach them on the remoter stretches. However, it's really worth taking camping kit as this must be some of the most spectacular camping in the world and it'll give you the freedom to explore the stunning lakes of Tso Kar and Tso Moriri on the Tibetan plateau.

● **Permits** Not required for the main Highway, though an alternative (and more demanding route) from Upshi to Pang via Mahe Bridge, Tso Moriri and

RIDING HIGH – CYCLING IN THE DEATH ZONE

Roads at high altitude are often graded for badly-tuned goods trucks, and as long as the surface is reasonable, cyclists won't find themselves out of breath even when pedalling uphill above 5000m. It's strange, but trekking or just walking up stairs are far harder work – the heart races after little perceptible exertion and the lungs feel short of breath. From 2500m upwards our bodies initiate physiological changes to adapt to the lower atmospheric oxygen, such as breathing deeper and faster, and increasing the heart rate.

Acute Mountain Sickness (AMS) occurs when you ascend too high too fast – as most of us do, for example when flying into Leh (3500m) or Lhasa (3600m). A mild headache, feeling off your food or finding it hard to fall asleep are nothing to worry about in themselves, but are all symptoms of mild AMS, and a warning that you need to acclimatize fully (ie stick at this altitude until the symptoms disappear) before ascending further.

For the world's highest roads, head to the Himalaya. Tibet and India have several sealed roads over 5000m, though India's boast (backed by the Guinness Book of Records) that Khardung La pass in Ladakh is 5602m and the 'world's highest motorable road' is incorrect: the road only reaches 5353m, and there are higher roads in both Tibet and Bolivia. Other legendary high-altitude roads are the Karakoram Highway between Pakistan and China (4693m at the Khunjerab Pass), the Manali-Leh Highway in India (five passes including 5300m Taglang La) and the Friendship Highway between Tibet and Nepal (six passes including 4945m Yarle Shung La).

To cycle among, and over, the world's highest mountains is a fantastic and constantly varied experience; on the KKH alone, the jaggedy ice castles of the Karakoram lead to the smoothly rounded, ancient Pamirs, which drop past two-humped camels into the desert oasis of Kashgar and the fringes of the Taklamakan Desert. The light in this thin air is strangely clear and colours become extraordinarily vivid. At night stars mob the sky, creating a panorama as impressive as the daytime, earthly views. Many cyclists find that despite the lack of oxygen, these 'high quiet places' are strangely energizing, and a great contrast to the fabled travellers' cities which await the end of a high-altitude trip: Kashgar, Lhasa, Kathmandu – where all things are available (especially chocolate!), but the stillness and the grandeur of the mountains feel a world away.

Laura Stone (photo © Tracey Maund)

Tso Kar currently requires an Inner Line Permit, available only in Leh. Areas are opening up all the time so check, as this is a beautiful and extremely remote region.

● **Road conditions** Roughly 75% of the Leh-Manali Highway is tarmac. Tar-blackened roadcrews and rock-cracking women crouched at the side of the road will become a familiar sight. Early in the summer, river crossings can be wild and wet, though landslides are infrequent.

● **Direction** Despite the fact that Leh lies 1500m above Manali, most cyclists do it the hard way by starting from the south. For many, the road stands as a rite of passage from the Indian subcontinent – the heat, dust and crowds – to the remote and ancient kingdom of Ladakh – the heat, the dust, the silence. Apart from its romantic appeal, this direction allows for proper acclimatization. Beginning in the south, the passes rise steadily from 3978m (Rohtang), to 4883m (Baralacha La), 5060m (Lachlung and Namika La) and peaks at 5328m (Taglang La). And it's not so masochistic as it seems – tentless cyclists from Leh face a 2000m climb from Upshi to Taglang La, followed by a sprint across the Morey Plains before reaching the first food and water at Pang, 125km away. And that's only on the second day…

● **Planning** Many travel to the Indian Himalaya specifically to cycle the Manali-Leh Highway. Three weeks is sufficient time to arrive in Delhi, reach Manali then ride. Once in Leh, daily flights across the Great Himalaya and Zanskar ranges return to Delhi, weather permitting.

Lahaul, Spiti and Kinnaur

Boasting scenery just as spectacular as the Manali-Leh Highway but with only a few Tatas a day, the Spiti Valley is a much less explored corner of the Himalaya. At an average elevation of 4570m, above which 6000m peaks and glaciers glint under a high-altitude indigo sky, the valley possesses some of the most important gompas in Tibetan Buddhism, including the thousand-year-old monastery of Tabo near the border with Tibet. Initially more demanding than Manali-Leh since little of the road is metalled between Gramphoo (at the base of Rohtang) and Kaza, 137km to the east, the awesome scenery and spectacularly situated gompas will easily compensate. Kinnaur, south of Spiti, is a narrow valley carved out by the Sutlej River as it flows west from its source near Mt Kailash in Tibet. The villages perch high up the valley sides, watched over by snowy 6000m peaks such as Kinner Kailash, south of Recong Peo. During late August and September all three valleys will be a fruit-fest for the hungry cycle tourer – with fresh peas, apricots, apples and pears filling the trees and markets. With time to explore, the turquoise, mountain-fringed lake of Chandra Tal is only 10km from Kunzum La and offers fantastic camping. Other detours include the scenic side valleys of Pin and Sangla and the characterful stone-built villages of Kibber and Nako.

Kunzum La (4335m). Tracey Maund and Colin Champion say they won't get out of bed for less than 4000m. © Colin Champion

- **Duration** Three weeks to one month, starting and finishing in Manali.
- **Best time** June to October.
- **Permits** At present foreigners need an Inner Line Permit to travel between Tabo in eastern Spiti and Recong Peo in Kinnaur, though it looks like this may end soon. The seven-day permit can be obtained in either Recong Peo or Kaza, depending on where you're coming from. Either way, you'll need three passport photos, photocopies of your visa and the personal details pages of your passport. Set aside an afternoon for shuttling between the police station and the magistrates' office. Checkpoints are at Sumdo, Chango and Jangri.
- **Road conditions** Road quality varies enormously, from an astonishingly bad stretch of boulders and river between Chhatru and Batal in Lahaul to silky tarmac in Kinnaur. The road-crews and their barrels of tar are inching their way westwards from Kaza, though it's still a good 130km before the next decent stretch of road at Gramphoo. To the east of Kaza, the road quality is generally excellent. During summer this entire region is prone to landslides which can close the roads for days and cut off entire valleys. While Tatas and motorbikes have no choice but to sit it out, cyclists can hop, skip and jump across the rocks and mud like the locals. Sometimes crude pulley systems are set up to ferry people and their belongings across chasms until they are bridged again. Traffic in Lahaul and Spiti is more likely to have four feet than four wheels, though it's heavier on the Hindustan-Tibet Highway in Kinnaur.
- **Direction** From Delhi many cyclists catch the train up to Shimla then cycle east through Kinnaur up into Spiti. At Rohtang you can either drop south to Manali or continue north-west towards Keylong and Ladakh. Not only does this give you the chance to experience one of India's classic train journeys, it also allows you to build up altitude gently through Kinnaur, before tackling the Kunzum La at the far end of Spiti. The other choice is to catch a bus from Delhi to Manali (14 hours plus), then immediately do the two big climbs (Rohtang and Kunzum La), after which it's downhill all the way. That's unless you want to loop back to Manali, in which case the Jalori Pass, just west of Rampur, is a shortcut back to the Kullu Valley.
- **Planning** You can cycle Lahaul, Spiti & Kinnaur as a loop from Manali in just over three weeks, but if you want to visit Chandra Tal and investigate the side valleys of Spiti and the hill villages of Kinnaur, then allow for a full month.

Leh–Srinigar Highway

Once rivalling Manali-Leh as the classic ride, this route has been cast into shadow by the continuing political tensions in Kashmir. The road, which skirts the Line of Actual Control between India and Pakistan, has been the target of Pakistani shelling and crossfire, while bombs and shootings continue in Srinigar and between Drass and Kargil. All the same, every year cyclists decide to run the gauntlet, usually without incident. The road is heavily militarized with increasingly frequent police checkpoints as you approach Srinigar – the upshot of this is the excellent condition it's kept in. It's also spectacularly beautiful – with pea-green glacial rivers, crumpled mountainsides like rhino hide and the wonderful gompas of Lamayuru, Alchi, Likir and Basgo. West of the Zoji La, the barren Ladakhi landscape is supplanted by the lush and pretty Vale of Kashmir.

One possibility is to cycle half of Leh-Srinigar, until Kargil. The 240km can be comfortably covered in three-plus days, provided you don't lose yourself

TRIP REPORT
INDIAN HIMALAYA

Name Laura Stone
Year of birth 1976
Occupation Writer/photographer (www.himalayabybicycle.com)
Nationality British
Other bike travels Holland and Himalaya

This trip Indian Himalaya (Manali–Spiti–Kinnaur–Manali)
Trip duration One month
Number in group Two
Total distance 1000km (625 miles)
Cost of trip US$150 (land cost only)

Longest day 120km
Best day Reaching Chandra Tal
Worst day Crossing five landslides and a 2000m pass and then getting everything stolen by eight-year-old kids
Favourite ride Side route to Chandra Tal
Biggest headache Turning up at school assembly to ask for stolen kit back. Waiting on roadside for three hours while they appeared from all directions, each with one item!
Biggest mistake Letting the eight-year-old kids carry our panniers
Pleasant surprise Three students from Mandi who learnt of our plight and helped us. As they said, 'Every hand has five fingers. Each finger is not the same'. Their kindness left a deeper impression than the kids' trickery.

Bike model Thorn Nomad
New/used One year old
Modifications None
Tyres used Schwalbe Marathon XR tyres
Baggage Setup Ortliebs – 2 front, 2 back, handlebar bag, tent strapped on rear rack
Wish you'd brought Nothing
Wish you'd hadn't brought Trekking shoes, the minidisc which broke

Bike problems None
Accidents None but riding carefully because arm still in splints
Punctures One (two-inch nail)
Same bike again Yes
Recommendations The water filter was worth the weight. Also, consider a BOB trailer

Road philosophy Be open to invitations (except the one to carry your panniers ...) Try to balance your gut instinct (which is usually right) with an open mind. Talk to people!

wandering around the lovely gompas. Once in Kargil, you have the option of cycling down the rough Suru Valley – overshadowed by the lovely Nun Kun Massif (7000m-plus) and bristling with glaciers – to Padum at the valley head, from where you can trek over the Zanskar range to rejoin the Manai-Leh Highway at Darcha eight days later.

Manali to Dharamsala

Home of the Dalai Lama and the heart of all things Tibetan in India, Dharamsala is an excellent place to wind up a trip, especially if you've spent time in Ladakh and Spiti. Regain any weight you've lost by learning to make momos, thukpa and Tibetan bread, gen up on Tibetan history and current affairs, study meditation and yoga, or maybe meet the Dalai Lama or the Karmapa – there's loads to do, and it's only 12 hours by bus to Delhi. From Manali a lovely backroad climbs high along the right bank of the River Beas, through the wooden-and-slate houses of Naggar and Jagatsukh before dropping down to Kullu and the main Highway.

From Bhanjar, take another back-road (again, a high road) to Drang via Kandi. Instead of the traffic of the main road, this route spirals up through terraced hillsides, above buffalos cooling off by the river, and chillis and sweetcorn lying out to dry in the sunshine. From Drang, the main road rolls its way across a series of valleys before dropping down to the vast Kangra plain, which stretches to the horizon. Dharamsala lies above this on a ridge and the colourful McLeod Ganj, where most travellers stay, is another 9km (and 500m in altitude) further up the hillside.

China

The idea of bicycling into China and across its breadth is a daunting one but numerous bikers have done it in recent years. Arriving from the west, China is barren and desolate and many roads are unpaved. Camping is the norm and the riding is undoubtedly 'expedition' level in terms of the gear, supplies needed and the adversity experienced. For specifics on eastern China see p.129.

Not actually the Friendship Highway but it sure feels like it. © Robb Maciag.

Crossing from Central Asia

It's possible to cross into the western province of Xinjiang in China from Kazakhstan but the roads in China pass through extremely desolate country with vast distances between towns. Most of the tiny volume of traffic crossing into China goes through either the Torugart Pass or Irkestam Pass to the south-west. Torugart is the easier pass in that it is closer to Bishkek and a better road. Irkestam is a nice ride from Osh but is much further south than Bishkek and is also a minor road, not that cyclists would mind. It's a good continuation from the Pamir Highway (see p.108).

Torugart has always been the more important crossing but it has a couple of disadvantages that do not appear to be about to change. First, private transport, including bikes, is not allowed in the approximately 18km no-man's land between border stations. Second, on the Chinese side, you have to take some form of public transport to Kashgar, which means booking in advance. The justification is that Torugart is not recognized as an official entry point into China for tourists but in reality, the rule is there to benefit travel agents and taxi drivers in Kashgar. There are always exceptions and someone occasionally gets through on their own – but this unsatisfactory situation has been going for a long time now.

Irkestam has no such restrictions – it is just a bit further away for many travellers. There is great interest in the Qolma Pass, which should open at some point between Tajikistan and China, but whether it will be open for tourists rather than just locals is another matter. Such a route would link directly to the eastern end of the Pamir Highway, and become Tajikistan's first road link with China. All three passes – Torugart, Irkestam and Qolma – lead to Kashgar, also known as Kashi, in the Xinjiang province of China.

Kashgar to Mt Kailash – clandestine cycling

China extends further west than the Tibetan border into the Xinjiang province populated mostly by Uighur Muslims, though Beijing continues to relocate ethnic 'Han' Chinese there. Kashgar is the regional capital and while all recent building has been in the Chinese style, the city has a very multi-ethnic feel arising from its position on the Silk Road and the influence of its last non-Chinese leader, Yakub Beg, an Islamic fundamentalist Uzbek general who was ousted by the Chinese in 1877.

Once in Kashgar, it's a matter of loading up on fuel and pot noodles for the journey east. The most formidable route of all, the road from Kashgar east past Mount Kailash to Lhasa, where it joins the Friendship Highway, scarcely drops below 4000m for most of the route and has seventeen major passes, the highest being the breathtaking 5250m (17,220ft) Satsum-La pass marking the Chinese-Tibetan border. From Kashgar to Lhasa expect to take six to eight weeks to cover the 2900km – even extremely fit cyclists are averaging only 50km each day.

The first great challenge when heading east from Kashgar is to leave the area without attracting the attention of China's Feds, the thoughtfully-named Public Security Bureau, who may try to turn you back at Kharghalik, 250km down the road. Try the usual tactic of passing through in the middle of the night, but watch out for guard dogs; they're going to get wise to this. The road then rises into the Aksai Chin area, land claimed by India but annexed by China in 1962. Not a permitted area to be in, but your chances of being caught are fairly low as it is too inhospitable to establish a permanent post. At Ali, 1350km from Kashgar and the first decent-sized town in Tibet, come clean with the Chinese authorities by paying a fine and hopefully obtaining a permit for the region.

Every rider passing through Tibet from the west plans to stop at Mt Kailash (see p.235) and while there most hope to perform a *kora*, the ritual

Returning from Everest Base Camp.

55km circumambulation of the mountain considered the holiest place in the world for Hindus and Tibetan Buddhists.

TIBET

Tibet is the ultimate expression of self-supported bike touring: the chance to get to places which cannot be reached any other way, for there is little public transport, foreign private vehicles are forbidden and many roads are in any case impassable by car. Anyone who actually rides into Tibet has earned their stripes; if you fly in you'll have a more sudden exposure to altitude.

Riding in Tibet demands the utmost physical fitness and preparation for both you and your bike. Supplies and backup transport cannot be relied upon. If there for a week or two expect to lose significant amounts of body weight; riders returning to Tibet often try to bulk up before arrival – not just in muscle but body fat too.

Entry points

Flying into Lhasa is an easier option than sneaking in from 'mainland' China: but at 3650m expect some acclimatization. This can be easier if you take a train from Xining to Golmud then a bus into Tibet and Lhasa (the rail line to Lhasa should be open by 2008) – a good option if you're starting from the east.

Riding up the Friendship Highway from Nepal is basically a non-starter unless you're in a group, but people have formed such groups in Kathmandu and been given visas as long as they had a support vehicle and guide.

The eastern roads from Dali in Yunnan (near Vietnam and Laos) or from Chengdu in Sichuan are hard going as they cross the Mekong and its tributaries with plenty of ups and downs and are well-policed to repel individual travellers. Entering from the Karakoram Highway (see p.109) in Pakistan at the Khunjerab Pass may be one of the best bets, though in times

---

TIBET HEALTH WARNINGS

Altitude Be careful to acclimatize properly before heading for the first high passes.
Sun Put zinc paste on exposed parts of your body.
Weather A blizzard can trap you in a bad spot if you are not careful.
Rivers During the monsoon, there may be some very wild rivers to cross.
Flash floods Be careful not to camp too close to river beds: during heavy weather they can rise by metres in a very short period of time.
Landslides and rock falls Sounds crazy, but in the east, this is a very nasty hazard.

Truck convoys Visibility can drop to zero when large numbers of trucks whip up clouds of dust.
Dogs Crazed from starvation, huge Tibetan mastiffs sometimes attack without cause.
Stone throwers Violent beggars who sometimes bombard you with rocks unless you hand over what they want. Blame the package tourists in the Landcruisers for this.
High passes Plan ahead in order not to have to stop in a switchback section where you can't pitch your tent.

Janne Corax

TIBET VISA TIPS

Many people have asked me about how to pass from China to Tibet, whether they need a visa for Tibet and so on. The Chinese government regard Tibet as just another of their autonomous provinces and therefore there are no borders as such. Entering from other Chinese provinces you will not even notice that you've passed into a new province while in some other places there is just a border marker or a sign showing the geographical border.

• The situation is fluid – it pays to stay updated.

• A visa for China is also valid for Tibet.

• Though I've never tried, I've been advised never to state 'Lhasa' or any other destination in Tibet on my application in order to get the visa without hassles.

• The normal length for a Chinese visa is three months though you can get six-month business visas in Hong Kong.

• If you have a problem getting a three-month visa (or longer), go to your embassy and ask them to write a letter of introduction, stating that you need a long-term visa.

• Visa extensions in Tibet are hard to get. Of the major cities in central Tibet, Shigatse might give you a seven-day extension. In the outback, some of the major cities can extend your visa, but the catch with that is that you're probably not allowed to be there in the first place, so you'll probably have to pay a fine and risk bicycle confiscation before you can apply for an extension. As an anecdote I got a 22-day extension in Bayi. My request was 90 days and the PSB started by offering three days.

• In Kathmandu you can get a 90-day visa without any hassles but to enter Tibet from Nepal by air is another story; you have to book an expensive tour. The Chinese embassy here has different rules from any other embassy and the rules for getting a visa usually include booking a tour to Tibet.

Janne Corax

of border tension, bike riders are forced to take a bus from the Chinese border to Tashkurgan, missing one of the longest and most scenic downhills in the entire Himalaya.

Visas

How much riding you get to do in Tibet will be governed by your visa situation. Visa renewals in Tibet are possible but not assured, especially outside Lhasa. The PSB office at Ali may give an extension but cannot be relied upon. The term of your initial visa for China may vary, typically from between one and three months. Asking for a long visa and specifying Tibet in your application could blow your cover. The situation often changes and varies depending on which embassy you apply to, so keep up to date by looking on internet forums such as 🖳 www.tibetoverland.com and work out a strategy before you go.

Wars anywhere in the region, Islamic unrest, Tibetan unrest or political problems in Beijing can cause the fragile modus vivendi between independent travellers and the authorities to be suspended. During the US invasion of Afghanistan, independent travellers were hastily put on buses and trucks and taken out of Tibet.

Tibet biker's notes

Janne Corax

Tibet has the reputation of being a mystical place and was once thought to be where Shangri La was to be found. Beautiful scenery, interesting culture, challenging riding and the feeling of being on a real adventure make it the most interesting destination for cyclists.

TOP CYCLING AREAS IN TIBET AND WESTERN CHINA

For cycling, these are the places I'm most keen on, in no particular order:

● The transition from the Taklamakan Desert to the first big mountain ranges in the west
● The desolation and emptiness of the Aksai Chin plateau
● The Mt Kailash, Lake Manasarovar and Mt Gorla Mandhata areas
● Crossing the Trans-Himalaya/Gangdise mountain range
● The multiple passes where Tibet and Xinjiang provinces meet

● Views close to the Tanggula Pass
● The transition from the high plateau to the lowlands of sub-tropical Nepal
● The views of the high Himalayas, particularly the Big Four (Makalu, Everest, Lhotse and Cho Oyu)
● Rawu Valley
● Namche Barwa region
● Riwoqe Pass area
● The entire Yunnan Highway

Janne Corax

Maps

The best plan is to buy a Chinese map in China and use a Western one as a back up. Usually the Chinese atlases are far more accurate when it comes to distance but they look pretty unexciting without topographical information. Another advantage of having a Chinese map is that you can ask directions from local people by pointing at the map. Xinhua bookstores are best for a wide selection of good atlases. The thick brown truck-driver's bible is still the best option. The most useful one with a Western name is *China Tibet Tour Map* by the Mapping Bureau of Tibet autonomous region. It's very good, even if it looks cheap and simple.

Climate and the seasons

The climate varies greatly in Tibet. In general, winter runs from November to mid March, spring from mid-March to mid-late May, summer from late May to mid-August and autumn begins mid-August and ends in November. In addition, the spring wet season runs from March to mid-May. This mostly applies on the approaches from the lowlands in the west, Nepal and all over the east. Late summer/fall wet season runs from mid-June to late August. The west can be hell all over at this time, especially if the monsoon reaches over the Himalayas. The approaches from the west, Nepal and the east may be blocked for weeks and are in general really dangerous. Landslides, flash floods and storms kill quite a few people every year. The west is much colder than central Tibet and the winter arrives much earlier north of the Gangdise mountains than on the southern side: it was a real shock to get over the Semo Pass and arrive in bitter cold on the northern side.

When to go

Spring and autumn are by far the best seasons. The summer can be good but if there's a strong monsoon you may end up battling serious mud or even landslides. Winter is for those with a real sense of adventure and those who are prepared for cold weather, heavy blizzards and waist-deep snow on some passes. The east gets much more precipitation than the west but the west is much colder and there are no deep warm valleys to take a break from the cold.

Costs

Bring lots of cash, not travellers' cheques, as there are few banks. I would never consider a budget higher than US$10 per day. Usually, if you're cycling alone, the average ends up ranging between US$2-5 per day, depending on the area; the west is more expensive. Sometimes you're in places where the nearest bank is weeks away. Remember that prices can be quite steep in some distant areas and in extreme cases you may even be charged for hot water. Check out how the truck drivers handle these situations and then try to pay about the same. If camping a lot and cooking your own food, you will not spend much money even if the prices are higher.

I usually also stash Y1500 (about US$185) for 'unexpected costs': fines, for example, or if you get injured and have to hitch with a truck (there are very few free rides up there). You can change dollars in Ali/Shiquanhe (although you'll get a bad exchange rate if counting the fine in order to be able to change it here in the first place), Lhasa, Shigatze, Bayi, Gyantze, Nagqu, Qamdo, Zhangmu and possibly Lhatze, Saga and Nyalam. In some other places you can change on the black market. I've heard the PSB has higher fines now. Before paying a fine, demand to have a look in the law book (English version), especially if you think the price is a bit steep. Also let the PSB officer state which crime you're being charged with. Be polite but firm about this. Sometimes they back off and let you go when you demand this.

Accommodation

The obvious choice for most cyclists is to camp. On most of the routes you'll find places which seem as if they're custom-made for pleasant camping. According to Chinese law you are not allowed to camp but no-one seems to care. If you like being left alone by curious truck drivers or shepherds, you can always find a place where your tent isn't seen. Certainly, on the Friendship Highway it's a good idea to keep a low profile and not camp where you can be easily noticed because of the risk of theft. You'll also avoid the annoyance of having someone sitting outside the tent begging for hours.

The alternative to camping is the often abysmal truck-stop hotels along the way. They are usually severely overpriced: a concrete or clay room with old and worn-out beds, often set so close they look like one huge bed. Filthy, flea-infested blankets, a candle and sometimes a thermos of hot water complete the picture. Chain-smoking room-mates who constantly seem to cough their lungs up is the norm and in winter time a smoky little heater loaded with yak dung adds to the fug. Watch out for furious guard dogs and falling into the toilet pit when going to the toilet at night. In the bigger cities there are hotels where, like everywhere in China, you get what you pay for.

Food

Contrary to what most people think, food is not a problem in the region. There are normally shops within a couple of days' cycling and, if not, you can always stop at any settlement and buy tsampa, sugar, salt and other basic foods.

Travelling in winter makes it a bit harder to find food in some areas:
● Along most of the popular routes (Friendship Highway, Golmud Highway, Kashi – Kailash – Lhasa) there are few longer hauls without food – sometimes a day or two but seldom more.

- The Northern Route (Ali/Shiquanhe – Gerze – Tsochen – Raka) has some stretches of 3-7 days where it's impossible to buy provisions, depending on the distance you cover per day and in which season you travel.
- In the east there is plenty of food along the way but you have to be more careful about being noticed by the PSB, so it's not always practical to eat in a restaurant.

In general, Chinese eating places are safer than the Tibetan equivalents with regard to hygiene standards. Fresh vegetables are available in the bigger cities, especially if there is a large Chinese population. In the smaller villages and at truck-stops you can always buy fresh vegetables straight from the restaurants, but prices can be steep.

It's usually cheaper to eat a vegetable dish in the restaurant. The army biscuit/noodle diet is for those who decide to cook for themselves, people going for the longer hauls or those travelling in winter, when many truck stops and restaurants are closed.

Water and fuel
Water is not generally a problem and I've very seldom come across an area where there is no water for more than 50km. There are some drier periods and at the beginning or end of winter you may have to melt snow. The closer to the northern parts of the plateau – the Chang Tang region – the more brackish and salty lakes you'll encounter. As long as you stick to the roads, you can always flag down a truck and ask for water. A water filter may come in handy if you want to play it safe, but in general the water is OK to drink in most places.

Bring a multi-fuel stove. Gasoline and diesel can be bought from motorists and in towns along the way. Paraffin/kerosene is also available but usually harder to find and of poor quality.

Closed areas
As in other parts of China, there are some places which are off-limits to foreigners. You can either try to get an Alien's Travel Permit at the PSB (Public Security Bureau) or go without a permit. The former option can be costly or you may be denied a permit. The latter has the obvious disadvantage of the possibility of being arrested by the PSB. Closed areas fines can be Y200-1000 (US$25-125) and you'll be made to leave the area. If caught in some of the

Way off the beaten track in Kerriya Shankou,
Western China. © Janne Corax.

more sensitive areas or if the PSB people take a disliking to you, you may have your gear (including your bicycle) confiscated.

There are occasional crackdowns and sometimes open areas become closed without notice. Usually the Golmud Highway is the only sure bet and the Friendship Highway is usually safe to cycle from Lhasa to Kathmandu. The east is full of checkpoints and closed areas regardless of which route you take. The Yunnan

TRIP REPORT
SOUTH ASIA AND CHINA

Name Paul Woloshansky
Year of birth 1954
Occupation Bike Mechanic, Travel Writer
Nationality Canadian
Other bike travels Asia, North and Central America, Australia

This trip Nepal, India, Malaysia, Thailand, Laos, Cambodia, Vietnam, China
Trip duration One year
Number in group Two
Total distance 17,500 km (10,940 miles)
Cost of trip US$6100 (US$25 a week each, airfares, insurance, souvenirs, and postage for four parcels sent home)

Longest day 170km
Best day Too many to choose from
Worst day First day out of Kathmandu: 75km of climbing on loose gravel, nervous soldiers pointing guns, no food
Favourite ride Rajasthan, Tamil Nadu, and Kerala in India; northern Lao; northern Yunnan in China
Biggest headache Katadyn Mini Water Filter
Biggest mistake Should have taken more memory cards for camera
Pleasant surprise Universal goodwill shown to us everywhere we went
Any illness Heat exhaustion in Malaysia, upset stomach in Lao

Bike model Tech Pulse MTB
New/used New
Modifications DT spokes and Sun Rhyno Lite/Mammoth rims; Brooks saddle; new chainrings, chain and cogsets and all bearings repacked a month before we left.
Tyres used Specialized Hemisphere Armadillos: very slow and tread peeled off. Replaced with Avocet Cross tyres we'd brought as spares: excellent, fast, hard-wearing.
Baggage Setup 2 rear panniers; waterproof bag on top of the rack
Wish you'd brought Less! We ended up discarding/mailing things home

Bike problems Front derailleur – rode about 1500km without it
Accidents None
Punctures About a dozen
Recommendations Malaysia is more oriented to vehicular traffic, and the heat so intense we both had headaches.
Advise going straight from Chennai to Bangkok, and spending more time in China (Tibet!)
General tip 700c tyres are very hard to find; I'd advise taking a bike with 26" wheels, both for tyre availability and use on unpaved back roads – in Asia the most fun

Highway may be the easier in terms of checkpoints. Western Tibet has two routes (the Northern and Southern, see below) and the bottleneck on both is in Ali/Shiquanhe, where you pay a fine and get your permit but after that you're allowed to cycle on.

Routes

These are the most common routes:

- **Golmud Highway** Relatively easy cycling on good asphalt. High passes but no long climbs and relatively easy gradients. A good route to start with.
- **Friendship Highway** Mostly easy cycling on a combination of gravel and asphalt roads. Some higher passes and a couple of rougher climbs depending on which route you choose.
- **Southern Route** Kashi (Kashgar) to Lhasa via Mt Kailash. Rough cycling in the western part, with long hard climbs. Sandy and pretty bad road conditions exist in the areas in between Mt Kailash and central Tibet. Hazardous route during the rainy season.
- **Northern Route** Kashi (Kashgar) to central Tibet, using the northern alternative instead of passing Mt Kailash. Long hauls in the rugged and desolate north. Hard road conditions and rough and high passes. Longer between food stops.
- **Yunnan Highway** Some parts are now being sealed but it's still a hard route. Long, hard climbs almost every day and an ever-present danger of being hassled by the PSB. The rainy season and the spring melting season sometimes make this route completely impassable.
- **Sichuan Highway** Hard route which can be combined with the Yunnan Highway. Long hard climbs and heavy police presence. If the Yunnan Highway is closed because of floods and landslides, this may be an alternative.

Lhasa to Kathmandu

A trip through Tibet would not seem complete without a visit to Lhasa, which is why your time in Tibet and visa arrangements need to be planned carefully. Besides the famous attractions of Lhasa, Kym McConnell suggests numerous other rides in the Lhasa area which would keep you fully occupied for several weeks, visiting monasteries in the area or riding to Lake Nam Tso at 4760m.

Many first-time riders in Tibet choose to leave Tibet on the Friendship Highway. It's logistically as hassle-free as anything in Tibet and there is a fair amount of bike traffic. Although the quality of the road and facilities steadily improve, it is still a difficult route, with altitudes, dogs, stone-throwing kids, high winds and food poisoning all routine hazards. Don't take it for granted that you'll get through and don't take it as personal failure if weather, lack of stamina or stomach troubles cause you to flag down a bus or truck for a lift. The rewards of this spectacular ride – Shigatse and Tashilhunpo Monastery, the Kumbum at Gyantse, the side trip to Everest Base Camp and Rongbuk Monastery (permit required for the area) and then the world's longest downhill run, a descent of 4200m in 160km – will be lifelong memories. Just pray that you don't get headwinds to spoil that fabulous ride.

(Opposite) **Top:** Tibet – Rattling down from the Chakpa La. **Bottom:** North-west China – Idyllic campsite beside Karakul Lake. (Photos © Cass Gilbert).
(Overleaf, double page): An inspiring vista in eastern Kyrgyzstan, near the border with China. (Photo © Janne Corax).

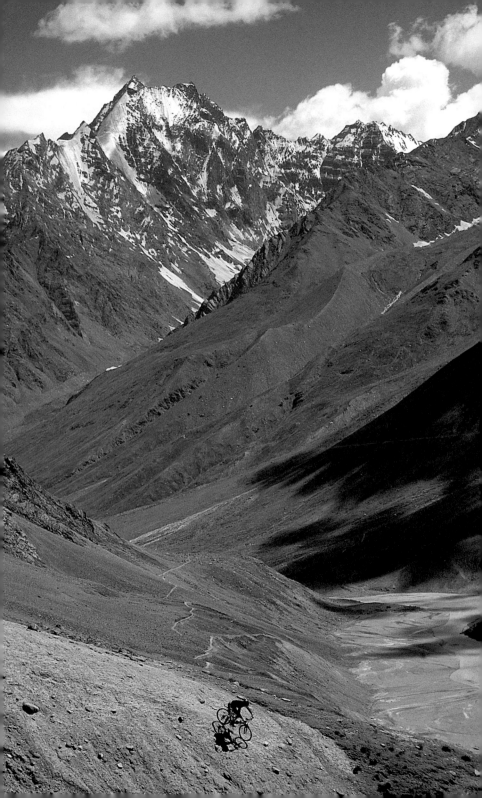

EASTERN CHINA

Peter Snow Cao

The populous half of China is a never-ending mass of cyclists of all shapes and colours, and it offers a multitude of opportunities and challenges to the visitor. Despite the language barrier, people are friendly and helpful, travel is inexpensive and relatively safe, and with a good map, a few words of Chinese and an open mind one can travel the country easily.

The cultural highlights of China, where history is measured in thousands of years, are both rich and diverse: the Great Wall, Tiananmen Square, Dunhuang Grottoes, the Giant Buddha at Leshan and the Shaolin Temple, birthplace of kung fu.

Basics for bikers

In mainland China, traffic uses the right-hand side of the road, but Hong Kong and Macao use the left-hand side. Major roads outside the cities are mostly asphalt; they're concrete pavement in the cities. Note that in remote areas some national highways are not paved. Also, China is rapidly upgrading the highway system, so there may be long stretches under construction. Many major urban roads have separate bike paths. Expect to encounter a variety of people, vehicles, bicycles, tractors and animals using the roads, even in remote areas.

Earthquake zone, China.
© Robb Maciag.

Cycling in China is significantly different from cycling in most Western countries. Cyclists must never assume they have the right of way. Drivers of motorized vehicles (including motorcycles, cars, trucks and especially buses) generally assume that cyclists will yield right of way to them, regardless of the situation. If a vehicle honks frantically behind you, it is best to move off the road as soon as possible. One of China's traffic laws requires that drivers warn pedestrians, cyclists and other drivers that they intend to pass by using their horn, which can be deafening at times.

Most drivers are relatively accurate, if slightly aggressive. They also tend to pass closer to cyclists than drivers in the West. With the recent rapid increase in the number of private vehicles, it is best for cyclists to keep a respectable distance and give way rather than stand their ground because they think they have right of way. Bear in mind that China has more than 100,000 road deaths annually.

Finding spares for your bicycle can be difficult. Standard 26" mountainbike tyres are available virtually everywhere but 700c will be found only in a few specialist shops in major cities such as Beijing, Shanghai, Chengdu and Kunming. In better shops Shimano components (or copies) are the norm. Guangzhou has the greatest selection and offers the best prices on new bikes.

(Opposite): Going off-road in Spiti (see p117), India. (Photo © Laura Stone).

Accommodation

Hotels for budget travellers are plentiful and inexpensive. China uses a five-star system to rate hotels with the five-star hotels charging Western prices. Getting into inexpensive digs is a matter of learning what to look for and then bargaining hard. Prices for hotel rooms are always negotiable, sometimes as much as 50-60% off posted prices, with 20-30% off a more common discount except during the May 1 and October 1 holiday periods in popular tourist destinations.

The quality of the hotel is mostly dependent on its age; the older it is, the worse condition it will be in. The cost of a budget hotel room in the big cities will be US$20-40. Dormitory beds for Western travellers are available in some big city hotels for US$3-10. Outside the big cities, cheap hotel rooms can be had for US$8-20 and there are guesthouses used by long-distance truckers with dormitory beds for US$2-5. In some places the local police will require Westerners to stay in 'approved' tourist hotels, despite the central government's mandate to the contrary.

The traveller hotels and guesthouses are most useful to the budget traveller, although many owners will not have any experience in dealing with foreigners. In the back-country it's possible to stay with local families if you're able to establish a good rapport with the family. An experience like this can be a very interesting way to learn about how the local people live but it can also be very draining: you will definitely earn your keep by providing entertainment for the family and friends for the duration of your stay! The men will always want to drink alcohol with the male traveller and a refusal is seen as a huge snub.

Camping and food

Camping is relatively unknown in China. Nevertheless, wild camping is possible in some mountain and desert areas but be prepared for inquisitive visitors regardless of how remote you may think the location is.

'Wild' camping in Canton – behind a gas station. © Robb Maciag

For the touring cyclist, Chinese food is cheap and delicious. Breakfast in southern China usually consists of noodles, while in the north, dumplings are the mainstay. Lunch can be with rice, noodles or dumplings. Vegetarians will have to be persistent in their no-meat requirement; stating that you don't eat meat is like saying you don't breathe air. Even if there is no visible meat, vegetables are often cooked in meat fat with pork fat being ubiquitous.

Average daily costs for food in inexpensive restaurants will be US$5-10. All running water in China must be filtered or boiled before consumption. Boiled water will always be provided in large thermos flasks in any hotel or guesthouse free of charge. Bottled water is readily available from shops everywhere for US$0.15-0.40 per 500ml bottle.

TAKING BIKES ON TRAINS AND BUSES

Touring cyclists can take their bikes on trains by going to the freight section at any train station. There is no requirement to box the bike but, left unprotected, it will probably suffer surface scratches. Metal mudguards will likely be dented. It is recommended that everything be removed from the bike before shipping it since small items such as bells may be pilfered en route. Also, removing the pedals and rear derailleur prevents train personnel from taking joy rides on your bike around the station.

The process for shipping is time-consuming: expect to spend an hour or two getting help from someone in filling out forms. The cost is usually about half the cost of the hard-seat ticket, and they will ask if you want to insure it. There is a maximum amount of insurance for bicycles of about US$1000. Bikes shipped by train generally get sent on a slower freight train rather than on the passenger train so you will have to ship your bike ahead of time if you want to pick it up when you arrive at your destination. Usually a day or two before is sufficient, depending on the length of your train trip.

Taking the bus with a bicycle is becoming increasing difficult as the bus system transforms into a US Greyhound-style service with small under-coach luggage compartments instead of the roof racks that were

Actually a Laotian bus, but you get the idea.
© Robb Maciag.

ubiquitous years ago. Bikes that can be dismantled into a compact size will be allowed on these buses if there is room. Sometimes the driver will allow the bikes to be placed in the aisle of the bus, particularly if it is not full. Charges for bikes vary considerably from nothing to half the price of a seat on the bus. In the countryside, there are usually small old buses that serve the local farmers with racks on the top. These buses are very slow, stopping anytime to pick up or drop off passengers, but are generally quite willing to accommodate putting a bicycle on the top rack. Sometimes a small fee will be charged for doing this.

Edward Genochio

TOURING NOTES

Edward Genochio

China offers a vast range of touring opportunities, from historic city-hopping in the east to village-to-village explorations in the interior, to hard-core mountain and desert traverses in the west.

Get a map of China and draw a line running from Heihe (Heilongjiang province) on the Russian border in the north-east to Tengchong (Yunnan province) on the Burmese border in the south-west. The area to the south and east of that line comprises 43% of China's land area, but is home to 94% of the country's population. It is crowded, intensively cultivated and relatively low-lying. To the north and west of the line, with 57% of the land area but only 6% of the population, China is virtually empty with vast ranges of grassland, desert, high mountains and plateaux.

Your China touring experience will be very different depending on which side of that line you choose to ride. If you want to see villages and teeming cities, ride on good roads and find decent accommodation every day, head east. Camping in the east is usually difficult because nearly all flat land is either under intensive cultivation, built on or flooded. In any case it is hard to find a spot away from prying eyes. If you're more into adventure/expedition cycle touring, go west, but be prepared for unpaved roads, more extreme conditions and long stretches with zero facilities.

The road network in southern and eastern China is extensive and in most parts good. Things thin out considerably as you head towards the wilder west. China is divided roughly 50-50 between endless plains and plateaux (which can get dull to ride) and steep and rugged mountains, so start your route planning with a good topographical map. For detailed route planning and on-the-bike navigation, though, you'll want to get hold of a Chinese road atlas.

Incidentally, most roads in China have regular toll-booths but as a cyclist you are exempt from paying and can slip round the side. Some river crossings marked as bridges on the map are in fact served by ferries, on which you can take your bike for a couple of Yuan.

Road Atlas of China

The best single-volume coverage of the whole of China is the *Zhongguo Qiche Siji Dituce* ('China Auto Driver's Atlas'). It comes in a tidy portable size and individual pages can be teased out without too much difficulty so they'll fit in your handlebar bag map case. If you're handy with a needle and thread you can unpick the binding stitching and lift the pages out in six-sheet bundles, which you can then sew back together. That way you can keep the pages you need in your map case, while burying the rest of the atlas at the bottom of your panniers.

The maps show virtually every road in the country and are reasonably accurate – though take the hard-to-make-out distance indicators with a pinch of salt. They show rivers but no relief other than the odd spot-height, so you'll probably want to use the atlas in conjunction with your topographical map.

The atlas is sold in Xinhua bookshops across China (there's one in every town) and comes in a burgundy plastic cover, with a small gold steering wheel on the front. It's updated annually.

G-roads

G-roads are the great national trunk roads. If you're covering long distances it's likely you'll need to use them for at least part of your route. Expressways are being built at a frantic pace across the country, in many cases running semi-parallel to the old G-roads. While the expressways are closed to cycles, they draw off a lot of the long-haul traffic, making the G-roads more pleasant to ride.

Almost all G and smaller 'S' provincial roads, as well as most 'X' county roads have pretty reliable kilometre markers on which the road number is also painted; unlike in some countries, they count in one direction only, so the kilometre-numbers are the same whichever direction you're headed. For G1-series roads, km0 is always Beijing; for G2-series roads, km0 is the north end; and for G3-series roads, km0 is the east end.

G-roads are generally kept in good condition though in mountainous areas this can vary and in the rugged west don't expect them to be paved. Where there's no parallel expressway, G roads can be major trucking routes and not much fun to ride, especially near major cities in the east. Often, though, they have generous cycle lanes, which offer some protection from the heavy traffic, but in which you will compete for space with local inhabitants on bikes, tricycles, micro-tractors and, increasingly, mopeds.

Picking refuelling or overnight stops from the China Road Atlas takes a bit of practice, because its basic symbol for a settlement can represent anything from a hamlet with no amenities

At a time like this you'll want the *China Auto Driver's Atlas.* © Robb Maciag

to a large town with everything. If you want to be sure of finding services such as accommodation, a bus station, or a hospital, look for towns marked with a dot inside a circle. These are county administrative centres and are guaranteed at least to have a range of basic services including accommodation.

Dealing with closed areas in China

In the early days of China tourism, the whole country was 'closed' with the exception of specially declared 'open' areas. Gradually more and more areas opened up, with the result that nowadays you feel the few areas that remain unopened are simply administrative oversights. There is no official list of closed areas; instead, each province (in theory) maintains a list of open areas, so you can discover which areas are closed only by a lengthy process of elimination. Trying to establish whether the particular road you want to take crosses a closed area can take days of cartographic investigation – even if you actually manage to lay hands both on the open-areas list in question and on a map whose place-names tally with those on the list.

You can try going to the police in the provincial capital – they should be able to supply the open-areas list for their province and, if you're not the 29th cyclist in as many days to have asked for the information, you might find a friendly police officer with patience enough to go through the list with you and mark all the open areas on your map. Some cyclists have tried this approach but you can still come unstuck even if you try to do everything by the book. The open-areas list you are shown may be out of date – sometimes areas are closed again without notice; or the local police out in the sticks might not have been told that their area is open, so they'll try to haul you in anyway.

Touring extensively through eastern and central China, from the northern border with Mongolia all the way to Hong Kong in the south, I decided the best approach was to assume everywhere was open and hope for the best. I ran into trouble only once, in Inner Mongolia, when the police stopped me on the road between the Mongolian border and the town of Jining. They told me I was in a closed area, but let me continue on condition that I 'go straight to Jining and don't stop anywhere'. I know of other cyclists who have been fined by police in that area, so perhaps I got off lightly. If you know you're going through a closed area, you're better off sticking to the main road – you're less likely to run into trouble if you're clearly just 'in transit'. Yunnan in the south-west was the first province in China to declare itself open in its entirety, so

---

BIKING TO CHINA FROM HONG KONG

Bringing your bike into China via an overland border is not always simple. Coming from Hong Kong, you are not allowed to ride into the restricted area just south of the border, so to get to 'mainland' China you will have to put your bike on the KCR train as far as the border crossing at Lo Wu. You then push your bike across the footbridge and through the immigration formalities. Once you're through, you're bang in the middle of downtown Shenzhen and free to get riding. Going the other way, from China to Hong Kong, the same applies – once across the border, you'll have to take the KCR at least as far as the first stop (Sheung Shui). The excess baggage fee for taking a bike on the KCR is about US$6 or, bizarrely, half that if you take the front wheel off.

Incidentally, don't write off Hong Kong as part of your China tour. The northern two-thirds of the territory include some very fine biking routes on scenic roads. There are also some great designated cycle paths, including a well-signposted route along the seafront from Sha Tin to Tai Po. Lantau Island also offers some good day-ride routes, though Hong Kong might be a good place to ditch your panniers for a few days and let your touring bike be what it always wanted to be – a mountain bike. Contact the Hong Kong Mountain Bike Association (💻 www.hkmba.org) for details. Contrary to popular belief, you can ride your bike in Tsimshatsui and on Hong Kong Island itself, as long as you're happy riding in busy urban traffic. And remember (especially if you've just arrived from right-side mainland China) that they drive on the left in Hong Kong. You can cross the harbour to Hong Kong Island with your bike by taking the Star Ferry from Tsimshatsui to Wanchai. The other Star Ferry routes don't take bikes. **Edward Genochio**

---

there at least you can tour without fear of straying into closed territory. See 💻 www.bikechina.com/china-open-city.html for a list of open areas. The list is periodically updated as new information becomes available.

Mongolia

Edward Genochio

Like Timbuktu in Africa, the very name Mongolia invokes images of extreme remoteness but in Mongolia's case the image is still accurate. Today, thanks to the fall of the Soviet empire which used the country as a buffer state against China, you can find out for yourself. This is a country which has yet to shake off its nomadic origins. Outside the capital Ulaan Baator (UB) most of the population lives in *gers* (yurts or felt tents) and even the most rudimentary infrastructure is unknown. There is only one road, north from Russia to China via Ulaan Baator. Elsewhere intermittent tracks wind across the grassy plains from one settlement to another. If you can't get your adventure cycling rocks off in Mongolia it's time to try another planet.

If you're making that haul between Russia and China, the simplest route takes you from the northern border at Kyakhta (Russia)/Altanbulag (Mongolia) to Zamyn Uud (Mongolia)/Erlian (aka Eren, or Erlianhaote, in China). This way will take you through Ulaan Baator where it's easy to pick up a Chinese visa from the embassy there.

Crossing into Mongolia from Russia at Kykhta/Altanbulag is straightforward: the border is open every day and assuming your visas are in order you can ride across with minimal hassle. There are other border crossings from Russia into Mongolia further west from Tashanta (Altay Republic, Russia) to Tsagaanuur (in the far west of Mongolia) but this would be a seriously remote cross-country ride requiring very long range and stamina. An attractive option due to open soon is the crossing from Khandagayty in Tuva (Russia) to near Lake Uvs-Nuur in north-western Mongolia. The crossing from Mondy (Russia) to Khankh (Mongolia) would connect up a fine route between Lake Baikal (Siberia) and Lake Hövsgöl (northern Mongolia), if it were ever to open.

The last Edward saw of his tent and bike for a while – see p.225. © Edward Genochio.

For now, the simplest route into Mongolia from the north takes you on the road from Altanbulag to UB; a stretch of about 340km is on high-quality paved road, and you can't get lost so long as you stay on the metalled surface. If you are planning side trips on other roads, you'll need good gesticulatory communication skills or a GPS and a good map (try the American, half-million TPC series) because signposts are virtually unknown. But then, so are roads as we know them.

FROM MONGOLIA TO CHINA

If you're coming to China from Mongolia, the border crossing is a little more complicated. The Mongolian authorities may allow you to ride across their 5km section of No-Man's Land, but they'd rather you put your bike in the back of one of the many vans that shuttle between the border posts every day. Even if you do succeed in riding to the Chinese side, you'll be thwarted in your attempt to ride 'the whole way' from Mongolia to China by the border guards who will insist you load your bike into a vehicle, at least for the 200 metres or so between the two gates of their customs compound. Alternatively, it's easy enough to take your bike on the trains that run from UB to Erlian over the Chinese border.

CROSSING THE GOBI

At the time of writing the road and rail crossing at Zamyn Uud/Erlian is the only one on the long Mongolian-Chinese border open to foreigners. A brand new road is being built across the Gobi to connect the border to the Mongolian capital. When I rode the route in the autumn of 2004, 140km of road had been completed, leaving 550 roadless kilometres across the desert. Sometimes there are decent tracks; the trick is to work out which one heads for the border and which goes off to someone's ger behind the sand dune on the horizon. Sometimes the tracks become faint or disappear altogether for long stretches; get used to it, this is Mongolia. Unfortunately, where the tracks are clear and well-used, they're usually badly corrugated by passing traffic, so a bit of suspension makes riding more comfortable. Be rigorous about tightening your bolts out here when riding long distances on washboard surfaces. I lost a rack half way across the Gobi as a result of failing to do this.

It would be unwise to attempt the crossing without a compass or GPS – at least until the road is completed. Much of the way you can ride within sight of the railway line, so you can use that as your guide. Maps show the 'road' crossing back and forth across the railway, but in reality there are tracks on both sides and it is simply a matter of picking which track seems least bad. Invariably, the better track is on the other side of the railway. Storm channels running under the railway every few kilometres allow you to cross from one side of the tracks to the other when you feel the urge. Around 150km of the route goes through extremely arid dry desert with virtually no vegetation at all. For the most part it's stony desert, some of it not bad for riding on, but there are long sandy stretches where pushing is required, and lots of hidden sandy patches which will stop your bike dead and send you flying over the handlebars – to a soft sandy landing.

If you stick close to the railway, you'll find settlements of some sort every 50km or so, so carrying huge quantities of water may not be necessary, though given the high probability of getting lost for a while, it'd be wise to carry at least a couple of days' supply of water at all times. Plastic jerry cans can be bought at the 'Black Market' in Ulaan Baator. The piped water in the Gobi towns is pretty foul – it certainly needs sterilizing – but bottled water is also available.

Look out for half-buried lengths of barbed wire which seem to stretch across the Gobi and could put a nice hole in your tyre if you go over them. Keep an eye on the horizon, too, for approaching sandstorms. They are most common in the spring but can strike at any time – one descended on me in mid-September and lasted all day. There's not a lot you can do to avoid them but they can cut visibility to just a few metres and the airborne grit will shred your eyeballs in any case if you try to open your eyes. Your only defence is to lie low and wait for the worst to blow over. On the plus side, you'll find your bike is spotlessly clean the next day – all the accumulated dirt and grime is sand-blasted away.

At time of writing, the road heading north from Zamyn Uud extends only about 100 metres beyond the edge of town, so if you're coming from China you've either got to plunge straight into desert riding or you can put your bike on the train as far as Choyr to skip the toughest stretch of the Gobi.

Other than the road from Ulaan Baator north to the Russian border at Altanbulag, and the beginnings of the road south to the Chinese border, there's precious little tarmac in Mongolia. All maps show a generous network of roads covering the whole country, even distinguishing between 'highways', primary and secondary roads, but 95% of these are unsealed tracks and paths, not all of them bikeable.

South-East Asia

Felix Hude

Why cycle in South-East Asia? Well, there are lots of reasons: the landscape is beautiful, there's a very wide variety of routes, it's safe, the food's tasty but most of all, the people are genuinely friendly and welcoming. In this modern world of ours, this seems to be an increasingly rare phenomenon.

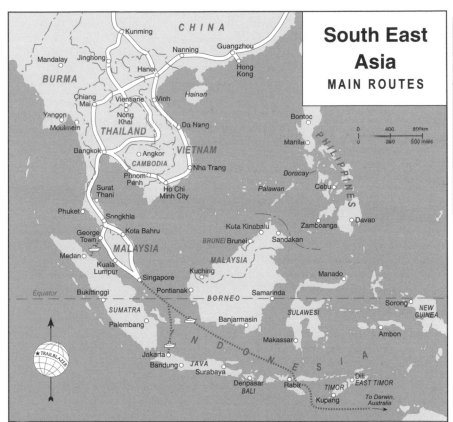

An extremely easy region for riders, with plenty of open border crossings and only one serious headache, Myanmar (Burma), whose government insists you fly in and out of the country. Otherwise, almost any rideable road is a good route and avoiding traffic is one of the main considerations. Bangkok or Singapore are probably the easiest places in the region to fly in and begin a circular tour, though consider taking a bus or train to get out of Bangkok, beginning your ride on quieter rural roads. Note that getting from South-East Asia to Australia generally involves flying as there is no passenger ferry.

THE UNKNOWN ROAD

To cycle in South-East Asia and keep the edge, you must be prepared to give up some day-to-day certainties and simply trust the winds. You need to be happy to stand astride your bike on top of a mountain and look down onto that unknown road snaking through the forest beside the river, open your arms wide and suck it all in. And then you just slip your feet into the pedals and launch yourself into it. This is really what adventure cycling is all about.

Felix Hude

Routes and border crossings

The area is politically very open nowadays. If you look closely at a map, you'll see that the roads run from country to country, across borders, across the whole subcontinent. You can cycle them all.

Crossing through the numerous border points should for the most part scarcely impede your progress. You can wheel your bike through most of them at no charge, with no tax, no forms to fill out and no proof needed of an onward plane ticket out of the country. However, there are a few border crossings that are not open to foreigners; the situation fluctuates, so you need to keep yourself updated.

You can start in Singapore and ride all the way to Flores in the eastern half of Indonesia, or go north to Bangkok and head to Hanoi through Laos and on to China, or start in Bangkok, ride across Cambodia to Saigon, and then go north to the DMZ (Demilitarized Zone), and cut back to Bangkok through Laos. Or start in Laos and ride all the way south to Phnom Penh along the Mekong. It's up to you!

Take note, however, that there is no land entry/exit in Myanmar (Burma) from anywhere that will allow you to travel into the heart of the country. You must enter and exit Yangoon (Rangoon) by air. Biking from South-East Asia to India or Bangladesh presents an insurmountable obstacle for the cyclist. There is simply no way around it, and if you want a tea and a chapatti in your favourite café in Delhi, and you insist on riding there, you'll have to go via China and Tibet.

MALAYSIA AND INDONESIA

You can take a boat out of Singapore south to Jakarta, get on your bike and just keep going. Ride across Java to Surabaya and head south over Mount Bromo for a day's climb through a science-fiction landscape. The traffic can be nightmarish in Java; I rode it once and never returned but with its green-on-green forests and smoking volcanoes, it's one of the most beautiful places on earth. Or you can head north through Pulau Madura, off the beaten track.

Roll south to Banyuwangi and cross into Bali for some Hindu culture and Italian food. You can cross Bali in a few days by either the north or south roads, and go up over the centre through Mount Batur in a day or two. It's a steep climb but the road is sweet, the view is exquisite and they sell pizzas.

Keep going across Lombok down the middle through Mataram or north over the more mountainous terrain along the coast road via Sengiggi. The traffic's thinner on the northern route but either way the local Muslim population will invite you into their homes for tea, enquire politely about your family and smile at you.

By the time you get to Sumbawa time has no meaning and the roads are extra quiet so try not to run over the kids that stand in the middle of the road waving you down. The road across the western half of the island through Sumbawa Besar is surprisingly flat but the eastern side is mountainous and will test your mettle but it's still a great ride.

Further east is Flores. It's got serious mountains and is built for serious bikers. But, having said that, it's perhaps the most gorgeous island I've seen in the whole Indonesian archipelago.

West Kalimantan

From Jakarta you can take a boat north to Kalimantan (Indonesian Borneo). From Pontianak in west Kalimantan you can ride east into the Central Kalimantan forests along easy stretches of river on good roads and through bustling trading towns. There's a unique mix of Javanese, Chinese and native populations (Iban, Dayak, Pinan and others), and churches; indeed, often more churches than mosques.

East Malaysia

From Pontianak you can head north through the mountains and cross into East Malaysia at Etikong. Note the shift in living standards. It's an easy and picturesque run, the roads are good and you can make it into Kuching, the capital of Sarawak, the south-western state of East Malaysia, in under a week. Apart from the occasional foreigner spotted in the major towns, the local people just don't see tourists out here, so you've got it to yourself. Keep going north-east in Sarawak through Brunei and up over the hills to Sabah. It's rugged and mountainous but this is by far, in my opinion, the best half of Malaysia. The people are wonderful, the country spectacular and it's a long way from Kuala Lumpur.

Sulawesi and Sumatra

From Samarinda you can cross easily into Sulawesi by ferry. The roads run in all directions out of Palu, on central-western Sulawesi, and a lot of it is mountainous. If it's virgin biking territory you're looking for, pick a route and ride it. You might run into the odd cyclist escaping the insanity of the modern world up on the north arm towards Manado. If you do, you'll have plenty to talk about.

From Jakarta you can also take a Pelni boat to Southern Sumatra and ride north to Lake Toba. The road is a mixed bag of hills and flat, and the traffic is moderate. Lake Toba, another spectacular science-fiction landscape, is the home of the friendly Christian Batak people.

From Lake Toba you can cross east over the hills, visit the orang-utan sanctuary at Bukit Lawang and push on to Medan. The road runs through dense forest, the traffic's not too bad and from Medan you can take the high-speed ferry to Penang on the west coast of Peninsular Malaysia. It takes five hours.

The road up along the east coast of northern Sumatra from Medan is flat and boring and the best route to Aceh is up the gorgeous north-west coast; you could call in at the offshore island of Nias on the way. The coastline is rugged, the road running beside the mountains on one side, and sandy beaches and rocky coves on the other. However, Aceh is off-limits at the time of writing because of political troubles and the more recent Asian tsunami. Worth visiting also is Pulau Weh, an isolated volcanic island beyond Banda Aceh (the capital of Aceh Province). It's as far north-west as you can go in Indonesia and it's close to paradise.

Singapore and Peninsular Malaysia

North out of Singapore you can head straight up the east coast of Peninsular Malaysia and into Thailand, and keep going until you hit Bangkok. It's an easy route, mostly flat, with moderate traffic and a friendly laidback local population, and it runs beside the South China Sea the whole way. Alternatively you can ride up the west coast of Peninsular Malaysia through Malacca, Kuala Lumpur and on to Penang. It's the populated side of the peninsula so expect busy roads and bigger cities; for my money, it's not the best choice.

THAILAND

From Malaysia there are four border crossing points strung across the border with Thailand, but the most picturesque routes are over on the east side through Kota Bahru/Tak Bai, or on the west side through Sadao.

From Kota Bahru/Tak Bai the road hugs the east coast all the way to Bangkok. It's flat and easy all the way to Surat Thani where you can take a small paved road that runs beside the railway tracks for the next 200 kilometres. It then comes and goes all the way to Hua Hin, passing through quiet towns and over a few hills, and past the odd beach bungalow perched on the cliffs overlooking the Gulf of Thailand. Past Hua Hin you're back on Highway 41 and the traffic into Bangkok can be heavy, so it might be worth taking the train from say, Petchaburi, into Bangkok.

If you're leaving Malaysia from Penang, you'll come up through Alor Setar and cross the Thai border at Sadao. From there you can get off the arterial road and weave your way over the hills north to Krabi on the south-west coast of Thailand and take a swim, then keep going all the way past Phuket (not recommended) and north to Ranong on the Myanmar border. It's an excellent route, taxing over the hills but forested, beautiful and you're never far from a beach. From Ranong you can slip over the border into Myanamar for the day (for a few bucks) if you're curious, but you're limited to a small kilometre radius.

Western and northern Thailand

You can take a one-way run north-west for a few days to Three Pagoda Pass on the Myanmar border. The road goes via Kanchanaburi on the River Kwai (of 'Bridge' fame) and then heads off through the mountains and along the flats and a last steep 30-kilometre hair-raising ride to the pass. It's almost worth going for the name alone.

From Bangkok you can get up to Chiang Mai in a couple of weeks and as long as you stay off Highway 1 through Tak things will go swimmingly. There are historic ruins, great food, first-class cheap accommodation and friendly people: a pretty good deal. It's mainly flat and as the minor roads are paved and in excellent condition you can pick and choose your route wherever you want.

If you head west out of Tak to Mae Sot, you can then ride north along the Myanmar border to Mae Hong Son, and approach Chiangmai from the north-west. And what a run that is! Mountains, wats, forests and the alluring scent of the beyond.

THAI TRAINS

We can't leave Thailand without mentioning the trains. Thai trains are without a doubt my fave form of motorized transport in South-East Asia. Clean, efficient, regular and with smiling staff. If you need to get somewhere quickly, this is the way to go, as long as the train has a luggage carriage. (Once upon a time you just carried the bike on with you and sat with it but, alas, things are changing.)

Provided there is a luggage carriage, hand your bike to the nice man in the snappy grey uniform and climb aboard, worry-free. Second-class sleepers have soft pillows and crisp white sheets and are, and I hate to say it, being an independent, rugged biking sort, awfully snug. But you shouldn't feel ashamed if you take a Thai train!

Felix Hude

Bangkok to Cambodia

Leaving Bangkok, the cycling route choices fan out at 360° – it really is the road network hub of South-East Asia. However, cycling into and out of Bangkok itself can be a nightmare and it might be worth taking the train, though make sure it has a luggage carriage. How far? Around 100 to 200 kilometres is a fair hop. Swinging east and south-east from Bangkok you can ride (or take the train) to the Cambodian border in a few days and cross at Aranyaprathet/ Poipet, Pakkard/Pailin, and in the far south-east corner at Klong Yai/Cham Yean (Koh Kong) in Trad Province.

North-east Thailand to Laos

From Chiangmai go further north along the flat to Chiang Rai and then hook right over the hills to the Golden Triangle and enter Laos at the Chiang Khong/Huau Xai border crossing. The whole of eastern Thailand (Issan) is a wide open plain, bordered by Laos in the north and east and Cambodia in the south. The Thai people here are of Lao origin (which means relaxed), and the towns and small country wats are quiet and welcoming. Many of the routes are on the flat and boring side but down along the Cambodian border the scenery is more varied and there are mountains; and it's devoid of tourists.

From Bangkok you can ride north-east through Issan to Nong Khai on the Mekong, an easy run, and cross over the river into Laos on the Friendship Bridge near Vientiane.

The Friendship Bridge, by the way, was built with (my) Australian tax dollars and you must cross by bus, bike no problem. I have, however, written several letters to the Laos Tourism Authority over the years suggesting that, considering my rather generous financial support, the seats at the front of the bus be reserved for cyclists – but I've yet to receive a reply. (The post is slow in Laos.)

From Issan you can enter Laos at Nakhon Phanom/Tha Khaek, Mukdahan/Savannakhet and further south at Chong Mek/Pakse.

LAOS

Looking at a map you'll see that where the flat plains of Thailand end at the Mekong, the mountains begin over on the Laos side. Northern Laos, north of Vientiane, is mountainous but in actual fact southern Laos, along Highway 13 east and south of Vientiane, is pretty much flat, including the routes across to

Ladies' crossing, Laos.
© Robb Maciag

the Vietnamese border. Highway 13 is the main north-south artery in Laos and it's in great shape – wide, smooth, paved and carries moderate to little traffic.

If you head north on Highway 13 out of Vientiane on your way to Luang Phrabang, you'll hardly be out of Vientiane before you're dropping down through the gears and climbing mountains and they won't stop until you're through Tibet and running downhill almost into Delhi. By then, you'll really need a tea and chapatti.

The roads deteriorate badly up past Luang Phrabang towards China, and if you've entered Laos from Thailand at the Chiang Khong/Huau Xai border crossing (east of Chiang Rai) conditions are variable and it's sometimes extremely rough and hard going. In fact the whole of the north of Laos is rugged but it's well populated and is a cyclist's dreamscape if you're up to it – and you'll certainly be up to it by the time you've cycled it. Take note that there's no crossing into Vietnam from northern Laos for foreigners. However, the border crossing to China is open.

East and south from Vientiane along Highway 13, things are a lot less intense. The road follows the Mekong all the way around into Cambodia and it's pretty flat until you get to Pakse way down in the south, where there are a few hills before the road levels out again towards the Cambodian border.

To get to Vietnam, you can strike south-east from Pakxan or north-east out of Tha Khaek and ride up the river valley and over the hills into Ban Nape and cross into Vietnam, and on through the rice paddies to Vinh. Or go east from Savannakhet to the little town of Lao Bao on the Viet border and cross over and climb up the hill to Khe Sanh. From there you drop down the other side of the Vietnamese Central Highlands, freewheeling all the way to the South China Sea along what in the Vietnam War used to be the McNamara Line just south of the DMZ.

The road is paved all the way east out of Savannakhet but prepare for culture shock at the Viet border. I love the Viets, I really do, but think of 'Donald Trump meets Yogi Bear' and you'll be getting close to where Vietnam interfaces (and I do mean 'interfaces') with Laos.

Savannakhet, by the way, is an easy going former-French headquarters and one of my favourite extended drink stops. You can sit on the bank of the Mekong at night eating noodles and chatting to sweet Lao teenagers and watch the relative madness unfolding across the river in neighbouring Mukdahan.

CAMBODIA

If you reach further south to Pakse (not one of my favourite extended drink stops) and keep going almost to the Cambodian border you can stop off at Don Khong Island right in the middle of the Mekong for a rather civilized three-day lunch break or go a little further on to Don Det Island and bang drums on

T R I P   R E P O R T
SIX MONTHS IN ASIA

Name Bridget Ringdahl
Year of birth 1974
Occupation Environmental Consultant
Nationality South African
Other bike travels South America

This trip India, Vietnam, Laos, South-West China, Tibet, Nepal
Trip duration Six months
Number in group Two for half the trip, then alone
Total distance 5400km (3375 miles)
Cost of trip £2000 (including flights: return to Europe, to Saigon, to Kunming, to Lhasa)

Longest day 160km
Best day Summiting Gyatso-la Pass and catching views of Everest North Face on the descent to Tingri
Worst day Near rape incident at truck stop in Tibet
Favourite ride Laos and SW China
Biggest headache Dogs and all the yak stuff: yak butter, yak milk, yak meat – yak yuck!
Couldn't do without Nice cheap clothes-scrubbing brush
Pleasant surprise The ever joyous, exuberant children along the way shouting 'helllllooooo', 'sabadee', 'sinchowww', 'namasteeeee' and even 'I love you'.
Any illness One day of the runs in India; septic wounds in Laos

Bike model Ridgeback
New/used New
Modifications None
Tyres used Knobbly ones that came on the bike
Baggage Setup Two Altura back panniers: excellent and moderately priced in comparison to other brands like Ortlieb
Wish you'd brought Sleeping bag

Bike problems Bearings going in the rear hub
Punctures Three
Same bike again Yes, and perhaps a shorter front bar so more upright
Recommendations Don't listen to what other travellers or the LP may tell you about the road ahead. Unless they're cyclists they have no idea what bikes can do!

General tip Rest days are vital for obvious reasons, but they also fuel the desire to get back on the bike. After 2 -4 days of rest I was always ready to head on.
Road philosophy Be impulsive. Trust your instinct. Get up and GO!

'... if you're looking for the raw Cambodia you'll need to turn off the highway'.
© Robb Maciag

the full moon. A few kilometres south of Don Det there are two border posts. If you want to catch a boat from the Lao-Cambodian border along the Mekong to Stung Treng and beyond, and it's a fair option under the circumstances, hang a right off Highway 13 at the nice big border-post sign just past the police post (you can't miss it!). However, if you want to ride all the way to Stung Treng, just keep going on Highway 13 in Laos until it runs out at the Cambodian border (and believe me, it runs out) at Voeng Kam. But be careful. The road to Stung Treng is only 50-odd kilometres but it's a tough leg.

I first rode Cambodia in 1998 and have very fond memories of looking down onto the roofs of cars as I pulled out and passed and hurtled on down that rough track they called Highway 6. The holes were big enough to swallow cars. In the late nineties, after a generation of chaos and mind-numbing tragedy, Cambodia was stumbling forward once again, and as you rode through towns and villages the local people opened their arms and gave you a heartbreaking welcome.

However, it's changed a lot, at least on the main thoroughfares, so if you're looking for the raw Cambodia you'll need to turn off the highway and claw your way along the dusty back roads (but that goes for the rest of South-East Asia as well). These days most of the main highways are paved, smooth and wide, and Cambodia is a relatively easy cycling option. They're also improving the roads at a frantic pace.

Cambodia transit

If you're simply crossing Cambodia from east to west or vice versa along Highway 5 (through Battambang to Phnom Penh) and Highway 6 (through Siem Reap/Angkor Wat to Phnom Penh), there's not a lot to it. Count the klicks and ride from town to town. It's safe, cheap, the people are friendly and trustworthy and there's zero danger from mines.

Out of Bangkok east to Aranyaprathet/Poipet, you can get the train to the border and cycle from there which is a good option. The only hiccup is the stretch of road between Poipet, through Sisophon and onto Siem Reap/Angkor Wat, which is still unmade and rough in parts. However, the accommodation and drink stops are good and it's a fair run. Angkor Wat, by the way, is a must-see. I'm not big on 'the sights' but, believe me, it's the Real Thing.

If you cross into Cambodia from Thailand at Ban Pakkard/Pailin, note that the road up to Battambang is not yet sealed though it soon should be. Even so, it's in reasonable condition and is an easy option.

Taking the motorboat over the Tonle Sap (The Great Lake) between Siem Reap and Phnom Penh is not recommended. It's overpriced and uninteresting. Better to stay on the bike.

Southern Cambodia

If you're coming from Khlong Yai south-east of Thailand through Koh Kong, the road south through Cambodia to Sihanoukville (Kampong Som) is not paved yet but is in good shape. However, it's a long stretch through the Cardamom Mountains from Koh Kong, so be prepared. But it sure is beautiful. From Sihanoukville you can go straight up Highway 4 to Phnom Penh but it's busy and not much fun, so a better option is to push east to Kampot and come up through Takeo. You can also visit the beach at Kep, which is not much good for swimming but a pleasant little spot, and cut north-east right from there to the Vietnamese border post at Phnom Den/Nha Bang through Kampong Trach. The roads are rough but it's a lot of fun. Note that it's not possible to cross into Vietnam at Ha Tien.

Western and northern Cambodia

From Sisophon you can head north through Banteay Chhmar along a rough dirt road and head further east on better roads beside the Thai border to Anlong Veng and go south to Siem Reap.

A few kilometres north of Anlong Veng is an extremely steep goat track of a road leading up to one of the Khmer Rouge's last strongholds and the site of Pol Pot's grave. You'd need to be Lance Armstrong on steroids to ride up it but if you're curious, leave the bike at the guesthouse in Anlong Veng and hitch a lift. Halfway up the hill is also the site of the only Khmer Rouge objet d'art known to man, a life-size rock sculpture of, what else, soldiers. Curious.

You can push further east to Preah Vihear Temple, another ex-Khmer Rouge hangout, perched spectacularly on the cliffs amidst the jungle on the Thai border. Again, you won't get up or down the mountain road on your bike without extreme difficulty but it's worth a visit.

You can then ride due south from Preah Vihear village all the way to Kampong Thom. However, take note that there's a long 70-kilometre stretch south from Choam Khsant to Tbaeng Meanchay that's as rough as rough. Super rough! There's nowhere to stop for drinks, no people and mines in the forest so don't wander too far off the track, but apart from that it's a heap of fun. It's possible to head further east from Choam Khsant along the Lao border to Stung Treng on the Mekong, but the roads are pretty rough and you'll need a good map. Even the local inhabitants don't know where the roads lead half the time.

Up the Mekong to Laos

From Phnom Penh you can go north through Kampong Cham all the way to Kratie on a new paved road but things fall apart beyond Kratie. The road to Stung Treng is rough and dusty but there are people and food so it can be done.

From Stung Treng to Voeng Kam at the Lao border the road is very rough, sandy and tough going with almost nowhere for food and drinks. Scenically it's totally uninteresting. A viable and fun alternative is to catch a riverboat from either Kratie or Stung Treng up the Mekong into Laos.

North-east Cambodia

You can cycle out to Banlung from Stung Treng along a poor road, so take extra water and plan carefully. Banlung is, strangely, quite a pleasant spot, stuck as

PART 2 – ROUTE OUTLINES

it is out in back-country Cambodia. Note that you cannot enter Vietnam at Tang Doc, east of Banlung. It's for local people only. South of Banlung the roads are mostly bad and it's a long way from Phnom Penh, so if you want to push further south into Rattanakiri Province take adequate precautions.

Beyond Kraek (about 70 kms east of Kampong Cham along Highway 7) northeast into Mondolkiri Province the road through Snoul and Sen Monorom is OK but again there are some long stretches between drink stops. Beyond Sen Monorom they tell me the road simply disappears, despite what the map says. One of these days I must get up there to check it out. Sounds interesting.

From Kampong Cham you can go east along Highway 7 and turn south and head to Neak Luong, or push 50-odd kms east to Kraek and weave your way south along the Vietnamese border to Svay Rieng. The road twists and turns and splits at various points, so you'll need to stop and ask directions at times and be prepared to spend half an hour every so often entertaining the friendly but bored Cambodian border police.

VIETNAM

If you're pushing on to Vietnam out of Phnom Penh, Highway 1 east to the Viet border at Bavat/Moc Bai and on to Ho Chi Minh City (HCMC/Saigon) is sealed and flat but a bit of a milk run.

Vietnamese border functionaries, by the way, are notoriously humourless and it's best to play it straight and leave the jokes for later. You can't cross into Vietnam at Chau Doc by road. You must go by boat from Phnom Penh or Neak Luong. The best option into southern Vietnam, in my opinion, is to cycle Highway 2 south out of Phnom Penh through Takeo, and cross the border at Phnom Den/Nha Bang, some 20km south-west of Chau Doc. Past Takeo the road turns to dirt and is rough in places, but it's a picturesque and fun trip through a quiet corner of Cambodia.

You can reach Saigon (HCMC) from Bavat/Moc Bai (due east of Phnom Penh), or along Highway 1 from Chau Doc (by boat from Phnom Penh) or by road up from Phnom Den/Nha Bang (down Highway 2 out of Phnom Penh through Takeo, entering 20km or so south of Chau Doc).

The Mekong Delta

The Mekong Delta in Vietnam is one of my favourite weekend cycling destinations and when I start spending too much time on the internet in Saigon I take off to the Delta for a few days just to remind myself that I'm a cyclist. But you've got to get off the highway and ride down the small roads that run along canals and tributaries of the Mekong. There's a whole network of single-lane roads to get lost on and you will still find, even today, places where the locals come out and look at you like you're the first white face they've seen since the day in 1972 when that hairy GI guy took off at full pelt down the road in the green jeep.

From Laos you'll probably be entering Vietnam at Lao Bao, and can easily turn south down Highway 1 and make it to Hue and Danang in a couple of days. If you've come from Ban Nape and then across to Vinh, you can turn north along Highway 1 and go straight to Hanoi.

Alternative routes

If you want to avoid the rip-offs in Vietnam, it's worthwhile studying the map and looking for other, less touristy, routes. You can cycle from the Khe Sanh (DMZ) down though the Central Highlands all the way through Buon Ma Thuot, and further to Saigon. It's not an easy run but it may be the price you need to pay for some peace of mind. And from Vinh you can travel up to Hanoi along the Lao border. Again, you'll need to work at it but if it's the essential Vietnam you're looking for, you may just find it here.

From Hanoi most folks head north-west to Sapa and beyond but you can ride west to Dien Bien Phu, or south-east down the Red River where the road keeps to the flats but twists around small hilltop temples on top, or even east – there must be something out there.

Japan

A few years ago Japan was an unthinkable destination for most bike tourers unless they had recently come into a large inheritance. It was seen as the most Westernized country in Asia as it was the most advanced and in terms of costs, dauntingly expensive compared with South-East Asia. How times have changed. South-East Asia is developing rapidly and environmental problems and traffic growth are now serious considerations in planning a tour there. Japan's experience has been completely different. Superficially Western in many ways and certainly wealthy, Japan has a unique culture and a very conservative character. Ancient rituals, interior styles and customs have survived amidst technological innovations and idiosyncrasies like multi-storey bike parks, capsule hotels, revolving-belt sushi bars and karaoke. Japanese people may feel their culture is under threat in the modern age, but to the visitor it appears to be thriving, creative, innovative and surprisingly accessible to foreigners.

Although there are plenty of tourist sites to visit in Japan, independent travellers on bikes can dig a little deeper and experience Japan on a level with the Japanese. In Japan, there is no 'foreigner pricing' and you will likely be forgiven for making honest mistakes and being inquisitive. You are on a par with the Japanese people; if they help or befriend you, they are not expecting any financial rewards, nor are they desperate to emigrate or likely to mug you in some back alley. For these reasons and many more, Japan is a traveller's paradise and is all the more rewarding for not having much of a budget traveller's network outside Tokyo. You have to figure it out for yourself, but Japan is for the most part relatively open to foreigners in areas where other Asian societies are not and Japanese people are surprisingly tolerant of *henna gaijin* – 'crazy foreigners'.

Getting to Japan

If you are travelling only to Japan, you will almost certainly fly there, most likely arriving at Tokyo's Narita Airport. Take the bus into the city. They will

© Matt Goodhind

take your bike for free in its box which is much easier than lugging it onto a train.

Long-distance travellers may prefer to take a ferry to Japan. The closest and cheapest point of entry is from Pusan, Korea's main port, to Shimonoseki at the western extreme of Japan's main island of Honshu, or Fukuoka, the beautiful capital city of the island of Kyushu. Ferries also connect Shanghai with Osaka and Kobe and there are ferry services between Vladivostok and either Niigata on the Japan Sea coast or Yokohama near Tokyo. Lastly, there is a ferry service from Sakhalin to Hokkaido.

Climate and seasons

Japan has a temperate climate, a relief from the heat of much of Asia, but it has some distinct features. It is a reasonably wet climate with lush vegetation, punctuated from June to July by the rainy season which extends across most of the country from the west and is followed by a hot summer. Hokkaido is cool and comfortable in summer and has a more challenging climate the rest of the year with heavy snow in winter. The autumn is typhoon season, with unpredictable and occasionally fierce but short-lived storms, and not a bad time to visit.

Expenses – surviving Japan

Japan's reputation for high costs is not entirely deserved and you've brought your own transport and accommodation. Your main expense is food and the occasional night with a roof over your head. Eating out in Japan is surprisingly cheap – simple meals cost around £2-£8 or US$4-15. At the cheap end, it's stand-up noodle bars but even revolving-belt sushi bars can cost as little as £1/US$2 per plate of two pieces.

Supermarkets may appear expensive, but that's if you are looking for familiar Western foods. Try some Japanese vegetables and things are much cheaper. These are easy to stir-fry. Japan is vegetarian-friendly and has many bean dishes such as tofu that are very cheap and nutritious. Seaweed is also healthy and cheap too but it's not easy to guess what everything is in a Japanese supermarket. If you like sushi, packs of assorted sushi are heavily discounted at the end of the day in most supermarkets, and it's still extremely fresh. There are many new food tastes and experiences to be had while travelling in Japan; a good guidebook or, at the very least, the vocabulary and phrasebook at 🖳 www.japancycling.org will help you get started on a culinary tour.

Youth hostels cost around £8-15 or $23-30. Youth hostels are full in the summer and public holidays, so book ahead. Japan Cycling has a hospitality list for overnight homestay possibilities with Japanese people. Never mind that it's free, the experience can only be a positive one and help you get an insider's view of Japan. The next ultra-cheap option is wild camping. This is

TRIP REPORT
ZURICH TO TOKYO VIA CENTRAL ASIA

Name	Patrik Wuthrich
Year of birth	1965
Occupation	Graphic Designer
Nationality	Swiss
Other bike travels	France, Italy, Thailand, Laos, Vietnam, China

This trip	Switzerland, Italy, Greece, Turkey, Iran, Turkmenistan, Uzbekistan, Kazakhstan, Kyrgyzstan, India, Nepal, China, Taiwan, Korea, Japan
Trip duration	Two years
Number in group	Two
Total distance	35,000km (21,875 miles)
Cost of trip	about $10,000 each

Longest day	170km
Best day	Cycling inside crater of Nemrud Dagi, Turkey
Worst day	Hit by bus on Grand Trunk Road, India
Favourite ride	Kashgar to Mount Kailash
Biggest headache	Hidden thorns in the tyres
Biggest mistake	Not taking enough time
Couldn't do without	BBC World Service
Pleasant surprise	Not caught by police in closed zones of China
Any illness	Homesick, but only a few seconds per month

Bike model	MTB – Cycletech Papalagi (www.velo.com)
New/used	Five years old
Modifications	No serious ones
Wish you'd fitted	Disc brakes, Rohloff SpeedHub
Tyres used	Schwalbe Marathon XR 26x1.95, good but too expensive; now Chinese Landmark Guilin Nylon ($3)
Baggage Setup	4 panniers, another on top of them and bar bag
Wish you'd brought	40GB mp3 player with all my CDs on it
Wish you hadn't brought	Frying pan, which I gave away

Bike problems	Rims, rims, rims ...
Accidents	One – collision with motorbike in Kyoto
Punctures	14 over 20,000 km
Same bike again	Not really, maybe a recumbent
Recommendations	Bruce Gordon Racks – expensive but eternal; SRAM Chains: cheap but strong; small compass on handlebars is useful, particularly in cities

General tip	The smaller the road, the more surprising the adventure!
Road philosophy	Go slow but don't stand still! (Old Chinese proverb)

PART 2 – ROUTE OUTLINES

not for everyone as it involves pitching your tent discreetly after dark in unused spaces as Rodger Grigsby describes opposite. Besides wild camping, asking the local policeman in his neighbourhood box – the koban – often works. The police may suggest somewhere and, in extremis, might even let you spend the night in the koban. Asking locals is always a good idea.

No matter how small your budget is, staying at least once in a Japanese inn is a memorable experience. There are also some 'pension'-type guesthouses in the country which offer bed and dinner at similar prices to inns, but with Western-style bunk beds and dormitories.

When wild camping, look out for public baths, known as *sento*, for a place to wash and warm up. This is a very respectable old tradition dating from the time when houses did not have baths or people could not afford to heat sufficient water. Sentos all charge a standard rate for the area. In Tokyo it costs just £2/US$4 and it's another great Japanese experience that ordinary tourists miss out on.

Roads and riding conditions

The Japanese drive on the left-hand side of the road. There is not a lot of space in Japan; most of the land is mountainous but don't let that put you off. Unlike most other nations, they understand that precious space has to be shared and drivers are respectful of bicycles – if they have seen them. It's one country in Asia where might is not right. There may be an element of surprise in seeing bikes on some roads and cyclists should be as considerate as they expect drivers to be.

You will do most of your riding on the road, but bikes are allowed on the pavement or sidewalk, though you would be expected to ride slowly. All bikes in Japan should have bells; they are used and appreciated as a courtesy to pedestrians. In the country look for narrow paved farm roads that may be headed the way you want to go. These can extend for miles and may even lead you into the next valley or onto unpaved roads. A rear flashing light will give you peace of mind when passing through the many tunnels through the mountains and along coastal roads.

WHERE TO GO

Start by buying Kodansha's *Japan: a Bilingual Atlas*, which also has good city maps and has Japanese names spelled in the Roman alphabet. If you are a keen camper and like wild scenery, Hokkaido is the place for you. Plenty of wide open roads and an easy to follow circuit around this large island combined with cool summer temperatures make it ideal for bike touring. Jens Olsen's website, 🖳 www2.gol.com/users/jolsen/onsen/index.html, which looks at Japan's *onsen* (hot springs), lists 18 free outdoor natural hot springs in Hokkaido.

Tokyo is busy but traffic is bearable and you can find minor roads parallel to main roads going in the direction you want that have far less traffic. It's a quiet city. Kyoto is more manageable by bike and the temples are spread out around the edges and in the surrounding hills so a bike is useful to visit them. To the south of Kyoto is the ancient capital of Nara, which has historic monuments well worth a visit but is only a small town and easy to get around. Coastal roads are busy in some places as, like Italy, the interior is mountainous

---

WILD CAMPING TIPS

I've camped on the top of castle-moat walls, in the foyer of big-city art museums, in Shinto shrines and under the eaves of Buddhist temples. Lighthouses always offer a good spot nearby, and it's hard to beat Japanese beaches. Most towns, large or small, have a river running through or by them, and along those rivers there is inevitably a park, sports field or croquet court, and nobody seems to care if you camp there. In smaller towns, the city park, if it's on the coast or near a wood, is also good. Look for rest-stop shelters near parks and along beautiful 'tourist' stretches of coast. These covered pavilions have a table, and many have running water too. I often pitched the tent under these, using it for privacy and bug proofing, while letting the structure protect me from rain.

Rodger Grigsby

---

and the coast is a natural place to build towns and roads. The Izu peninsula west of Tokyo is a beautiful region and has many hot springs and a good coastal road with views of Fuji. The island of Shikoku is much quieter and is known for the 88-temple pilgrimage – a fine combination of mountains and coastline. Kyushu, on a larger scale, has volcanoes and national parks in the interior and is much easier for camping.

Generally, Japan gets friendlier as you head out from Tokyo, especially to the west. Japan Cycling has produced an excellent 1930km route between Tokyo and Fukuoka in Kyushu that consists of roads chosen for cyclists and passing through areas foreign visitors might wish to visit. The route includes Nikko, the mausoleum to the first Shogun and one of Japan's must-see destinations, then passes through the Japanese Alps before descending to the heartland of Osaka, along the northern coast of Shikoku and then through rural lands to Fukuoka. The route, guidance notes and all maps needed can be found on Japan Cycling's website.

JAPAN END-TO-END

Roy Sinclair

Pedalling Japan end-to-end had been a long-time dream. We had loosely planned a course along the Japan Sea on the west coast of Hokkaido and Honshu. For variety we included a detour through the Japan Alps in Nagano prefecture. In Kyushu we visited Nagasaki and later took a highland route through southern Kyushu to Kagoshima Bay.

Despite its huge population, sometimes dense traffic, hundreds of road tunnels, mountains, and a summer of typhoons, Japan soon manifested itself as an agreeable bike traveller's country. We often stopped to chat with people. `My time is my own, please come and visit my house,' one woman working in a rice field told us. Good intentions of an industrious pedalling day were often, and delightfully, foiled by Japanese hospitality. A bike-shop proprietor told us, ruefully, he saw few bike travellers these days. 'Young Japanese people prefer to stare at a computer all day.' Convenience stores provided most daily needs. Breakfast, typically an *onigiri* (seaweed covered rice ball with filling of salmon, pickled plum or fish roe) and canned hot coffee, was early. The post box outside the store improvised as a breakfast table.

PART 2 – ROUTE OUTLINES

TAKING BIKES ON TRAINS

You can break a lot of rules in Japan but you will never get a bike on a train unless it is in a bag. There are no guards vans on Japanese trains; most people send large luggage by baggage-delivery services. A little expensive, but convenient. Hence you will be the only one on the train with your bike. A bike bag can be bought before your trip or you can find a large but pricey one at Tokyu Hands (interesting hobbyist department store found in major cities) for Yen14,000 (about £70).

Pedals, wheels and handlebars and perhaps racks must come off to fit the bike in the bag. In every Shinkansen (bullet train) carriage, there is a space behind the last row of seats which will take a bike. For local trains you can carry on your bike and should have no problem on buses either. It's not done by Japanese people, who send their bikes on by baggage-delivery services, but your situation as a foreign visitor will be understood, if not sympathized with.

Along the Japan Sea we detoured through the narrow streets of shabby fishing villages. In Tottori prefecture (in western Honshu) we temporarily abandoned bikes to climb Mount Mitoku where the curious Nageire-do Temple clung precariously to an alpine cleft. It was built in 706 AD.

We stayed at YHA hostels, business hotels, cycling terminals – which were like upmarket backpackers – and we camped. We also slept in railway stations and, on one occasion, on a station platform. A ritual was an end-of-day call at the hot spa or onsen. Bicycle travel had reduced life's needs to basics and we could feel content.

In a larger town or city we would generously reward our efforts – sampling the local cuisine, beer, *sake* (rice wine), or *shochu* (sweet potato wine). Beer, served in large chilled glasses, accompanied by a simple dish of boiled green soy beans (*edamame*) was an excellent entrée followed by a glut of dishes, among them grilled tuna, fried noodles and thinly-sliced lightly-cooked beef. Foods also challenged. *Motsunikomi* was a stew of cow guts; *fugu* was a blowfish delicacy and deadly poisonous if not cooked correctly; and *natto*, a paste of fermented soybean, was a test for any foreigner. A Japanese woman told me, 'It smells like shit'.

Urban riding, necessary for a length-of-the-country ride, was tedious. Wide, cluttered footpaths were shared with pedestrians and dare-devil commuter cyclists. Japan also provided bike riding at its best. And there was always the unexpected. A steep descent in southern Kyushu saw us hitting the brakes as two human-sized monkeys bounded across the road.

© Roy Sinclair

I particularly enjoyed the ride beside Kagoshima Bay, gazing at the beautiful volcano Mount Kaimondake, on the final stretch to the Sata township. Sadly, we had to succumb to taking a bus on the final eight kilometres to the cape. Bicycles were unreasonably banned from this narrow, steep, but little used privately-owned road. Next day we crossed Kagoshima Bay by ferry, paused at Nishi Oyama – Japan's southernmost train station – and rode high above the stunning southern ocean before turning inland on a stiff climb to Chiran, best known for its Kamikaze Pilots Museum.

The bike ride concluded at Kagoshima city where we easily fell in with the colourful Ohara autumn festival. Costumed telecommunication workers insisted we participated in draining their bottles of sake. What better welcome could we have wished for at the conclusion of a 72-day bike ride of almost 4000 kilometres?

Australia

Despite being the flattest continent, the sheer size of Australia makes it a daunting prospect for those hoping to ride a large chunk of the country. Even the determined few who circumnavigate the country have only seen the edges. Away from the 'bitumen' (as they call sealed roads out there) the great outback remains a tough and dangerous proposition despite the obvious appeal of thousands of kilometres of desert tracks. The distances are so great, the summer temperatures so high and the water supplies so limited that cyclists are bound to have a safer time riding in the south-east and south-west corners of the country. Here the temperate climate and short distances between settlements are much more forgiving for cyclists. Head for the southern coastline such as Victoria's Great Ocean Road, leaving plenty of time to head inland on tracks such as the Mawson Trail (🖳 www.southaustraliantrails.com/pdf/mawson.pdf) or, in Western Australia, the ancient karri forests and the developing Munda Biddi Trail (🖳 www.mundabiddi.org.au) running from near Perth to Albany on the Southern Ocean.

Basics
Most Australian states have a compulsory helmet law for cyclists, which means this is a two-hat country – the other one is for sun protection when not riding. Visas need to be obtained outside the country but North Americans and most Europeans can get an Electronic Travel Authority (ETA) online which does the job. A standard visa is for three months but you can apply for extensions of up to one year within Australia.

Australia has an excellent camping scene, with caravan parks in most small towns around the country. The selection of bike parts is not great outside the big cities, especially if you need something touring related. The website Bicycle Fish (🖳 http://users.chariot.net.au/~gloria/) is one of the best resources for touring Australia and for a good read try Roff Smith's *Cold Beer and Crocodiles: A Bicycle Journey into Australia,* all the better for not being written by a hardened world tourer. As for which guidebook, well in Australia you barely need one. That said, most lemmings drop onto the Lonely Planet at terminal velocity, but the Rough Guide is as good and has much better jokes!

TRIP REPORT
LONDON TO NEW ZEALAND

Name	Tim Mulliner
Year of birth	1973
Occupation	Environmental Scientist
Nationality	New Zealand/UK
Other bike travels	Europe, Central America, Japan, Australasia UK, Canada, Scandinavia, France, New Zealand

This trip	London to New Zealand
Trip duration	14 months
Number in group	One
Total distance	24,115km (15,072 miles)
Cost of trip	€5000

Longest day	224km
Best day	Cycling through Zagros Mountains, Iran
Worst day	Stuck in hotel room in Iran having put my back out
Favourite ride	Turkey – friendly people and hassle-free travel
Biggest headache	Visa extensions in China
Biggest mistake	Boring coastal road in Thailand
Couldn't do without	Small photo album of family and friends
Pleasant surprise	Getting my book of the journey published: *Long Ride for a Pie*
Any illness	A month of bowel problems in Pakistan

Bike model	Condor custom-made road-style frame (steel), mountain bike brakes, gears and wheels
New/used	New
Modifications	(see Bike model, above)
Wish you'd fitted	Shimano: worldwide availability. Also simple down shifters instead of all in one brake/gear levers
Tyres used	Specialized Nimbus Armadillo 1.5's and Specialized 1.75's knobblies: both excellent tyres
Baggage Setup	Ortlieb: 2 front, 2 rear & 1 handlebar bag
Wish you'd brought	Walkman
Wish you hadn't brought	Iranian aeronautical maps: bulky and useless

Bike problems	Internal mechanism of gear/brake lever snapped, broken racks, two split rear wheels
Accidents	None
Punctures	20, though none in first 7500km
Same bike again	Yes, very comfortable for the long distances

General tip	Don't commit to covering ground in a certain amount of time, anything can happen and it probably will.
Road philosophy	Laugh at your misfortune. If you can't you'll struggle. It's often in the worst of times that best things happen

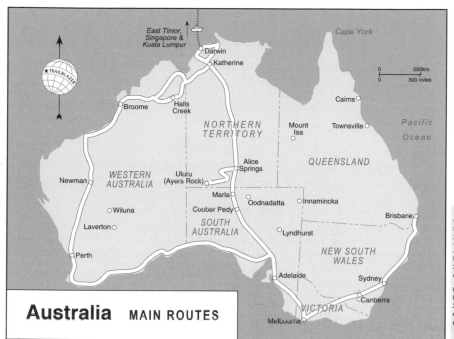

Australia MAIN ROUTES

THE NULLARBOR PLAIN

Tim Mulliner

The Nullarbor crosses a vast limestone plateau stretching 1200km across the southern Australian outback, between Norseman in the west and Ceduna in the east. Even then, these two settlements are little more than remote one-horse towns – in fact Norseman happened to be named after a horse that kicked up a gold nugget. Either way, depending on winds and your single-mindedness, it takes about seven to twelve days to ride the Nullarbor.

A major misconception about this road crossing is that it's nothing but an empty desert that stretches as far as the eye can see. While this may be true of the plateau further to the north, the scenery and landscapes viewed from the road are spectacular and the sealed section is far from tree-less, despite the Latin origins of its name. Eucalyptus forests give way to scrub land where saltbush, spinifex and bluebush dominate and for several hundred kilometres the road parallels the high cliffs of the Southern Ocean before heading inland.

Besides the superb scenery the Nullarbor is full of wildlife. Flocks of parakeets move from tree to tree with much commotion, their flashes of bright feathers and loud chattering a lovely alarm call after the silence of a quiet night's camp. In the distance a couple of kangaroos are gently gliding over the ground and you watch them in amazement before being startled by a violent shaking of bushes on the opposite side of the road: an emu's wobbling backside is all you can see as it crashes through the bushes.

As the day warms up, the aptly named 'blue-tongue' lizard stands its ground in the middle of the road poking its tongue at you. It's one of the many weird and wonderful reptiles to be seen on the Nullarbor. Giant wedge-tailed eagles are a common sight too, circling around waiting to swoop on the latest truck-mashed roadkill. At night by the campfire, the noise of those trucks muffled by the trees and shrubs around you, the howl of a distant dingo sends a shiver down your spine, compelling you to edge slightly closer to the flames.

Food and drink
Food between Norseman and Ceduna consists solely of roadhouse mush: burgers, chips and cooked breakfasts all thawed from frozen in a deep fryer or a microwave. For a ravenous touring cyclist this is seldom a thing to complain about (look on the bright side; the high oil content will help lubricate your joints) but the distances between the roadhouses, the longest being 200km, mean additional provisions are needed. At some of the roadhouses you can buy overpriced supplies and at Eucla, on the WA/SA border there's even a shop but it pays to stock up at Norseman or Ceduna. Note the meat and veg quarantine when crossing the state borders and remember that there are no banks though 'EFTPOS' card facilities are common at roadhouses.

Water can be a problem. Some friendly people at the roadhouses will take pity on cyclists and fill water bottles for free. At the ones that don't, you can try the water from the taps in the toilets. Despite signs saying that it's not safe to drink I never had a problem though it was rather salty at times. The only other option is to buy bottled water at the roadhouses, as long as you don't mind paying nearly three times more per litre than you'd pay for petrol!

Cycling the Nullarbor accounts for only about a third of the distance between Perth and Adelaide. It's a long grind with a lot of empty stretches, but there are some highlights along the way that are worth the slog. Apart from water shortages the biggest danger is from road trains – multiple-trailer trucks up to 50-metres long whose drivers may not share your alertness for the scenery until it's too late. Give them plenty of room and if necessary get out of their way – they are much less manoeuverable than you are.

Cooking on the Nullarbor
Don't be fooled into thinking this is 'only Australia'; even the Nullarbor can get very hot during the summer and right across the outback inexperienced tourists regularly get in trouble and die from the heat. Even this far south temperatures above 40°C are common in the summertime and to save water and energy you'll need to rise before dawn, rest during the hottest part of the day and then ride until sunset. The summer I rode it was said to be one of the coldest on record, although after Asia I found the dry hot climate quite bearable – until one particular day.

I had just met up with Manfred, an Austrian cyclist and we were puzzled how all the roadhouse staff we'd met were complaining about how cool it was; around 40°C – hot but bearable. Then the mercury started to rise. When Manfred and I awoke at 6am it was a pleasant 20°C. By 8am it was 32°C. By 10am it was 40°C. We kept riding and hit the hundred-kilometre treeless plain that signified the 'true' Nullarbor. There was no shelter so we kept going. By

11am it was approaching 50°C and half an hour later the mercury was still rising. We spotted a roadhouse shimmering in the distance, dumped our bikes in the shade of the forecourt and made a dash for the air-conditioning restaurant. Inside we collapsed in a heap at one of the tables and proceeded to gulp down iced coffees just as soon as they could serve them. 'Bit warmer today isn't it, boys?' said the man behind the counter.

SOUTH AUSTRALIA AND VICTORIA

When you enter South Australia opportunities open up. The state is home to much of the country's best wine and has the 900-km Mawson Trail, a network of minor roads, unpaved tracks and forest trails linking various points of interest and suitable for sturdy touring- or mountain bikes. It's one of the easiest and most interesting ways to get a flavour of the great interior of Australia without undertaking some of the long desert tracks which are beyond the touring range of human powered vehicles.

Melbourne in neighbouring Victoria is one of Australia's great attractions and is considered to be its most cycle-friendly city with almost 1000km of bike paths. It's therefore an excellent city to pick up bike parts and camping gear and the stepping-off point for the ferry to Tasmania and the Great Ocean Road. At only 284km, the latter is perhaps not satisfying enough for some, but given the size of the country, an excellent way to sample its delights as few people have time to see it at a bicycling pace.

AN OUTBACK TOUR

Chris Scott

Like it or not, Australia is defined not by its shady forests where squirrels gather their nuts, but by the gritty, lip-cracking outback, populated by laconic

PART 2 – ROUTE OUTLINES

SOUTH-WESTERN AUSTRALIA

If you're crossing the Nullarbor towards WA, or even if you've landed there in a spaceship, at Norseman turn south, away from the thundering road train route and towards Esperence where the storm-swept beaches of Cape Le Grand and the Southern Ocean await. Westward from Esperance is an exposed and mildly hilly ride to Albany, usually against the wind and offering little beach access or much else of interest. Nevertheless, unless you're pining for Kansas and Oklahoma, avoid venturing further inland hereabouts – it's nothing more than an interminable man-made prairie of cross-grid byways linking wheat farming towns that time and most other things have forgotten.

West of Albany is where the real pedalling treats await. Alternatives to the main coastal highway (including the Munda Biddi Trail; see above) begin to proliferate and on the

way past Denmark to Walpole there are more lovely granite-fringed bays matching Cape Le Grand.

Walpole marks the eastern edge of WA's famous Tall Timber country – at least what the loggers have not turned to pulp. Even in the heat of summer the shady byways towards Northcliff, Pemberton and Nannup offer idyllic riding on or off the bitumen, though by the time you near Collie or Bunbury the party's over and you'll do best to seek out the quietest routes to Perth or hop on a train.

No matter how much you may be attracted to the hardcore romance of riding the sunburned outback further north, it is these temperate corners of Australia – including the more populated equivalents in South Australia, Victoria and Tasmania – that offer the most agreeable riding downunder.

Chris Scott

individuals whose self-worth stems from being a big fish in a nearly empty bowl, or where young families convince themselves that life in an isolated mining town has its perks.

With limited dawdling – or better still, lifts across the really boring sections so as to enjoy some quality time off – a 7000-km tour from Perth to Adelaide via Darwin could be done in three months – just about the length of the cool season in the far north and the interior, as well as the duration of the average tourist visa. During this time you're unlikely to experience any rain or even see a cloud. There are no gradients to speak of and – excluding wet season cyclones – little wind in the tropics, but obviously plan your water supplies judiciously and avoid riding at night; drunk, drugged or just plain dozy drivers are a menace and, anyway, there's nothing to see.

Riding up here away from the busier eastern states is the only true way of experiencing Australia's mind-boggling spaces. Try to set out at the end of the summer and ride into the cool season to give yourself the best chance of not 'going troppo'.

Costs and food

With just about everything coming up by road train or ocean barge from the south, the under-populated north is expensive and roadhouses are notorious for their limited range of overpriced and poor-quality fare. This is where your taste buds will hark back to Asia where a wholesome, freshly-cooked snack for the price of a box of matches is never far away. Make the most of the fresh produce found in the supermarkets of the big towns; there are no more than a dozen along the entire route. If you make it to Darwin, check out the sizzling oriental take-aways at Mindil Beach Market on a Thursday night.

Apart from tourists on day-rentals, few locals cycle in the far north; it's just too hot at any time of year and too awkward to carry more than a slab or two of beer. Don't expect a useful stock of essential cycle spares anywhere other than Darwin and maybe Alice.

Bush camping

Obviously you'll end up camping out in the bush and not through choice. A tent's waterproof qualities will be wasted up here but the light mesh of an inner tent – effectively a free-standing mozzie net – is very useful. It gives you the peace of mind to sleep without being tormented – literally or psychologically – by insects, reptiles and other things that bounce around the bush at night. Most of the world's species of venomous snakes are found in Australia and all reptiles are more active in the heat of summer. However, it's worth remembering that they have little to gain by sidling over and biting you as you're too big to eat. They will only do so when threatened but it is worth acquainting yourself with the difference between harmless but sometimes huge pythons (usually broader headed) and venomous snakes.

As anywhere else in the world, do yourself a favour and make sure you camp out of sight of the highway, particularly when you're near towns as bored and drunken idiots may be on the prowl for something or someone to harass.

To the Top End

It's 4000 kilometres from Perth to Darwin and, of the two sealed routes, the inland Great Northern Highway rejoining the coast near industrial Port

Hedland will give you as much outback as you can stomach – even if you're still only halfway to Darwin, let alone Adelaide. Mile for mile, the attractions of the longer and busier North West Coastal Highway are just too insignificant at pedalling velocities and, apart from the Shark Bay area and the North-west Cape and the Ningaloo Reef, beach life is less alluring than you'd expect.

By now firmly in the cloudless tropics, Port Hedland to Broome is a 700-km legendarily monotonous stretch, with up to 300 kilometres between road-houses (150 to 200km being the norm up here) and with no other services *of any kind*. Get used to these kinds of distances and make sure your brain is in good shape because, unless you've mastered the art of velo-meditation, you'll be doing a lot of thinking. Typical wintertime temperatures up here are in the low to mid-thirties centigrade, more further away from the humid coasts. You'll find Broome expensive but an unusually charming town (considering what's come before and what lies ahead) with a cosmopolitan pearling history. If you don't mind communing with regular tourists, it's well worth a break.

From nearby Derby to the Northern Territory border many travellers, two-wheeled or otherwise, mistake the Gibb River Road – slicing across the Kimberly plateau – as a short cut. A short cut it is: to a sack-full of broken bicycle parts. However, the Gibb River Express bus service (🖳 www.gibbriverbus.com.au) does the mostly-corrugated 700-km Derby-Kununurra run most days and will carry your gear or even you and your bike as far or as near as you like. With short excursions off the Gibb to some lovely croc free gorges and waterfalls, and a good (if expensive) range of homestead accommodation, it's more interesting than the highway to the south but will be a very tough ride without support.

Even in the coldest months the so-called Top End of the Northern Territory, through Timber Creek to Katherine and Darwin is never less than hot, though humidity keeps temperatures in the low thirties in Darwin itself. If heading up to Darwin and coming back via Kakadu, take a chance to ride the 120-km stretch along the quieter Old Darwin Road between Hayes Creek roadhouse and Adelaide River.

The menace of crocs and a large tidal range makes the beaches around Darwin nothing special but Kakadu National Park is nearby, and an all-sealed 450-km excursion east to Jabiru and back out south-west to Pine Creek takes you past many of the park's natural and cultural highlights. Alternatively Litchfield Park is nearer the main southbound highway, offers fewer expectations and plenty of croc-free swimming holes.

Down the Track – Darwin to Adelaide

With 4000 clicks already under your belt, it's only another 3000 down to Adelaide along the Stuart Highway, aka 'the Track'. You'll want to get cracking and make the most of the cool season in the interior because it's here that the frame-cracking, brain-melting summer temperatures will soon cause problems. Scenically, distances are galling when measured on a scale of 'things to see and do', but this is the nature (and to some, the wonder) of outback Australia. If it all gets too much you have a chance to leapfrog down the road a bit on the daily buses and twice-weekly trains now running between Darwin and Adelaide.

PART 2 – ROUTE OUTLINES

Excursion to the Rock

If you get there before October when the hot season returns, the Central Deserts around Alice Springs offer one of the few worthwhile excursions along the Track – the 750-kilometre detour to Ayers Rock. If your bike can handle a 200-kilometre section of corrugated track, the best route takes you out along the rolling West MacDonnell Ranges with many inviting waterholes, and past the mysterious crater of Gosses Bluff by which time the dirt section is well under way. At the junction for Hermansburg to the east, set your sights west on Kings Canyon where the bitumen resumes – it's about 150 km of rim-cracking washboard along the Mereenie Loop Road with daily traffic but no services whatsoever.

From Kings Canyon Resort, you're back in tour bus country, but even then the road passes through lovely stands of desert oak as well as a couple of roadhouse/cattle stations in the 300 kilometres it takes you reach the Rock. Sure it's an expensive tourist trap but be prepared to plop your world-weary cynicism into the special bins provided at the park entrance: the elemental brooding mass of Uluru will mesmerize you, not least because you've pedalled here the long way from Perth.

The Rock is a dead end (although 4x4-supported cycle tours do run along the all-dirt Great Central Road south-west back to WA). Mere unsupported mortals must backtrack 250 km along the at-times unnervingly narrow Lasseter Highway to the Stuart Highway. From here it's a ride through the most arid parts of northern South Australia for another fortnight or so, all the way to Adelaide, a cup of tea, a biscuit and maybe a haircut.

New Zealand

Roy Hoogenraad

Despite some wind and rain that come from being in the 'Roaring Forties', New Zealand is popular with bikers, especially the west coast of the South Island – which happens to be the area most affected by showers rolling off the Tasman. The scenery here is spectacular; snow-clad alps, glittering fjords, steaming volcanoes and humming sub-tropical forest. Travellers arriving from overseas get a three-month visa on arrival and many of them find it barely enough to cover just one of the two main islands.

If you have a month or less visit the South Island. You can take your bike on the few passenger train services, though it's easier to bring your bike on the many private-bus services. This gives you the flexibility to choose a region, do the ride you want in the time you have, and take the bus back to where you fly out.

(**Opposite**): Off-roading in the Indian Himalaya. (Photo © Cass Gilbert).

(**Overleaf, double page**): World map.

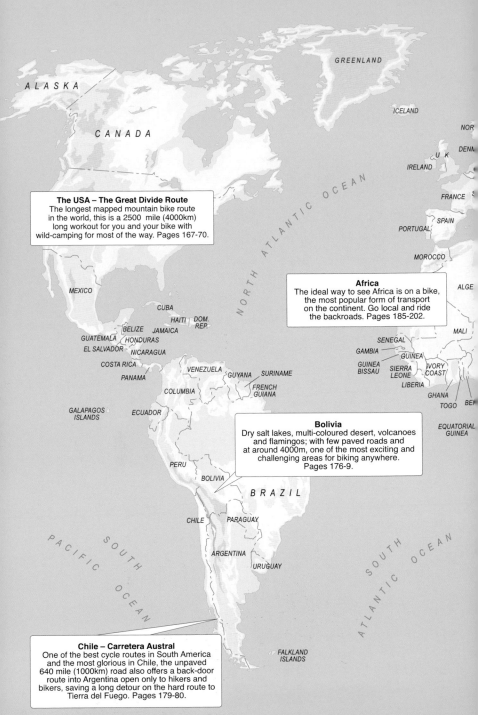

ARCTI

GREENLAND

ICELAND

NOR

U.K

DENM

IRELAND

FRANCE

ALASKA

PORTUGAL

SPAIN

CANADA

MOROCCO

ALGE

The USA – The Great Divide Route
The longest mapped mountain bike route
in the world, this is a 2500 mile (4000km)
long workout for you and your bike with
wild-camping for most of the way. Pages 167-70.

Africa
The ideal way to see Africa is on a bike,
the most popular form of transport
on the continent. Go local and ride
the backroads. Pages 185-202.

MEXICO

CUBA

HAITI | DOM.
REP.

BELIZE | JAMAICA

GUATEMALA | HONDURAS

EL SALVADOR | NICARAGUA

COSTA RICA

VENEZUELA | GUYANA | SURINAME

PANAMA

COLUMBIA

FRENCH
GUIANA

GALAPAGOS
ISLANDS

ECUADOR

SENEGAL

GAMBIA

GUINEA
BISSAU

GUINEA

SIERRA
LEONE

IVORY
COAST

LIBERIA

GHANA

TOGO

BEI

MALI

EQUATORIAL
GUINEA

PERU

BOLIVIA

BRAZIL

Bolivia
Dry salt lakes, multi-coloured desert, volcanoes
and flamingos; with few paved roads and
at around 4000m, one of the most exciting and
challenging areas for biking anywhere.
Pages 176-9.

CHILE | PARAGUAY

ARGENTINA

URUGUAY

PACIFIC
OCEAN

SOUTH

OCEAN

SOUTH

ATLANTIC OCEAN

NORTH ATLANTIC OCEAN

Chile – Carretera Austral
One of the best cycle routes in South America
and the most glorious in Chile, the unpaved
640 mile (1000km) road also offers a back-door
route into Argentina open only to hikers and
bikers, saving a long detour on the hard route to
Tierra del Fuego. Pages 179-80.

FALKLAND
ISLANDS

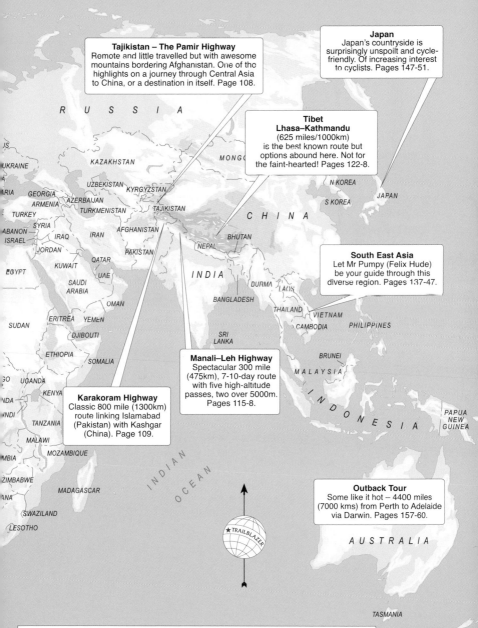

Tajikistan – The Pamir Highway
Remote and little travelled but with awesome mountains bordering Afghanistan. One of the highlights on a journey through Central Asia to China, or a destination in itself. Page 108.

Japan
Japan's countryside is surprisingly unspoilt and cycle-friendly. Of increasing interest to cyclists. Pages 147-51.

Tibet
Lhasa–Kathmandu
(625 miles/1000km) is the best known route but options abound here. Not for the faint-hearted! Pages 122-8.

South East Asia
Let Mr Pumpy (Felix Hude) be your guide through this diverse region. Pages 137-47.

Manali–Leh Highway
Spectacular 300 mile (475km), 7-10-day route with five high-altitude passes, two over 5000m. Pages 115-8.

Karakoram Highway
Classic 800 mile (1300km) route linking Islamabad (Pakistan) with Kashgar (China). Page 109.

Outback Tour
Some like it hot – 4400 miles (7000 kms) from Perth to Adelaide via Darwin. Pages 157-60.

★ TRAILBLAZER

The Adventure Cycle-Touring World
Selected Highlights

A circuit of the South Island is what many long-haul bikers go for, and they're likely to spend three months doing that. You could get round in less time, but there is a lot more to see than just main roads. New Zealand's greatest treasures are off-road and if you like hiking, try to do some of the famous hikes as you make your way up, down or around the coast; the national parks are far too good to miss.

New Zealand's roads are narrow and in places crowded, especially so on the main road around the South Island. Buses and trucks can pass by faster than any cyclist would like, and there are also a lot of old cars well past their scrap-by date which look none too safe from a cyclist's point of view. So, as in most places, you'll be aiming for the minor roads and including some unpaved roads if your bike doesn't mind. Again, as elsewhere the jewels are mostly off-road and the closer you can get to that, the more you will enjoy the country.

Don't rule out the North Island, which bicyclists find quieter and less touristy than the South Island. Although not mountainous, it is hilly in the north and not much easier riding. It is less windy than Fiordland but anywhere near Wellington gets blasts of winds coming from the west. There are so many good places to discover that there is no point in worrying about missing something, or following a specific route. Travelling at a bike's pace, you will have time to stop and ask local people along the way.

North America

It's tempting to overlook North America as an adventure cycling destination; many riders are looking to sample the culture so familiar to them from films and TV. But there are some meaty long-distance challenges, including the world's longest mapped off-road route. Canada itself is the world's second largest country and one of the emptiest; ninety per cent of the population live within 100 miles of the US border. North of that you have all the forests, rivers, distances (and insects) of Siberia, but without the checkpoints.

There are as many routes across the continent as there are roads, the smallest of which are traffic-free. The best of these have been mapped by the Adventure Cycling Association (🖳 www.adv-cycling.org), who supply route guides for all of them. Here we focus on the Great Divide Route, the toughest and probably the most satisfying trail on the continent for adventure riders, and the Pacific Coast Highway, the most commonly taken route for riders coming down from Alaska to Mexico or beyond. Other ideas include the ride up to the Arctic Ocean, either to Inuvik up the Dempster Highway in Canada, or up the Dalton Highway in Alaska from Fairbanks to Prudhoe Bay.

(Opposite) Top: If it's a sugar boost you need you'll have no problem getting it in South America. (Photo © Bryn Thomas). **Bottom:** Big Sur, California – see p167. (Photo © Cass Gilbert).

TRIP REPORT
ALASKA TO BAJA

Name	Stephen Lord
Year of birth	1959
Occupation	Author
Nationality	British
Other bike travels	London to Athens and around Europe, USA and Japan, Tibet and Nepal

This trip	Alaska, Canada, USA, Baja California (Mexico)
Trip duration	Five months
Number in group	Two
Total distance	6000km (3750 miles)
Cost of trip	£3000 each including flights and gear binge

Longest day	140km
Best day	Every day in Northern California
Worst day	The day the hotel owner slashed partner's tyres to try to make us stay another night
Favourite ride	Big Sur coast, central California
Biggest headache	Crazy drivers in California and Mexico
Biggest mistake	Riding the Pacific coast in August (vacation time)
Couldn't do without	Espresso maker
Pleasant surprise	Incredible friendliness in Oregon; great campsites
Any illness	Strained muscles from overdoing it

Bike model	Dawes One.down (www.dawescycles.com)
New/used	Four years old
Modifications	Switched to Tubus racks, no wobbling after that; Brooks saddle (appreciated it every day)
Wish you'd fitted	One gear lower!
Tyres used	Specialized Hemisphere 1.95" – they made the bike ride like a hearse but lasted 10,000km
Baggage Setup	Four Ortliebs, handlebar bag and tent on the back
Wish you'd brought	Forgot fuel pump; had to mail order one in Alaska
Wish you hadn't brought	Nothing

Bike problems	Rear rim wore out and cracked
Accidents	None
Punctures	One each
Same bike again	A higher quality bike would be nice
Recommendations	The West Coast must have the freshest air in the world and the campsites and ocean views can't be beaten

General tip	If your gear won't fit in four panniers, leave something out. A light bike is a real pleasure to ride.
Road philosophy	A ride is never just a ride

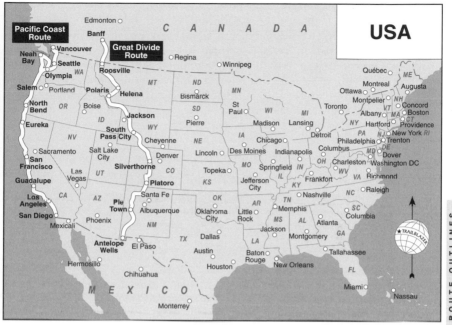

CANADA

Paul Woloshansky

Canada's stunning northern wilderness is almost entirely empty of human inhabitants and a magnet for those in search of adventure. A tour to Canada's lonely places requires careful planning and equipment to compensate for widely scattered services, so it's not unusual to see tourists on heavily-laden bicycles. Aside from the usual tent, sleeping bag and cooking gear, it's necessary to have a wider range of clothing options to deal with climatic extremes.

A good practice is to anticipate all types of weather: Alberta, for instance, has more days of sunshine than any other province, but in the past has received snowfalls in every month of the year (thankfully, not the same year!). This variation in climate might be difficult to comprehend while you're eating fresh peaches at a road-side fruit stand in British Columbia's Okanagan Valley, with the temperature hovering around 35°C; yet a week later the breezes off the Athabaska Glacier between Lake Louise and Jasper in Alberta's Columbia Icefield may chill you to the bone.

A cyclist touring the breadth of Canada will also have to deal with prevailing westerly winds and therefore the usual and easiest route is from west to east.

Terrain

British Columbia is mountainous, and an eastward tour originating in Vancouver will soon have you climbing over the spine of the Rocky

Mountains, whichever route you take. Low gearing is a necessity as the hardest cycling on a west-to-east tour will occur right at the beginning, before your legs have had a chance to harden up. Roughly speaking, Canada's prairie region stretches from the BC-Alberta border to the Manitoba-Ontario border; any hills you encounter will be mere bumps compared to what you've already ridden over. Ontario's Pre-Cambrian Shield is an older range than the Rockies but doesn't present the same challenge to a cyclist. Touring Canada's east coast presents obstacles that are common to coastal tours everywhere: plenty of short, steep climbs and descents that mark drainages to the ocean.

Bear country

Wild camping can be a pleasurable feature of bicycle touring in Canada, although campgrounds are common. Wherever you choose as a stop for the night, you have to be cautious about food storage. Campgrounds in bear country will often have bear-proof food lockers available; food caches accomplish the same thing for wild campers. This necessitates hauling food bags on a line up over a tree branch, ideally a hundred metres or so from a campsite. Eating away from where you sleep is another good idea.

Forest fires regularly devastate the Canadian wilderness so fire bans must be respected – use a stove for all cooked meals; they are mandatory for some of Canada's backcountry.

Yukon Territory

The Yukon plays a large part in Canada's mythology: its gold rush of 1896 was a catalyst for the development of the west and for Canada as a nation. Read the poems of Robert Service to get a sense of those times and ride the only tour in Canada that ends above the Arctic Circle, in summer's perpetual daylight.

It's possible to take a ferry up from Vancouver through the spectacular inland passage to Skagway and then ride to Whitehorse in two days. Otherwise, the ride from Vancouver will take a couple of weeks and passes through forested mountains with settlements up to 150km apart. Most road traffic goes on the Alcan highway and cyclists prefer the much less busy, part-gravel Cassiar Highway. The winds are generally from the south in the short summer riding season, but are not necessarily so strong as to prevent anyone riding south. Whitehorse is the starting point for canoe trips on the Yukon river to Dawson City, or ride your bike up the Klondike Highway. Dawson City is considered a must-see, famous for the Klondike Gold Rush and reachable only by this all-gravel road – or on the Yukon river itself.

The Dempster Highway begins just east of Dawson City, ending 736 kilometres further north in Inuvik on the Arctic Ocean. It's remote, all-gravel, and a spectacular ride, first passing through forest and leading to bare mountains as you reach the Arctic. Along with bears, caribou and muskox there are provincial campgrounds along the way (complete with bearproof lockers) and a hotel at the halfway point – just the bare minimum to get you through.

USA

The USA has done more than most nations to preserve its wild spaces and make them available to outdoors people such as cyclists. Much of the western USA is publicly-owned land with parks and campgrounds. If you're headed south, the Pacific Coast route is the most likely option for getting to Mexico but the Great Divide ride along the Continental Divide (more or less the crest of the Rockies) is a destination in itself – for this allow the whole summer. It's wild enough and certainly remote but with excellent free-camping possibilities the whole way and much easier logistically than a similar ride anywhere else in the world.

Visas: a caution for bikers

Post 9/11, immigration procedures have tightened considerably and are still changing, so your research before you arrive and check with immigration staff – who are often more helpful at small border crossings between Canada and the USA. First, the normal limit without a visa is 90 days – it might save trouble later on to get a longer visa if you have a long run in mind, say Alaska, Canada, back into the USA and on down to Mexico. Second, watch out if you leave the USA by road: you may need to hand in your I-94 arrival card though this may not be the case if you intend to re-enter the US, for example if you are just passing through Canada between Alaska and Seattle. Unless you want to end up in solitary at Guantanamo Bay, the only way to be sure is to stop and check your documents with US authorities before leaving.

PACIFIC COAST HIGHWAY

Just as California's coastal Highway 1 is considered by many to be the most beautiful drive in America, the Pacific Coast Highway from Vancouver to San Diego is perhaps the best road tour in the USA and must rank among the top bike rides in the world. The climate, the ocean, scenery, campgrounds, cities and also the ever-helpful tailwind are an unbeatable combination.

About half of the route runs right next to the ocean with fabulous views,

Denali National Park, Alaska.

sunset watching at many campgrounds and countless beaches for picnic lunches. Although the altitudes aren't great, the road is rarely flat or straight. But it's an easy ride in terms of logistics as food, water, gear shops and camping are never far away. Highlights include the coast itself, especially Highway 1 around Big Sur. Many people find Oregon to be the most friendly state but the big cities of California – LA, San Francisco, Santa Barbara and surf-town Santa Cruz are a big draw for bikers, and there are campgrounds on the coast close to or in all these cities.

When to go

Owing to prevailing winds this route is strictly southbound and from May onwards the land is at its greenest. Allow two months to get to San Diego near

HOMAGE TO REPACK ROAD

If you fancy some dirt riding, Marin County, north of San Francisco Bay, is the birthplace of mountain biking and many early brands and models were named after local features. It was here in the late 1970s that Gary Fisher and Joe Breeze tested their fat-tyred hybrids down the famous Repack Road (a turn-off on the Pine Mountain loop) – so-called because they had to repack the wheel bearings of their old hub-braked bikes after each descent. Local bike shops have info and maps, or go to 🖥 www.marintrails.com/biking.

Other dirt excursions

There are many easier but just as scenic off-highway routes in the area. Generally, only doubletracks are open to bikes and they are serious about enforcing their 15mph speed limits; rangers patrol with radar guns, fining cyclists on the spot.

Mt Tamalpais (2500ft) is another great ride. Don't be put off by fog – ride through it to win fantastic views of the clouds below, perhaps punctured by the top of the Golden Gate Bridge or the skyscrapers in downtown San Francisco.

Samuel P Taylor State Park is hidden away amongst redwood trees, and to the south of 'Mt Tam' is the Marin Headlands Hostel, set in a rugged location far from towns (stock up on food first, you'll want a couple of days here). It's the kind of scenery and location our friend Kerouac wrote about in Dharma Bums, isolated and surrounded by hills. A tunnel saves you some legwork if you want to get through the hills to Sausalito, or to the bike trail that runs from Mill Valley into San Francisco.

South of San Francisco and less than five miles short of Santa Cruz, Wilder Ranch State Park is well worth a stop for mountain biking on the thirty-odd miles of mixed-use trails in and out of forest overlooking the Pacific. The website 🖥 www.virtualparks.org has some mouth-watering pictures for bikers as well as excellent maps.

---

the Mexican border. It will get hot in places but there'll be a cooling fog at times and you're never far from the coast after you pass through San Francisco. Avoid July and August: holiday traffic, busy campgrounds and heat.

Autumn is the other great time to go, as the roads are quieter, the weather is still dry and comfortable and there's little coastal fog. Camping and riding in coastal fog is well worth experiencing as it's part of the microclimate of the redwood trees that flourish in a moist environment and keep temperatures cool in the summer by retaining humidity.

Maps and camping

Washington, Oregon and California each produce a free road map, found at tourist offices, and Oregon goes one step further by publishing a map especially for bikers showing detours to avoid high-traffic areas and steep hills. The Adventure Cycling Association (see above) produces a five-map set for the ride with a lot of useful information, including vertical scale charts, information which rarely features on American road maps. The bike route is well signposted all the way – the free maps will be adequate.

To enjoy this ride to the full plan on camping as all the state parks are away from development and it's a chance to camp by the Pacific Ocean for peanuts. Most parks reserve hiker/biker sites for a few dollars and you'll not get turned away from these campgrounds.

Highlights

In Washington the route avoids Seattle by taking an island-hopping course across Puget Sound, but try to make a side visit to Seattle, a bike-friendly city and home to REI, the world's largest camping store. A detour round the less visited Olympic peninsula is the wilder option, with a chance to visit Olympic National Park and the unique temperate rainforest alongside the ocean.

Oregon has probably the best setup for bikers on the coast, with the best campgrounds reserved only for us at inexpensive prices. Ancient cedar forests and coastal fog all add up to the allure of the Pacific North-west. By the time you get to California three adjacent parks, Redwoods NP and SP and Prairie Creek SP have some excellent mountain biking trails right along-side the ocean. It's a great place to ride without your panniers, among some of the tallest trees in the world. Next comes Humboldt State Park and the Avenue of the Giants, leading through some of the last virgin Redwood stands along a winding 30-mile trail.

Highway 1 starts just north of Mendocino and runs for 650 miles, one third of the whole border-to-border run. It's winding, narrow, rarely flat and often windswept with awesome ocean views for most of the way. It's a tough road for motorhomes but great for bikers who can stop without causing a lawsuit-inducing pile-up.

San Francisco and Santa Cruz are great for a few days off the bike and then comes Big Sur, an 80-mile section of cliffs where Jack Kerouac famously flipped out. Stock up on food and wine, it's nothing but you and the ocean for a couple of days. The route will take you safely through LA mostly by the beaches, then past more great surfing country until you reach San Diego.

RIDING THE GREAT DIVIDE

with Scott Morris

Created in 1994 by the Adventure Cycling Association (ACA), the Great Divide Mountain Bike Route (GDMBR) is the world's longest mapped off-road route, a 2500-mile network of unpaved tracks following the Rockies from Roosville on the Canadian border in Montana, through a corner of Idaho, then Wyoming, Colorado and New Mexico, ending at Antelope Wells on the Mexican border. Over that distance you'll clock up over 200,000ft of total elevation – nearly seven Everests – and lately 220 miles have been added up to Banff in Canada, passing through several national and provincial parks that certainly won't give you nightmares.

It's a fabulous unending treat of mountain-bike riding that will take three months – a blissful summer of riding and camping each night in a remote, off-highway setting. It's usually possible to ride from town to town, but perhaps the greatest appeal of this route is the chance it gives you to camp for free on public lands, passing through towns only for lunch and provisions.

The ACA sells the maps and a book that make this trip a doddle, though the latter is not strictly necessary. You can also download GPS data for the trip. The route itself is unmarked, it's the map that shows the way so you'll need an accurately calibrated bike computer so that when the map says 'turn left at 3.5 miles', you hit the mark.

Scott Morris flies the flag to celebrate Independence Day. © Paula Morrison

Terrain

The scenery is mostly 'Big Sky country' rather than closed-in valleys and you'll be continuously exposed to the power of nature and mountain weather on the Great Divide. It's a mix of ranchland and forest. The route passes no more than 60 miles either side of the Continental Divide, and gradients are not so bad, with only one or two short sections where everyone will have to push their bikes for a half mile or less.

Scott Morris's website (http://topo fusion.com/divide) breaks down the route as 870 miles of climbing average 5.4% grade (gradient), 951 miles of descent at an average 4.9% grade and 735 miles on the flat. This is almost perfect mountain-biking country, giving you long, easy downhills. The average elevation is around 6000ft or 1800m.

Although there's almost no traffic there's plenty of washboard, rocks and loose gravel and you'll easily get through two sets of tyres. The weather is typical of the high country: snow is always possible, high winds from any direction, thunderstorms are a certainty towards the south, but more often than not it will be brilliantly sunny and very dry.

When to go

The best season for riding the Great Divide depends on which direction you ride. Most riders go south where the earliest possible start dates are typically mid-June. Snow can linger on the high passes in northern Montana until July, but the route itself is usually clear earlier. Another consideration is the seasonal rainstorms in New Mexico; several portions of the route become impassable after hard rain, so it is best to travel through New Mexico in late August or early September. Northbound riders should start in late May to avoid the heat, but it's not advisable to start too early or you'll encounter snowed-over passes in southern Colorado.

Gear considerations

You will see a lot of BOB Yak trailers (see p.53) on this ride, towed behind full-suss bikes. Glacier Cyclery in Whitefish sell and rent them. A BOB makes for less rattling than a pannier set-up – if you go with panniers, use the strongest you can get and check bolts daily. Front suspension will greatly reduce fatigue; it's practically a must, and your spine will thank you for a suspension seatpost too.

A petrol stove would be the best choice. If you cannot find small cans of white gas, outdoors shops will often refill your fuel bottles cheaply. Outside towns mobile phone coverage is poor throughout the route. Carrying a bear spray (easily bought there) will give some peace of mind in Montana.

Route highlights

Starting from the north, the route begins in beautiful forested mountain and lake scenery and the lowest elevation of the entire route. Whitefish is the first decent-sized town with a bike shop and camping shops. Well worth a stopover. At Holland Lake, a simple US Forest Service campground backs on to Holland Lake Lodge, which has a bar, restaurant and sauna that should be open to non-residents. Lincoln is your next stop with a campground, then a long ride across country to Montana state capital Helena where the museum is a must-see. The old copper-mining city of Butte is a few days south and is also worth a tour. The route moves into more open country, briefly crossing a deserted corner of Idaho into Wyoming.

The trail runs into strikingly beautiful country near the Grand Teton mountains. This is a good spot for a detour to the town of Jackson for some R&R, cunningly avoiding the first major pass in the process. Towards the Great Basin, an enormous bowl in the Continental Divide from which no water escapes, the land becomes more barren and tree-less. The ACA advises carrying three gallons of water for the Great Basin, but that seems excessive for an overnight bivouac. Take a chance on one gallon and you'll easily make it to the town of Rawlins the next day. The one water source marked on the map, where most people camp, is not water you'd want to drink except in an emergency.

Cruising the Great Divide.
© Scott Morris

From Rawlins you begin climbing into Colorado. The landscape changes drastically from wind blown deserts to cool pine forests. If you aren't a climber, you'll sure be one after riding through Colorado. Fortunately, most of the climbs are on firm, non-technical dirt roads. After crossing the Colorado river at the ghost town of Radium, you'll climb several more high passes before reaching the most urbanized area of the route, Silverthorne. The hordes of bustling tourists and shoppers will seem out of place, but the area is host to world-class mountain biking trails, and is worth the stop.

From Del Norte, Colorado, the route begins its longest and highest climb to Indiana Pass, just shy of 12,000 feet. The reward for the climb is sweet; on the far side lies a wonderland of high-alpine scenery that'll have you reaching for your camera. Not long after the tundra and alpine meadows the route travels through the superfund cleanup site and Summitville.

In New Mexico the climbs are as big as Colorado, but the riding turns more challenging. However, by the time you're there you'll be ready for it. The route in New Mexico is more remote, less travelled, and easily as beautiful as any other portion of the route. Be ready for some rough riding and lack of services. Towns are further apart and water becomes a serious concern.

After descending out of the pine- and fir-covered Jemez mountains into the town of Cuba, the route traverses a remote stretch of desert BLM land featuring deeply eroded arroyos, tall cliffs and interesting rock formations. You're unlikely to see another person, apart from another Great Divide rider, on this section. Eventually, after climbing back into the ponderosa pine forests of Mt.

> ### ALL CHARGED UP
>
> Fifteen miles after crossing into Wyoming from Idaho, the trail meets a main road (north to Yellowstone, south to Lake Jackson) with gas station, shop and ranger station. There is a natural hot spring a few miles north of here identified by detailed maps in the rangers' office.
>
> They'll warn you that the water has a high level of radioactivity and is not good for bathing, but I met a bike tourer who'd just spent two nights camping next to the pool and soaking in the hot water. Now able to ride at night without flashlights, his rationale was that it saved on batteries.

Taylor (10,200 feet), you'll have a blast of a descent into the town of Grants on the historic Route 66.

Grants was once a booming mine town, but as with many towns on the Trail, it has metamorphosed into a service-based economy after the bust that inevitably followed the boom. You'll find more than enough services to stock up on supplies for a long stretch of service-less riding. The next major city is Silver City, some 250 miles away.

The route now traverses El Malpais (the badlands) south of Grants. Cinder cones erupted in this area, covering the plains with black volcanic rock. It's rather beautiful, and makes for some pleasant cycling. Before reaching Silver City you will run into a place whose name says it all: Pie Town. Eat as much as you can.

The Geronimo Trail follows a narrow corridor between the Aldo Leopold and Gila wilderness areas. An off-route hike (no bikes in the wilderness) here leads to some stunning vistas. After riding on the Continental Divide itself for a few miles, the route drops to the Mimbres river valley where a hefty off-route climb leads to the impressive Gila cliff dwelling national monument.

Silver City is another large mining town long since bust and picking up the pieces. But it offers everything the touring cyclist needs after a few days in the wilderness. The 120 miles from Silver City to the Mexican border at Antelope Wells features typical Chihuahuan desert terrain, treeless and desolate with a unique, quiet beauty. If there isn't a headwind, you'll glide the last miles of pavement to the border station with ease.

Baja California and Central America

Many riders bike the 1000-mile Baja peninsula on their Alaska to Cape Horn run. Going south as winter approaches, it's an easy continuation of the Pacific Coast ride, with dependable tailwinds on the ocean side and ferries from La Paz at the southern tip of Baja back to the Mexican mainland. Entering Mexico after the USA is a stark contrast: the riot of colour, new sounds, food and language. Some find it a shock, especially Tijuana, but it's really Mexico-Lite, an easy region to get by in using only English, or to work on your Spanish in preparation for riding through the heart of Mexico and into Central America.

Preparations

Most riders simply stick to Highway 1 the whole way and spend three or four weeks on this ride. Camping is the way to go, allowing you to enjoy beaches and the desert scenery. There are good camp spots, but for wild camping, buy plastic gallon jugs of water for your overnight needs. A map is necessary for planning your daily distances and knowing where to locate provisions; truck stops on the desert sections are your lifeline and make good campsites – just ask if you can camp in their grounds. There are always tiny shacks offering food and water at the mid-point between towns.

The road is fairly good and the sections with potholes are continually being worked on. Nonetheless a strong bike (only 26" tyres are found in Mexico) will carry extra water when needed and protect you for those times you have to jump off the road as a bus heads right at you.

It's understood that if someone is waving an empty water container by the side of the road, they need water and that's what you do if you get into difficulties. Mexicans mostly buy their drinking water in shops that will fill any container you bring in. It's the cheapest way and plastic gallon jugs are not expensive.

You won't find any stove fuel other than unleaded gasoline in Baja, at places often far apart, though you could probably make a litre of white gas bought in San Diego last the whole way if you eat out once or twice a day.

Visas

At the border you need to get a visa good for travel beyond Ensenada about 100km down the road. This costs $20 and you need to stop and ask for it. There

PART 2 – ROUTE OUTLINES

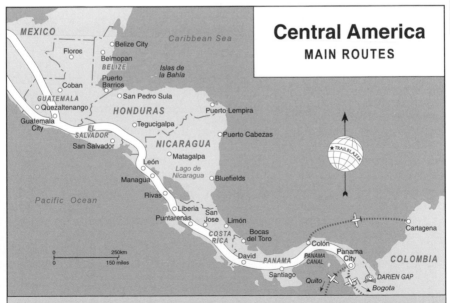

Central America
MAIN ROUTES

MEXICO
Flores
Belize City
Caribbean Sea
Belmopan
BELIZE
Coban
Puerto Barrios
Islas de la Bahía
GUATEMALA
San Pedro Sula
Quezaltenango
HONDURAS
Puerto Lempira
Guatemala City
EL SALVADOR
Tegucigalpa
San Salvador
NICARAGUA
Puerto Cabezas
León
Matagalpa
Managua
Lago de Nicaragua
Bluefields
Pacific Ocean
Rivas
Liberia
San Jose
Limón
Puntarenas
COSTA RICA
Bocas del Toro
Cartagena
0 250km
0 150 miles
David
PANAMA
PANAMA CANAL
Colón
Panama City
COLOMBIA
Santiago
Quito
DARIEN GAP
Bogota

Riders generally travel on the Pacific side of this region, owing to its better climate than the Caribbean and because most bikers are heading south and have taken a westerly route down Mexico. It's not necessarily an easier route – there are 4000m peaks in Western Guatemala.

On the road in Baja

will be a checkpoint further on where you will have to show it. As you leave the USA, make sure you hand back all the papers stapled in your passport to US authorities.

Safety
Riding down the Pacific coast of the US, people will often tell you to 'watch out' in Mexico. Most likely those people have never been to Mexico; it's no more dangerous than parts of the US. There are army checkpoints on the road and the police nowadays are much more reliable than in the past; the days of bogus fines are over. Nevertheless, as has already been said, camp in places where you cannot be seen from the road.

What to expect
It gets hotter and drier as you go south, and less populated. After Tijuana, you're on a quiet road near the ocean until Ensenada, which you'll reach in a day's ride. Plenty of blue ocean, blue skies and sandy hills and a slower, quieter pace compared to California to the north. Northern Baja is farmland and the roads can be fairly busy but there's a shoulder to ride through the worst of it. Dirt roads lead down to the beach and some great surf camps run by gringos.

They say that Baja really begins after El Rosario, when the road heads inland and upwards through the unique ecosystem of the Central Desert; many cacti such as the Boojum tree are found only here. Time then to strap on a few gallons of water and camp amongst them – easily done behind the many rock formations.

Southern Baja sees the road cross over to the Sea of Cortez side. High winds are possible at any time during the winter months, from any direction, and may blow for a couple of days. They're more common inland or on the Sea of Cortez side. There's great beach camping on this side and many other diversions – birds, fish, diving and kayaking. To the south, the ferry runs from La Paz over to the mainland for you to continue down the Pacific Coast.

The camping is good all the way and most campgrounds have hot showers. Hotels are not great value and there are no hostels. In the desert sections we asked at truck stops, ranches or houses if we could camp on their land and were never refused. It's less hassle than finding a wild camp spot amid all the cactus and thorns, but bikers who camped wild in the desert enjoyed the stars and silence at a small risk of scorpions and snakes. Food is always cheap and surprisingly fresh – street food is often the best. Mexican food is one of the world's great cuisines and Baja is known for fish tacos. Small roadside stands also sell *ceviche* (marinated raw shellfish), which is also amazingly fresh and wholesome. And however hot it gets, you're never far from a cold beer anywhere in Baja.

CENTRAL AMERICA
To the south of Mexico the Indian population increases as do the mountains; it's a great preparation for South America as you reach altitudes of over 3000m

in Guatemala. Cyclists rave about the friendliness of Mayan villages in Central America. You may be wary of crime, but the travellers' network is there to warn you of troubles ahead. With several borders in short succession there's petty bureaucracy to deal with; almost a quaint touch as the sums involved are not great. One of the worst offenders, Honduras, stretches from the Atlantic to the Pacific, so there's no avoiding it, but it's only a day ride through Honduras from El Salvador to Nicaragua if you're not in the mood to get stiffed for something else. Costa Rica will be a shock – a return to the developed world and light-skinned locals, American tourists and very few *indigenistas*. Beautiful beaches and national parks precede your big decision how to get across the Darien Gap to South America. Panama itself is well worth a visit to cross the canal, ride across to the Caribbean or Pacific, then see Panama City itself, from where most riders fly on to Colombia.

South America

South America offers an extreme range of environments and topography: mountain passes rivalling the Himalaya, frozen deserts and extensive salt lakes in Bolivia, tropical raintorests of course, and the spectacular peaks of southern Chile leading on to the wilds of Patagonia and Tierra del Fuego. For the most part it's good cycling country with decent roads and positively European standards in places like Chile and Argentina.

Brain-out driving in the poorer Andean countries is the biggest hazard. The weather runs to extremes – sub-tropical in the north to sub-Antarctic in the far south, so climate considerations will determine when you'd want to travel in each region. On the other hand, with the complications of mountains, it's impossible to avoid all bad weather so riders on long trips need to be prepared for just about everything.

COLOMBIA, ECUADOR AND PERU

Colombia, is it safe? The fact is that, yes, it's potentially dangerous but it's also one of the great experiences of South American travel, known for its vitality and heartwarming hospitality. Unfortunately, a combination of political separatists and the drug trade make security unpredictable and kidnappings are a risk. Pedal-powered gringos generally look poor enough to be overlooked as kidnap victims, but keep your ears and eyes open wherever you go.

Though more stable politically, Ecuador can still be a rough ride with reports of hold-ups in the poorer south. However, along with neighbouring Peru, the legacy of the pre-Columbian civilizations and colonial Spanish era, and the

On the Via Panamericana.
© Bryn Thomas.

T R I P   R E P O R T
QUITO TO LIMA

Name Bryn Thomas
Year of birth 1959
Occupation Travel writer and publisher
Nationality British
Other bike travels France, Italy, Spain, Portugal

This trip Ecuador and Peru
Trip duration Three weeks
Number in group One
Total distance 2165km (1350 miles) – OK, nothing compared with the other contributors in this book!
Cost of trip £150 plus flight

Longest day 136km
Best day Cycling out of the Andes and down to the Pacific
Worst day Crossing the Sechura Desert
Favourite ride To Inca ruins of Ingapirca in southern Ecuador
Biggest headache Cycling into burning hot wind in northern Peru
Biggest mistake Not having time to do a longer trip and continue through the Andes in Peru
Couldn't do without Star chart to work out constellations in the clear skies
Pleasant surprise That the bike made it
Any illness None

Bike model Elswick Hopper racing bike
New/used 25 years old
Modifications Replaced wheels with thicker 28" steel wheels, new tyres, new chain and five-speed deraillieur
Wish you'd fitted More than five gears
Tyres used Cheapest Indonesian tyres and inner tubes
Baggage Setup Three plastic Ecuadorian shopping baskets ($1 each); old rucksack laid across carrier
Wish you'd brought Nothing
Wish you hadn't brought Faulty stove; making fires to cook on was easy

Bike problems Carrier stay broke: welded back on in next village
Accidents None
Punctures None – surprising given amount of glass on roads
Same bike again Possibly; it was fine for a short trip where I was never too far from a village if things had gone wrong

General tip Improvise! Don't spend more than you need to on your kit. A cycling adventure needn't be either a fashion display or a competition: I met an Argentinian cycling from Buenos Aires to Mexico on an old bike with one gear. He thought my bike decadence personified.

South America
MAIN ROUTES

WEATHER AND SEASONS

From the tropics to tundra, South America has an extremely varied climate – humidity, heat and rain in the north and formidable winds and cold from Bolivia southwards, owing either to the altitude or to the southern latitude in Patagonia. Most of the continent is in the southern hemisphere, so anyone riding down from North America will most likely find themselves arriving as South America approaches winter. This means heavy rains for much of the tropical zone, though winter is the favoured season for the altiplano of Bolivia. To ride in one continuous journey, it's hard to avoid bad weather at some point. Some riders begin their journey in Buenos Aires to avoid the tropical region altogether, and many choose to visit only one part of the continent so they only need prepare for one region rather than carrying gear for every situation.

Seasonality is less important than altitude for the northern Andes; it's too close to the equator. In Patagonia, the season is very short. Late spring through to early autumn is the time to visit Patagonia, though the winds are strongest at this time.

conspicuously indigenous populations make these two countries (and adjacent Bolivia) among the richest experiences on the continent. Against this, Peru has some of the best scenery, especially to the south towards Lake Titicaca and Bolivia, where the jewel-like lakes and snow-topped volcanoes of the altiplano begin.

BOLIVIA TO PATAGONIA

Ivan Viehoff

Looks like ice but in fact it's salt.
© Antony Bowesman

From La Paz in Bolivia to Tierra del Fuego at the foot of the continent, Andean altitudes and Patagonian gales will in turn leave you panting and take your breath away. The combined natural wonders of the mountains, the altiplano and southern Chile's glaciers all add up to the cycle-touring cream of South America.

Bolivia is South America in a coca nutshell: high-altitude deserts, volcano-studded salt pans and the glaciated peaks in the Cordilleras ranges right down to the lush mountain forests of the Yungas and the Amazon jungle.

What to expect

Any cycling trip in Bolivia is going to involve its fair share of hills and unpaved roads, and the important thing is to manage your expectations – 50km or 60km is often plenty for one day. Bolivia retains more of its historic culture than any other Latin American nation but the days of finding villages where no one speaks Spanish are pretty much over. Nonetheless, avoid wearing Lycra shorts and other forms of clothing that make you look like a Martian.

La Paz sits at 3600m (11,800ft), about the same as Lhasa in Tibet, and if you're flying in you'll need several days for acclimatization. Entering Bolivia from Brazil, Paraguay or Argentina offers the best chance of acclimatizing at a natural pace. Coming in from the Chilean side gives you an extremely rapid climb with few obvious stops until you arrive on the altiplano, with little immediate descent except by retreating.

With such varied topography and altitudes, Bolivia's climate ranges from tropical in the Yungas and eastern lowlands, with lush forest and a long wet season from October to April, to the hyper-arid altiplano and cordillera to the south. This high desert region has strong winds and cold nights, permanent snow above 4600m and a polar climate above 5500m. The best time to travel in Bolivia is in the drier months of May to September, though it is the cooler season. Altitude is a greater influence on temperature than time of year.

Supplies

In much of the country finding food is not a problem and the institution of the lunch stop, small roadside cafés offering a fixed two-course lunch, is great for cyclists. Expect to find little in the way of food up on the altiplano and certainly little variety; bring what you can from larger towns or from home if possible. It can be hard work to find water so your water-carrying capacity needs to be at least 15 litres as it's no place to be caught out.

Central highlands and eastern valleys

The highlands between Potosí and Oruro, stretching southwards towards Tupiza are, according to the local people, part of the altiplano but offer a rather different topography. This is a hilly area mostly above 3000m, cut through by deep valleys separating bare rounded mountains up to 5400m. The cycling here is hard work, always either up or down and at high altitude. But at least there is regular habitation to provide water and occasional supplies.

The Eastern valleys run from Cochabamba, Sucre and Tupiza where the Andes gradually fall away but remain cut through by deep river valleys. The

---

HIGH PLAINS DRIFTING

Some 500km from north to south, the Bolivian altiplano is an arid high plain trapped between two parallel Andean ridges: the Cordillera Oriental and Occidental. It slopes from around 4500m on the Chilean border down to the east. The wonderful bits include Lake Titicaca (3800m), beautiful multicoloured deserts criss-crossed by tracks and passes, the red Laguna Colorada and its famous flamingos, the arsenic green Laguna Verde, volcanoes such as Licancabur, the Dali Desert and dry salt lakes such as Chalviri and the Salar de Uyuní.

Bolivia also claims the world's highest road, on the volcano Uturuncu, but this unsurfaced track is now so poor that the claim is debatable at best. Altogether the altiplano offers a tremendous cycling adventure full of experiences and sights unattainable elsewhere on Earth. Cycling across the blinding white Salar de Uyuní salt lake is the oddest, coolest experience. The illusion of cycling on a polar ice cap is hard to shake off.

In the south-west there are some passes approaching 5000m in altitude, but generally roads are no more than undulating. The altitude certainly takes it out of you, no matter how well acclimatized you are, but long-dis-tance cycle tourists who stick to the 'path of least resistance' along the eastern edge miss most that is wonderful on the Bolivian altiplano. Tracks run across the plain but may not be marked on maps so this is the adventurous area to explore by bike. It's safer to stick with better-travelled tracks. If you stray west of Oruro or south of Uyuní you get into extremely remote areas where opportunities for getting supplies are limited or non-existent and water can be a serious problem.

There are no good maps of this area, making navigation difficult. Update your map from the Internet before you go and carry a compass.

Touring tips for drifters

• Take glacier glasses or strong sunglasses with sideshields.

• Use car petrol for stove fuel; allow about a litre per week.

• Refugios rarely offer food – carry several days' worth of dried food, depending on your route.

• Carry two days' water as lakes are mostly saline or volcanically poisoned. Treat refugio water with iodine. There are refugios at Lagunas Blanca and Colorada, and Quetena, Alota, Villa Mar, Isla Inkawesi and Uyuni.

• GPS receivers can be useful; look for waypoints to download from the web.

• Wide tyres are best for riding on the sandy desert tracks.

• Don't overestimate how far you can ride in a day – 60 km is good in the mountainous desert areas.

• The corrugated altiplano roads will test the strength of all your gear, especially wheels and racks. It's no place for a breakdown.

• There are lots of sharp cacti around – bring a repair kit for your air mattress.

Steve Pells & Antony Bowesman (photo © Antony Bowesman)

THE MOST DANGEROUS ROAD IN THE WORLD

The Inter-American Development Bank has thoughtfully classified the La Paz to Coroico road as the 'Most Dangerous Road in the World'. It descends 3300m over 65km from the 4600m pass at La Cumbre, 24km northeast of La Paz, to Yolosa down in the jungle, but still at 1300m. From Chuspipata, the last 35km of this hair-raising descent is a rough track where the road hugs the left-hand side of the mountains, sometimes with a very weak embrace. Every year many people plunge to their deaths when their vehicles go over the edge.

In Bolivia, traffic drives on the right. However, from Chuspipata traffic drives on the left to give downhill drivers a better view of how close their wheels are to the edge. However, priority is given to ascending traffic so when there is not enough room to pass it's the downhill vehicle that has to reverse up to a suitable passing place.

I'd arranged to meet my friends for the 95km ride to Coroico. One of them felt that to merit the 65km, 3300m downhill run we had to earn it, so we set off to climb 24km and 1000m to La Cumbre pass. The climb wasn't so bad, taking less than four hours at a steady pace. A number of bike-tour companies rushed past us on their descents, gazing at the four mad people doing it the 'wrong' way.

The other side of the pass was cloudy but we could still hear the yelps of exhilaration coming from somewhere far down below. So we turned round, poured some holy water on our brakes and set out to join them.

The first 30km of the descent was wild. The road was sealed so we were coasting at over 50kph (30mph). The clouds would part high above our heads revealing the ghostly shadows of cliffs. At one point the clouds were racing up from the valley below, to spill over the road like a wave.

A little further and the road turned to dirt. The sides of the mountains got steeper and in front of us a big yellow sign warned us to drive on the left. This was it, the scary part. It started to drizzle and the road became really slippery but one of us shot off at high speed, his eyes alight with adrenaline. There were huge rocks on the road and at times we had to stop to let trucks coming up pass by. We teetered on crumbling sections of earth, the trucks grinding up between us and the wall, while trying not to look at the massive drop inches from our feet. The vegetation had changed so quickly we hardly noticed but already, even at 3000m, we were in jungle. Large, broad-leaved plants and brightly-coloured birds were all around.

The final stretch was much wider, allowing vehicles to pass easily, although there were still big drops into the valley below. The road turned to thick dust with hidden rocks and we hurtled down at 40kph. Every time a vehicle passed, we were enveloped in a thick suffocating cloud. We rode into Yolosa and spotted all the downhilling day trippers waiting for their lift uphill for the next stage to Coroico. As for us, we had food on our mind so we found ourselves a cheap hotel for a couple of bucks and called it a day.

Antony Bowesman
(photo © Iris van den Ham)

valley bottoms are generally around 1200m to 2400m, with intermediate passes up as high as 3600m. The contrast between the cactus-covered hillsides and green cultivation of the better-watered valleys is extraordinary. Cycling remains hard work because of the ups and downs but altitude is less of problem and supplies and water are also easier to find. With a distinctive culture reflecting the particularly benign climate, this is the best area to buy chicha, a maize beer.

The Yungas

With their enormous height differences the Yungas will appeal to the downhill mountain biker. The roads are notorious, with tour agents providing transport and renting mountain bikes for riders who want to experience the 3300m drop from La Paz down to Coroico. The long-promised new road has still not been opened, so currently cyclists still have to share the dangerous route with trucks and buses.

A two-week circuit ride is possible from La Paz down to Coroico then upriver to the gold-prospecting villages of Guanay and Mapiri (a boat can take you up the Coroico River), after which you follow the Consata River back up to Sorata and the altiplano. Directions, a sketch map and much more useful information can be found at 💻 www.irisentoreopreis.nl/mapiri_map.shtml.

CHILE

The main attractions of Chile to the tourist, cycling or otherwise, are its well-managed national parks – among the best-preserved natural environments of South America. Here you can find true wilderness and a great variety of scenery, from hyper-arid desert in the north-west to rainforest and glaciers further south. Austral Chile (formally known as Aisén) is one of the most wonderful cycle-touring regions in the world, though you need a bit of luck with the weather. However, paradise is far from continuous and in between these idyllic retreats are busy main roads, dreary farmlands, monotonous deserts and many uninteresting towns. Fortunately, efficient and surprisingly cheap transport is available to carry you and your bicycle between the beauty spots.

Chile has a developed network of excellent paved roads and that network is being rapidly extended. Most Chilean unpaved roads are dreadful; you need the strongest panniers and racks you can find. Fortunately, a few unpaved roads of special interest to cyclists appear to be more regularly maintained, in particular the section of the Carretera Austral from Chaitén to Puerto Aisén and roads in Magellanes, the far south.

Border crossings

The Santiago to Mendoza crossing is a major route between Chile and Argentina. It can be ridden either way in about two days, but would require a high level of fitness if you were riding from the Chilean side, even though you would probably have the prevailing wind at your back. There is a tunnel at 3185m where bicycles used to be bussed through, but for purists the old dirt road over a 3800m pass has now reopened. Nearby, Mt Aconcagua, South America's highest peak, is sometimes visible to the north just above Puente del Inca on the Argentine side.

The Carretera Austral

The Carretera Austral, a largely unpaved road running for over 1000km from Puerto Montt in the north to Villa O'Higgins in the south, is regarded as one of the best cycle routes in South America. To make things more interesting for adventure cyclists, in recent years a new border crossing has opened between Chile and Argentina that enables backpackers and the hardiest of bikers to cross at the southern end of the Carretera Austral to El Chaltén in Argentina and Mount Fitzroy. This saves you from many hundreds of kilometres of backtracking and crossing over into Argentina and a long stretch of the infamous gale-infested Ruta 40 in order to continue the journey south. In most areas the climate is comparable to that of Fiordland on the west coast of New Zealand, so expect plenty of rain (and almost as many bugs) but greater rewards. In a normal year November and December have the least wet weather.

The Carretera Austral has little traffic, mostly buses and rented cars, but there are adequate facilities all the way down, including good campgrounds. The route passes through or near numerous national parks and includes a couple of ferries to carry you across the fjords. There are ferry connections for longer journeys and you could cut the journey in half and return by ferry from Puerto Chacabuco, halfway down the Carretera. The ferries between Hornopirén and Chaitén operate only in January and February, so at other times take a ferry from Puerto Montt or Quellón to Chaitén, or come via Futaleufú from Argentina.

Coyhaique is the largest town on this route. To the north are hot springs at Puyuhuapi and at Futaleufú there's white-water rafting on rivers; a huge glacier calving into the sea at Laguna San Rafael can be visited on boat trips from Puerto Chacabuco.

The southernmost stretch of the Carretera has the driest climate in this region – some 300 days of sunshine a year. The road becomes a simple track ending at Villa O'Higgins and the Argentine border south of there. It's generally held to be the most beautiful stretch of all and a bike will give you greater freedom than any other form of transport to take in all those views.

The crossing into Argentina involves taking a boat across Lago O'Higgins. In the summer season the boat may be running daily (check at ⌨ www.villao higgins.com/hielosur.htm). You then exit through Chilean customs and trek up a tough 15km climb carrying your bike or part-dismantling it to sling on rented horses. After you pass through Argentine customs at the top of the hill you can take another boat down Lago Desierto to a campsite and then it's a 40km trail to El Chaltén, your base for exploring the Mt Fitzroy area.

Torres del Paine
Despite the almost unendurable winds, the far south is popular with cycle tourists because of the access to the wonderful Torres del Paine and Tierra del Fuego. Cold weather lovers will be in their element: summer maximum temperatures are typically about 16°C and frosts are possible almost all year. Rain turns to snow above about 500m all year round though rainfall is modest except in the western areas of Torres del Paine and the south of Tierra del Fuego. Expect three-minute squalls at any time. Winds are generally from the west and frequently very strong so it's preferable to cycle south-east from Puerto Natales to Punta Arenas, crossing by ferry to Tierra del Fuego. Predicting how long a journey will take is hard because of the wind factor. Midsummer is attractive because of the long daylight hours, especially December before the hordes get there. However, March and April can also be wonderful as the gales die down and the sun breaks through more regularly.

ARGENTINA
Argentina provides the cycle-tourist with a wonderful variety of landscapes including wilderness. The Andes in north-west Argentina present a high-alti-

TRIP REPORT
BOLIVIA, CHILE AND ARGENTINA

Name Antony Bowesman
Year of birth 1962
Occupation IT Engineer
Nationality British
Other bike travels China, Pakistan, India, Nepal

This trip Bolivia, Chile, Argentina and Cuba
Trip duration Seven months
Number in group One
Total distance 8112km (5070 miles)
Cost of trip US$2500 excluding flights

Longest day 168km
Best day 50km along a disused railway in Bolivia
Worst day 121km in cold rain in Patagonia
Favourite ride 450km from Uyuni (Bolivia) to San Pedro de Atacama (Chile)
Biggest headache Sand and corrugations
Biggest mistake Cycling into Shining Path guerilla area, Bolivia/Peru
Pleasant surprise Less headwinds than expected in Patagonia
Any illness Flu (one week in Bolivia)

Bike model Thorn EXP
New/used New
Modifications No modifications but this is a custom-built bike
Wish you'd fitted Heart rate monitor
Tyres used Two Vredestein Spider 1.9"; Three Panaracer Pasela Tourguard 1.75"; Vredesteins a tight fit – hard to take on/off. Panaracers best on paved roads, but generally not well suited to this trip
Baggage Setup Ortlieb: Bar bag, 2 rear roller plus panniers, 2 front roller plus panniers, Pannier/rucsac converter
Wish you'd brought MP3 player
Wish you hadn't brought Panaracer tyres. Ortlieb rucsac converter

Bike problems Cracked front fork crown – discovered 2 years later!
Accidents A couple of minor spills
Punctures 14
Same bike again Yes
Recommendations Suunto X6HR for some great stats; Terra Nova Voyager tent is a great size for 1 on a long trip

General tip North-South has more favourable winds than South-North.
Road philosophy Be flexible. Don't go mad trying to save weight; on some rides you have to carry water for several days.

tude desert punctuated by volcanoes and canyons and the roads are among the best in South America, though there are serious on- and off-road challenges. But this is also the land of macho Latinos and bolas-swinging gauchos. Crazy driving is a constant threat to riders in Argentina; keep your eyes open for cars on the wrong side of the road, overtaking when there is no room, turning right in front of you and other such hazards.

Camping
Wild camping is customary and easy; organized campsites cost no more than a few dollars a day and usually have hot showers. Many small towns have municipal campsites or a balneario (a swimming pool or waterside location where it is usually possible to camp), and these are often free, though expect facilities to be primitive.

North-west Argentina and the border with Bolivia
The north-western part of Argentina is an interesting transition zone to the altiplano to the north. Here you're among colourful canyons and cacti, the colonial cities of Salta, Jujuy and Tucuman as well as numerous high passes, including the highest road pass in the Americas: the Abra de Acay between Cachi and San Antonio de los Cobres, west of Salta (allegedly 4895m). There are also several passes of around 4000m into Chile and this is the better side to start from. The Quebrada de Humahuaca, also known as the Camino Inca, has much to see along the way – the multi-coloured ravines are famous – and is a UN-approved acclimatization route for those headed north to Bolivia.

Santa Cruz region
The desolate and windswept plains to the east of the Andes are similar but windier than the Chubut region to the north. You won't forget cycling in Santa Cruz though it's tough to predict which will linger longer in your mind – the amazing Andean views or the endurance test posed by the winds and roads. Be prepared for extraordinary winds (generally from the west), large temperature fluctuations (summer maximums up to 40°C), enormous arid plains where the absence of a view continues unaltered for hundreds of kilometres, and large distances between food and water supplies. Apart from dying of thirst you will find the most demoralizing of these is the wind. You can take five minutes to 'cycle-sail' to the shops and 30 minutes to get back, and that's on an average day. On a bad day cycling on a level paved road is actually not possible. But there are wonderful places to visit such as the Perito Moreno glacier, the Fitzroy area, and the Bajo Caracoles area with Cueva de las Manos (prehistoric hand prints and cave paintings) and Andean lakes. Also, as an adventure cyclist, you'll have the perverse satisfaction of having endured the conditions. Late summer into autumn is a good time to go, as calm intervals

Fitzroy in southern Argentina.
© Antony Bowesman

become more common. Río Gallegos, however, is an industrial town, not somewhere to linger.

Ruta 3 – the uncyclable route
From Comodoro Rivadavia to Río Gallegos it's a flat paved road and so should be rideable, right? Wrong. All but one of the cyclists I met who tried to cycle the 800km Ruta 3 gave up. One pair ran out of water. The others couldn't handle the wind and the unchanging scenery. On the positive side, failure need not be terminal; when it all gets too much there are lifts to be had.

The Ruta 40 gales defeat another cyclist.
© Antony Bowesman

Ruta 40 – not much easier
They say you'll never forget cycling Ruta 40. This unpaved road receives some maintenance these days, so it's not as terrible as it used to be but the prospects of a lift are poor. As the local people observe, not even the birds fly this way. However, there is now a tourist minibus service in season (subject to demand), so you may be able to hop onto it when the wind gets to you – and it will. You shouldn't have to go further than 150km between water supplies, though that's a long way under the extreme conditions. For supplies it is possible to detour to Gobernador Gregores but this adds another 60 galling kilometres.

Tierra del Fuego
Tierra del Fuego is a surprising jewel after the barren, gale-swept plains of Patagonia. Around 100,000 people live in the Argentinian half (another 3000 live in the Chilean portion), but nearly all inhabit the two towns of Río Grande and Ushuaia. The north is grassy steppe while the central area is an attractive transition zone of small wooded hills and lakes, where llama-like guanacos inhabit the amazing red- and yellow-coloured pastures. The south has a forested and glaciated mountain range comparable to that of Norway, with wintry weather on tap on any day. It is extremely windy of course, though less so once you get into the hills. Since winds generally come from the west and are stronger in the north, it's better to ride to, rather than from, Ushuaia, and to arrive via Porvenir rather than Punta Delgada. Don't feel too bad about not cycling out of here as getting here will have been no small ordeal. In the mountains weather conditions can deteriorate badly at surprisingly modest altitudes, as in Scotland.

Ushuaia itself occupies a dramatic setting with opportunities for trekking, wildlife watching and boat trips in the Beagle Channel. Its location makes it relatively expensive, and at the height of the summer it gets crowded and is a gathering point for adventure motorbikers around New Year. The best time to visit would be in March or April.

PART 2 – ROUTE OUTLINES

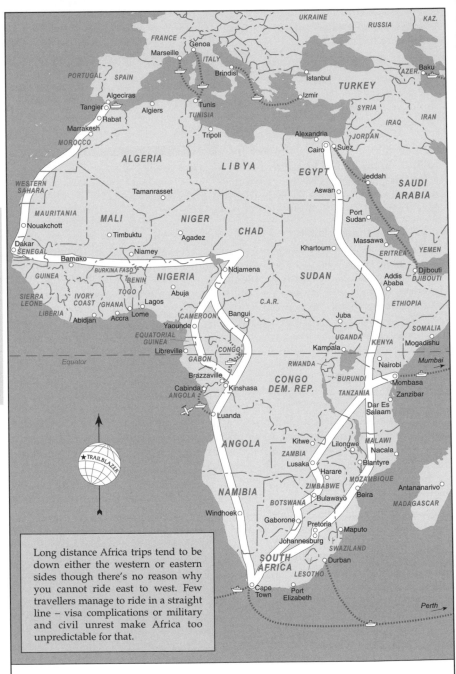

Long distance Africa trips tend to be down either the western or eastern sides though there's no reason why you cannot ride east to west. Few travellers manage to ride in a straight line – visa complications or military and civil unrest make Africa too unpredictable for that.

Africa   MAIN OVERLAND ROUTES

North Africa

Raf Verbeelen

North Africa may not be the most popular destination for cyclists, but it's climbing the ranks, with Morocco as the front runner. From Mauritania to Egypt, this region offers anything a biker could want. Just a short distance from Europe you'll find wild mountain ranges, sunny beaches and marvellous desert landscapes, often very close to each other. And if you want culture, besides historic mosques and medrassas, much of the northern coast is scattered with Roman antiquities, not to mention the pharaonic heritage of Egypt. Most riders return home raving about the rich culture and great hospitality of the people. Also, you'll never pay a fortune; many places are accessible on inexpensive charter flights and you can travel on a modest budget.

For further information *Sahara Overland* (also from Trailblazer) has ten pages on cycling; or visit my webpages: http://users.telenet.be/verbeelen.

Climate
Even if you keep to the Mediterranean, summer is a season to avoid. The high temperatures will become dangerous owing to your water needs. Winter temperatures are generally pleasant but can be cold and rainy. The transitional seasons are in most cases the best choice in the north, especially if you want to cross the Moroccan High Atlas where the higher passes are closed because of snowfall. Temperatures can drop considerably at night; bring warm clothes and a good sleeping bag. If you plan to cycle to sub-Saharan Africa (see p.193) you're better off starting your trip in early autumn.

Muslim mores
The version of Islam you'll experience in North Africa is far less strict than that of the indigenous Arab countries further east, and even less so in the less sober black African Islamic countries of the Sahel. Nevertheless, it's appropriate to wear baggy clothing – long sleeves and trousers – and not expose bare skin. There is some debate about cycling in lycra shorts but from my experience it seems no problem to wear them, for a man at least, as long as you're actually cycling. People mostly regard you as a sportsman anyway. However, attitudes may differ from region to region, so be cautious in your dress as you move into new territory.

Muslims regard other religions with much respect but atheism is not appreciated. During Ramadan, when Muslims don't eat, drink or smoke during the day, it's considerate not to do those things in public, though as a traveller (and a non-Muslim) you are permitted. Keep in mind that during this month it can be hard to obtain food before late afternoon in some places.

When you get away from the tourist enclaves you'll be surprised by the hospitality of the people. The Berbers are famous for this, though some will take advantage of this reputation and try and sell you a carpet you don't need!

During your trip you'll almost certainly be invited to have tea, a meal or even stay at someone's house. When this is the case, a little gift in the form of some tea, sugar, sweets or a present for the kids will always be appreciated.

Food and accommodation

Outside the tourist areas, where you can find any degree of Western luxury, your choice is limited to the local hotels which can range from very nice and clean to holes. They are, however, always cheap. Campgrounds are usually nothing to get excited about and wild camping is no problem in rural regions; just keep a low profile or ask a farmer for permission. In remote areas put up your tent out of sight but even then don't be surprised if someone turns up out of nowhere out of curiosity or to invite you to their village.

Food is very good but in the poorer or desert regions you'll have to take what you're given which can become quite monotonous. Dates are found everywhere and are very nutritious snacks for cyclists. In the towns and villages you can also buy pasta, rice, canned food and fresh vegetables, but the more remote the village, the more expensive and the more limited the choice. Hygiene standards are not the same as in the Western countries, so keep your eyes open and pray!

Alcohol is forbidden to Muslims but this is not observed by everyone and it is certainly available in tourist centres. In Libya, however, it's illegal to bring in, let alone drink, any alcoholic beverage at all.

Safety and health

Northern Algeria aside, the North African countries are safe though you have to be alert as you would in any big city or tourist spot. In general theft or violence against tourists is far less common than in Europe.

Some visitors are driven crazy by the endless hassling that goes on in Morocco, Egypt and to a much lesser extent, Tunisia. This is mostly restricted to tourist hotspots. The general advice is to be firm without losing your good humour towards the hustlers. Don't let it cause you to turn your back on the people or you will miss the genuine hospitality offered by most of them.

Health precautions are not too demanding and medicines are available in towns. It's sensible to get medical advice from your doctor or a travel health specialist and essential to check the country-specific requirements before you leave. In most cases your tetanus and hepatitis injections and a basic medical kit will do. During your stay you're most likely to encounter a degree of diarrhoea which can result in dehydration. Don't neglect the symptoms. To be on the safe side, stick to bottled water unless you have a good stomach. Rabies is present so avoid petting dogs and don't let them bite you. Some dogs can be persistent but in most cases you get rid of them by speeding up. If not, an aggressive attitude or a stone can help (see p.24).

Roads and stones

Roads are in reasonable condition. African drivers don't have a very good reputation and cycling in the big crowded cities like Cairo is an adventure on its own. Where you have a choice, plan to ride on secondary roads; traffic outside the big roads is mostly very light. Unsurfaced tracks or pistes offer a good alternative for exploring the countryside, providing they are not too sandy.

Reports of stone-throwing children are not unknown in these countries but in most cases it's nothing more than a local kids' game, although someone badly hit would disagree. Once I sat by the roadside in the little Egyptian town with a local teacher who threw little stones at his own pupils cycling past! In Morocco's Draa Valley an attempt to chase after some stone-throwing kids ended up in a football game with them and an overnight stay in the house of one of

Egypt's Western Desert.
© Raf Verbeelen

their parents. In Morocco, however, you'll wish that the tourist who started to give pens to the local kids had been stoned before he ever started...

THE SAHARA

A successful bicycle trip in the Sahara starts with careful preparation and a realistic knowledge of your physical and mental limits. A look at a map such as the Michelin 741 can generate over-ambitious plans like crossing the central Sahara. Although it has been done, it's an expedition to be undertaken only by very experienced and committed riders. For the majority of us, other routes on the fringes of the desert can be far more rewarding but even then, it all comes down to knowing the difficulties that can be encountered and to be prepared for them.

Major concerns for cyclists in the Sahara are the climate, remoteness and the terrain or track surface but the primary concern is that water resources are far apart and a cyclist's range is limited. Even in winter you will need 5-10 litres of water a day. However, if you envisage having to push a loaded bike through soft sand, you don't want to take much more than 20 litres in total. An easy calculation brings us to an absolute maximum of four days' range in winter with no washing. The distance covered on an average day in the desert can range from 100km or more on asphalt with a tail wind to a mere 10km or less pushing through soft sand with that same wind blowing in your face.

The wind is another concern for cyclists and, as we all know, heading for hundreds of kilometres into the wind can make one crazy, so keep this in mind when planning long stretches in the open. The main wind direction in the vast spaces of the Sahara is from the north-east but don't rely on this.

In addition, political problems can make some tours impossible. The Moroccan–Algerian border has been closed for many years and there are restrictions on independent travel in Algeria and Libya, even on highways – though one can be lucky and sneak out.

Your bike

If you go off the surfaced roads the best bike is a tough mountain bike on fat tyres. Bring spare parts and tools, too, because it will be hard or impossible to find anything decent over there. On the other hand, there are little bike-repair shops in most towns and you'll be amazed what they can fix, albeit in a Heath Robinson way.

TRANS-SAHARA ROUTES

There are two main cyclable routes across the Sahara at the western and eastern borders of the desert. The Atlantic route, running along the coastline out of Morocco via Western Sahara to Nouadhibou in Mauritania, became fully sealed in early 2006. It's the easiest route but scenically the least attractive. Visas for Mauritania can be obtained in Casablanca or at the border (slightly more expensively). At the moment the longest waterless stretch is the 160km from Chicas to Barbas, between El Argoub and the Mauritanian border.

The Nile route is the harder way. From Aswan in Egypt one has to take the ferry over Lake Nasser to Wadi Halfa in Sudan. Once past the Sudanese bureaucracy you can cycle and push the 400km along the Nile to Abu Dom. You will encounter plenty of soft sand, especially past Dongola. The thorns will test your tyre-repairing skills. But the people are incredibly hospitable and if it becomes too much you should be able to get a lift or take the train. From Abu Dom a tarmac road goes to Khartoum.

Raf Verbeelen

What to bring

Needless to say you should take the absolute minimum – your load will be big enough with your water provisions! Light shirts with long sleeves, sunglasses, a hat or local scarf, sun-cream and lip balm provide protection against the sun. You may be planning to take a Camelbak with you for carrying water but be aware that wearing a few kilos on your back can become quite unpleasant after a while. You can buy bottled water and put the bottles away somewhere on your racks or in your bags. The water can get unpleasantly warm during the day but it cools off at night.

If you plan to camp, light self-standing tents are best. Speaking from personal experience, just make sure the tent can't be blown away by always leaving something heavy in it! As you won't always be able to find wood, a fuel-stove is a must.

A rope will prove very useful for getting water out of a well where nothing is available. You can then get the water out with your waterproof pannier. Note that the technique is none too easy and it's a good idea to take a lesson or two with a local. Navigation requires maps and compass and even a GPS unit. Small binoculars may come in handy, too, though make sure you have experience in using all of these items before you set off!

In the desert

Once you're out in the desert, the success of your trip depends on economy of effort and good navigation. To save your strength and resources, rest in the shade during the hottest hours of the day and sip your water continually rather than drinking one full bottle every few hours.

When the track becomes too sandy, you're lost. Have a laugh with your companion who will eventually fall down when stuck, drink some water, and start to push your 40kg loaded bicycle through the soft, deep sand. Convince yourself that it's the most normal thing to do on a hot day while all the crazy others are having a swim and a drink at the lake.

MOROCCO AND WESTERN SAHARA

Morocco's awesome range of landscapes makes it great cycling country. What's more, once you can see past the persistent 'guides' and hustlers in

some cities, you'll discover an amazing hospitality among the people. The
only region to avoid for the first-timer
is the Rif region in the north from
which all kinds of drug tales come.
Generally the south of the country is
more relaxed than the north.

As there are infinite options buy a
good map and guidebook to plan your
route. If things don't work out on the
road, it's never a problem to put your
bike on a bus. The four imperial cities
of Rabat, Fez, Meknes and Marrakesh
are all certainly worth a visit. If you

Thirsty work, cycling in the Sahara: you'll
need to be able to carry a lot of water.
© Raf Verbeelen

want to visit the south of the country, Marrakesh is a great starting point, from
where you can cross the High Atlas to end up at the borders of the Sahara,
where you'll find green palm trees, beautiful kasbahs and strange ranges like
the Anti-Atlas and Jebel Sahro. Never forget that parts of Morocco are very
mountainous!

If you're up to cycling in the desert and are very well prepared, the stretch
from Tan Tan near the Atlantic coast via Assa, Tata, Foum Zguid and Tagounite
to the dunes of Merzouga at the Algerian border is a great Saharan ride and
just about manageable on a bike. Contrary to remarks on the Michelin and
IGN maps, the stretch on the piste between Tagounite and Merzouga is not
forbidden, though not to be undertaken lightly.

MAURITANIA

This country is usually crossed on the way to sub-Saharan Africa rather than
seen as a destination in itself. Although the cycling possibilities are limited, it
certainly offers some great rides. From Nouadhibou close to the Moroccan border the new tarmac road to the capital, Nouakchott, should be finished by
now. If not, or if you want a rewarding detour in the desert, you can take the
iron-ore train east to Choum. The ride in an open wagon is free. From Choum
you can try to cycle or get a lift south-east to Atar and from there a sealed road
runs south to Nouakchott. The Adrar region around Atar also holds possibilities for off-tarmac riding, including a visit to the old Islamic towns of
Chinguetti and Oudane.

From Nouakchott one can head into Senegal, which should be quite
straightforward except for the intimidating border crossing at Rosso, or into
Mali via Kiffa or Nema along the 'Route de l'Espoir', a harder route because
of the state of the road and encroaching sand.

TUNISIA

Tunisia may have an unwelcome 'Ibiza factor' for the adventure cyclist but
inland it offers many sights to see and is a relaxing place to travel in. It con-
tains the tail end of the Atlas ranges in the north, the Sousse plain with
Kairouan in the east and the Sahara with the Grand Erg Oriental in the far
south. This said, the Erg rules out off-road cycling, so for a desert adventure
you're much better off in Morocco. Nonetheless, the region around the Chott

> ## TRANS-AFRICA TIPS
>
> • You need patience and infinite flexibility. Africa is not to be rushed and you have to expect delays.
>
> • Never hurry, for 'sweat means death' is the advice local people give for desert travel.
>
> • Always stay in a good humour at roadblocks or checkpoints. Don't become angry and don't provoke people who could lock you up or worse. Patience will help – if they think you are in a hurry, it could prove more expensive.
>
> • Be subtle if you have to bribe – 'perhaps a little gift would smooth the situation...'
>
> • Do not take a 'no' for a no and have patience with your goals.
>
> • To avoid encounters with hyenas, it's best to avoid camping altogether. I purchased a spear and a long dagger which gave me peace of mind and enabled me to sleep better.
>
> • Don't enter villages after dark. Either arrive before dark and ask to stay in the village, or camp outside in a place you will not easily be seen. Don't light fires or burn candles.
>
> **Sebastian Eissing**

El Jerid offers some nice rides and one should also be able to reach the oasis of Ksar Ghilane, not far from the fabulous mountain villages between Matmata and Chenini. And the sea will never be far away.

EGYPT

If you want to visit Egypt with your own vehicle, do it with a bicycle! Car drivers rate Egypt among the most difficult and bureaucratic countries for temporary vehicle importation but for a cyclist things are breeze. However, cycling along the Nile and in the Sinai can be restricted by the police, who may insist you join a convoy. To avoid this, you can always try to skip round the checkpoints or talk your way past the police.

An alternative to cycling along the Nile is to take the Oasis Circuit into the Western Desert. Starting at the Giza Pyramids, a 1400km loop takes you via Bahariya, Farafra, Dakhla and Kharga to Luxor, all on tarmac. On the way you'll pass a range of desert landscapes, the 'White Desert' being the most striking and if it becomes too demanding there are daily buses between the oases. Once in Luxor it should be possible to cycle independently to Aswan.

ALGERIA

Algeria's glory days as the Saharan destination of the eighties are long gone, mainly on account of the civil war in the nineties. Tourists returned to the south at the beginning of the new millennium but after 32 tourists were taken hostage in 2003 travel restrictions followed and hope of a renaissance has waned. Independent cycling is not allowed these days; more's the pity, because the country has much to offer.

To avoid the northern part of the country one could enter close to Nefta in Tunisia and head west to Timimoun or south to Djanet, a dead end but a great ride, or along the trans-Sahara highway to Tamanrasset. The route via In Salah, Tamanrasset, In-Guezzam to Arlit and Agadez in Niger is a straightforward way to cross the Sahara but distances are huge. Even if it were allowed, it's a long haul south to Tamanrasset on tarmac. Between Tamanrasset and the border at In Guezzam tarmac is being laid, but they've been at it at least 25 years! And from In Guezzam to Arlit in Niger is another 250km of piste.

T R I P   R E P O R T
ZAMBIA, NAMIBIA AND BOTSWANA

Name Mike Hutton
Year of birth 1977
Occupation Clinical Scientist
Nationality British
Other bike travels Uganda, Tanzania, Zambia, Ethiopia, Namibia, Botswana, Scotland

This trip Zambia, Namibia, Botswana
Trip duration 102 days
Number in group One
Total distance 3000km (1875 miles)
Cost of trip About £1500 including flights and beer

Longest day 164km, Caprivi Strip, Namibia, escaping from elephant country
Best day Cycling alongside the Luangwa river, Zambia
Worst day Cycling with Giardiasis, Myombe, Zambia
Favourite ride Luangwa valley, Petauke–Lundazi
Biggest headache Tsetse flies
Biggest mistake Unplanned 90km detour to the DR Congo
Pleasant surprise Zambia – beautiful people and beautiful country
Any illness Giardiasis, malaria

Bike model On-one Inbred
New/used Nine months old
Modifications Custom build, butterfly bars, Tubus Logo/OMM Sherpa racks, Mavic EX721 rims, XT hubs, Brooks B17, Avid front mechanical disc, XTR v-brake rear
Tyres used Schwalbe Marathon XR Evo 2.25" – without a doubt the best tyre for touring in Africa. Resists most African thorns and lasts forever.
Baggage Setup Karrimor Kalahari rear, Ortlieb Roller Plus front
Wish you'd brought Blow torch for the Tsetse flies, more spare chains
Wish you hadn't brought Nothing!

Bike problems Broke Tubus rack several times, short chain life, poorly sealed pedals
Punctures Two
Same bike again Same bike
Recommendations I've found that chain wear when cycling African dirt roads is astonishing. I plan for only 3000km per chain. Take plenty of spares!

General tip Take to the dirt roads and explore Africa, there are so many wonderful places that cycle tourists have still not found.

TRANS-CHAD

N'djamena is a three-way junction for Trans-Africa travellers. To the west lie Lake Chad and Nigeria, to the south, Central Africa and to the north and east the vastness of the Sahara. For over three weeks I had tried to extract a Sudanese visa from the embassy here. I finally decided to cycle back to Europe via West Africa instead of Sudan when, at last, I was summoned to the consulate in Abeche to get my visa. I had learned my lesson again in Africa: be patient and you may well get what you want. I went to the market the same evening, bought some dates and two kilos of rice and set off next day.

At times I consumed 15 litres of water a day in this hottest time of the year. I always consulted locals about the quality of their wells and where the water was too brown, I sieved it through a scarf. The habit of asking for the next well on your route is vital. Knowing this, you decide on the amount of water you want to carry. Water is most crucial but it can be galling to carry an additional 10 litres that you won't drink through deep sand. I tried to make up for the loss of salt with loads of dates, an all-round food, and salted peanuts; both are available in the little villages which were typically about 50km apart.

Each morning I would get up and leave as soon I could make out the terrain. I pedalled eagerly into the morning hours but after the first sunbeams came over the horizon I had to force myself to continue. Increasing headwinds from the east arose during the morning. A six-metre-long turban worked as protection against the baking 50°C winds and the sand. In Chad I usually pedalled no later than 9am. If I hadn't made it into a village by then, I made my tent into a shadecloth and pitched it in a wadi. Arrival in villages always aroused considerable attention. I could get spicy sweet tea, refreshing mangoes and cook my meal; then I stretched out on a straw-mattress under a tree. Thanks to the authority of the village headman I could get some rest before continuing in late afternoon, riding well into the night, sometimes in bright moonlight.

There were weekly markets, the big event for nomads and villagers alike. At little food stalls I could stock up my saddlebags with dates, nuts, fruit and rice for onward travel. The deeply corrugated ruts on the vanishing road made me bump along slowly. Beyond Um Hadjer the road disappeared altogether. Sometimes nomad children appeared suddenly and helped push my bike through deep sand. Long thorns and hot sand complicated walking in sandals. There was lots of tyre patching!

Sebastian Eissing

You'd have to count on the minimal traffic to supply water, which is risky. Don't even consider the infamous Tanezrouft piste to Gao in Mali on a standard bike because of the complete lack of water as well as the risk of banditry. Note that both routes have been cycled in the past, the latter on a specially-engineered three-wheeler. For off-road enthusiasts prepared for a big adventure, the beautiful region around Tamanrasset offers the best possibilities, assuming that one day the accompanying guide restrictions will be lifted.

LIBYA

Although Colonel Gaddafi is opening up his country to tourism, independent travel without guides has become restricted, though some get away with it. When this changes, it will be the north of the country, with the cities of Tripoli and Benghazi and various archaeological sites, that will offer the most rewarding cycling, though note that the driving along the north-coast highway is infamously dangerous. The rest is desert, particularly the Fezzan of the southwest, which is accessible on good sealed roads and worth visiting, although the road to Kufra in the south-east is ruined.

(Opposite): Morocco – see p.188. An enticing (if you're at the top, that is) mountain road in the High Atlas. (Photo © Cass Gilbert).

Sub-Saharan Africa

Sebastian Eissing

The real Africa begins south of the Sahara and it is not a continent to be rushed even if that were possible. It is best explored as a single destination in one long trip in order to appreciate the variety of desert, jungle, forest and the many peoples and cultures. On my second African trip my itinerary was determined according to various rainy seasons but on a long Trans-African tour it's not possible to avoid every inconvenience of climate. I took a ferry from Genoa to Tunis in December and crossed Tunisia and Algeria in two months. Having looked in vain for a riding partner to get through the notorious Hoggar route of several hundred kilometres of desert to reach the first Sahel nation and Black Africa, Niger, I obtained a visa for Niger in the southern Algerian city of Tamanrasset and a visa for Nigeria back in Tunis.

Zebra crossing, Zimbabwe.
© Kenichi Kuroe

I took a small road leading further south from Agadez to Zinder, parts of which were very sandy and which forced me to push. In this area, you may come across clans of Peul nomads, the gypsies of West Africa. Once a sandstorm hit me hard and I was forced to stay with a Peul family I befriended. Arriving in Zinder I had to decide whether to continue south to Nigeria.

Nigeria

Nigeria struggles with the consequences of overpopulation. People are often extremely friendly – the friendliest anywhere in Africa. Dots on my map indicating villages turned out to be huge cities. At no point did I ever feel unsafe in Nigeria though I travelled only in the north; the south is less safe. Main roads have asphalt surfaces and the hotels are reasonably-priced and easy to find.

Cameroon

Before entering Cameroon check if you need a visa or if you can get one upon arrival. Arriving at the border, I almost got turned back to Abuja in Nigeria to get the visa – a big detour! Cameroon is magnificent, Africa in miniature, offering everything from desert to jungle. I enjoyed most of all the northern mountains around Maroua and east of Garoua, the Alantika mountains, riding along the Faro River and the road around Mt Cameroon and the jungle south of the

(Opposite) Top: Mali – after the rains have come. Bottom left: Traffic hazard warning, Zimbabwe. Bottom right: Local welders fixing a bike rack, Tanzania. (Photos © Kenichi Kuroe).

PART 2 – ROUTE OUTLINES

capital, Yaounde. The friendly population makes it a great country to ride through. The heat builds up towards the rainy season. I had avoided the big heat of the Sahara, but now faced temperatures hovering around 40°C in the shade in April in the Sahel nations.

Hotel standards in Africa can vary considerably but I always found budget hotels in towns or cities for around $3. In Douala I got what I paid for: a hovel built of cardboard no bigger than a garage and a bucket of water to wash with. During the night a couple crashed through one of the cardboard walls.

In general, Africa is not as cheap as Asia, perhaps with the exception of Egypt, Ethiopia, Malawi and Nigeria. You could get by on US$300 a month unless you indulge in luxuries. In Yaounde I tackled three consulates, two immigration offices, two harbours and three minor offices within a day – all for a one-month visa extension. Yaounde is the best place to get visas for Gabon, Congo-Brazzaville (as opposed to DRC) and Equatorial Guinea.

Central African Republic (CAR)

Leaving Cameroon southwards, you've got several options but make sure your documents are in perfect shape before you leave Yaounde! The easiest route would bring you into Gabon at the town of Bitam and on to Libreville. Taking a river barge on the River Ubanghi from Banghi in the CAR to Brazzaville is another option. There are roads leading into Congo south of Yokadouma. I opted for probably the most adventurous version through the Congo Basin: malaria attacks, bribe-demanding soldiers and crawling, biting, stinging insects.

Congo–Brazzaville

From Djoum in Cameroon to Ouesso in Congo-Brazza' expect overgrown footpaths and many scratches to your skin and gear. There were butterflies, monkeys and birds I couldn't see but I enjoyed the concerts they gave. Termites attacked and tiny flies, known as fourou, bit mercilessly on exposed skin.

In small pygmy villages I found rest and often experienced great hospitality. I was even invited to join a group going hunting. I could pitch my tent or take an empty hut in the chief's compound, sometimes paying a little sum in return. I made sure I closed all tent zippers to avoid an invasion of mosquitoes, snakes and scorpions. My daily diet consisted of fresh meat and manioc wrapped in leaves and a wide variety of fruits. But be careful: if there's a morsel of meat in the tent, you'll be invaded by ants.

When you've had enough of pedalling, try some paddling. © Kenichi Kuroe

I had to crawl under monstrous tree trunks or lift my bike over to continue along the paths. Speed and distance were not concerns any longer; to get through became the only goal. I was enticed by the pristine beauty of this land and fascinated by the contentment of the people.

I pushed on. Once I heard a growl and a rustle and suddenly a gorilla stared at me from five metres, scratched his belly and strolled on. National parks like Odzala or Ndoki

---

'CHIN CHON' AND OTHER HILARITIES

An Oriental travelling through Africa can expect to be greeted with cries or chants of 'Chin-chon' in many countries. Africans see Chinese movies and assume we're all Chinese. Walking through Accra's markets, I was followed by shouts of 'Chin-chon' wherever I went. Having to listen to these words more than ten thousand times, it was hard to avoid going mad. Pedestrians would burst into laughter when they saw me. When I walked into a shop, it was the beginning of great excitement for them – even shopkeepers would scream 'Hey chin! Chon chin! Chun wan!' A couple of times I completely lost my temper!

Kenichi Kuroe

---

would be excellent destinations for viewing wildlife. Thanks to the flexibility of my bike, I could dump it in a dugout canoe for a few days and drift down narrow streams. I'm not the type who's driven to cycling every single kilometre in order to claim 'I've done it all by bike'. Africa's public transport system offers rewarding experiences.

Arriving at the Ubanghi River, I decided to remain on water rather than be prey to soldiers on roads. For eight days, from Impfondo to Brazzaville, I travelled on an overloaded barge stuffed with 280 cows and a varying number of passengers, crammed on like refugees. After the barge ran aground on a sandbank 50km before the final destination, I pummelled my way through ten roadblocks and entered Brazzaville.

After so long in jungles, I enjoyed the hectic scene of an African city. The hub city of Kinshasa was 5km over the Congo River. It's one of the worst borders in terms of bribery and security. Try to have at least one trustworthy accomplice to guard against pickpockets while squeezing through a mass of shuffling bodies and shouting, while fat customs officers try to get their share of your money.

Congo (DRC)

Kinshasa can be intimidating at first as it's very hard to find budget hotels with basic safety requirements. Your best bet might be Matonge, the busy nightlife district. I was excited to explore 'Kin' on my bike and soon came to feel very safe and comfortable, making excursions with my bike into the most crowded market of Africa.

Rumours are that barges will operate again upriver to Kisangani which would allow a travel connection between west and east Africa. However, owing to current conflicts between tribes in the eastern DRC, this passage cannot be regarded as safe.

Another 'block' between west and east exists in southern Sudan, where a long civil war has recently ended. Some daredevils have made it through southern Sudan from the CAR to Uganda. My own plans to cross the DRC towards Lubumbashi were shattered by demands for US$400 for crossing the diamond-rich province of Kasai Occidental. So instead I flew there for $100 and continued into peaceful Zambia.

Congo – bribes and money

I got caught in bad weather in southern Congo and had to linger in a thatched-roof village for days. Thick mud from the roads clogged the tyres. As I recalled

THE IMPORTANCE OF BICYCLES IN SUB-SAHARAN AFRICA

In countries such as Malawi or Zambia, Ghana or Nigeria, many communities depend on bicycles. Almost every village offers some sort of repair shop, with spare parts – for Chinese or Indian bikes. One can often use narrow bike paths between villages leading through dust and scrub. They have the advantage of being more direct and having smoother surfaces than the broken roads – and of course they're less dangerous and polluted.

A bike may be used to collect water daily from wells, sometimes as far away as 10km. Bikes transport farm goods, animals from distant fields and serve as transport to get to distant markets. In Congo I met traders travelling in groups, transporting as much as 160 litres of palm oil on their battered bikes for up to 400km! Smugglers use bikes for easier access over remote borders in neighbouring countries. For example, in Cameroon smugglers cross over to Nigeria to buy cans of petrol, which is far cheaper there. Other traders use bikes to travel from village to village, loading them like Christmas trees with goods. The bike not only plays an important role but in many African communities it's the sole mode of transport and the reason these small villages survive.

Sebastian Eissing

in former Zaire, ten years ago, big trucks got stuck in the bog for weeks so I knew I could not continue.

All over Africa I had used the same three Michelin maps: 741, 745, 746 and, apart from in the Sahara, I found them adequate for my needs and for the most part reliable. However, the road surface indications are often wrong and the distance markers inaccurate. I'd ask local people about unknown roads ahead, though expected the answers to vary tremendously, with estimates ranging from 2km to 150km.

Military checkpoints became more frequent before the border to Gabon. Continual demands for bribes in return for passage or invented papers only spurred me on. False compliments, threats and implorations are the tools of the trade: 'You have a driving license for the bicycle? No? Ah bien, alors, pay US$200! No? US$100, vite! No? A T-shirt then, or how about medicine?' The trick is to amuse them (and yourself) without complying or provoking. Remember, local travellers also get held up. What you need is lots of time. Never become loud or emotional, remain friendly but firm. Produce a document from your nearest embassy stating you are protected – even observed! Don't show any of your money. Hide it in several different spots, in the seatpost, handlebar or in your underpants. Crossing Africa, you are forced to carry a certain amount of cash (best in either Euros or US dollars). ATM machines are often limited or non-existent and travellers' cheque commissions may be as high as 90% in Equatorial Guinea or 50%, in Sudan. Figure out how much you'll need to spend until the next reliable bank on your itinerary.

Drunken, bored soldiers will search your bags and may try other means to infuriate you. This is one reason why I didn't carry valuables. If nothing works and you feel at a loss despite being in the right, offer them – in a subtle way so as not to suggest a direct bribe – a 'gift to smooth the situation'. After all, they have the power to deprive you of your liberty or even inflict further damage to you and your bike. Before risking too much, turn back, try another border crossing, improve your papers or persuasive powers – or decide to travel elsewhere.

ZAMBIA AND SOUTHERN AFRICA

For days I cycled on remote roads from Lubumbashi in the DRC through dry bush country into Zambia alongside traders on their Chinese bikes. In villages I ate 'foufou', a mixture of mashed maize with water and sometimes meat. On one occasion I had boiled rat. A famine resulting from a drought in parts of southern Africa forced people to rely on UN supplies and to shorten their rations. It

Stumpjumper meets African elephant.
© Kenichi Kuroe

demanded sensitivity to share what I could and not to display my wealth. The first town, Solwezi, had takeaway restaurants and supermarkets but who could afford them?

You need not fear marauding soldiers and roadblocks in southern Africa. In Zambia, you could cycle into parks like Luangwa and Kafue. I had no time for game watching as I sometimes had to find my path through deep grass and around piles of elephant-dung. Warthogs, antelopes and monkeys fled in terror. I was often asked: 'What about the animals?' 'Don't disturb them, respect them, and they will leave you alone!' was my reply. This applies even to elephants, crocs and other dangerous beasts. Cheetahs never go for humans unless threatened, they prefer antelopes and smaller game and, believe it or not, during the night the tent is a barrier they seem to accept. [Note from editor: take local advice before sleeping out in game parks!]. To avoid encounters with snakes I never rummaged in the sticks in search of firewood after dark. Make noises when moving in high grass! Snakes usually want to escape from you – after all they can't eat you! When invited into huts, try to sleep in your tent to avoid scorpions, snakes and other tormentors.

I enjoyed the wilderness! Here, man was still dominated and surrounded by nature. But then another serious plague descended with a monstrous ferocity: tsetse flies! I had to wear all my shirts as a shield from their stabbings. As soon as I stopped pedalling, they fell upon me.

Visas for eastern and southern African countries are all easy to obtain, usually upon arrival at a border or, as in the case of Tanzania, by applying at an embassy in the nearest capital.

I cycled on the shores of Lake Malawi and the Mulanje Mountains and cruised on into the Tete sector of Mozambique. Despite corrugated roads, I loved this landscape of vast, dry bush. To avoid landmines I stayed in villages. Portuguese is spoken widely in Mozambique and Angola, and it is relatively easy to pick up the basics. French is useful in Madagascar, Central and West Africa. English is widely spoken in East Africa, South Africa, Nigeria and Ghana. Kiswahili in East Africa, Afrikaans in South Africa, Lingala in the Congo and Hausa and Wolof in West Africa are all major African languages.

While cycling through the Congo 10 years ago, I caught Guinea worm, which was treated in a tropical hospital upon my return to Europe. Bilharzia was also diagnosed. It's generally not safe to wade through standing water or

Seb's Iron Horse.
© Kenichi Kuroe

bathe in it or, of course, drink it! I didn't have a water-purifier with me and trusted the advice of the local people and used the many newly constructed wells of many NGOs all across Africa. And if I wasn't certain I boiled or treated water with chlorine pills.

I cycled up and down the Zambezi River and took a little ferry from Cabora Bassa Dam to Zumbo. Despite 45°C, hippos and crocs prevented me from taking a refreshing bath. The hardships of cycling in unimaginable heat or on bad roads didn't get easier in southern Africa. Although you could always stay on asphalt roads all the way from Nairobi to Cape Town, I preferred the hard but more interesting back roads.

One of my worst experiences of brain-shaking, frame-shattering corrugated roads was in northern Namibia, one of Africa's wealthiest countries (though only in a 'per-capita' sense). After eight months of not meeting any other Western traveller I enjoyed fully equipped hostels. Places like Nkhata Bay or Cape McClear in Malawi, Lusaka or 'Vic-Falls' in Zambia, 'Dar' or Moshi in Tanzania or Cape Town in South Africa are ideal places to meet up with fellow cyclists and to exchange information. The Etosha National Park in Namibia's north would have been great for game, especially so in the dry season, when animals congregate on the remaining waterholes. Namibia is better cycled in southern Africa's winter though I had ice on my tent during my first trip. But the second trip, around October, was unbearably hot.

Southern and East Africa caters well for tourism in any category of course. Any cliché Western tourists harbour about Africa may be served up in Kenya, along the coast of Tanzania and in South Africa. Sadly, most Africans don't distinguish between a bike traveller and a two-week all-inclusive tourist. I often found myself a target for unemployed thugs roaming cities like Nairobi, Mombasa and Dar Es Salaam. Here I appreciated my mobility in comparison with that of most travellers with clumsy backpacks. A place which first appears as a haven for holidaymakers can turn into a nightmare and stand in stark contrast to the rest of Africa.

Angola

After endless research and consulting Angolan refugees, the embassy and NGO websites I concluded that, following the peace treaty of April 2002, Angola would be the next place to travel in. I got my Angolan visa in Lusaka for US$20. Angola is likely to undergo many changes in visa requirements in the near future, probably with stricter regulations. Visas are currently available from the Angolan consulate at Mongu, Zambia and Matadi in the DRC for US$80 for 15 days. You are likely to need a letter from your embassy.

Angola was so new and different! Tanks stood alongside roads. They reminded me of the invisible danger of landmines so I stayed away from bridges, ruins and abandoned roads and refrained from bush camping. I was even worried about having a pee in the bushes.

AFRICA ON A CHINESE STEEL HORSE

In the summer '94 I backpacked through Turkey and decided at short notice to go on to Syria. In the old market in Damascus I fell in love with an old Chinese steel bike, loaded with carpets, battered by rust and somehow twisted, its spokes were fit to grill bulls on and the back carrier could carry an elephant. The seat resembled a couch and instead of flimsy brake cables it had metal rods. I purchased this curiosity, strapped the backpack on and set off. I travelled to Jordan and pedalled on via the Sinai to Cairo.

In Cairo, word spread that the classical Trans-Africa 'Cairo-Cape Town route' was open and Sudan, Eritrea and Ethiopia were welcoming travellers. I got the Sudanese visa easily in the embassy and within three weeks cycled through Egypt and took the last ferry to sail for the next few years on Lake Aswan.

In northern Sudan I plunged into another world, so different from tourist-infested Egypt. For weeks I cycled along the pristine shores of the Sudanese Nile, which gradually makes its epic journey in continuous bends bringing life to the Sahara.

In Eritrea I had as many as 37 punctures in a single day! Hopes of a new nation inspired Eritreans; the mood was extraordinarily positive in 1994. I pushed the bike on through deep sand on the way to Djibouti along the coast. In the Simien mountains, shortly after the monolithic rock-hewn churches of Lalibela, the fork broke for the first time. Samburu nomads chased me in northern Kenya. It is still recommended that

travellers avoid the area between Moyale and Marserbit.

In the former Zaire I cycled for weeks on muddy roads and paths to Kisangani and came into close contact with pygmies, took a dugout canoe up the Congo River and lugged around bundles of worthless Zairi banknotes. By constant wading through standing water, I picked up the Guinea worm. On a campsite in Harare in Zimbabwe I was robbed of my modest gear, leaving me with no more than the trustworthy old bike. The Namibian desert fascinated me with magical shapes and surprised me with chilly nights. I was 300km short of my final destination, Cape Town, when the fork broke a second time on a corrugated road.

Countless times I had been told the bike wouldn't make it. My travel speed wasn't much different from that of other bike travellers. In good conditions I pedalled 180km daily. I had completed 16,000km through Africa on a piece of rust in 17 months. I had no concerns for spare parts, for in virtually every African village I could get my bike fixed. I carried no more than a spoon, a nail, and a pocketknife for tools. True, repairs were common; daily, to say the least but I wasn't in a race; I travelled. Although I don't regard such a bike as suitable for the Sahara, for long distances or for areas without villages this episode confirms that no fancy gear or bike is necessary. With the right attitude, everything is possible!

Sebastian Eissing

Village markets were basic and shops didn't exist. Colonial houses were in ruins. I found the rocky highland was more pleasant to travel across than the bush land of the plain with its suffocating heat. Whenever I stopped for provisions or shelter I was surrounded by groups of curious people making it impossible to move on. For years, white men were seen only on armed trucks. Yet people warmed up gradually, once I had the chance to use my Spanish, which allowed for some contact with the Portuguese speakers. My presence was regarded as a clear sign that things were getting back to normal.

The cities all had a very lively atmosphere, a mix of vibrant Africa and the buzzing culture of the Portuguese ancestors, all neatly caught in a time-warp. Although there were sidewalk cafés in abundance, it was often difficult to find groceries. However, outside the cities there were new markets, stocked by trucks from South Africa, which had virtually everything – for a price! Some cities like Huambo or Kuito were badly marked by the war. Angola is not cheap if you demand certain standards. The few hotels in the cities were costly. In

---

JESUS CHRIST ON A BIKE!

'Jesu Christo, Jesu Christo!' people shouted when seeing me riding on my bike. In Africa, a white traveller gets called many different names – and a bicycle traveller in particular, for we happen to cross so many people's paths during our trips. We arouse hopes, fears and other emotions among curious and open-minded Africans. In East Africa I heard 'Muzungu', in the Congo 'Mondele', in Sudan 'Faerancha' and in West Africa I heard 'Toubabou', or 'Yovo' in Togo. On the other hand, exclamations like: 'Hi John, give me your bike' were common in Nigeria.

Sebastian Eissing

---

small towns or in the countryside I could easily stay in friendly police posts or with town mayors. I did not venture to the north-east where rival gangs still battle over diamond mines, keeping instead to the coast. In Luanda you could get visas for any neighbouring country without trouble. North of Luanda the coast offers some stunning beaches, especially around Mukkula. From Soyo I took the weekly ferry to the Angolan enclave of Cabinda and from there cycled on to Pointe Noire.

MADAGASCAR ON A LOCAL BIKE

Simon Hill

After six weeks of travelling around central and eastern Madagascar on public transport, I finally decided that I had had enough when, after getting up at 6am to be at the taxi brousse (minibus) station by 7am, I then had to wait three hours for the minibus to leave. As a keen touring cyclist I'd been missing my bike anyway and I realized that I could have cycled about 40km in those three hours of waiting. The frustration grew as, crammed in on one of the middle rows of seats in the van, I found even viewing the wonderful scenery was a neck-straining operation. I resolved to buy a bike immediately on my return to the capital Antananarivo (known locally as 'Tana').

Madagascar had been flooded with cheap Chinese mountain-style bikes and it seemed as if every shop in Tana was selling them. The basic specifications are all similar but the accessories, names and colours vary widely. As I wanted one for touring, I chose a bike with a luggage rack and mudguards for the princely sum of Fmg480,000 (about $77). The deal is that you buy the partly assembled bike from the shop and then have it 'finished off' for a further Fmg12,000 by one of the lads sitting around outside. You need to inspect the bike carefully although it's the assembler's job to make sure that it's all OK. I had to take mine back four times in the first hour to mend a broken chain, have the brakes properly assembled and the gears adjusted twice.

My route was to be from Tana to Tamatave on the east coast and on to Soanierana–Ivongo, a distance of about 520km. Leaving Tana presented the first problem as a combination of steep hills, heavy traffic, cobblestones and pollution make riding grim. So I took a taxi (with bike in the back) to Gare Routier Ampasampito which is located in the outskirts and right on the main road to Tamatave (the RN7). With my rucksack strapped to the luggage rack off I pedalled. The traffic for the first few kilometres was fairly heavy but this soon thinned out as the road rose and fell over some big hills. After 47km I spent the night in a grotty room at the Manja Motel in Manjakandriana.

The next day was spent cycling to Moramanga (64km), still with plenty of climbing involved but with an excellent downhill stretch following a forested river valley, passing the Mandraka Nature Reserve. There then followed a very steep descent over the edge of an escarpment, before the track flattened out for the next 35km into Moramanga. Unfortunately at this point the bike's rear derailleur fell apart. Unable to mend it, I got a lift into Moramanga where it was fixed for Fmg10,000. Although the bike was now going again, I also decided to get a new chain as the repair to the original one left it a bit short and it sometimes jammed when changing gear. Buying and having this fitted, plus adjusting the wheel bearings, cost the grand sum of Fmg15,000, a couple of bucks.

I really liked Moramanga. There's a good choice of hotels and restaurants and an excellent market but after two days it was time to leave. The road to Andasibe also has its share of uphills but it was only 28km. This proved too much for the bike as the bottom bracket (crank) seized up halfway there. I managed to free it and when it was stripped down later the reason was obvious: no grease had been used when assembling it. There is a very popular national park in Andasibe with plenty of tourist facilities for the weary cyclist and so it was well worth a couple of days' stay to view the forest and wildlife.

One thing I've learned as a touring cyclist is not to trust information from local residents as most of them have never travelled more than a few kilometres from their home. Such was the case when I left Andasibe where everyone assured me that there was nowhere to stay before Brickaville, a mere 112km away. Fortunately they were wrong and I found some very basic bungalows in Manambonita after only 80km of hard up-and-down cycling. This was the end of the Central Highlands and in theory the 160km I'd just ridden should have been easy as Tana is at 1600m and I was heading for the coast. In practice far more time is spent climbing because the road crosses innumerable ridges and valleys.

The 32km ride to Brickaville was a pleasant early morning stroll after the exertions of the hills. Brickaville is a basic town with no tourists but with a great market, food and bike-repair shop where I had a full service for another Fmg15,000. The bike had done only 100km since the last service but because of the very low quality of the components the bearings needed to be tightened and regreased and everything else adjusted. Here I discovered that the headset had also been assembled with no grease. Although I carried enough tools to do minor repairs it wasn't worth kitting myself out for every eventuality as it was so cheap and much easier to use the local service. As preventive maintenance is unheard of in Madagascar I would be met with amazement when I asked them to have something done to my bike which was already in far better condition than any of the local ones. One reason is that the locals never ride long distances. They couldn't believe that I had ridden the 200km from Tana and was up for another 300.

Brickaville to Tamatave is 105km, fairly hilly and, apart from some basic bungalows 13km from the end, there is nowhere else to stay, making it a long hard day. From Tamatave, though, the ride is much easier, following the coast and numerous beachside accommodation options along the way. I then took the boat to Ile Sainte Marie, paying Fmg10,00 for the bike. The total distance from Tana was about 520km, the road was in very good condition, traffic light and the ride very enjoyable; I can thoroughly recommend it.

Once on Ile Sainte Marie, I found having my own bike a real advantage. Bike hire is about Fmg30,000 per day and foreigners pay four times the local fare for taxi brousses. Having a bike meant that apart from touring the island, I could also ride into town for cheap breakfasts and shopping, which allowed me to save up to 60% on hotel bottled-water prices.

Not wanting to take the bike home, I approached a number of bike-rental places who expressed an interest in buying it; however, in the end I sold it to an Austrian traveller for Fmg350,000. Over the five weeks I owned the bike, I reckon that I spent a further Fmg100,000 on servicing, spares and repairs, so all in all the bike cost me about US$40 – well worth it.

BYO and some tips

If you are thinking of doing any serious cycling in Madagascar, bring your own bike as the local ones are of very poor quality and don't come in large sizes. However, if it's your only option, don't let my story put you off as buying a bike is cheap. In any case it's much better to be with a bike than without.

If you do decide to buy, here are a few tips. Go for a standard mountain-style bike (these are virtually the only bikes for sale in Madagascar now), preferably with luggage rack and mudguards. A rear-view mirror is a useful addition. Avoid state-of-the-art features such as suspension or V-brakes as they are very poor quality, potentially dangerous and spares will be impossible to get in out-of-the-way places. Even if the bike is brand new, get it thoroughly serviced as soon as possible and that includes all the bearings. Buy enough tools to mend punctures and do basic repairs and check daily that all nuts, bolts, screws, etc are tight. Remember that on long descents the brakes are inadequate so keep your speed down. Don't wear your rucksack as this makes you very unstable; strap it on the luggage rack. These bikes are not strong enough for serious off-road use, particularly if you are carrying luggage. When you buy a local bike, always expect the worst and you won't be far wrong.

TRIP REPORT
ROUND THE WORLD

Name	Alastair Humphreys
Year of birth	1976
Occupation	Cycling round world (www.roundtheworldbybike.com)
Nationality	British
Other bike travels	Karakoram Hwy, Mexico to Panama, Istanbul to Rome, Buenos Aires to Lima, Land's End to Jo'G
This trip	UK to Istanbul, through Middle East, Cairo to Cape Town, Patagonia to Alaska, Russia through Siberia, Japan, China, Central Asia to Europe and UK
Trip duration	Four years, three months
Number in group	One
Total distance	73,600km (46,000 miles)
Cost of trip	£7000
Longest day	240km
Best day	Cycling to Petra on Christmas day
Worst days	(1) Stone throwing and abuse almost led me to quit in Ethiopia (2) Sleeping in a tent at -40°C, Russia
Favourite rides	Jordan, Sudan, Lesotho, Chilean Patagonia, Alaska, Japan, Kyrgyzstan
Biggest headaches	Punctures ad nauseam, visas for ex-USSR countries
Couldn't do without	Discman, travel poetry book, book of inspirational quotes, sketch book, small square of foam to sit on
Pleasant surprise	Realizing that (1) I wouldn't be shot in Sudan and (2) that I was actually going to enjoy Sudan
Any illness	Decided I would eat and drink anything and ride my luck, and I was fine. Only ill one night.
Bike model	Specialized Rockhopper
New/used	New
Modifications	Blackburn racks – but they snapped!
Tyres used	Schwalbe Marathon XR
Baggage Setup	Two big back panniers, two front panniers, dry bag on top of rack, granny basket
Wish you'd brought	Puncture proof tubes, SW radio, girlfriend
Wish you hadn't brought	So many clothes
Bike problems	Snapped frame, three snapped wheels, no gears from Malawi to Cape Town (except by changing gear with a spoon), no brakes, snapped Blackburn racks (mended with string & spoon), 6 sets of tyres, lots of punctures and Mavic spokes that always broke
Same bike again	Very happy with steel-framed Rockhopper and Brooks saddle
General tip	England to Cape Town worked out at exactly 50km a day if I included restdays. A good benchmark?
Road philosophy	If you were to die right now how would you feel about your life? Don't succumb to temptation and take that bus! It doesn't have to be fun to be fun.

Europe en vélo – 1929

In 1929 air travel was almost non-existent and only the wealthiest Americans and Europeans continued to cross the Pond in the great Cunarders, the luxury liners, as the first part of their Grand Tour of Europe. Some students did take the equivalent of a gap year, however, the more enterprising and less rich working their passage as did **Jean Bell** *who kept a diary of his travels.*

21 May 1929 – Shoving off
Clad in cap and gown, my friend Amos Culbert and I joined our classmates last Wednesday in Faculty Glade and marched to the stadium where we were awarded diplomas with the degree of Bachelor of Arts by the President of the University of California. Today we sailed through the Golden Gate as members of the crew of the American Hawaiian Steamship Company freighter, *California*, outbound for New York via the Panama Canal. My BA is reversed to AB (Able Bodied Seaman); Amos's rank is Mess Boy.

24 June 1929 – Across the Atlantic
We've set sail from New York aboard the *MS Josiah Macy*, an oil tanker flying the Danzig Free State ensign and, for this trip, under charter to the Standard Oil Company of New Jersey to pick up in Venezuela a cargo of crude oil destined for Antwerp, Belgium.

8 July 1929 – Arrival in Antwerp
We seem to have taken an extremely long time getting here but the seaman's pay which got us to Europe puts us quite a bit ahead of the game financially; the voyage finally ended, the crew paid off.

We stand alone on a dock in Antwerp in the late afternoon and are not quite sure what to do next. Obviously we must get into town, find a room, get something to eat. A street car is sitting empty in the street, apparently at the end of its line. Amos looks at me. I'm the one who took French lessons at U.C. So...! I pick up my bag and approach the trolley. The conductor is watching me with curiosity. 'Pardon, Monsieur,' I gulp, 'Nous voulons aller au centre de la ville.' He stared, then smiled brightly and reached for my bag: 'No problem, mate, this trolley will take you there.'

Deposited in downtown Antwerp, our next goal is to find a place to sleep. This, to me, poses no problem. I have spotted a number of windows in which a small sign is tucked which reads 'Chambre à louer.' I am pleased that my French vocabulary is up to this translation.

We knock at one house. Monsieur le Propriétaire opens the door. 'Oui?' He looks us over with a puzzled frown; I explain haltingly, 'Pardon Monsieur, nous avons besoin d'une chambre pour la nuit.'

A very long pause followed by a deluge of incomprehensible French which I fail to understand. Fortunately, the patron is very patient and eventually light dawns: his chambre is for rent day or night but only by the hour! It is available for almost anything but sleeping. I could see him thinking, 'Why not? A few easy francs.' Without haggling

Our first nights in Europe are spent in a brothel – asleep

I accept his price so our first nights in Europe are spent in a brothel – asleep.

9 July 1929 – Buying bicycles

Tired as I am after our journey I find it difficult to drop off. Everything is so quiet. On a freighter (or tanker), the crew's quarters usually are located as far aft as possible. The steering engine is directly overhead and it is active every minute of the voyage day **and** night. We'd got used to it. So Amos and I are up with the birds and become very early patrons of the ever-present pâtisserie 'just around the corner.'

After breakfast, we set out in search of a bicycle shop. The call of the open road is strong and we're anxious to be on our way, really to begin our vagabonding abroad. Judging by the bicycle traffic we are seeing at this early hour, we should have no difficulty finding one but buying those bikes proved to be one of the most hectic linguistic trials we were to encounter in all of our travels.

Within the first three or four blocks we have turned up a choice of several very nice-looking bike shops. Through their big, glass-front window, we examine the bikes carefully. We like them all, but Amos and I agree that the Rijwielen & Triporteurs offering, 'The Golden Lion', seems the most attractive. We note the address: Lange Beeldeenstraaat, 106 and plan to return at 8:30 when the shop advertises that it will be open for business.

At first glance, these Belgian bicycles look just like our bikes back home. Two wheels, two pedals, one chain, one seat, all that a cyclist needs for around-town riding; our plans for making a long-distance ride, however,

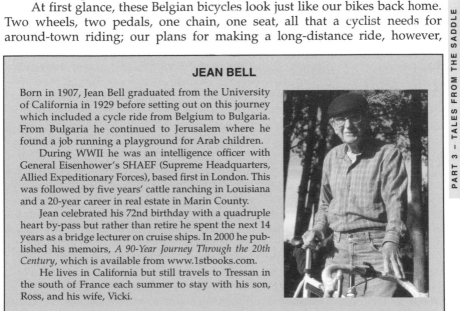

JEAN BELL

Born in 1907, Jean Bell graduated from the University of California in 1929 before setting out on this journey which included a cycle ride from Belgium to Bulgaria. From Bulgaria he continued to Jerusalem where he found a job running a playground for Arab children.

During WWII he was an intelligence officer with General Eisenhower's SHAEF (Supreme Headquarters, Allied Expeditionary Forces), based first in London. This was followed by five years' cattle ranching in Louisiana and a 20-year career in real estate in Marin County.

Jean celebrated his 72nd birthday with a quadruple heart by-pass but rather than retire he spent the next 14 years as a bridge lecturer on cruise ships. In 2000 he published his memoirs, *A 90-Year Journey Through the 20th Century*, which is available from www.1stbooks.com.

He lives in California but still travels to Tressan in the south of France each summer to stay with his son, Ross, and his wife, Vicki.

PART 3 – TALES FROM THE SADDLE

Brakes on these bikes consisted of a lever mounted on the handlebar which, when squeezed, activated a pad on the front wheel which served to slow down progress ... more or less.

require a luggage rack. We also would like to have a coaster brake and a tool kit which will permit us to make emergency roadside repairs. Obviously there is a need to upgrade our vélos for long-distance traveling. The salesman calls in the mechanic and we explain why we need a rack. We will probably be cycling to Paris, we tell them. Their eyes pop open when we mention Paris as a possible destination. The mechanic nods, 'Oui. C'est possible.' With a rack mounted over the rear wheel we now have a place to lash our 'carry-on' luggage. I use quotes to emphasize those two words. In 1929 the phrase had not yet been coined, let alone airplanes developed to accept such paraphernalia.

Our next request. 'Can you install coaster brakes?' Here we foul out. What in the world is the French for 'coaster brake?' That took some doing; I'm not sure that we ever really got through but eventually we drew a 'Pas possible,' followed by a vigorous shake of the head. We gather from his response that this technology apparently has not yet crossed the Atlantic from west to east. With the sale of two bicycles at stake, I am sure they would have willingly complied with our request had such brakes been on the Belgian market. Brakes on these bikes consisted of a lever mounted on the handlebar which, when squeezed, activated a pad on the front wheel which served to slow down progress ... more or less. But the lack of coaster brakes, at that moment at least, did not seem worth wrestling for, so we skip to our next request: single tires.

A word of explanation at this juncture in our negotiations may simplify the problem for the reader who never has had a paper route. As a ten-year-old paper boy my bike had two tires, one in front and one at the back. There was no inner tube. After mounting a tire on the rim, you simply squeezed a container of 'Never Leak' into the casing. This provided very effective puncture control. During all the time I had a paper route, I never took either tire off its rim.

There was no inner tube. After mounting a tire on the rim, you simply squeezed a container of 'Never Leak' into the casing.

What the Belgian bike offers is a tire **and** an inner tube on each wheel. When you get a puncture with this set-up, prepare to remove the wheel from the frame, take the tube out of the casing, repair the puncture and then put it all back together again. A ten-year-old newsboy can quickly convince you which system of puncture control is preferable.

Well, 'win some, lose some'. We would get the rack but struck out everything else. And, oh yes, the price. Would you believe it, their grand total selling price per bicycle,was 1100.25 Belgian francs ... the equivalent of US$25, all of which we recaptured when we sold them in Bulgaria some four months later.

I don't know why the rims on the wheels of my bike are wooden; Amos's rims are metal. Some thousand miles later, the significance of this difference will become clear.

The rims on the wheels of my bike are wooden; Amos's rims are metal. Some thousand miles later the significance of this difference will become clear.

Weight and simplicity are significant factors in long-distance cruising. Our plans for the road are to wear blue jeans, blue work shirts and tennis shoes. Our baggage includes changes of shirt, underwear, socks and pyjamas, also a blue-knit 'UC' sweater. Add maps, camera and film, a water bottle ... the list grows with astonishing speed.

Ah yes, let me not forget to mention the $300 letter of credit Mom had tucked away with my passport and seaman's papers. Incidentally, this map mentioned above, is a Rand McNally pocket map of Europe and the Near East which I had bought in a New York drug store. This funny little map guided us all the way across Bulgaria and, eventually, to Jerusalem.

One might ask, 'What did you do about your good clothes?' (Translate that to 'city' clothes). I think that we came up with a very ingenious solution. When moving from one major metropolis to the next, we simply pack our 'city' clothes in our one suitcase, take it to the Bureau de Poste and mail it to ourselves care of General Delivery, Brussels (or Paris or wherever.) This became standard operating procedure.

The real high spot of our days in Antwerp centered around the old Gothic cathedral of Nôtre-Dame with its spire towering above the crooked little cobblestone streets. Down one of the dustiest of these we tramped guided by the tower which is visible in almost every quarter of the city. In fact, the guide book says the tower can be seen by people in Brussels 30 miles away. Nôtre Dame is old and brown and gothic, friendly in its huge way, rubbing shoulders with little shops and overlooking the ocean-going vessels docked in the Scheldt River in its front yard.

At this point, our itinerary is surprisingly vague. We plan to leave Antwerp heading north to the Netherlands and after several days practising (cobblestones were in use long before bicycles were invented), visiting the cathedral and acquainting ourselves with Belgian beer, we felt ready to take off. Our plan is to bike north into Holland, then swing east and south again to reach Brussels.

Amos on his new Golden Lion bicycle, in Belgium

When moving from one major metropolis to the next, we simply posted our city clothes on to await our arrival.

11 July 1929 – off to Holland

Our first morning on the road is a dismal affair ... fog, heavy mist and light rain ... in the summer time? Shades of California weather. When we left California, we had no thought of rain in the summer. We cross the border just before noon. School is out for lunch and the clatter of wooden shoes is deafening.

This first day out we reach Dordrecht. It is all the storybooks tell about a Dutch town. Having found sleeping accommodation, Amos and I go out front to the street. I cross to the other side and touch the building opposite. Holding both arms out sidewise to my body, and with Amos doing the same on his side of the street, we find that we make a human link completely across the street. Talk about a tight fit! Imagine trying to drive an American-size car on such a narrow street.

12 July 1929 – Sunday traffic

The next morning's ride is a tourist's delight. We bypass Rotterdam but spend time enjoying Delft. It is Sunday and beyond Delft we whirl into a tangled stream of bell-ringing bicycles bound for the beaches. Everyone rides a bike in Holland, even mother and father. If baby is small he is carried under one arm or placed in a basket on the front handlebars. And the young couples out for the day – how they do that on their bikes without landing in the canal I do not know! By late afternoon we find ourselves trapped in heavy bicycle traffic hurrying home after a day at the sea shore. How Amos and I escape a collision with the speeding mass I will never understand. Moving handlebar to handlebar about six riders abreast, we form a formidable stream of traffic. And the noise! Every bicycle seems to be equipped with a bell.

We meet some boy scouts and they question us about our country: 'Are New York skyscrapers really fifty storeys high?' 'Is your friend a cowboy?' 'What means your jazz song, "There ain't no sense in sitting on the fence"? Perhaps it will cost him nothing to sit there on the fence?'!

13 July 1929 – Amsterdam

I have one major goal in Amsterdam: to see the Rijksmuseum and that famous painting by Rembrandt, *The Night Watch*. All by itself the sight of this memorable canvas pays off the time and effort of getting there. That accomplished I enjoy standing on one of the little bridges over a canal watching all the boats go by.

We decide to make an effort to end each day in a small town ... the smaller the better for a number of reasons: 1. The prices are more subject to bargaining. 2. The prices are usually lower. 3. Probably most important, your host is not so busy with other guests and an evening with him around the fire is a heart-warming experience. Some of our most interesting nights have been spent with the host and his wife. Their questions are exceedingly interesting and, hopefully, ours are too. Perhaps the best advice a traveler gets is 'Avoid stopping in big cities.'

> **Perhaps the best advice a traveler gets is 'Avoid stopping in big cities.'**

14-15 July 1929

Our first night out of Amsterdam, we reach Volendam. If you have read *Hans Brinker and the Silver Skates*, think Volendam. It is a Dutch town in every sense of the word. The dress of both men and women is pure Dutch. The houses, as in so many Dutch towns, are jammed together. The streets are narrow and paved with cobblestone. The smell of the sea is everywhere.

On the ride next day to Hoorn there are many delays as bridges are raised for tall-masted ships. There's also a delay for some ducklings that have fallen into a lock. The mama duck makes a great fuss as she runs back and forth on the top of the lock. A string of barges is held up as the ducklings are rescued.

So much for Holland. We have a long ride ahead of us to Brussels. Two days of rather strenuous pedaling land us in Leuven, just north of Brussels.

22-23 July 1929 – the Somme

West of Brussels are two very, very old cities, Ghent and Bruges. Of the two, I vote for Bruges with its bright and very colorful cathedral and interesting canals. We continue south, a long, long bike ride to the River Somme. We pass a great many large cemeteries. Even after all the years since WWI damaged cities still seem to be everywhere. Amiens, on the River Somme, was the scene of some of the war's bloodiest conflicts. But its chalk-white cathedral comes as a surprise. In contrast to so many cathedrals built in the Gothic style of the times, the edifice is white both inside and out.

23 July 1929

Noontime found us, like Goldilocks, lost in the woods outside Amiens. We were hungry, very hungry. Eventually we reached a promising peasant dwelling. An old lady in a black apron and white lace cap was feeding the chickens as we drew near. We told her we were hungry and wonder if she could sell us something to eat. What is outstanding in my memory of these strangers whom we approached with requests for favors such as this was their almost universal smiling and obliging aquiescence. Wiping her hands she said lunch had finished but if the messieurs would care to wait? We would! And while she podded peas and peeled potatoes for our three-course lunch we sat in her kitchen, spoke bad French and told her of our travels and of America. What a lunch! The little old lady fluttered

> **What is outstanding in my memory of these strangers whom we approached with requests for favors such as this was their almost universal smiling and obliging aquiescence.**

about, anxious that everything please us. When we left, we gave her 14 francs and she waved us on our way with a cheerful 'Bon voyage'.

With such experiences are the scrapbooks of vagabonds filled. Nothing stereotyped, nothing pre-arranged by a travel agency, nothing staged for its effect on tourist pocketbooks. Only a desire to please, a warm glow of friendship which steps across barriers of race and language. Such are the true joys of wandering.

Nothing stereotyped, nothing pre-arranged by a travel agency, nothing staged for its effect on tourist pocketbooks.

We pass the plain of the Somme and after some strenuous biking reach the River Seine and Rouen. We visit the cathedral and, with bowed heads, stand at the spot where Joan of Arc was burned at the stake.

25-28 July 1929

At Mont-St-Michel our bike meters register 1486 kilometers (991 miles) for the three weeks from Antwerp: an average of 50 miles a day biking time without a real rest since we had set out. No wonder we're tired and declare a moratorium on biking and dirty clothes! Our auberge proprietess is shown our pile of laundry. It will be ready tomorrow; imagine our pleasure to find that starching and ironing are *compris*. To think that American tourists go abroad and return home complaining bitterly about foreign service!

We continue south, our objective the Loire River. Crossing Brittany we pull up to a small inn hoping for dinner and a night's sleep. A very attractive hostess quizzes us while we eat her scrambled eggs. Her eyes light up when she finds that we are American. After a cognac and considerable conversation, it becomes apparent that she is ' interested.' Not professionally, but obviously it has been a long time since an American has graced her bed. She clarifies the situation: 'Pas deux hommes'. She reaches into a pocket for a coin. She looks at me 'Que dis-tu?' Things are happening faster than I am used to. 'Heads', I call. I lose. Taking Amos's hand she turns as she heads for the door. I have never forgotten her words: 'Quand tu veux quelque chose, demandez à son nom'. I had a lonely night in which to make the translation: 'When you want something, ask for it by name.'

The Loire is a beautiful area, the playground for the kings of France. One of my greatest pleasures here is to reach Chenonceaux, and we see the remains of the castle from which Joan of Arc departed on her ill-fated quest for God and Country. We find, most unexpectedly, the grave of Leonardo da Vinci (so far from home) and we see an inscription on a window pane by François I which reads, (I translate) 'Woman is fickle and foolish is he who trusts her.'

30 July-5 Aug 1929 – Paris

Paris is everything one expects including its prices which stretch our purse to its limits. But we resisted the concern about our dwindling supply of cash. We eat cheaply on the Left Bank of the Seine to save for tickets to see *Carmen*, a night at the Follies, the Eiffel Tower, Napoleon's Tomb and, of course, The Louvre. My memory of Paris is that my feet never touched the ground. I am sure that Amos and I were walking on air. My most poignant memory of Paris? Perhaps, if I had only one choice, it would be to stand at the foot of a broad staircase at the Louvre and find myself face to face with that incredible statue, the *Winged Victory of Samothrace*.

We leave Paris with regret. But so much still lies ahead. Our next objective is the Rhine River. Our selected route passes through Rheims, Verdun, Nancy and then to Strasbourg on the Rhine River with Germany waiting for us just across a bridge.

The World War has been over for barely eleven years. We have grown up reading newspapers about the 'Huns'. When we reached the Cathedral at Rheims we saw clearly the damage inflicted by German gunfire. We saw the damaged cities. We remembered the gold stars on flags in so many windows at

Rush hour 1929 in a town in northern France

home. I do not think that either Amos or I was fully prepared for what we saw.

8-15 August 1929 – Germany

We cross the River Rhine on a short bridge linking France with Germany. Strasbourg is a very busy port for river barges which are towed up and down this busy waterway. We worked our way down to Bonn as crew on several of these barges and in the evenings got free lessons playing cards with the German crew. We disembarked in Bonn, having made a detour of about 150 miles back towards our starting point in Antwerp.

16-28 September 1929 – Austria

What a lot of ground for two college boys to have covered in approximately two months!! Belgium, Holland, France, Germany! And now we are preparing to head south towards Vienna and the Alps. Then probably down the Rhône River valley to Marseilles and home. Consider that all this travel began only two days after we received our diplomas. I wonder what we would have thought if we had known in advance what really was going to happen? One thing about Amos and me, we are more than willing to 'dream big'.

You would think that Switzerland with all its mighty mountains would have been a bigger draw but from Bonn we will head back up the Rhine to Frankfurt, on to Nuremberg, down to Munich and on to Salzburg. I am glad to have seen Salzburg: it helped me appreciate *The Sound of Music*.

29 Sept-2 Oct 1929 – Vienna

I knew absolutely nothing about Vienna as far as its history, its geography or its architecture are concerned, but I had been exposed to the beautiful *Blue*

Danube and to Strauss's lovely waltzes. Our first night 'in town' we attended the opera. I forgot to write down what it was but it was a horribly hot night and all the swells up in their boxes took their dress coats off.

Two days later, with a cup of café crême, Amos picked up a copy of a morning newspaper and idly started thumbing through it.

'Oh! Oh!' he muttered. 'Aren't the McCowans there?'

'Where?' I asked, not particularly interested.

'Jerusalem.'

'Yeah, Beatrice and John are there with their folks. Dr McCowan is head of the American School for Oriental Research. What's up?'

'This piece' he waved the newspaper in his hand, 'says there is a strike going on between the Arabs and the Jews.'

I am still flippant. 'That's great. Let's go see them. You can see Beatrice and John. I'll go see the strike.' And this desultory conversation actually ended up with our setting off for Jerusalem.

With great good luck we manage to buy deck passage on the last river boat to leave Vienna for the year. We have deck passage for a five-day trip down the Danube. We will disembark at the last port of call in Bulgaria. The sailing date is my 22nd birthday, 2 October 1929. Our only map is the Rand-McNally pocket map of Europe and the Near East which I had casually bought in that New York drug store. (I still have it, a happy reminder).

7-14 Oct – Bulgaria

We disembark at the 'city' of Russe, last port of call before our river boat ties up for the winter across the Danube in Romania. We are prepared to encounter a new language but caught completely off guard to find out that a new alphabet adds to our confusion. Cyrillic script is strange to Westerners' eyes. How does one read a menu or a road sign? In Russe we find no paved streets, no high-rise office building, no street cars. Somehow we find a place to sleep. And we are served dinner after invading the kitchen and pointing to the items we wish to try! For the first time in our lives, we hear the muezzin call to prayer.

After breakfast the next morning, we make a quick tour of the 'city'. In the distance we can see a blue ridge of mountains. We know that we will have to cross them eventually and, with some foreboding, take the first (and only) road out of town leading south. Later that morning at an outdoor market I purchase an Astrakhan cap of black lamb's wool (This cap is still resting on a shelf in my closet, having served time as unusual headgear for formal occasions in San Francisco).

We had expected to find paved roads. We did! They were paved with a six-inch layer of yellow dust which concealed both rocks and dust.

We expect to reach Svilengrad in three days. The map shows a 'very good road' most of the way. Seven days later we drag into Svilengrad cussing all Bulgarian road maps. We expected to find paved roads. We did! They were paved with a six-inch layer of yellow dust which concealed both rocks and dust.

Our road leads away from the river towards Varna, up over the brown hills into the blazing sun. We push our bikes for an hour, choking in the dust raised by overstuffed carts loaded with curious peasants, crying babies, nondescript bundles; carts drawn by buffalos, cows or donkeys, yoked in all sorts of helter-skelter teams. The wagons are rickety affairs with wobbly wheels and luridly painted red and yellow sides. Always, several dogs trot behind.

Bicycling is evidently not the accepted mode of transport over lonely Bulgarian roads. We nearly cause a runaway or a smash-up each time we meet or pass an animal-drawn vehicle. The beasts shy into the ditch or climb the bank as their frantic drivers shout strange oaths and jerk helplessly at the reins. Even the dogs slink under the wagons as we pass.

By mid-afternoon we have reached the foothills and begin what promises to be a long, steep climb. Suddenly there is a very loud bang and I find myself sprawling over the handlebars into the gravel. My wooden rim has shattered when my tire exploded and the inner tube is tangled in the chain. So ... here is our very first accident in all those long miles from Antwerp.

> **Suddenly there is a very loud bang and I find myself sprawling in the gravel. My wooden rim has shattered ...**

Amos rushes to my rescue, examines me for anything broken and gets me up on my feet. What a mess! To say that I am shaken up puts it **very** mildly.

Have you ever tried pushing a loaded bicycle backwards **and** on one wheel? It seems that I have been pushing forever when we finally reach the small village of Razgrad. We eat our first meal since dining on bread and sausage the night before. That accomplished, we show the waiter our bike. He is all smiles and indicates that we should follow him. About a block up the street we come upon a bicycle shop. To our great surprise we are greeted in very passable English. Here, in the middle of the Balkan Mountains, we have found a bike shop owner who had put in some 15 years as a waiter in Chicago and only recently returned home to retire.

Our needs do not faze him. 'Of course I can get you a new wheel'. He will phone in the order and we should be ready to roll in two days. 'Two days?' I am very dubious. I had seen no phone lines; nor had we encountered either a UPS or Fed Ex van on the road.

With two days to kill we busy ourselves getting acquainted with this tiny Bulgarian village. Apparently our arrival's timing could not have been better. They are in the middle of pressing grapes and the young girls in town are 'tramping out the vintage.' We sample the results of their handi-

Crossing the Maritza River on a series of plank bridges

(foot?) work and find it meets our needs most adequately; fresh roasted lamb was on the restaurant menu that night. Oh boy! Did we ever live it up in this tiny village.

Believe it or not, my damaged wheel is replaced and I am as good as new (I refer to the bike and not to my body.) We bid goodbye to all our friends (by this time it seems that we have become old friends with everybody in the village) and after some three hours of steep hill climbing, we reach the pass. Some three thousand feet below lies a broad valley through which the Maritza River flows gently, reminiscent of the Los Angeles River in late summer time.

We make a long and very careful coast down the south slope to the valley floor. We are still riding after the sun set. A half-moon low in the west gives us enough light to ride by. Often we pass campfires partly blotted out by the black figures of men sitting around them. Dimly we can see the animals and wagons. Fierce dogs rush out, barking furiously, snapping at our heels but clever enough to dodge our kicks. We carry stones to keep them at a distance. At midnight it is too dark to go on so we lay down by the roadside.

The road closely follows a train track, which leads us to Svilengrad on the Greek frontier. However, what had started out as a bright sunny day has developed into a very wet rainstorm. Our dirt road is a mud puddle and we end up riding bumpety-bump down the railroad track wet, cold and very muddy finally reaching Svilengrad in the very late afternoon.

Over dinner that night we make several strategic decisions:
1. Amos is committed to entering law school and time, for him, is running out.
2. I have no wish to tackle a bike ride all alone across the Middle East.
3. We have investigated Third Class train fares and found that the cost is barely more than walking. So we sell our bikes (for 2500 leva, quite a bit more than we had paid for them new in Antwerp) and, just after midnight, we board the Orient Express as it passes through Svilengrad bound for Istanbul.

Here our biking adventure ends and so I leave you standing on the railroad tracks watching our train's lights disappearing into the night. After a stay in Jerusalem I returned home via Egypt. My nine-month trip around Europe, Asia and Africa cost a total of $265.67, almost all of which I managed to cover in various jobs along the way. Not as tourists, or statesmen, or students but as *wandervogel* we 'did' the Old World on a minimum of cash and a maximum of exuberance.

A 90-Year Journey Through the 20th Century by Jean Bell is available from www.1stbooks.com.

PART 3 – TALES FROM THE SADDLE

By the Great Pyramid at Giza

The Colonel's Trousers

Between February 2004 and January 2005 **Edward Genochio** *cycled 20,500km (13,000 miles) from Exeter to Hong Kong. His route ran via Russia where he foiled an attempted mugging and crossed swamps infested with giant horseflies in Siberia but it was near the Russian-Kazakh border that the following incident occurred.*

I t's the best feeling you get on a bike. The wind is on your back and you're flying down a hard-packed dirt road. You haven't seen a car all day. Your wheels are spitting kilometres out the back, and the world feels good.

Out of nowhere, a car horn blasts me. Russian drivers are generally pretty friendly and like to offer a bit of encouragement to stray cyclists. I glance over my shoulder and see a battered maroon Lada kicking up dust behind me; I think the driver is waving. I wave back, smile, and, since the blood is pumping this morning, kick the pedals a little harder. It is that kind of day – I feel good enough to give a Lada a good run for its money.

> **It is that kind of day – I feel good enough to give a Lada a good run for its money.**

I hit thirty, maybe thirty-five kilometres per hour. It feels fast, exhilarating, on my heavily laden tourer. The steppe blurs on either side as I burn down the middle of the track. The Lada revs harder to keep up, and the driver raps out a rhythm on his horn. I wave over my shoulder and give him the thumbs-up, not looking back.

The engine sound gets closer and soon the car pulls alongside, two wheels up on the grass. The driver hoots and his passenger waves. I smile and wave back, easing over to the right to give him space to get four wheels on the track.

The waving doesn't look quite right. The window comes down and it's definitely more a flagging than a waving; in any case, he's starting to squeeze me up against the right bank. 'Tormoziy', the passenger orders me. ('Stop.')

EDWARD GENOCHIO

Born in Belgium, Edward Genochio read archaeology, anthropology and geography at Cambridge, graduating with 'a lousy degree but reasonable frisbee skills'. His first major cycle expedition was this trip from England to China but he had such a good time he decided to ride home rather than fly. Supporting several charities he set out on the 25,000km return journey via Central Asia in September 2005, aiming to arrive back in Britain in November 2006. Visit his entertaining and regularly-updated website – www.2wheels.org.uk – for updates on the journey and look out for his forthcoming book: *But isn't there a Bus?*

Sandwich and champagne to celebrate his arrival in Hong Kong.
(Photo © Colin Beere)

Somehow I don't think we're racing any more. Something is wrong; these guys are going to bike-jack me. Better to stop than risk being run off the road at speed; I hit the brakes.

I've got my feet on the ground, straddling my bike, waiting for what's coming and running through in my mind how I'm going to get out of here once I've been relieved of my money, passport, and bike. The passenger gets out of the car, followed by another taller man, dark and moustachioed, who has been in the back behind tinted windows. The tall man shuffles towards me. His boots don't seem to fit.

'Federalnaya pogranichnaya sluzhba,' he announces, while placing on his head a high-peaked cap, the sort that goose-stepping guards used to wear as they drilled in Red Square – only his is battered and tatty to match his Lada. He raises his right hand to his forehead and offers me a shaky salute. 'Vashy dokumenty, pozhaluysto.' (Your documents, please.)

His cap bears the badge of the FSB, the new name for the KGB – same guys, same caps, different badges.

His cap bears the badge of the FSB, the new name for the KGB – same guys, same caps, different badges. So if this is a robbery, it is an elaborate one. I hand over my passport; he examines it, upside-down, for a while, and looks puzzled.

'Is there some problem?' I ask.

'What is your nationality?'

'British.'

'How do you mean, British?'

I begin a lengthy explanation of how I, despite having an Italian surname and being born in Belgium, came to have British citizenship.

The Man in the Cap frowns. 'Your restricted area pass?'

I do not have one. I have never heard of a restricted area pass. I don't even know that I am in a restricted area. 'I have a visa in my passport.'

The driver gets out of the car to join his friends in poring over my Russian visa. The visa is printed in Cyrillic, so at least now they can decipher my name.

'Genry,' announces the driver.

I nod. This has happened to me in Russia before. Henry is my middle name; it is rendered Genry in Russian. The Russian authorities always seem to pick on my middle name. Perhaps it is easier to pronounce than Genochio.

'Genry,' takes up the tall man, who seems to be in charge. 'Genry, we will report to our base that you are British. Please wait a moment.' He reaches into the car and gets on the radio.

'We have intercepted the man on the bicycle. He claims to be British.'

After a pause, a response crackles over the speaker. 'Please repeat. He claims to be what?'

'British.'

Another pause. 'Nonsense. Any documents?'

'Yes, a passport. British.'

'A British man on a bicycle. Does he think we are stupid? Bring him in'.

'This is ridiculous. A British man on a bicycle. Does he think we are stupid? Bring him in.'

The tall man turns to me. 'Genry. You must follow us. Your documents will be checked at the base.'

The passport goes into his pocket, and the three get back into the maroon Lada. I clip into my pedals and follow as they u-turn and drive back. Their dust trail gets in my face, so I let them get ahead a little. We're going into the wind now; I curse them loudly for spoiling a perfect day's ride.

Twenty minutes later we turn off the road into a tiny settlement: a handful of wooden cottages and a disproportionate number of telegraph poles. The car pulls up outside a compound – it is surrounded by serious-looking barbed-wire topped fencing– a world apart from the rickety efforts that mark off the vegetable plots around the cottages. The driver leans out of the window and yells. 'Open the gates, for heaven's sake. It's us. We've got the British cyclist.' The gates are opened by a soldier with a Kalashnikov round his neck. The car drives in and they beckon me to follow.

Half an hour later, I am sitting in the lieutenant's office. He explains the situation. I have entered a restricted border area without a permit and with dubious documentation, and am being held by the Border Troop division of the FSB ('formerly the KGB', he emphasizes) on suspicion of illegal entry and possible involvement with contraband, narcotics, espionage or terrorism, until my situation can be clarified. He is courteous and offers me a cup of tea and a biscuit.

'What is the name of the Queen of England?' he asks.

'Elizabeth,' I answer, doubting whether that will be enough to secure my immediate release. I think of the inside page of my passport, which is sitting on the lieutenant's desk. Her Britannic Majesty's Secretary of State Requests and requires in the Name of Her Majesty all those whom it may concern to allow the bearer to pass freely without let or hindrance...

I ponder the wisdom of drawing this to the attention of my hosts, and decide against.

Two people are brought into the room. 'Do you know these people?' asks the lieutenant. There is a man in a dirty tracksuit, mid-thirties probably, smoking nervously, and a girl, pretty in a Russian peasant kind of way, no older than twenty.

'No. I have never met them.'

'Good. They will be our witnesses.' The lieutenant passes a piece of paper under their noses, and tells them to sign it.

'Now, let me explain your rights,' says the lieutenant, turning to me. 'Under the constitution of the Russian Federation, you have the right to remain silent. You have the right not to incriminate yourself or your relatives. You have the right to speak in your own language. An interpreter will be provided by the state if you request one.'

'Good,' I say, speaking for the first time in English. 'Then I will speak in English. Do you understand English?'

'No,' says the lieutenant, in Russian.

'Then I wish to exercise my right to an interpreter,' I say, in Russian.

'There is a problem. Nobody in this village speaks English.' This does not surprise me. 'In fact, the nearest English speaker may be several hundred kilometres away. It could take several days to arrange.'

'And in the meantime?'

'In the meantime you will remain here. It might be more convenient to proceed in Russian.' A white cat slinks into the office. 'Cat,' says the lieutenant, in English, and smiles. 'Do you insist on your right to an interpreter?'

'Let's start in Russian and see how we get on.'

'Good. First we must examine your personal belongings. Then our interrogator will question you in detail.'

The examination of personal belongings began. It was about four in the afternoon. It was still underway at three the next morning, when the witnesses, who had been hauled in off the street to see fair play, were finally allowed to go home. We began with pockets, then moved on to my handlebar bag. Panniers came last.

The money part was embarrassing. I was a couple of months into a 10-month ride, and was carrying a lot of cash. I had to count it all out in front of the witnesses, who had probably never seen a dollar bill, let alone a wad of 1,237 US dollars. I expect it was worth more than they earned in a year in a depressed-looking hamlet like this. The lieutenant wrote 1,237 US dollars down on his form.

Cycling through Europe on the way to Russia, I had accumulated a wallet-full of odds-and-ends from a dozen currencies. 840 Serbian dinars, I counted out, hoping that the witnesses would realize that this really was small change, not another foreign-currency fortune. 24 Hungarian forints. 10 Moldovan bani. A quantity of Ukrainian currency whose name I had forgotten. Each passing currency seemed to deepen their suspicions about me.

Credit cards were next. A couple of bank cards were easy enough to explain, and I think a long-since-expired 'Young Person's Railcard' didn't raise too many eyebrows, but I came unstuck on a Youth Hostel Association membership card. I think it was the 'Association' part he didn't like. It sounded faintly secretive, conspiratorial, underground.

When all my valuables were accounted for and neatly listed on the lieutenant's form, I was asked to sign my name at the bottom, confirming that this was a true and complete statement of all the money I had in my possession. I signed, sat down again, and noticed I still had something in a back pocket. It turned out to be a one-forint coin, a souvenir from Hungary.

'What is that?' asked the lieutenant.

'It is a one-forint coin. A souvenir from Hungary.'

'Why did you not declare it earlier?'

'I'm sorry, I forgot about it. It was in my back pocket.'

'You declared 24 forints. In fact you had 25. We must start again.'

'Can't you just change the 24 to a 25 on your list?'

'Impossible. Crossings-out are not allowed. People will suspect something improper. We must re-write the whole list from scratch.'

'But that's ridiculous, it's only a forint, it's scarcely worth a kopek. It's only a souvenir. Here, look, I'll give it to you as a present, keep it, it will save you having to re-write the list.'

The lieutenant looked gravely at the witnesses, and then at me. 'Genry, I should remind you that bribery is considered a very serious matter in Russia. We will begin the list from scratch.'

So he wrote out the list again, this time with 1,237 dollars, 840 dinars, 10 bani, and 25 Hungarian forints to my name.

'We will now go outside, and examine your other belongings.'

The kit-check was, shall we say, thorough. It threw up a few surprises for me: I found things buried at the bottom of my panniers that I had quite forgotten about, untouched in two months on the road – an indication, if nothing else, that I had not yet perfected the art of travelling light. Watched by the witnesses, the lieutenant, the interrogator (who was warming up for the grilling I was due once the inventory-taking was over), and the bored soldier with the Kalashnikov, I went through my belongings, pannier by pannier, and item by item. The blond interrogator wrote them all down on his list.

I found a pack of envelopes in my stationery bag. 'Envelopes,' I declared.

'How many?' snarled the interrogator. The lieutenant had courtesy and had betrayed an occasional hint that he realized the absurdity of the whole process. The interrogator had neither of these charms.

I counted my envelopes. There were 22. 'Twenty-two,' I said.

'Are you sure? Count them again,' said the blond man.

I counted again. 23 this time. 'Oh, I'm sorry, twenty-three.'

'Twenty-two or twenty-three? We must be precise. Count them again!'

It came to 23 again, so I settled on that. The interrogator read out as he wrote down: 'White paper envelopes, 23, in cellophane wrapper.'

Next up was an orange plastic groundsheet. The interrogator wanted to know its dimensions, and what kind of plastic it was made of. I said I didn't know, and made him unfold it for himself if he really wanted to know. He was officious, petty, and a creep, and would have made the perfect gulag sadist in darker days.

It was now dark, a clear starry night that was becoming cold. The male witness chain smoked. The girl started to shiver in her little summer dress. The lieutenant ordered the soldier to fetch her a coat from inside the guard-house.

I had a stack of business cards from various contacts. The interrogator wrote down: 'Business cards, various. To be examined in detail later'.

Next out of the pannier (it was like playing

He was officious, petty, and a creep, and would have made the perfect gulag sadist in darker days.

He wrote down 'Fork, metal-type, with prongs, four'.

lucky dip) was a fork. 'A fork,' I said, placing it on the growing pile of stuff on the table, confident that this would be a non-controversial item.

The soldier came out of the guard-house just in time. Draping an oversized military great-coat over the girl's shoulders with exaggerated gentility, he looked at my fork and sneered, in perfect imitation of the interrogator, 'How many prongs?'

The witnesses laughed. I laughed. The lieutenant allowed himself a smile. The interrogator sat stony-faced and tried to salvage his dignity by pretending it hadn't been a joke at his expense. 'Well, answer him! How many prongs?'

'Four,' I told him, straight-faced, so he wrote down 'Fork, metal-type, with prongs, four.'

After several hours' hard work, the interrogator had perhaps the most complete listing of a cyclist's baggage ever produced. I asked him for a copy, thinking it might make a useful planning check-list for other cyclists. He told me that this investigation was not being conducted for my benefit, and that the personal interrogation would now begin.

I was taken into the guard-house and shown into his office. He had things set up properly. A bare light-bulb hung from the ceiling. He sat behind a bare desk on a big chair. I was sat in front on a little stool.

He wanted to know where I was born, what school I had attended, what subjects I had studied, what grades I had obtained, where I had worked, and the names of my employers. He wanted a list of every country I had ever visited, with dates. Everything went into his little black notebook. He wanted to know where my father was born, in what year, on what date, and where he had been to school, and what jobs he had done. He wanted to know why I was riding my bicycle along the Russian-Kazakh border – ah, a sensible question at last – and who was paying for my trip and where had I obtained my visa and whether I had been to Russia before and if so where and when and whom I had met. He wanted a country-by-country account of my bike ride so far. The lieutenant came in to observe. I told the interrogator that I had come through Moldova.

'The colonel will come down from headquarters to continue the interrogation in person in the morning'.

'Where is Moldova?' he asked, about a country that had, a dozen years before, been part of the Soviet Union. I told him that it was between Ukraine and Romania.

'So it is part of Russia, then,' he said.

The lieutenant intervened. 'Moldova is an independent republic. You should know that. I have been on the radio with the colonel. He has instruct-

ed that we allow Mr Genry a few hours' sleep. The colonel will come down from headquarters to continue the interrogation in person in the morning.'

This came as a relief; it was already 3 a.m. I was particularly pleased when the lieutenant assigned the comfortable sofa at the back of the interrogator's office to me, to the obvious annoyance of the interrogator. A soldier brought me a set of clean, freshly-starched military bedding.

The colonel arrived in the morning, demanding breakfast. He had been driven several hundred kilometres through the night on rough roads to get there, accompanied by his driver and an oleaginous side-kick whose job was to laugh at his jokes and to play the straight-man while the colonel did the funny lines in set-piece routines.

An ethnic Tajik but a Russian nationalist, the colonel was, above all, hungry. He preferred gestures and sound-effects over conventional language, and used them to reel off a string of anecdotes at which everybody present, all subordinate to him, felt obliged to laugh – led, of course, by the greasy side-kick.

The colonel invited me to join him for breakfast. The lieutenant chivvied various orderlies to knock together a platter of cheese, salami, cakes and bread, but only the colonel seemed interested in eating. I didn't feel too guilty about tucking in either. It wasn't as though I had invited myself in.

'This is interesting, really very interesting. Tell me, Genry, do you know the films of James Bond, the famous British secret agent?'

The colonel sized up the situation pretty quickly. 'So, you are an English gentleman. Riding your bicycle across Russia. This is interesting, really very interesting. Tell me, Genry, do you know the films of James Bond, the famous British secret agent?'

I nodded.

'Well,' the colonel went on in Russian, uncharacteristically free of wild gesturing and guttural sound-effects. 'My friend and I' – he indicated his side kick – 'were giving the matter some thought during our long journey to investigate your case here. And we have reached the conclusion' – he paused for dramatic effect – 'we have reached the conclusion that in none of the James Bond films does the hero use a bicycle as his preferred means of getting about. We therefore think it unlikely that you are a British spy. Besides, I received my counter-terrorism training from a British officer on secondment to Moscow, and he did not ride a bicycle either.'

The side-kick smiled. The colonel turned to the lieutenant. 'Lieutenant, your interrogator tells me that he is not convinced by Mr Genry's story. What is your opinion? Have you seen the James Bond films?'

'Yes,' said the lieutenant, adding, 'Ya Bond – Djeymz Bond', quoting the secret agent's Russianized catchphrase to back up his claim.

'And do you believe that our foreign guest here is also a secret agent? Perhaps his real name is also Bond – Genry Bond?' The colonel was smiling.

'No, I think perhaps not.'

'I am inclined to agree with you. However, we must ensure that both the sheep and the wolves are satisfied.' He turned back to me. 'Genry, in Tajikistan, we like to keep both the sheep and the wolves satisfied. In this case, you are the sheep and we are the wolves. For our part' – his face became serious – 'we should reprimand you. You were apprehended while riding your bicycle in a restricted zone near the very sensitive border between Russia and Kazakhstan. Entering this zone without a permit is an offence under the

'...punishable by a fine of not more than 5000 roubles or imprisonment for two weeks. Do you understand the gravity of your offence?'

criminal code of the Russian Federation, and is punishable by a fine of not more than 5000 roubles or imprisonment for two weeks. Do you understand the gravity of your offence?'

'I am sorry if I unwittingly broke the law,' I replied.

'Good. Now, I am reprimanding you for what you have done. That is to satisfy the wolves. However, I believe that in your case your crime does not warrant further punishment. You will not be required to pay the fine or go to prison. That is to satisfy the sheep – in other words, you. Shall we have some more breakfast?'

The blond interrogator, who had been sulking at the back of the room, sensed he was about to lose his quarry. 'Colonel, I have not yet had the opportunity to examine in detail the collection of business cards which were found among the suspect's possessions,' he whined.

'I think that can wait until after breakfast,' replied the colonel, who proceeded to polish off the last of the biscuits as he launched into a story about the time he was serving in Kamchatka. It was a clearly a familiar story to the side-kick, who knew in advance when the laugh-points were coming. The colonel was giving an explicit account of his sexual performances with the local maidens, using graphic gestures rather than words, banging his fist into his palm with mounting enthusiasm. His tea-mug was half-way to his lips when he reached a crucial climax in the story. The fist came down, the mug came down, and, as hot tea sloshed over him and his audience, his mug flew across the table, cracking a plate and sending a shower of salami onto the floor.

His mug flew across the table, cracking a plate and sending a shower of salami onto the floor.

The side-kick, the lieutenant, the interrogator scurried to mop up and restore order to the breakfast table, but the colonel didn't seem at all put out, continuing his story unperturbed as hot tea dripped into his crotch. He paused to examine a slice of salami which had landed near his shoe, and decided it was too dirty for human consumption.

'Zdes yest sobaka?' he asked, waving the salami vaguely: Do you keep a dog here?

Then, suddenly, a long-forgotten English lesson must have leapt from his memory. 'Dog!' he exclaimed, in English, beaming at me.

'Nyet,' replied the lieutenant. 'Yest koshka. Cat.'

The lieutenant smiled nervously, perhaps aware that his insertion of the English word 'cat' looked like an attempt to up-stage the colonel's 'dog' – perilously close to insubordination.

'Fifteen all,' I said. A Siberian girl had just won Wimbledon – I hoped a spot of tennis would diffuse the tension.

The colonel didn't seem to mind. He gestured to the interrogator to go and feed the salami to the cat, and resumed his breakfast.

'Do you want to know how I knew you were not a spy?' the colonel asked, munching on slab of bread and cheese. 'I will tell you. It wasn't just the bicycle. MI-5' – he pronounced it mee-5 – 'give their agents decent trousers.' He pointed to where my trousers ought to have been. I had forgotten that the morning before my arrest I had split my trousers while bending down to pack up my tent. The split must have widened as I pedalled my bike, because now, I discovered, they were completely open from crotch to knee. I had been interrogated by the KGB with my underpants blowing in the wind.

'I will make a deal with you. Unfortunately I cannot permit you to continue riding on this road. But your trouser situation is very bad. Ride back the way you came, and turn right when you reach the main road. In two or three days you will reach our headquarters. You can't miss it. It's behind a kebab shop. Call in there and ask for me personally.'

The colonel finished his breakfast; the lieutenant gave me more forms to sign, confirming that everything had been done by the book, that I confessed my crime and accepted my reprimand; the interrogator brooded in his office, sharpening pencils with a pocket-knife. Twenty-four hours after I had been

Modelling the donated FSB Border Guards jacket and trousers, accessorized with the colonel's own belt.
© Edward Genochio

picked up, I was free to go. In the dusty compound courtyard was a concrete pillar inscribed with an outline map of the country and the Border Guards' motto: 'The Borders of Russia are Sacred and Inviolable'. They let me pose for a photo in front of this totem, but, on grounds of national security, wouldn't pose themselves. Everybody (apart from the interrogator) wished me schastlivovo puti – bon voyage. The soldier with the Kalashnikov told me to take good care of my four-pronged fork.

A couple of days later, around noon, I found the colonel's kebab shop and, round the back, the FSB headquarters. The sentry told me the colonel had just gone out for lunch. I sensed I was in

The soldier with the Kalashnikov told me to take good care of my four-pronged fork.

for a long wait. At half-past four the colonel's jeep returned. The burly Tajik strode out, holding his belly, followed by his side-kick. 'Ah yes, Genry. We were expecting you,' he said, passing me a neatly-folded FSB Border Guards uniform. 'Here, try these on.'

I lugged on the jacket. It had a sleeve badge bearing the Border Guards' insignia. It was a perfect fit, but the beltless trousers were a little slack around my waist. The colonel thought for a moment, then pulled the belt from his own trousers and handed it to me. 'Don't worry, my trousers will stay up,' he said, patting his belly. 'I've had a good lunch. Oh, and just keep that uniform on at all times, and you shouldn't have any more hassle from the authorities in Russia.'

I pedalled off towards the Urals, with the wind on my back.

☆☆☆

I was only 2000 miles short of the end of my 13,000-mile bicycle journey to China when something really bad happened. I lost my bike.

In truth, I didn't exactly lose it. It was stolen from me as I slept. But this was not your ordinary cable-cutting bike theft. Plenty of cycle tourists have had their bicycles nicked, but I think I have the distinction of being the only one to have had his bike stolen by a horse.

But this was not your ordinary cable-cutting bike theft.

It was the small hours of Sunday morning. I was camped on the riverbank not far from Ulaan Baator, asleep in my tent. And then, suddenly, my tent collapsed on top of me. The sound of tearing canvas quickly gave way to the beat of galloping hooves.

My bicycle had been ripped from the tent, to which it had been locked, and dragged away by a four-legged bike thief. The galloping faded into the distance as, still half asleep, I struggled to escape the tangled remnants of my tent. I fought my way into the outside, and found myself standing in the silence and darkness of a moonless night, bikeless and alone. The evening before I had welcomed this darkness for the views it allowed of a spectacular meteorite shower. Now, I was afraid: afraid that whoever it was – assuming the horse hadn't been acting alone – would be coming back soon for the rest of my belongings. I worried especially they would get my diaries, precious to me but worthless to anyone else. Gathering my thoughts and as many of my remaining possessions as I could carry, I went to hide behind a low ridge, and waited to see if anyone would come back. A few minutes passed. Nothing; everything was still, quiet and dark, just the gentle sound of the river flowing by, a few yards from where my tent had been.

... [Reaching the road in the darkness Edward manages to find a policeman] ... After several minutes of theatrical mime, sound-effects and jumping up and down, I felt I was beginning to get the message across: I sleep (two hands under head), in tent (triangle shape in the air), man on horse (Monty Python-style coconut shell noises) steal my bicycle (rotate fists in front of chest). (Why do people always mime 'bicycle' by pedalling their hands like that? It looks more like Chinese shadow-boxing than anything to do with a bicycle).

The two uniformed men nodded, climbed into a car, and beckoned me to follow. We drove wildly across the rutted steppe, feeble headlights barely picking out the large rocks that littered our path.

'Which way?' mimed the driver.

'I've no idea,' I mimed back. 'We've been spinning so much I've lost my bearings.' I spun my finger in the air.

The driver spun the steering wheel.

'No, no, no, we have already been spinning enough, I mean. We don't need to spin any more.' It is hard to do tenses in mime – past, present and future merge.

A bang, a crunch of metal and a sudden stop announced that the car had hit a trench. The policemen climbed out to inspect the damage. I climbed out to inspect the trench – I recognized it as the one into which I had fallen and nearly broken my leg an hour or two earlier, a hundred yards from where my tent had been.

Over by the riverbank we found the remains of my tent. The policemen walked up and down, tutting. After a while, tutted out, they climbed back into the car. I wondered what clues they might have uncovered in the course of their tutting. Perhaps they would send for a forensic team to comb the scene of the crime, taking hoof-prints and collecting mane samples for DNA analysis. In any case, they remained tight-lipped.

As the first hints of dawn began to lighten the eastern sky, a jeep arrived from police headquarters. They drove me back to Ulaan Baator as I contemplated completing my bicycle journey without a bicycle.

It was August. Iraq was in the grip of violence. Thousands faced starvation in Darfur. But, for some reason, news editors liked the story about the Englishman who had his bike stolen by a Mongolian horse. The story appeared in newspapers and on television around the world. Since I had foolishly failed to arrange for TV crews to be present at the time of the robbery itself, I had to re-enact it for the cameras a few days later, in broad daylight, in what remained of my tent, on a pavement in down-town Ulaan Baator. I suppose when they got back to the studio, they mixed in some library footage of a horse galloping away with a guilty expression on his face.

Thanks to the media coverage of my plight, I quickly received not just one but five offers of replacement bikes from companies back home. Should I accept just the one and carry on with my journey? Or accept all of them and set up a bike shop in Ulaan Baator?

I was touched to receive hundreds of email messages from strangers, many of them fellow cyclists, who had heard about my predicament and wanted to sympathize. I had one very angry message from a Mongolian, who told me that his country makes the news internationally only about once a year, and that the last thing it needed was for its 2004 slot to be a story that cast Mongolians in a bad light. I felt bad about that. Let me set the record straight here. Mongolia is a beautiful country, and, with one notable exception, everyone I met there was extremely friendly and welcoming.

Losing the bike wasn't really so bad in the end. Marin sent me a nice new one. But I also lost something much harder to replace – a pair of official-issue Russian Border Guard trousers.

For details of Edward Genochio's forthcoming book, *But isn't there a Bus?*, see www.2wheels.org.uk

Nouakchott for Christmas

Between August 2004 and April 2006 **Luke Skinner** *and* **Anna Heywood** *cycled 29,169km from London to Cape Town raising money for Link Community Development, a UK-based charity working on education projects all over Africa. After 3600km of trouble-free cycling in Europe they crossed the Strait of Gibraltar to Africa for the Saharan section of their trip: 4500km from Fnideq (Morocco) to Dakar (Senegal), spending Christmas in Nouakchott in Mauritania.*

The Rock of Gibraltar is such an unmistakable feature that even the geographically challenged cannot fail to recognize it. There was no mistaking, either, that its hulking silhouette was receding rapidly as we peered rather anxiously from the upstairs lounge of the Ceuta-bound ferry. Tearing our eyes from this last European landmark, we turned to try and make out the approaching North African coastline. With 3600km of cycling and four countries already under our (somewhat tightened) belts, we were feeling pretty pleased with ourselves. Mild trepidation heightened, however, as we disembarked and headed for Fnideq, the entry point to Morocco. We had left London on 1st August, our destination was a little way off ... South Africa. The temptation to jump back on a ferry bound for Spain was suddenly very strong. What if we had bitten off more than we could chew? How would we cope with the unpaved roads, traffic, terrain, germs, not to mention the unfamiliar language, customs, religion and food? What if it was all just too hard or, perhaps worse, what if we could cope but it was just no fun? A mental procession of kicking camels, rabid dogs, hostile locals and pettifogging officials marched relentlessly through our minds as we saddled up on African soil for the first time ...

> A mental procession of kicking camels, rabid dogs, hostile locals and pettifogging officials marched relentlessly through our minds ...

Food over fear. We momentarily put worries to one side as we attempted to spend our remaining €4.49 in a supermarket – Ceuta is a tiny Spanish enclave, hence the use of the Euro. Adding up the prices of items as we went, we soon reached €3.67, but then followed a fruitless five minutes of aisle-pacing before Luke emerged triumphantly, clutching a bag of *pain au chocolat*. 'I've got it! I've got it! 82 cents' he yelled, to the understandable consternation of the staff. Exuberance turned to embarrassment when we reached the till and discovered we were somehow seven cents short! A local man shoved some coppers our way to speed things along and, muttering thanks, we beat a hasty retreat.

At the border the pettifogging officials were far too busy investigating and unpacking lorries and cars to be concerned with small fry like cycle tourists. So, our passports stamped, we sailed through the barriers and began to thread our way through the mêlée. Decrepit, bright blue Mercedes taxis filled the potholed road, bumper to bumper and three lanes deep. In between, and far down the pecking order, came wheelbarrows, donkey carts, child-porters and...cyclists. We emerged unscathed onto the coast road, however, and even saw a few camels grazing by the roadside. We didn't see another for hundreds of kilometres so suspect these are stationed here to impress upon the traveller that Europe is now far behind! After guzzling a glass of mint tea containing about three handfuls of sugar, we felt sufficiently revived to push on to Tetouan, where we stumbled into the hotel recommended in our Rough Guide.

That evening, we forayed out for a ramble in the medina and a *couscous* dinner – well, you can't expect an entirely cliché-free first day in Morocco, can you. On our return, with the sunlight streaming in through our third-floor window, and the hubbub of the cafés far below, we heaved a sigh of relief. Our first day had passed without incident and suddenly we could relax and look ahead with eager

LUKE SKINNER & ANNA HEYWOOD

Anna Heywood was born in 1980, the youngest of three sisters, and grew up in Germany and Yorkshire. She read archaeology and anthropology at Cambridge, where, among other things, she met Luke and avoided early-morning lectures by taking up rowing. Before setting off on this trip she worked at the Museum of London.

Luke Skinner was born in Wales in 1979. Graduating from Cambridge with a degree in Zoology he moved to London to work for a travel company but remains deeply patriotic, particularly when it comes to the rugby!

They kept a detailed written and photographic record of their recent trans-Africa trip on their website: www.africabybike.org.

anticipation once again. Fearing arrest by the Serious Crime Squad for illegal possession of pork in a Muslim country, Luke had gobbled his *mortadella* sandwiches with undue haste as soon as we arrived. In the process, the supermarket receipt fell to the floor and showed that we had been overcharged for the sliced meat by seven cents – the robbers! With faith in our mental arithmetic restored, we fell into an exhausted and contented sleep.

Perhaps we were a little over-the-top to worry about clandestine pork consumption, but by the end of our first week in Africa we were well aware of how seriously Moroccans take their religious duties. Unwittingly, we had arrived in the country a couple of days before Ramadan, the Muslim month of fasting, began. This, we thought, might cause problems. In the ten weeks since leaving London, we had developed our (already impressive) ability to consume a huge volume of food every day. How could we hope to cycle 1500km a month (our self-imposed target) if we had to go without food from sunrise to sunset? Mercifully, we soon found out that travellers and infidels do not have to observe the fast, so we were dually exempt.

Travellers and infidels do not have to observe the fast so we were dually exempt.

PART 3 – TALES FROM THE SADDLE

In fact, Ramadan proved to be a fantastic time to travel through Morocco. While we weren't up to a full-on fast, our attempts to get into the spirit of Ramadan were very well received. It really wasn't too hard to respect the rules even though we needed regular, and not infrequent food stops! In many ways it was a boon to be on a bike – we could stop in the middle of nowhere and sit behind a tree to eat our lunch, and invariably we would arrive in a town at dusk just as everyone was sitting down to their bowl of *harira* – a delicious, thick soup. From our appetite every evening it probably appeared that we had been fasting like good Muslims all day! We were given honey-covered pastries, dates and glasses of milk, plied with mint tea, invited to dinner, and presented with still-warm home-made bread in various towns and villages throughout the land. All through the holy month, from Fes to Khenifra to Casablanca to Marrakesh, the hospitality never wavered and calorie-starved tempers never seemed to fray. All the more amazing in the touristic towns, where insensitive visitors gobbled and smoked at any hour while tolerant Moroccans cooked, and served and observed ...

During the lengthy period of preparation that precedes a long cycle tour, you have ample opportunity to pore over maps and study that moth-eaten school atlas. Somehow, certain land borders, geographical features or latitudes stick in the mind as 'key points'. For both of us, the ferry crossings – first the Channel and then the Straits – were significant points of no return but for Anna, it was mountains. Surmounting Port D'Envalira, 2408m high and just inside Andorra, had become established in her mind as a make or break moment. Despite wobbly legs, she made it, and yet it was a similar scenario with the Tizi'n'Test pass in the High Atlas. On a frosty morning in November we left our room (hotel might be stretching it a bit) in the little village of Ijoukak and started the climb. Stands of fruit and walnut trees gave way gradually to pine as we climbed higher. Sheer rock walls rose up dauntingly on one side (and fell away even more dauntingly on the other) and patches of snow appeared on the road.

... we were on top of the world.
The descent was something else,
a white-knuckle ride that drops you 1600m in the space of just over an hour.

Despite the strenuous climb and the warm sunlight, goose pimples appeared on Anna's skin. She had been having premonitions about cliff-edge plunges and friable road surfaces giving way. It was something of a personal epiphany for her, then, when at 2.30pm we reached the pass in one piece. To have dragged yourself up a mountain by pedal power alone, wondering all the while who the hell has filled your panniers with concrete, is the most fantastic feeling. Looking across valley after valley, to the smooth, snow-blanketed peaks that form the highest points of the High Atlas range, we felt as though we were on top of the world. The descent was something else, a white-knuckle ride that drops you 1600m in the space of just over an hour. As we whizzed round the bends, we were vaguely aware of a few reddish insects overhead – feeble harbingers of the coming hordes, as it turned out ...

We met countless examples of the kindness and hospitality of the Moroccan people (and later, the people of many other countries), whether being invited into their homes, asked to share their dinner, or offered cold drinks or sweet tea as we passed through their villages. Halfway through our longest day so far, having left Goulimine early in the morning, we were again brought face to face with this genuine kindness. Anna had been startled by a dog emerging from the sandy scrub some distance from the road and giving chase. While trying simultaneously to speed up in order to escape and give the hound a blast of the 'Dog Dazer' to send it packing, she lost control of the bike, careered across the road, clipped Luke's back wheel and – well, went flying. Within minutes, by the time Luke had come to a stop and dumped his bike by the side of the road, the first helpers had arrived. The road couldn't be described as busy

> **... she lost control of the bike, clipped Luke's back wheel ... and went flying.**

– there had rarely been more than one car in sight at any time, but seeing the accident every single passing vehicle either slowed down to ask if we were OK or stopped to offer assistance. Very soon, a small group had collected Anna's bike and various débris (Dog Dazer, waterbottle and headlight were scattered across the road along with her panniers, some ripped, others intact), brought Luke's bike back and helped us to the verge. Anna, badly shaken by the experience, just wanted to be left alone, while Luke was reluctant to miss a potential lift until her condition had been established. Fortunately one of the passers-by was a pharmacist who offered tubes of painkilling gel gratefully received and some indeterminate tablets which Anna politely declined. It gradually became clear that although very sore, with cuts, grazes, and a bruised shoulder, Anna was in no immediate danger and probably needed rest more than anything; after accepting some bottled water from another Good Samaritan, we thanked everyone, turned down numerous offers of assistance, and settled quietly by the roadside to allow Anna to get over the shock. Two hours later we continued on our way, and although Anna remembers it vividly as the most painful 60 kilometres of the whole trip, made it to Tan Tan soon after dark – for a few days R&R in a welcoming hotel.

We came closer to accepting a lift a few days later. Another early start saw us leaving Tan Tan as the sun rose and heading south on the first stage of the desert crossing. Almost as soon as the reddish tint left the sky though, we began to notice a few grasshopper-type insects surrounding the few scrubby bushes lining the road. They looked like the insects we'd seen as we descended from the High Atlas a few weeks previ-

City walls, Chefchaoen, Morocco.
© Luke Skinner.

PART 3 – TALES FROM THE SADDLE

Little did we know that we'd soon be in the thick of that very plague!

ously, and we assumed that they were the remnants of the locust plagues in Mauritania which we'd heard about from home. Little did we know that we'd soon be in the thick of that very plague!

As the day went on, though, things became more obvious. The few insects by the roadside became clouds overhead, the reddish coating to the bushes became a red slush, as insects crushed by passing vehicles covered the road. Pretty soon, vehicles began stopping as they saw us – southbound vehicles to offer lifts, northbound drivers to warn us that things became worse further on. Estimates for the size of the cloud ranged from a few dozen kilometres in length to over a thousand, and the prospect of riding through the plague for days on end didn't appeal. When a Moroccan lorry driver offered to load the bikes onto his cab and take us to Laayoune, we were certainly tempted. Stubborness prevailed though, and we pressed on. And as the day went on, the plague did indeed get worse. The carpet of crushed insects on the road became thicker, the clouds in the sky became denser, and to add insult to injury a headwind picked up, reducing our speed to about 12kph and ensuring that we would be on the road for hours. As vehicles passed us, they threw up clouds of dead and half-dead insects from the road and sprayed them in our faces. In the strong wind the locusts couldn't make headway in the air, but were crawling along the ground and took flight as we approached, inevitably being blown into our bodies, and exposed arms and faces. We wrapped cloth across our mouths to avoid the horrific prospect of inadvertently eating one, and hunched down in the saddles to avoid direct hits. Around midday we stopped to have our passports checked by a group of bemused policemen who invited us into their hut to shelter and drink tea. Inside, things were better, but occasionally a locust would make it through a gap in the roof and drop onto someone's head. Before long it was time to press on.

It's hard to describe how mentally exhausting it was. By the time we reached our overnight stop shortly after dark, we'd lost count of the number of locusts we'd flicked off our bikes, panniers and ourselves. We had stopped several times to eat, but always pressed on within minutes as we couldn't stand having the insects crawling over us and our food. Equally, though, we had to stop and rest every couple of kilometres to recover from the strain of being bombarded by the hordes. By then, the

By then, the road was inches deep in dead bodies...

road was inches deep in dead bodies, and the metallic odour of crushed corpses was added to by those which had died after landing on our spokes, or been carried along the chain and crushed among the sprockets. Our clothes were spattered with red pigment, and it would take hours to remove all traces from our bikes. It truly was a disgusting experience we hope will never be repeated – yet we both agree we're somehow glad we didn't take that lift ...

Perhaps we had become unconsciously attuned to Islam by the time we reached the little nation of Guinea Bissau, with just under 9400km on the odometer. It certainly seemed like a long time since we had seen pigs – and yet here they were in abundance! Luke's thoughts turned to bacon butties, while Anna's vegetarianism precluded such daydreams. Anna's vegetarianism has, in fact, precluded quite a few things, like goat stew, mutton *tagine*, camel *brochettes*, chicken soup... In North and West Africa (not to mention Spain), a vegetarian is a phenomenon to be regarded with a mixture of disdain and pity.

A vegetarian is a phenomenon to be regarded with a mixture of disdain and pity ... 'Eh bien, vous êtes vegetal'!

More often than not restaurateurs will offer chicken, then fish, before finally accepting that these are not suitable and exclaiming in frustration, 'Eh bien, vous êtes vegetal'. It might be wise, if you are a veggie and bound for Africa, to cultivate a taste for omelettes (ubiquitous and usually deep fried), as well as an ability to turn a blind eye to chicken stock and, well, small bits of meat in 'vegetarian' dishes. Of course, on the bright side, this lack of suitable main meals gives you licence to binge on coriander and onion pancakes (Morocco), bean fritters (Senegal), sugar-encrusted doughnuts (Guinea Bissau) and fried plantain (Mali) and a myriad of other high-calorie roadside foods. Throughout the region we found cheap and delicious fruit – bananas, mangoes, papayas, apples, oranges, dates, figs and pomegranates, although our appetite for the latter waned considerably after we found one infested with tiny maggots. Extra protein for the veggie, eh? The lack of veggie fodder makes the good meals all the more memorable though. We ate delicious crudités in desert-bound Nouadhibou, found pizza from a wood oven in the highlands of Guinea, were amazed by a beautiful vegetable stew in a sleepy backwater in The Gambia and gulped down icy gazpacho in hot and dusty Segou in Mali.

Western Sahara is a vast swathe of the Sahara Desert, bordered by the Atlantic Ocean. This territory is occupied by Morocco and inland the Mauritanian border area sees heavy troop deployment, banditry and guerilla warfare. Following improve-

Excellent road despite the camels! Western Sahara.
© Luke Skinner.

PART 3 – TALES FROM THE SADDLE

ments in the security situation, we had hoped to take an inland route from Laayoune to Bir Moghrein and thence to Chinguetti, deep in the desert interior. As we arrived in Laayoune we noticed a plethora of shiny, UN 4x4 vehicles – never a good indicator of peace! Then, investigating the possibility with the Ministry of Tourism, we got the feeling no one was very keen on our planned itinerary, and we were informed that the military would certainly not issue the necessary *laissez-passer* without putting up a fight. Then a parcel from Anna's

Near Dakhla, Western Sahara.
© Luke Skinner.

sister, containing French maps of the border area, was 'lost in transit'. We thought perhaps someone was trying to tell us something. Fighting the military in a garrison town, figuratively or otherwise, didn't appeal, and so we reluctantly admitted defeat and took the coast road.

Sand to the left, ocean to the right, tarmac before and behind, we often get asked if it wasn't monotonous. Unexpectedly, maybe, our days through the Western Sahara and into Mauritania stand out as some of the best of the expedition. In the desert there are fewer distractions, the landscape is uncompromisingly vast, the merest change in the weather immediately apparent (including **rain**, yes in the Sahara), the light is somehow clearer, the air purer. We were on a major (though not always surfaced) highway the whole way so were hardly blazing a trail through a virgin dunescape, but even so water sources were infrequent and life seemed to be stripped of inessentials.

At times like this we wondered how lone cycle tourers cope with the physical and mental challenges of such an environment. A stiff headwind blew for days and we took turns to 'break wind', two pairs of hands made pitching and striking camp quicker; when one of us had a stomach bug or felt exhausted, the other took charge. It's not that we set out to test our relationship to destruction, but 1800km of desert puts most 'teambuilding exercises' into perspective.

One of the many advantages of unsupported cycle touring is that you realize how little you really need to survive. By Day 130 (our journal was starting to read a little like a Big Brother log book) we had given up on shampoo and shower-gel, deciding that we might as well simplify things a little. Soap

It's strangely comforting to hear the words, 'This is the BBC', when you're sitting in a freezing youth hostel in the High Atlas ...

for us and 'Omo' (West African shorthand for noxious detergent in powder form) for clothes, bikes, cooking utensils... The downside of this downsizing is that you can't carry lots of weighty tomes, and we found we really missed reading, both being bookworms. Our shortwave radio, a present from Anna's sister, provided some relief. It's strangely comforting to hear the words, 'This is the BBC', when you're sitting in a freezing youth hostel in the High Atlas or lying awake on a hot, humid night somewhere in Burkina Faso. Getting away from it all is, you might think, the aim of a 20-month trip through Africa, but sometimes you crave that link with home. Never more so, in Luke's case, than when the Six Nations was in full swing and the Welsh were on the ascendant. Despite fairly scant coverage of the tournament on the beeb (cricket and football gobbling up most airtime), we could get the scores each weekend.

Demands for pens, money and sweets are never far away. Tellingly, it was never the poorest people who were the most vociferous. We often enjoyed incredible hospitality from impoverished hosts who would have been affronted had we offered money. Yet the villages on which aid money had obviously been lavished and in the more well-to-do areas (all things being relative, we're not talking Porsches and indoor swimming pools, of course), the demands for hand-outs were far greater. Sometimes we were mobbed by forty children at once, other times pestered for hours by a determined individual. In Morocco, the phrase was economical 'Bonjour bon-

Camping near the Golfe de Cintra, Western Sahara.
© Luke Skinner.

bon', in The Gambia even the greeting was superfluous and they just shouted 'give me minty'! From Mauritania onwards we constantly heard 'toubab, toubab' (perhaps the best translation is 'whitey') and it was a relief to reach Guinea Bissau simply because the word was different – 'branco'.

It was at times difficult to keep an open mind, a smile on our faces and to refrain from being rude, hostile or dismissive. We discovered that moo-ing or baa-ing at kids as we rode by had the twin benefits of making us and them laugh! Poking fun at ourselves or appearing foolish often diffused a 'give me, give me' situation. Once the kids had forgotten we were toubabs (and thus walking ATMs in their eyes) they usually forgot all about needing a pen, and became shyly inquisitive about our bikes. Favourite bits of the bikes included the pedals – so tiny! – especially if we obliged by clicking our cleats in and out, and in and out, and in and out and ... enough! Earnest murmurings among the boys as they struggled to calculate the number of gears were matched by equally intense mental struggles on our part as we tried to work out the Arabic, Wolof or Mandinka word for '27' to put them out of their misery! Finally, everyone passed round the Dog Dazer and had a go at pressing the button, shrieking with delight as a red light appeared and a tinny whine could be heard. Such entertainment from such simple things! Locals were probably equally bemused by our fascination with birds, trees and architecture that were exotic to us but to them perfectly ordinary.

By the time we rolled into Nouakchott on Christmas Eve 2004, five months after leaving London, we had overcome a crash, a plague of locusts, sand too deep to ride over, a snapped tent pole and a dozen other minor disasters. Christmas Day was a unique experience, with a morning stroll along the beach (and a dip in the Atlantic for Luke) followed by a lunch of fresh pastries to compensate for missing out on the traditional festive food. We had kept at bay a feeling of sadness – brought on by being so far from home at Christmas – by tuning in to the service from Kings' on the BBC World Service, singing carols as we rode along and conjuring up our ideal Christmas dinners. Just as well there was no one around to hear us!

Postcards from a pilgrimage

Beat Heim *cycled 22,650km from Lucerne to Guangzhou in 2005, via Mt Kailash. As he says, 'I don't want to break records, prove anything to anyone, nor am I presenting the products of a sponsor. I do it because I want to fulfil a dream, because I love the adventure and because I want to see the people and the land along the way. One of the goals of this trip is Mt Kailash, the holiest mountain in Tibet and for Hindus and Buddhists, the holiest in the entire world. For many years I have been fascinated by this place and so this journey is also kind of a pilgrimage. A journey to myself ...'*

January 2005 – Bosnia-Herzegovina
The border crossing to Bosnia Herzegovina is strangely spooky. Just before the border there are mine clearance teams working.

'If the wind comes from the mainland, the weather will be good', I was told. I have good weather but the headwind is strong with snowdrifts and a windchill far below the -12 degree air temperature. Even with three pairs of gloves I can't keep my fingers warm. I dig through waist-height snow away from the road to find a place for my tent.

January – Greece
Sunrises are nowhere more beautiful than over the Aegean Sea. Flocks of flamingos and pelicans accompany me in the early morning – a dream! I cycle along a big lagoon where over 200 species of birds spend the winter.

BEAT HEIM

Beat Heim lives in Lucerne, Switzerland where he works as a software engineer while planning assaults by bicycle on the world's big mountain ranges. On his website – www.betzgi.ch – Beat lists 36 passes over 5000m (16,404ft) he has conquered by bike and he probably has around 25 more to add from his latest trip.

February – Turkey
The customs officer wants to see the papers for the bike. When I laugh and shrug my shoulders he asks me to come inside for a cup of tea: I am in Turkey! But at the border the snow is back. Wind and road-clearing have created some 2m-high snow walls either side of the road but on the second day a strong, warm wind starts to blow from the south. I virtually sail towards Istanbul, the often stormy side-wind making it difficult to stay on the road at all.

After 14 days hunting around Ankara I'm the proud owner of five new visas. Georgia holds the record for issuing a visa in 15 minutes, while Uzbekistan is quite a bit slower at seven days. Caucasus and Central Asia here I come!

March – Georgia
In Kutaisi I go up to the cathedral and with an Orthodox priest and three others, slowly downing a magnum of homemade wine, we watch the sun set.

May – Iran
Only 20km into Iran and I've been invited for tea, had to pose for pictures and give autographs, have an accommodation offer for the night and been given a soft toy. I am totally overwhelmed.

June – Uzbekistan
I have been cycling far too long across endless flat plains. I can hardly wait to get into the mountains. On the way to Samarkand I constantly scan the horizon until I can finally make out mountains in the distance. After almost six months and nearly 12,000km I have reached Samarkand, at the foot of the Pamirs!

July – Tajikistan: Pamir Highway
Crossing the 4000m altitude mark is like entering a different world: my world! Nowhere is the air as clear, the colours as intense, nature so untouched and the silence so complete. During the summer months Kyrgyz herders set up their yurts on the few green spots, letting their yaks, cows and sheep graze.

August – Kyrgyzstan
It's a sort of Christmas for me in the middle of August. I receive a big parcel that my parents have sent for me: spare parts for my bicycle. The bike now looks almost new again. It has been incredibly reliable in the past seven months: three flat tyres and a broken rack eyelet were the only problems in 13,600km!

October – Mt Kailash, Tibet
It's difficult to describe the feelings you have if you have just reached the goal for which you have invested all your time and energy for more than eight months – I am totally overwhelmed. I sit next to the road and cry for joy. I am utterly happy.

The highlight of every pilgrimage to Kailash is the kora: the three-day circumambulation of the mountain. I leave the bicycle in Darchen and begin the walk. I make a little side trip and camp right below the north face. A few hundred metres behind my tent the vertical face rises 1500m in perfect symmetry to the peak. It is without doubt the most spectacular place I have ever camped in! That night I hardly sleep. For hours I gaze up into the starry sky and the north face lit up by the moonlight – what a spectacle! And if it had been just for this one night all the effort of this journey would still have been worth it! My dream really has come true.

Mt Kailash by moonlight © Beat Heim

In 260 days I've cycled 15,500km: all the way from home to Kailash, every single metre. (Except the crossing of the Bosphorus in Istanbul, where I was not allowed to cycle, something I won't forgive the Turks for for a while ...).

November – Everest Base Camp, Tibet

I take a little-used road to Everest and am soon unsure whether I am still going the right way. Finally a truck comes and I ask for directions – everything OK. But when the truck goes on I stand motionless unable to believe what I am seeing – the truck drives right over my bicycle! In this one moment my world collapses. When I can finally react, the truck is gone and I can only examine the damage: the back wheel is totally twisted, at one point the rim is squashed and is broken for about 8cm, the rear derailleur is in pieces, the whole frame has shifted about 8cm, one pedal is twisted and the mounting of one pannier is ripped off. A passing jeep takes me back to Dingri. When I arrive at the same guesthouse I'd just left everyone stares speechless at the wreck I bring back.

When I was here eight years ago, my freewheel broke and I never made it to Everest Base Camp. Now this! The event has triggered a sort of act of defiance. For the next eight hours I am hammering, screwing and welding like crazy. After the sun has gone down I am ready for the first test ride. Of course it's not perfect. The pedal is not straight sand the gears hardly work at all. The broken rim has been rebuilt using a flattened Coke can and I cannot use the back brake. In Shigatse I am sure to get some spare parts, but what to do now? Should I skip Everest again? Against all rationality I head for Everest Base Camp.

I cycle as carefully as possible but the road is anything but gentle to my bike. On the way the rear rack breaks off and the rear derailleur falls into pieces twice more. But I get there. It is a victory of the will against all odds.

That Everest is a big mountain I knew, of course. But when I finally stand in front of it, it takes my breath away. I am at the Base Camp at 5170m but in front of me the Rongbuk face rises up yet another almost vertical 3500m!

December – Farewell Tibet

On the same day that I see the last yaks on the high plateau of Zhongdian, I catch sight of the first water buffalos by the Yangtze River. Everywhere there are fields. I pass through many beautiful villages. But they soon get bigger and I have difficulty in finding a place to put up my tent.

January 2006 – Approaching Hong Kong

Eighty km before Hong Kong, exactly one year after I started on this journey, I suddenly have terrible pain in my stomach and have to stop in a hotel. After several days in bed I finally find a doctor who examines me properly instead of just giving me pain killers and infusions. I don't know yet what the problem is, but they say surgery is necessary – immediately! Fourteen days later I leave the hospital on shaky legs. Behind me lies an intestine operation and on my belly I sport a brand new 'XL-zipper'!

If you've lost your belief in the good of humanity these days I can only say take your bike and go cycle the world. It's one of the great experiences to discover that, in fact, most people are incredibly friendly, helpful and hospitable – everywhere!

Small hazards in South America

After gaining a prize-winning masters degree in economics from Oxford, Ivan Viehoff worked on consulting projects for 11 years before setting out on an open-ended sabbatical. His trip lasted 14 months, beginning in Chile and ending in Burma (Myanmar).

I was 35; I was single; I was totally screwed up and stressed out; my hair was falling out. Why was I working every hour the devil sends? What was the money for? What was life for? I might as well give up and get far away to South America with my bicycle.

'You'll be back in three months,' said my therapist. 'You need me.'

'I can't come with you,' said my old cycling friend Simon, 'Zeneca Pharmaceuticals don't approve of career breaks.'

'You'd lurve Australia,' said George, the office Australian.

You'll be back in three months', said my therapist. 'You need me'.

'Don't forget to take a packet of condoms, ' said Brendan, a concert-going friend, ever practical. 'I'll be lucky to need them,' I thought.

Anne said nothing. She didn't even know. She was my ex-girlfriend but that didn't stop us checking each other out from time to time ... just to make sure. But the last time really had been the last time. Finally, it seemed, I could start forgetting.

I went to the airport to catch my deeply discounted one-way flight to Santiago, Chile; my mother shed a few tears. Waiting through the traditional three-hour delay, I went to Boots to buy a packet of condoms.

☆☆☆

My first moments in Chile are hardly welcoming. Leaving Santiago airport onto a busy dual carriageway, a two-inch nail instantly spears my tyre. Hundreds of cars are honking horns with people hanging out of their sunroofs, waving flags and shouting. Ten kilometres later I have another puncture but my spare tube is already used. Dripping in the humid 30°C heat outside a stinking butcher's shop, I have to make three attempts to get a

IVAN VIEHOFF

Ivan Viehoff is a consulting economist and treasurer of the Rough-Stuff Fellowship (www.rsf.org.uk). He was previously Seneschal of the Oxford Arthurian Society. Ivan spent a year cycling the Andes and has been to many other tough places on his bike. He has published articles on cycle touring, cookery and industrial policy and enjoys mushroom hunting.

PART 3 – TALES FROM THE SADDLE

patch to stick. Every 100 metres there's a junction with traffic lights and soot-belching buses cutting me up. I am heading for a hostel, but when I get there I obviously have the wrong address. Standing by a park in the late afternoon sun, three policemen jump out of a car and arrest a man just 20 metres from where I am standing.

In mid-evening the city erupts. The 12-lane Alameda is completely blocked. The noise of horns and chanting washes all around. A political demonstration? Revolution? No, a football match. Chile beat Bolivia 3-0. The afternoon's madness was but mild anticipation for this. Welcome to South America!

☆☆☆

I take a trip to Valparaíso, an attractive seaport 100km from Santiago. Here, in the main square, a young woman starts chatting to me. She tells me her name is Carla and volunteers that she is 28. Carla is *morena*, the colour of the dominant racial mix of colonist and native. I rather fancy her brown skin, her strong arms, her smallness. Within an hour she is showing me the contents of her handbag. A while later and I have an offer of marriage.

Within an hour she is showing me the contents of her handbag. A while later and I have an offer of marriage.

Carla wants to leave the poverty of Chile. I can start by taking her to Santiago with me. There is no illusion about what might be on offer back in my hotel. I want to believe what she says. I am alone and lonely in a distant land. I have my packet of condoms. But eventually I twig: I wonder who has bought her smart new clothes and her yellow suede shoes. Firmly I take my leave, lying as I promise to send a card. I have only her photo as a memory of my prudence.

☆☆☆

I phone Kathryn, a Kiwi backpacker I had met on a stop-over in Buenos Aires. 'You've got to meet José,' she said, 'I met him last night. He's a real Chileno cyclist, mad about the countryside. But don't mention Argentina.' So it is that a Chileno I had never met and his Irish friend, Iain, take me out to dinner in an Argentinean restaurant in a wealthy suburb. We talk about cycling in Chile. It is made clear to me that Chile has all the great scenery I need; Argentina isn't worth the candle. We just eat its food.

It is made clear to me that Chile has all the great scenery I need; Argentina isn't worth the candle.

A few days later, when my excess baggage finally arrives, I am on an overnight bus down to the green Chilean south, the land of volcanoes and lakes where the monkey-puzzle trees grow. But just now looking out of the bus window into the grey dawn and grassy fields, I could be at home in England. This is supposed to be an easy start, a paved road into the foothills. But things are rarely that simple. For 20km the road surface is under repair. Immediately I can see that things are not altogether right with the bike; things are bending that shouldn't bend; rack screws are working loose.

At lunchtime the next day I am freezing in a bus-shelter. The rain is pouring down and only a little higher in the hills it is snowing. This is supposed to be practically summer. A man arrives and invites me into a warm building for a hot drink. He is the headmaster of the village school. He invites me to lunch, then dinner. I help his daughters with their English, and I stay the night.

I learn of the poverty of his village. Malalcahuello is a peasant agricultural community. Today small-scale agriculture is uneconomic and animals wander the village uncared for. The logging and road-building employ only a fraction of the community. The village is surrounded by national parks and nature reserves but there is no tourist industry here yet. The population can no longer support itself. Five years ago a volcano rained down ash on them. The village had to be evacuated for a month and a year's crops were lost.

☆☆☆

In the morning mist the volcanoes are still hidden. I get a hitch through a single-track tunnel, allegedly the longest on the continent. It used to be a rail tunnel, but today cars drive on gravel with the rails still showing through. We have to wait half an hour to get a slot in our direction.

The intermittent road surface soon runs out for good. I replace a loose rack bolt with a stronger steel one. I turn onto a minor road to climb a pass. There is still snow on the ground at the top, among the monkey-puzzles. On the descent the first bottle-cage sheers off. The others will follow within days. As afternoon arrives the sun occasionally shows its face and I see parrots chattering in the pines.

The front rack sheers its new bolt. The scenery is changing to grassland. Goats wander past. I wave at gauchos on horses. And then suddenly I am on the ground, and the momentum of the bike gives me a blow in the chest I will feel for a month. The front pannier rack flexed into the wheel and is now twisted round the axle. An hour later, time I can ill afford this late in the day, I am back on the road with all my luggage piled on the back rack.

Suddenly I am on the ground, and the momentum of the bike gives me a blow in the chest I will feel for a month.

I am lost. The junction isn't on the map. The village isn't on the map. There is no one to ask. I guess the way. Finally I find someone to ask. The people round here are the Mapuche, marking off their home-fields with lines of thick rough-hewn stakes. I am going the wrong way.

The dogs are a pain. Approaching another Mapuche village there is a huge black dog in the road. I am expecting trouble because I am barely going faster than walking pace on this hill. As I get closer the dog turns into a thin pig and trots off. Finally I make the remote resort village of Icalma, just a scattering of rude buildings, with one primitive guesthouse, and uncarpeted candle-lit rooms. I've missed dinner, so I set up my camp stove in the garden.

In the morning sunshine I enjoy the tranquility of Icalma lake, right on the Argentina border. 'You can't go this way,' a local calls. 'It's flooded. You'd be better to go to Lonquímay.' Back the way I have come. A detour of hundreds of kilometres. I'd rather cross to Argentina. I bet he's exaggerating. Sure enough, the muddy wading lasts only a few hundred metres and is no more than shin deep. The road is the worst yet, but the scenery the best. I get clear views of Llaima volcano, which I have been circumnavigating for the past three days.

© Ivan Viehoff

A couple of days later I hole up at La Torre Suiza, a hostel run by Swiss cyclists. Claudia makes real muesli for breakfast. The dining room has a fine view of Villarrica volcano. Since it is always raining, they have stuck a picture of the volcano on the window, so you know what it looks like. They show me their bicycles with many times re-welded front racks. You need a good steel rack they tell me. But they do not know how to get one in Chile. I buy a primitive rack from a bike shop that wouldn't look out of place in a 1930s' period drama. It is a rear rack, but somehow we fit it on the front. I buy a thick woolly jumper in the handicraft market.

A few days later I pass through ever poorer villages and struggle over a rough pass over the shoulder of the volcano. The monkey-puzzles and southern beech are of a size unknown in England. They astonish me and drip on me. The weather is bad again, and there are no views. The new rack flexes like it is about to snap off on every pot-hole. Arriving in Pucón, a more up-market resort, I find a more modern bike shop. I buy a more modern rack. It is a Taiwanese copy of the real thing. It's alloy, but perhaps it will do for a while.

☆☆☆

The roads always get worse as you get near the border.

Curarrehue is a traditional colonial village up a terrible road. The roads always get worse as you get near the border. This time I am truly on my way to Argentina. I am still not happy with the rack and I want to see if they have better bike shops over there before I go to really remote places.

I'm directed to the only guesthouse. They point at the Big House, an enormous yellow-painted wooden affair. I am not sure I believe it. A maid greets me at the back door. I am at the right place. The price is high, but I am stuck. A rivet in my pannier is broken, and a workman says he will lead me down to the cobbler. As we walk down through the front garden, a parade of twelve men come the other way, two by two. One at the front is wearing a suit and tie, the first I have seen since Santiago, and he looks more like an accountant than a farmer. 'That's the *dueño*,' says the workman. 'And the others?' 'They're his men.' 'What do they do?' 'They collect the rent. He owns all the land round here.' The cobbler has no rivets to mend my pannier. We fix it back at the house with a nut and bolt. As time passes, I will fix every rivet in my panniers in this way.

As I cook my dinner in the kitchen, the dueño comes in and chats to me for a while. Although in his forties, he isn't married, which is unusual in Chile. He eats *en familia* with his men. They are served by the maid, the only woman

I see in the house. Upstairs, next to the guest room, there is a dormitory where the men all sleep. This is the traditional pattern of rural control in Chile which Allende strove to break so disastrously 25 years ago.

☆☆☆

It takes most of the day to climb the pass to Argentina. The road hasn't seen any recent maintenance and it is a mess. The border lies under the shadow of Lanín volcano, the tallest of the region.

It's different in Argentina. The dense forests and green fields give way to more open woods, and then to arid plains of steppe grasses and spiny cushion plants, the *pampa patagónica*. The houses are brick, not wood. Cars stop and people lean out to pass the time of day. The better-kept towns could be in Europe. The prices could be European too. In Chile practically all the travellers are outsiders, but in Argentina most of the travellers are Argentinians. It is not just the greater wealth of the country, for in truth the difference is not so large, but it is symptomatic of a more worldly view. The *chilenos* live in a narrow strip between mountain and sea, desert at one end and ice at the other, isolated from the world, with little thought of broadening the mind, and little thought that the outside world matters except as a market for their products. The *argentinos* live on a vast wide plain, just as remote, but dreaming of the world outside, somehow forgetting that they need to find an economic *raison d'être* if the trips to Paris are to carry on.

> It's different in Argentina ... The better-kept towns could be in Europe. The prices could be European, too.

Near the chocolate-box resort of San Martín de los Andes I climb the pass of Arroyo Partido, the divided stream. The rivers on each side of the pass somehow join in the middle. One side goes to the Atlantic, the other to the Pacific. The beautiful Siete Lagos (Seven Lakes) road starts here. My new rack soon shows its distaste for its terrible surface. As I fix it up for the fourth time, I spot the design fault the Taiwanese copyists have added to the original specification.

In Bariloche I stay in a hostel run by Belgian cyclist Carlos Vlaene. The bike shops in town cannot fix my bike. But he tells me of a frame builder just outside town. When he isn't playing the saxophone, Miguel Nitzsche works out of his garden shed to build custom bicycles with home-made tools. And he does a line in custom steel racks. I am rescued. I cannot believe my luck.

☆☆☆

Back in Chile the sun is now shining on the volcanoes and lakes. I am riding through flat farmland but the roads are still terrible. After a hot day I empty my water bottle and a small unidentified animal, about the size of my thumb comes out, cooked. Its presence explains the persistent bowel trouble I have been suffering. I am almost sick when I see it. I ask the landlady for bleach.

In the morning there is a small earthquake and I cycle off into the sunshine.

> Its presence explains the persistent bowel trouble I have been suffering.

PART 3 – TALES FROM THE SADDLE

A little light cycling in Kyrgyzstan

Igor Kvose *does not believe in carrying one gram more than is absolutely necessary: his packing list is on p.247. He made this Central Asian circuit through Kyrgyzstan, into China (Kashgar) and back on an ultralight bike with less than 10kg of luggage. Unfortunately, at the end of this trip he suddenly found he had even less.*

An experienced traveller would hide in shame if he got his wallet nicked in a picturesque market; so would a hard-core cyclist who got his bike stolen while sending home victorious e-mails at the end of a successful trip. What should I do then, when both happened to me and a dog bit me as a bonus? Now that several months have passed since my round trip in Kyrgyzstan and Xinjiang I've come to terms with the shame meted out by cruel destiny and my story is a warning to others!

I've come to terms with the shame meted out by cruel destiny and my story is a warning to others!

The plane in Bishkek early in the morning. My luggage and bike arrived safely and I assembled it without too much attention from the Kyrgyz taxi drivers. I was a trifle jet-lagged but decided not to waste a day so started cycling into the mountains right away. During a short stop in Bishkek to send e-mails and buy water, I noted that quite a few sewage covers had gratings running parallel to the road or were missing altogether; it'd be a quick end to my trip if I hit one of those, so I hurried out of the city. Soon the temperature rose to 40 degrees C and a few hours of unpleasant riding on a bad road with heavy traffic ended the somewhat idealistic picture I'd built about this trip. Towards the end of the day I found a flat space to lay my tent and went to sleep feeling pretty disillusioned.

I rose to a wonderful morning. After the first easy 20km the climb toward the Too Ashuu pass started and soon the gradient was not dropping below 7%. A quick descent on the other side was ended by strong headwinds but by the next morning the wind had gone and the road was climbing gently toward the Ala-Bel pass. Pastures with horses and yurts lined the road and a family invited me inside for a cup of tea and a demonstration of milking a mare. I reached Toktogul by 4pm. I found a cheap hotel, with no running water but with a curious toilet with two holes: one in the ground and one in a chair, apparently a concession to those weak-kneed foreigners.

The fine ride continued the next day with a smooth road and spectacular scenery along an artificial lake. I stopped for tea and fried fish, which some Uzbek businessmen offered me. Soon after starting the next morning, I ran into a roadblock caused by a landslide and then I got my first front flat tyre – the first for 5500km. Snake-bite again – I really ought to buy a better pump. Apart from that it was a great day, not truly easygoing as the road was undulating all the way, but fine scenery and some speedy descents made up for the climbs. Just before a dam a series of unlit tunnels with some deep potholes varied the already interesting day. After the dam it was as if I'd hit an invisible wall: broken asphalt, potholes, gravel and roadworks suddenly reduced my speed by half. I didn't know at that time that it was going to last more or less to the Chinese border. I stopped at a *stolovaya* (restaurant) for a tea and *pilmeni* (meat dumplings in soup). The manager invited me to share a watermelon and asked me the usual questions: (1) Why am I riding a bike? (2) Am I getting paid for that? (3) Why am I alone? (4) Why am I not married?

After Tash Komur came a 30km stretch of roadworks. It was evening already when I came to Kochkor Ata. The first part of the next day went in pushing the bike along a rough road with innumer-

IGOR KOVSE

Igor Kovse is a civil engineer living in Ljubljana. He discovered bike touring at 35 years of age, jumping in at the deep end with a trip to Iceland. The year after his Kyrgyzstan trip, Igor attempted the route from Kashgar to Kailash but had to give up after breaking a collar bone. He still tours ultralight on racing bikes.

able Ladas beeping and zooming past me at an incredible speed. I had a thought: maybe that's a religious issue; maybe there's a sentence in the Koran which says 'Thou shall not see heaven if thou drive at 90km/h or less'!

A good road continued from there on, albeit with a tough climb, at the end of which I was, to my surprise, already in Ozgon. Finding a *gostinica* (hotel) was easy, but finding an open one was not so simple. A friendly, well-dressed guy came and invited me to stay in his office while waiting for the hotel manager to wake up. We talked a bit, I worked on his computer a bit, then he gave me four pages of his freshly-started novel to translate from Russian to English and asked me to send him the translation by mail. I had a glimpse at the novel's title: *shorpo* (a lamb soup). Maybe that was a cookbook.

The road to Osh was catastrophic. The 10km section of roadworks was the culmination of evil. I was relieved when I saw a sign: Osh 3km. There was an irrigation stream at the edge of a cotton field where I washed off the dirt and sweat of the day before entering the city. I sent some e-mails and then went for a hard-earned beer.

The road rose gently but steadily. There were lots of opportunities to stop and freshen up in the river that flowed in the opposite direction. Around noon I stopped for a watermelon which I shared with two Kyrgyz men. Then came Chyrchyk pass, not too hard and with a bowl of *kumis* (mare's milk) waiting for me at the top. When I rolled over the top, awaiting the splendid joy of descending, I encountered one of those stone sections where your downhill speed is about the same as the uphill one. Halfway down the rear rim started to wiggle; I assumed it had gone out of true in these

A bowl of *kumis* (mare's milk) was waiting for me at the top.

rough conditions. I later discovered that the rim was OK but the tyre had worn down at one spot near to the tube, and then twisted. Finally the road improved a bit and I coasted towards Gulcha with the temperature increasing with every turn. I got into hot and shadeless Gulcha around 3pm. I found a very cheap *gostinica* (hotel) and met two Kyrgyz girls who spoke excellent English. They were there on a 'Golden Goal' project, educating the villagers about the procedures and risks of leaving the country to find work in Kazakhstan or Russia. I patched the tyre with duct tape from inside and the next day I rode carefully, inspecting the tyre every few kms; it took the pounding just fine. That was the day of the Taldyk pass. Quite a difficult climb on a truly terrible road surface – a thick layer of dust covering pebbles and potholes. Fortunately this time the road was paved on the downhill side, so I let go of the brakes all the way to Sary Tash where I raced directly into the arms of the gostinica's owner who carried me and my bike inside to a cosy warm room with hot tea and not-so-hard-to-break bread.

The final stretch to the Chinese border at Irkestam awaited me next day. A checkpoint at the end of the village, then a slow, careful ride; frequent glimpses of the White Mountain range of Eastern Pamirs and whistling marmots kept me company. I almost made it trouble-free, until 7km from the border when the rear tyre finally blew out. I changed it with a folding spare but soon had another flat. I walked the final kilometre to Nura village, where I got to wash off the dirt and get a meal, a room and watch news in Russian on TV.

It was a quick ride to the border the next morning, but not without trouble, for careful as I was, I had one more flat in front and I even fell, scratching my elbow and knee. Crossing the border was straightforward and soon I was riding on the paved, smooth and quiet Xinjiang highway. I loved the vast desert feeling about it and felt all my bike-related troubles were over.

It was an interesting day with some good Chinese food in a restaurant with live fish swimming in a tank in the toilet

The road to Kashgar had more climbs than I expected, but it was an interesting day with some good Chinese food in a restaurant with live fish swimming in a tank in the toilet, a Tour-de-France-like race when I realized Kashgar was 50km farther than I had calculated, another front flat, a night search for a hotel in a surprisingly large town and finally a shower, clean clothes, dinner and a beer. After 12 days of cycling I took a rest day to try some sightseeing and walking along the wide Kashgar streets. I looked for a 700 size tyre and found one which was quite expensive but unfortunately too wide for my racing bike. One day of rest and frequent expeditions up and down the stairs to my room on the fourth floor exhausted me enough, so I decided to go cycling on the Karakoram Highway (KKH) the next morning.

After about 80km of good roads, not so good roads, and frequent and unnerving bypasses because of road works, I came upon an amazingly smooth road up the Ghez canyon. It was a true delight. I enjoyed the rest of the day pedalling along the gentle incline with beautiful views of the wide Ghez river bed, steep rocks on the right and colourful mountains on the far left side. At the end of the day, when the gradient became steeper, I found a place for my tent beneath the road in a valley with an outlook on Kongur Shan massif. Good cycling followed next day up to Karakol Lake. This place didn't impress me much, maybe because of the cloudy day and after a quick stop to get some oil for the chain, I continued further up the unnamed pass, actually the highest point of my trip, slightly above 4000m. As I was on the top, black clouds started to gather from the Tajik side and I hurried down towards Tashkorgan without much delay. The following 50km were quite an adrenalin ride, since I was pushed by the strong wind preceding the storm on the paved but potholed road. At times when I reached wind speed at about 40km/h, it was a strange and exciting feeling racing down in a complete lull trying to avoid frequent holes and stones.

As frequently happens, the best day was followed by one of the lowest points of the trip. I set out on the return trip to Kashgar. Leaving the river valley and coming to the vast plain, I saw a kind of 'tourist resort' with a few yurts and tables on the grass and decided to treat myself to a morning tea in a chair under the sunshade. As I parked my bike and turned to the stalls, a dog rushed silently from behind, grabbed my left calf, shook and grunted for a moment and then ran away. It all happened so quickly that I only noticed it was a white dog. It had dug its teeth quite deeply into me. I washed the wound with a few litres of water, covered it with plaster, took some antibiotics (actually an anti-malarial drug – hardly an antidote to rabies!), and ate and drank something while waiting for the bleeding to stop. Then I just went on towards Kashgar. It was slow pedalling against the gradient and slight wind and everything was worsened by the pain in my leg that grew worse towards the end of the day. By the time I got to Karakol lake I was not able to walk properly. I arranged for accommodation with dinner and breakfast and I rode a bike for the few metres between the yurt and the huts rather than limping that distance. The night in the yurt was warm despite not being heated. Not surprisingly I had some troublesome, irrational dreams. I intended to cycle to Kashgar the next day, however at 7am it was grey, cold and rainy outside. As often happens in the mountains, the weather changed abruptly; the sun was shining by 9am and fortunately the pain in my leg lessened a bit.

Approaching Kashgar I somehow managed to miss the right road and I arrived at the hotel at night yet again. This time I got a room on the 5th floor – good exercise for my leg!

Next day I got a Chinese lady at the hotel to write down a message for a doctor about the dog accident and my wish to get a rabies shot. The clinic happened to be near the hotel. The nurses and the doctor were all delighted, amused even, when they saw the note, they took a look at my leg, cleaned and bandaged the wound and gave me some antibiotics. This was not exactly what I was looking for, but it appeased me for the rest of the day, until I searched on the internet under

A dog rushed silently from behind and grabbed my left calf ... It dug its teeth quite deeply into me.

The nurses and the doctor were all delighted, amused even, when they saw the note.

PART 3 – TALES FROM THE SADDLE

I searched on the internet under 'rabies' and found some alarming news ...

'rabies' and found some alarming news about the spread of this disease in China the previous year.

Next morning I went to the clinic again, insisting that I get a vaccine. A number of translators with varying degrees of knowledge of English filed before me, until finally a man came by for whom a connection between the words 'dog' and 'disease' was not unknown. The doctor and the nurses suddenly became enlightened, shouting at me that I should get a shot as soon as possible. After three hours they got the vaccine and gave me the first shot. I took the remaining four ampoules after some bitter discussion and their unwillingness to give them away. Then I sorted out my taxi for the Torugart pass, bought two syringes in order to give myself the next two shots and went for a meal, quite satisfied with the way I had arranged things. I had a few days before the Torugart trip. Most of the time, I just walked up and down the same streets on a tour of Kashgar. One day I'd had enough of this and cycled about 60km eastward. On the way back I stopped at Kashgar bazaar – and someone stole my wallet.

I stopped at Kashgar bazaar – and someone stole my wallet.

On the morning of the Torugart trip I gave myself the second rabies shot in the shoulder. This was the first time I had ever done such a thing; it was not without trouble, but there was not much blood and I was generally very pleased about the 'professional' appearance of the whole procedure. The Torugart trip went smoothly with the guides on both sides assisting with border formalities. There was heavy rain on the Chinese part of the trip, a few times cars barely got through the torrential flow across the road and I was more than relieved I didn't have to cycle this part.

I gave myself the second rabies shot in the shoulder ... there was not much blood.

At the Torugart pass the rain stopped and I chose to cycle from there on. That was not the best choice: as soon as I began cycling, the rain started, then turned to snow and it was not long before I was wet and cold, riding on a bad gravel road full of puddles. As if someone was testing my limits (hey, you someone, show yourself!) I had a rear flat and after I'd fixed it in rain, cold and mud, the front tyre went flat too. I pulled in to the house nearby in search of shelter to fix the flat, but after we had exchanged a few words, I decided to stay for the night for 100 soms (US$2.50), including some tea and food. Again, not the best choice, I guess. The kids of this family (I nicknamed them Frankenstein) started rummaging in my backpack as soon as I left it unattended. They even stole some of my tools, but it took me two days to find that out. Inside the house tea was served with nan, and then vodka came to the table. Many people entered and left the room and I was not clear who the master was in this house. It turned out to be a very quiet man who only became aggressive when everybody left. In the morning the man was quiet, apparently his anger had evaporated together with the vodka during the night. Still, the housewife demanded double the agreed sum for their services. We settled for something in between and I left their home with decreasing esteem for the people of this land.

The main adventures were behind me, so it seemed, and I cycled on mostly rough roads towards Bishkek. I was sceptical about everybody, I didn't answer any more greetings, the 'hello' and 'tourist' shouts, I didn't look at people and I hastily threw stones at the dogs that frequently ran towards me. There was another pass above 3000m – the Dolon pass – and after that it was just rolling down, but in much colder and more changeable weather than I had started in about one month earlier. I also gave myself another rabies shot: a very messy thing it turned out to be this time.

> **I felt in control, victorious and self-confident. I should have known that's when the most unexpected and bad things happen.**

After a few days of rattling on rough surfaces I came to Bishkek and found a good place to sleep. The next day I set out to explore the city. I cruised along city streets, watchful both for minibuses that can pull in and out in front of you at any time and the potential danger of falling into sewage gratings. But I felt in control, victorious and self-confident. I should have known that's about the time when the most unexpected and bad things happen. And it happened: I went to send some e-mails and left my bike locked, but not locked to a tree, fence or something immovable; from my computer I could even see the bike if I leaned a bit. But after five minutes I looked back and the bike was gone! My beautiful, reliable, fast bike!

ULTRA-LIGHT PACKING LIST

Igor Kovse shows how it is possible to ride for a month and camp with less than 10kg of gear. In fact, he had less than that as he includes the clothes he wore in the 10kg total. His total check-in weight for the flight barely exceeded 20kg, so he would have no excess baggage charges on a short-haul flight with a typical 20kg allowance. This was the gear list for his Kyrgyzstan trip:

Front		Rear	
550g	Handlebar bag	120g	2 x bungee cords
895g	Camera with batteries & zoom lens	830g	Rucksack
175g	8 rolls of film	1365g	Tent
80g	Monocular	840g	Sleeping bag
20g	Map, cut to include the route only	210g	Silk sleeping sheet
60g	Notebook, calendar and a pencil	155g	Foam pad
30g	Parts of guidebooks and other papers	60g	2 x underwear
100g	Gloves: right one is a mitt, the left one a lighter five-finger glove	80g	2 x socks
		120g	T-shirt
57g	Wool cap	330g	Cotton pullover
20g	Neckerchief	185g	Light fleece pullover
215g	Rain/wind jacket	370g	Long trousers with a belt
90g	Toothbrush, paste, liquid detergent, sunscreen	50g	Spare glasses in soft case
		120g	Medical kit, sewing kit
20g	Two dish washing cloths for towels	220g	2 x spare tubes
250g	Tool kit	195g	Spare tyre
27g	Mini flashlight	10g	Plastic bags
25g	Lighter, compass	**5260g = total weight at rear**	
30g	Pen water filter		
10g	Plastic bags		
2654g = total weight at front			

Recumbent research

Researcher **Maya Van Leemput** *travelled around different parts of the world by bicycle, with her partner, photographer Bram Goots, as part of a research project for Agence Future (www.agencefuture.org). Since the project concerned the subject of people's perception of the future they chose a futuristic-looking form of the bicycle – the recumbent (see p.35) – as their mode of transport. They travelled to no less than 30 countries on five continents, interviewing a total of 382 people from all walks of life about their ideas on the future. What follows are some extracts from Maya's diary.*

Cycling has several advantages. First, it offers great opportunities for contact with the local population. It gives you something to talk about, whether you are on the roads of Northern Europe, the plains of Senegal or the beachfronts of Australia. It helps to make you appear more 'human' in the eyes of the people you meet, particularly in the developing world. What they see is not a tourist emerging from a tour bus but a weary traveller who may need food, drink or shelter for the night.

On a bicycle you have a far better vantage point for gaining an understanding of a place than you could ever have travelling by public transport or in a car. You don't see just the two or three villages where you stop for lunch or spend the night but everything in between as well.

Our bicycles give us, as researchers, an added advantage since they're not run-of-the-mill touring bikes but futuristic-looking recumbent cycles. In many places we went to, no one had ever seen such a contraption before. In the context of our focus on the future, it is interesting to observe how people react to something that is entirely new to them.

MAYA VAN LEEMPUT

While finishing her Ph.D. thesis (*Visions of the Future on Television*) Maya Van Leemput set up Agence Future – www.agencefuture.org – the website forum dedicated to Future Studies, to consider questions such as: Where do images of the future come from? What do scientists, politicians, religious leaders and the media say about times to come? How do men and women, young and old, rich and poor, in cities, deserts, plains or mountain regions around the world, see the future for themselves and their children?

Her research forms the basis of a survey not of what the future will be like or how changes will take place in each of the locations included in the research but of what people think the future could be like, what they think it should be like, how they think changes might happen and the extent to which they think about the future at all.

She has contributed articles to several newspapers and magazines including *Science and Technology* and the Flemish newspaper, *De Morgen*. She lives in Belgium.

Egypt

We had waited for almost an hour on the dusty parking lot where people who saw our bikes for the first time without seats and with the handlebars askew were having heated discussions about how these machines work. They might as well have been spaceships. Someone makes the sound of a motor. We shake our head and point at our legs: 'This is the motor!'. With one foot up and ostentatiously gesturing steering with our hands under our hips we try to describe how our pride and joy really works.

> ... they were having heated discussions about how these machines work. They might as well have been spaceships.

Putting the bikes in working order after the bus ride we had lots of company again, grown men laughing like children at the idea of us on the machines before them. While Bram concentrated on the job in hand, ignoring the commotion around us, I used the few words of Arabic I knew to figure out how we would get to the village centre and to acknowledge the words of praise from the men eyeing up the machines. Half an hour later we rode off amidst cheers of 'Yallah!' and 'Goodbye!', due as much to our at last riding off in a recumbent position as to the delight of the audience at seeing that the bikes actually worked.

Europe

Before starting our 15,000km journey Bram enjoyed a week of turning the Street Machines into veritable 'expedition-beasts' at the HPVelotechnik workshop. Meanwhile I was writing and making what seemed like an endless list of last minute arrangements.

We travelled to Eastern Germany and then on to Poland. After some weeks in Warsaw, we spent time outside in Puszcza Bialowieska, the oldest forest of Europe where buffaloes roam. These animals are survivors, they are not free but stuck in time in the enclosure of a nature park.

After the Egyptian pyramids, we found ourselves once again amongst the ancient and the long-lasting. It dawned on us that what is old is more likely to continue than what is young and new: think of the pyramids, the sun, and for a counter example, think of start-up IT compa-

> ... what is old is more likely to continue than what is young and new: think of the pyramids, the sun, and for a counter example, think of start-up IT companies.

nies. Looking for the future we have to take the old as well as the new into account. Most of all, we have to be prepared to find the answers to our questions around every corner. Every new stretch of road, every curb, every hill top, affects our point of view, our expectations and our desire to explore.

West Africa

In Dakar, the capital of Senegal, we interviewed Tidiane Ba, the president of the world conservation society UICN and a biologist specialized in bio-diversity and drought. He gave us a metaphor about the direction mankind is going with the world: 'It is as if we are driving a car and are heading straight for a blank wall, what do we do? At the moment we are just trying to slow down,

We tried to get used to ... riding with an extra 14 litres of water each morning.

CO_2 emission norms, recycling waste etc but we are still heading in the direction of the wall. Unless we turn the wheel completely and head for a completely new direction, we will come to a full stop or crash'. Ba recommended we find out for ourselves what the conditions were like in the ever more dry Sahel. So we rode 900 kilometres through the sandy plains of the Fouta Torro region and tried to get used to drinking litres of lukewarm water every day and to riding with an extra 14 litres of water each morning.

India

From Madurai we rode eastward. It was after sunset before our stop for the night, Manalaparai, to be greeted by a line of bare-chested, drumming men. By the time we reached the roundabout at the edge of the town centre we were engulfed in a sea of sound: the shrill, piercing tones of more loudspeakers mixed with the honking and hooting of a large collection of buses. There were people everywhere, the streets were decorated with colourful lights. There was more going on here than the usual hustle and bustle, a full-blown festival was happening in this little town.

The policeman who kept an eye on the whole lot with a whistle in his

The large elephant came straight towards me ... and ... raised its trunk.

mouth directed us to the other side of town for a place to sleep. We rode on until we were completely surrounded by a heaving mass of people in a party mood. They received us with cries and laughter, a group of boys whistled after us. Suddenly the sea of people parted and we saw two elephants lumbering towards us in a gentle trot. The smaller, who was first, passed me but the large elephant came straight towards me and stopped less than a metre away. Sitting back on my bike, I was very impressed by the animal towering high above me. Then the elephant raised its trunk, showing me its big open mouth. When suddenly the trunk came down again, I was startled and shot to one side but the elephant had more experience in these kinds of things than I did and with a light tap the endearingly soft tip of the trunk landed on my head. Sitting on my bicycle I was blessed by a representative of Ganesh and I will never be afraid of an elephant again!

Cuba

We got to know Havana during the next couple of weeks and would return there for another three weeks at the end of our stay in Cuba. But a country is always more than its capital and to help us understand the Cuban reality we travelled east to Santiago with only 500,000 people, Cuba's second largest city. The place is buzzing with the sounds of instruments playing everywhere. We cycled away from Santiago, along the southern coast of the Sierra Maestra. Leaving town was fun. We hurtled steeply downhill towards the coast with people on the street shouting after us: 'Mamaa...que rico!' and 'Oh la la la Mamy!' As usual we'd hear someone burst out in uncontrollable laughter every once in a while.

Once we got away from town, we found ourselves in an almost ideal setting. On our left the deep blue sea, on our right the Sierra Maestra hills where Fidel and his comrades hid out in the years before the revolution. We saw the sea so turquoise that it made our hearts sing and rode alongside

Cycling by the sea, Cuba
© Maya Van Leemput and Bram Goots

bare-chested horse riders with big fat cigars in their mouths on winding roads along mangroves and mountain ranges filled with palm trees and big healthy grasses. The picture was perfect and so would the ride be.

Chile

The last leg of our journey started like most legs did: in a capital. The weather in Santiago de Chile was beautiful; most days we had clear blue skies with a pleasant winter sun. 'Exactly the kind of meteorological conditions that badly affect air quality in the city', said Pablo Ulriksen, the Director of the Laboratory for Atmospheric Modelling and Analysis, with whom we talked about pollution in his city. His lab is part of the Centro Nacional del Medio Ambiente. It measures and monitors air quality and is involved in guidance for policy decisions on environmental issues. According to Ulriksen air quality in Santiago has improved considerably in the last eight years but the city's geographic location enclosed by the Andes mountains, and its five and a half million population make it very difficult to make further significant progress into the future.

Further north in the province of Ovalle, the meteorological conditions have a very different kind of impact. Here they ensure a clear night sky with the brightest stars to be seen anywhere in the southern hemisphere. Some of the largest research telescopes on earth are placed on peaks of the foothills of the Andes mountain range, only a few kilometres from the ocean. In a nearby valley we set up camp on the flank of a hill, part of the grounds of a local farmer who had expanded into eco-tourism. We could oversee the whole of the farm with its vineyard. Grandma still owns it all, one of her sons runs the shop, her daughter is in charge of the campsite. Since there is now a tarmac road and a phone has been installed this place is part of modernity, even if four generations share the same small estate.

For information on the Future Studies project visit www.agencefuture.org

... this place is part of modernity, even if four generations share the same small estate.

Cycle-touring in Costa Rica

Michele Sanna *was a seasoned backpacker until this trip, his first experience of cycle-touring. He chose Costa Rica because it's a compact country and, as a biologist, he was keen to visit the national parks. At home in Italy he bought some panniers, did a little gentle cycling along (flat) roads and decided he was ready for his new adventure. The problems may seem obvious to an experienced cycle-tourist but we all have to learn some time!*

The first problem, even before leaving home, was the luggage: I tried to fit my kit into the panniers but the result was that I had to leave half of it at home. The second was on the first day. Outside the guesthouse where I spent the night in San José, I put the panniers on the bike and even though I'd left a lot of things behind, they were so heavy that the front wheel reared up. And this was related to the third problem: the hills! Costa Rica is crossed by the Cordillera Central, a chain of mountains that runs from north to south and sooner or later you have to cross over them. I asked the owner of the guesthouse what the climb was like and he replied that the week before a group of cycle tourists gave it up and came back to the guesthouse. That worried me but the following day when I was finally riding, sweating, being rained on and sometimes pushing the bike, it helped me because I didn't want to go back. It took me 10 hours to cover only 70 km, I arrived when it was already dark and I felt shattered, but I made it and that was the first unforgettable ride of a cycling career that took me all around the world over the next 10 years.

Costa Rica is a magnificent place to visit by bike: distances are short, traffic is light and the landscapes are wonderful; mountains, volcanoes, lakes and forests delight the eye. My tour was from San José to the north, staying on the east side of the Cordillera, to the border of Nicaragua and then back to south following the peninsula Nicoya, climb again the Cordillera and finish

MICHELE SANNA

Michele Sanna is a biologist and travel writer based in Milan. Since this Costa Rican trip Michele has taken his bike to places as far apart as Borneo, Africa and the Karakoram Highway. On his latest tour, to Mongolia, his bike broke down only 120km into the journey but a Spanish cycle-tourist returning home from Ulaan Baator kindly gave him his bike so he could continue his ride. He's pictured above outside a local papershop advertising the headline from *La Gazzetta*: 'In bicicletta sulle orme di Gengish Khan', just before his departure for Mongolia.

my trip in San José. It was August, the rainy season, but that didn't worry me much; mornings were almost always sunny but very hot with clear blue skies, while every afternoon there were heavy storms, usually when I had already finished the day's cycling.

The big effort for my first ride had to be rewarded and the prize was to see the volcano Arenal, which I reached after two days of

Arenal volcano © Michele Sanna

cycling. The night of my arrival there was a huge eruption and it was as if it was putting on a fireworks display just for me! In order to enjoy the show better, I cycled outside the town of Fortuna, but I took one of the worst risks of my travels: not because I was cycling alone in the middle of the night in a foreign country, but because in the middle of the road lay a snake called fer-de-lance, one of the most poisonous and aggressive reptiles in central America, and I saw it at the very last moment. It was explained to me later that, especially in the wet season, snakes love to lie at night on the road in order to recover the heat that the asphalt releases during these hours. It is never too late to learn, even if you have a degree in biology!

... fer-de-lance, one of the most poisonous and aggressive reptiles in central America, and I saw it at the very last moment.

The ride north was fascinating, wonderfully welcoming people and no cars to disturb me on the road. I found it quite strange because Costa Rica is, after all, a touristic place but the road to La Cruz, on this side of the Cordillera, is still safe from over-development: most road-users were locals riding horses. After a detour and a visit to the Refugio Nacional de Vida Silvestre Cano Negro, a very good place to see wildlife, especially caymans and birds and well worth the 40 km of unpaved road to reach it, I passed small villages before reaching the last 50 km of road to La Cruz. The road is unpaved and full of potholes that probably make a journey by car very uncomfortable, but not so by bike, as the slow speed allows you to avoid the roughness of the ground.

La Cruz is in the north of Costa Rica but, apart from the beautiful scenery on the Pacific coast, there is not a lot to see or do. Nevertheless I had to stop for two days because a strong hurricane hit the coast and that was the only time that rains didn't allow me to travel.

Going south, the first interesting place to visit is the Parque Nacional Santa Rosa, very important for naturalists because it encompasses several different ecosystems: dry forest, savannah, swamps and ocean beaches (Playa

Empty roads and lush vegetation.
© Michele Sanna

Nancite is the nesting home of the famous Olive Ridley turtles). But the attraction for the cyclotourist is that there is a road inside the park, with the possibility to make safaris by bike – and there is a lot of wildlife to spot. This is probably true during the dry season but not, as I discovered, during the wet one.

To enter the park there are two entrances, I chose the Murcielago Sector because it leads to the less crowded zone; as there were no campgrounds inside, I left my luggage in a guesthouse just a few km outside the park and, without heavy bags to carry, I started my safari: after a couple of km, with several shallow river crossings with the bike on my shoulders (that made me feel very adventurous), I sadly sunk in the mud with no way to proceed and had to go back to the guesthouse. I tried again the following day by the other gate, this time I could camp near the headquarters but there was no way to cycle in; even a 4-wheel-drive couldn't get past the mud. But what made me decide to leave the park happened at night. Around 6 pm it started to rain heavily and some hours later in my tent, which was not very waterproof, drops were falling from the roof. I tried to

I felt as if I was sleeping on something like a water mattress ... my tent was almost submerged by a new stream!

ignore them but then I felt as if I was sleeping on something like a water mattress, so I looked out and I discovered that my tent was almost submerged by a new stream! In the middle of the night, in the jungle under a strong rain I had to dismantle everything and look for a place to wait for the morning. The first spot where I sheltered was the bathroom block but the recent discovery that snakes love warm places made me decide to go and knock on the door of the rangers' bungalow; that, at least, was a good idea since, thanks to their hospitality, I was given a comfortable and dry bed.

A better national park for wildlife in Costa Rica is the Parque Manuel Antonio, 200 km south of Santa Rosa, but I didn't go there because it is really a touristy place, making me think of crowds of people pushing each other to take a picture of a scared monkey. Besides that, for a cyclist, to reach the park it is necessary to ride along the Carretera Interamericana, a very busy road with many dangerous trucks. The highway can be avoided by following the peninsula Nicoya, making the journey a little bit longer, but it still allows one to enjoy the beauties of the landscape. I also got a lot of satisfaction when I visited the Parque Nacional de Barra Honda, at only 20 km from the town of Nicoya, where I could see many howler monkeys, coatis, different kind of iguanas and a lot of invertebrates (and no people pushing me!). The elevation of the peninsula is fairly low, running mostly at sea level, so it means a climb of 2200 metres to cross the Cordillera Central again to reach San José. But after three weeks of cycling I felt myself very fit and ready to face the last challenge.

But all the training you might have done is no use if you have the great idea to go to dinner in a Chinese restaurant the evening before: if you get sick and vomit all night long, the following day will be a very hard day. That is, of course, what happened to me.

> **If you get sick and vomit all night long, the following day will be a very hard day.**

At the start I thought that after the first few pushes on the pedals and the fresh morning air, I would feel better, but when the first gradient came I started sweating as never before and my legs turned to jelly. Luckily that day I planned to cover a short distance, only 20 km to reach the northern point of Arenal lake, and so slowly, while refusing a lift offered me by a pick-up, I reached the small town of Tilaran, where I promised myself to stick to the boring gallo pinto and casado (rice and beans), that never made me feel so sick! To recover my energy decided to rent a room for three days and take a bus to the Reserve de Monteverde, the best preserved forest in central America. I still think it was the right decision, both to go there because the jungle was really beautiful, and not to cycle, as the 40 km to get to the reserve is a very long hill; the road is unpaved and rocky and it was raining most of the time. But sometimes, when I was looking out of the bus windows at the wonderful landscape passing by, without being able to stop and enjoy it more, I wished I was on my bike.

Three days of rest are very good medicine and I was really looking forward to jumping on the saddle again. After circumnavigating the fantastic lake Arenal, I reached Fortuna again, but this time the volcano was completely covered with clouds, telling me I had no more time to lose and that my duty was to reach San José. And that was what I did; this time I took another road, bypassing the towns of San Carlos and Zarcero, through magnificent scenery that seemed to be more Switzerland than Costa Rica, reaching the pass at 2200 meters and looking at the clouds below me with the satisfaction that I never got off the bike and pushed it (well, I didn't go to another Chinese restaurant the day before).

The last 50 kms to San José were an easy ride with my mind already busy thinking of what to tell the friends who hadn't joined me, but, above all, with a firm belief: after this experience, my vision of travel would never be the same – the bicycle would be my companion for the next years. And so it is!

> **My vision of travel would never be the same – the bicycle would be my companion for the next years. And so it is!**

The road to Everest

Dave Wodchis's trip to ride the Friendship Highway was fraught with setbacks. The first was before he'd even started: his original bike was stolen in Beijing. In Tibet, when the weather and his health turn against him, he's forced to alter his plans.

As I set off from the Banok Shol Hotel the Tibetan women who ran it wrapped a white scarf round my neck wishing me a safe journey to Mt Everest: a good omen as it turned out to be a pretty good day for cycling – cool and clear. I'm now camped about 90 km outside Lhasa at an elevation of 4100m, just below the Kampa La (pass). An army officer comes by to say hello, and there's also a Tibetan fellow camped in a big tent a little farther down. All I can hear is the scratch of my pen on the page, the sound of my breath, and the river rushing far below in the valley – and that's all.

All I can hear is the scratch of my pen on the page, the sound of my breath, and the river rushing far below in the valley – and that's all.

Camped on the west side of the mountain, I wake early as it's cold. My thermos of hot water prepared the night before is warm enough to make some instant walnut cereal I'd found in Lhasa and also a cup of instant coffee. When the sun comes around at about 9.30am, I head for Kampa La. The road is mostly smooth with a few streams to ford but my focus of the day is not to make the same mistakes I'd made climbing to Ganden Monastery. I stop a lot, have frequent drinks, take my altitude medication and breath deeply.

About 3pm I reach the 4700m Kampa La – and what a view! Yamdrok Tso (Lake) lies below surrounded by snow-capped mountains. Stunning! Four Tibetan women and a couple of Chinese soldiers cheer my arrival. Taking off the white scarf given to me yesterday I tie it to the line of other scarves and flags flying at the top of the pass.

☆☆☆

Arriving in Shigatse, I can't find the hotel where I was planning to stay, so I check in to the Sandrutze Hotel, a little upmarket with modern glass walled showers and, more importantly considering what happens later, central heating! The first full day in Shigatse is spent visiting the Tashilunpo Monastery, home of the Panchen Lama, second only to the Dalai Lama in the traditional order of Tibetan Buddhism. Unfortunately, I eat something bad somewhere, so I'm not feeling so well by the evening.

I eat something bad somewhere so I'm not feeling so well by the evening.

Later, my friends Pierre and Sonia knock on the door inviting me to dinner and we go for a

Chinese meal at a local/tourist restaurant. I say tourist, because they had an English menu that had prices just marginally higher than those on the Chinese menu. The manager said it was because they served a leaner quality of meat to the foreigners. I guess they also served leaner vegetables, as their price was also a little higher!

The next 36 hours are spent in gut-wrenching agony with excruciating stomach pains and the accompanying dysentery. Pierre and Sonia, who just happen to be doctors, convince me to take some Imodium and start a course of Ciproflaxin antibiotics. I begin to feel better but not well enough to start cycling again so Pierre, Sonia and the others start off from Shigatse a day ahead of me.

DAVE WODCHIS

Dave Wodchis is an event and video producer from Vancouver, Canada. Besides Tibet, he has toured by bicycle in South-East Asia, Northern Europe and Australia as well as in Canada on the west coast. Dave contributes to 🖳 www.worldsurface.com and his own site: 🖳 www.oneworldphotography.com.

I manage to pick up some more altitude medicine and while doing so have the opportunity to call in to a couple of hospitals. These aren't the first ones I'd visited in Tibet, as my hunt for altitude medicine had also taken me to the main hospital in Lhasa. If you are seriously sick in Tibet, get to Nepal, India, Beijing, or Bangkok, because you won't get much help in Tibet. Being sick, I'm far better off staying in my three-star hotel with central heating, than I'd have been lying in a freezing-cold hospital bed with filthy toilets and incompetent staff who would probably have ignored me.

I go shopping for more supplies and visit Shigatse's first department store. The experience is a reminder of how different is the retail experience in the modern world of elevators, automatic ticket readers, supermarket scanners, bar codes, anti-theft clothing tags, metal detectors and x-ray machines. Word had got out about the escalator in this department store, so locals and visiting Tibetans from the surrounding villages have come to try out this remarkable invention. Crowds of them arrive and head straight for the escalator, milling around at the bottom. After I'd done my shopping upstairs, I was coming

Word had got out about the escalator ... so locals and visiting Tibetans from the surrounding villages have come to try out this remarkable invention.

down the escalator and I saw a woman at the top afraid to grab the handle or step boldly forward. I remembered how my parents had held me by the hand as a young child my first time getting on and many more times until I got used to it. That was probably kind of funny to see as well.

PART 3 – TALES FROM THE SADDLE

☆☆☆

I've been warned that the road from Shigatse is dirt, so I have my dust mask ready to pull up over my mouth and nose when necessary. For the first hour or so the road winds along the valley and the surface seems pretty good. Then the headwinds begin to build. They keep building until there's a wall of dust blowing across the south side of the valley. My pace is slowing as I watch little tornadoes of dust blow around in the distance. Occasionally they cross the roadway in front of me. A small benefit of the wind is that it almost immediately clears the dust clouds sent up by passing vehicles. Unfortunately, the good doesn't outweigh the bad and things just get worse. Huge gusts of wind begin blowing and swirling around, bringing masses of dust that completely obscure the road. At times, I feel as if I'm in a massive sandblaster that pelts the exposed skin on my legs with tiny pebbles. There's nothing to do but stop, close my eyes, pull tight the dust mask and wait until the air clears again. The day the author of the *Tibet Overland* guidebook rode this route, it was 'a very pleasant ride'! The day I did it not only were there impossible winds but the Chinese army decided to throw in a few dust-churning convoys as well.

Huge gusts of wind ... bringing masses of dust that completely obscure the road.

☆☆☆

There's still some light left as I arrive in Sakya junction, but not much. A man tells me there's no place to sleep but the guidebook said there was a hotel nearby, and that accommodation was possible at a compound. I can't figure out where the hotel is – seeing only a small building set back from the road without much activity going on, so I opt for the Chinese Road Crew Compound. These buildings used to be the only building shelters for cyclists and other overlanders to stay in. The Chinese military guy in charge decides to let me stay the night. There will be no charge for this courtesy. He calls someone who opens up a barren concrete room for me and hands me a candle. After my sleeping bag and mattress are set up for the evening, they come by for a look, offer me the chance to join them for some food, and then say good night. It turns out to be a nice quiet, relaxing night.

... who opens up a barren concrete room for me and hands me a candle.

Waking up to the sounds of birds singing in the bamboo trees outside my window, the morning also brings a relaxing ride to the town of Lhatse, just 25km down the road. Along the way, I chase a few rogue kids, teach another group 'Head and shoulders, knees and toes...', and stop for tea at a military café. After checking out most of Lhatse's hotels, I settle on a courtyard place called the Dewang, just inside the town boundary. It's the only hotel in town with a hot shower to wash off all that dust from the last few days.

Just after I get my bags unpacked Pierre and Sonia show up. They decide to stay there as well and wait for their friend Chu. After lunch and a shower it's time to do some bike work. I have some bolts to tighten and Pierre has a tyre to change. Then we're off picking up supplies for the upcoming mega pass. On the way back we meet Chu. We discuss how to tackle this pass, Gyatso La, at an awesome 5220m. It's an 1100m climb with a distance of 38km to the peak. We decide to do it in two days, going halfway up on the first day, and then continuing on to the Mt Everest turn-off on the second day.

Leaving in the afternoon, it's a relatively easy ride, in fact, I don't even notice that we're climbing at all. Sonia has been quite sick the night before, so we're all taking it nice and slow. Cycling along the river we look for some campsites, finally settling on one around the road marker 5069, at 4405m. The night is cold and the truck traffic never completely stops.

After the sun hits the valley, we set off to tackle Gyatso La, our highest pass so far. The first part of the road there's a bit of a tailwind but soon enough it changes to icy headwinds. They're not that strong but certainly persistent. On reaching the top of Gyatso La, the biting wind is getting to me and I decide that I really can't face camping again tonight. That means I'll have to get a move on to find some accommodation. Sonia and Pierre plan to camp.

The descent is described as a 'brake burner' in the guidebook. Today it's anything but that: I find myself pedalling into strong icy winds, stopping every 10km or so to let my hands and feet thaw, check the distance remaining and calculate my potential arrival time in Baipa or Shekar. It seems I should make it before dark, but only just before. My water is running low and I resort to my quick energy snack – chocolate bars.

I get to Baipa around sunset. The first place I see is a rather dumpy, dirty dorm room – not what I hauled ass to find. I want a nice warm bed in a clean room, so I cycle up the paved road to Shekar. The sky is turning purple behind the mountains as I arrive at a hotel. After some noodle soup, I'm tucked under two large comforters, sleeping soundly until daybreak.

Shekar has a spectacular fort built up along a mountain ridge, and in the morning light the view can transport you to another time. A time when horses were the only form of transportation, when roaming yaks were massive wild creatures, and the Khan was the ruler of all the lands.

I leave Shekar around noon after cleaning my chain and dispensing with some unnecessary luggage like the oxygen canister I've never used. I ride down to Baipa and have lunch before going to pick up my entrance ticket for Mt Everest Conservation area. Going into the ticket office, I meet up again with Pierre and Sonia. They have yet to eat lunch and need to do some shopping so after waiting a while I set off for Chay ahead of them. There's a Chinese checkpoint along the way and my passport is checked but they don't bother with the travel permit.

At Chay there's a checkpoint for the Everest admission, and right next door is the home of a Tibetan who rents a backroom for cyclists and other

> The descent is described as a 'brake burner' in the guidebook. Today it's anything but that: I find myself pedalling into strong icy winds.

> ... dispensing with some unnecessary luggage like the oxygen cannister I've never used.

260 THE ROAD TO EVEREST

overlanders. Pierre and Sonia arrive a short time after I'm settled in and decide to stay, too.

The next day starts off all right although neither Sonia nor I slept very well at the altitude of 4260m. The new markers on the road to Everest Base Camp count down the kilometres from the main highway, starting at km101. Chay is at approximately km97, and it is here that we begin our climb over Pang La via a continuous series of switchbacks.

It's almost impossible even to just stand and hang on to the bike without getting blown over.

One of the side benefits of these switchbacks is that the headwinds become tailwinds as the road makes its abrupt turns on the way up the mountain. Everything seems to be going smoothly with very little traffic until we are about half a kilometre from the top. Then the winds become so gusty and strong, that it's almost impossible even to just stand and hang on to the bike without getting blown over or, worse, getting blown down the steep drop-off. After putting on more warm clothing and realizing that the gale force winds will not abate, we end up pushing up the last bit whenever the wind drops a little. At the top of the pass we endure the winds as long as possible while gazing at spectacular views of the Himalayan mountain range. There are some cross-country shortcuts on the downhill that allow me to cut out some of the switchbacks. Unfortunately, some of those shortcuts bring me to the edge of a roadway that's either four metres above me or four metres below, but that just means a bit more cross-country riding. At one point, I wonder if I'm still on the right road, because Sonia and Pierre are taking so long to pass me. It turns out that they had some bike problems caused by the rough surface.

On arrival in Tashi Dzom, I find a pretty good guesthouse. The room is cold but private and there's a good restaurant with a welcome English menu. Tibetan a difficult language to learn. My pronunciation is bad and a large number of Tibetan people are illiterate so you can't simply point to Tibetan script in a phrasebook in order to communicate.

Pierre and Sonia arrive about an hour later with bad news. A key bolt under Sonia's seat, the one that attached it to the seatpost, had broken. The vibrations from the road must have caused it to snap. There are tractors in much of Tibet so there is sure to be a bolt of some kind they can use to attach the seat. No way could she ride on without it.

The next morning's delay allows me to have a couple more helpings of fried potatoes and yak meat from the restaurant that served some of the most delicious food I sampled in all of Tibet. The ride that follows is warm and wind-free. This section of the road is extremely beautiful with very few villages and constant views of the Himalayas.

This section of the road is extremely beautiful with very few villages and constant views of the Himalayas.

Sonia and Pierre had thought to go on past Cho Dzong but turn back to the schoolhouse compound guesthouse after a couple of kilometres as the wind is picking up and making riding difficult. A trekker has already checked in to one of the guestrooms in the schoolhouse compound. Remarkably, because he's cut out about thirty kilometres by walking cross-country, and also owing to our extremely easy pace on this section, it turns out he's following the same schedule as we're following by bicycle but he's doing it on foot! It seems a bit disheartening.

He's following the same schedule as we're following by bicycle but he's doing it on foot!

After Cho Dzong, the road, although bumpy, provides non-stop superb views of Everest and the Himalayas. There's lots of time to stop and absorb it all in on the way to Rongphu (Rongbuk).

Sometimes misery comes on the road, and sometimes off. On arrival at Rongphu Monastery Guesthouse, a place that receives hundreds of tourists every week during the high season, I'm surprised that, even for Tibet, it's so disorganized, so unhygienic, and so limited in its services. The toilet is the most disgusting I've ever seen, with a mound of frozen shit piled so high it comes up through the hole in the floor. In the rooms the wash basins are full of dirty water and spit and the floors are still dirty. The other options are to virtually freeze in a tent or to stay in the semi-heated tent couches at Everest Base Camp.

The toilet is the most disgusting I've ever seen.

Following the first night of hygiene disaster survival, I make the journey on a brilliantly sunny day to Everest Base Camp, which is just 8km from the monastery. On arrival, I find that Pierre has just finished setting up his tent, and Sonia has made arrangements to sleep the night in one of the heated tents that serves tea and soup. Some mountain goats are grazing at the edge of the camp and Pierre is complaining about all the litter. When you see Everest and the surrounding area, it looks very mountainous but up close it's just loads and loads of rocks piled upon rocks that never seem to end. It looks dangerous and forbidding. Gazing up at the north face summit, it seems to have its own weather system with clouds swirling and masses of snow sliding down and then billowing up into the sky.

After another night in the Rongphu icebox I decide to attempt the shortcut road to Old Tingri back on the Friendship Highway. The guidebook describes it as more of a trekking route than a road. The turn-off is about 20 km from Everest Base Camp and then it's supposed to be 54 km to Old Tingri. Sonia and Pierre are also planning to ride to Old Tingri but they leave a bit later in the day.

After turning off the main Everest Base Camp road the way is at first quite smooth, then becomes nothing more than river rock before being submerged below a river. On the other side, rather than turning, I follow the road straight along which is a mistake. Backtracking, I head off in the right direction up a different hill, alongside the other river, and into the winds. After about ten kilometres I'm pushing the bike and I decide to head back down the valley for some shelter and try again in the morning when, with luck, the winds will have subsided. I just have no energy in my legs – no strength – and at this altitude the oxygen content is around 50% of that at sea level.

At this altitude the oxygen content is around 50% of that at sea level.

I run into Sonia and Pierre on the way down and let them know what I'm doing. They continue on for a bit before camping for the night somewhere up the ridge; I find a spot further down the pass near the river.

I wouldn't say I had a restful night but that's becoming quite common. Nevertheless it isn't that uncomfortable waking up in the majestic Himalayan landscape. I'm up and ready to go about an hour or so after the sun is shining down into the valley. Unfortunately, the winds are also up early. They're unceasing, the road is not improving much, with several sections running underneath streams, covered in ice in steep places and with rocks covering the surface in many areas. There are alternating periods of riding followed by pushing, waiting for the winds to subside, then more pushing, some riding, fording streams, resting, pushing again and then more riding.

After passing through a village and through another river I catch sight of Pierre and Sonia just ahead of me. I call out to them but the wind blows the sound of my voice far behind me. I keep going for another half an hour or so but after one more iced-over uphill section, my legs are without power, my lungs are struggling and I'm not having any fun. I have no idea of how far up this road goes, how bad it is, or even how far along I've come as my computer had been knocked out of order. I'm still suffering from diarrhoea and lack of sleep and it's time to call it a day. I decide to backtrack to the village and try to catch some kind of transport, at least back to the main Everest Base Camp road. Luckily, a jeep comes along and I get a ride to Rongphu where I'll have a good chance of catching another back to the main highway.

... my legs are without power and my lungs are struggling ...

The next morning I discover that a Swiss couple and a Korean guy are leaving by jeep a day early, so in just a few hours I could be on my way to Old Tingri. Both the driver and passengers agreed to take me, so by noon, we're bumping along the road to old Tingri – the same road I've now been up and down several times. It isn't a much better ride in the jeep but I'm glad that considering the weather and my condition, I had made the decision to seek transport. Thorsten and Pia from Switzerland are great company and I'm very grateful they let me join them in their jeep.

After lunch in Old Tingri, I get back in the jeep and keep going ... all the way to Kathmandu! My bike continues to endure the cold, this time on the roof of the jeep. While I miss the cycling and the freedom to stop at will, I don't miss the cold. Despite the challenges and the set-backs, I know those moments of serene cycling through one of the most majestic landscapes in our world will always be with me.

... those moments of serene cycling through one of the most majestic landscapes in our world will always be with me ...

Now I'm looking forward to getting healthy again, letting heal the many cracks in my skin made by exposure to the extreme wind. I'm also looking forward to espresso coffee, hot Italian pasta and everything else available in Nepal. Part of me had hoped to cycle all the way to Kathmandu but then I also wasn't originally planning to go to Everest Base Camp or getting sick, so I'll swallow my pride and call this the Ride to Everest – enough of an achievement for me to be happy with.

Bicycle wine

Alastair Bland *spent two months cycling in California and living off the land. There was an abundance of free grapes which he soon put to good use.*

*A*nd the wine', wrote Robert Louis Stevenson during his time in the Napa Valley, 'is bottled poetry'.

Such reverence for wine has not been lost on the modern connoisseur who considers it a miraculous potion, gently holding the glass and lifting it against the light to admire the shade of the vintage before taking a sip, ever so small. The connoisseur has spent numerous hours of training and refining a delicate palate and can detect even the slightest essences, which might be named raspberry, earth, cherry, smoke, oak, spice, vanilla, citrus, pine, hickory, peach, cinnamon, gooseberry, and anything else that sounds lovely to the ear. Wine: 'It's the nectar', as the connoisseur loves to say, 'of the gods.'

The process of making wine, however, is quite foul, if not offensive. The vintner infects some grape juice with a form of mold called yeast, and this stuff promptly goes to work eating the sugar. The cells go wild, feasting and producing alcohol and reproducing like bunnies until they all choke on their own excrement and perish at once. The poisoned corpses sink to the bottom and with that the nectar is ready to drink.

I am by no means a connoisseur of wine. I have, however, made wine at home, and last fall I even produced several gallons during a two-month bicycle tour of California. To save money on my trip, I never bought food. I cycled

ALASTAIR BLAND

Alastair Bland is a freelance writer based in San Francisco. A graduate of UC Santa Barbara, he studied anthropology and geography. Following this cycling trip in California he spent seven months in 2005 travelling through the deserts and along the beaches of Baja California, sleeping out and living off the land.

up and down the Central Valley, living peacefully off the land. Fig, almond, and apple trees could easily be found growing wild in roadside ditches but if I saw a tree sagging with fruit but on the other side of a fence, all I usually had to do was knock on the door of the nearest farmhouse and ask permission to pick some. The people I met were remarkably friendly and many times they brought out ladders and buckets and picked fruit by my side. Acquiring free grapes was just as easy.

They partied and feasted day after day in the plastic jug as I pedaled down the country roads ...

In camp – be it at a state park or behind a haystack – I crushed my grapes by hand and dribbled the juice into a plastic screw-top jug. Then I added a pinch of bread yeast from a small sack I carried, screwed on the cap, and called it a sealed deal. Contained in their warm world of sweetness, my yeast cell friends were immeasurably happy. They partied and feasted day after day in the plastic jug as I pedaled down the country roads of California. Often I had to loosen the cap a tad to release the pressure, and I'd say to my boisterous friends, 'Now, now, kids. Don't get too wild'.

But they never really listened. At night when it cooled down, so would the yeast but at sunrise the debauchery started up again. Such a lifestyle can only last so long, and after about a week my single-celled travel companions would all die quite suddenly of alcohol poisoning.

Tragic perhaps but this was not an occasion to mourn. Behind an old barn at dusk, I would kick off my shoes, strain the warm wine through a clean sock, stretch out my legs, and drink. Often the wine still bubbled slightly like cider – and it never let me down. It tasted good, in fact, and several times I got totally plastered before sinking into a deep slumber beneath the stars. Ah, wine: bottled poetry and the nectar of the gods.

I travelled 2500 miles on my tour of California, from San Francisco to Redding, south to Los Angeles, then north again, and through it all saw no place so beautiful as the Napa Valley. In the quaint little town of St Helena one sunny day in October, I pulled up to a fashionable-looking roadside winery with a sign in front that read, 'Free Tasting – Come on in!' I parked my vehicle outside, removed my helmet, and staggered in the door.

My eyes adjusted to the dim lighting and in a moment I beheld a half dozen wine tasters standing at the counter, delicately swirling their long-stemmed glasses, immersed in thought, surely trying to give a name to that oh-so-slight essence. Several pairs of eyes turned upon me, and I felt suddenly out of place in this society of well-dressed ladies and gentlemen. Yet they all smiled warmly at me, and one of three lovely damsels standing together at the counter commented, 'Nice day for a bike ride.'

'Even better day for some wine', I retorted.

'What can I get you?' the man behind the counter asked.

'Anything – just make it strong and on the rocks.'

He chuckled and poured me an itty-bitty little portion of red wine. 'This,' he said proudly, 'is what I like to call our nectar of the gods.'

I took a sip. 'Mm, the gods, indeed. But now you've got to try some of mine.' I thudded my sticky half-gallon bottle onto the counter and explained that it was five-day-old bike booze made from grapes I'd pulled down from the top of a huge fig tree by Lake Berryessa. The lovely damsel asked what varietal the grape was, and I said, 'Why, I don't know.' I suggested that she have a taste and decide for herself. I loosened the cap and swirled the bottle. A potent aroma filled the air. She giggled nervously and said she'd rather die.

She giggled nervously and said she'd rather die.

BICYCLE WINE – THE RECIPE

Ingredients

- **A bicycle** Mine's a Canadian MTB bought used in La Paz, Mexico. It is grey, has 21 speeds, and has been fitted out with three rusty baskets – one up front and two at the rear. It's a cool yet economical setup.
- **Grapes** Any sort will do and you can still tell the connoisseurs that your wine is a Pinot Noir or a Syrah or whatever because bike wine is always so rustic that no expert – should they dare taste it – could even hope to distinguish the true varietal of grape.
- **Yeast** A pinch of brewer's yeast is preferable but bread yeast will do the trick as well. (In prisons, you might note, the vintners among the inmates make *pruno* using common bread mould.)
- A plastic jug with a screw-on cap.
- A clean sock.
- A small, clean Tupperware container.

Method

1. Mash the grapes by hand in the Tupperware container.
2. Pour the juice into your plastic jug. A few seeds and skins won't do any harm. (Note that few things, in fact, can hurt the quality of this wine). Discard the pulp.
3. Drop a pinch of yeast into the jug and seal the cap loosely.
4. Let your yeast cell friends get to work. They will enjoy themselves immensely, having sex and eating sugar and making a big frothy mess of everything. Let them have their fun; they'll be dead in a week.
5. When the wine has ceased bubbling, filter it through your sock into your Tupperware container. Rinse the jug, pour the wine back in, seal the cap, and drink at will. (NB The wine will still be relatively thick – but this is bike-booze, and there is nothing quite like it.)

'Come on, now. About a million of my friends sacrificed their lives to make this stuff. I think you should do them the honor.' I held out the bottle, but the people stared at me in shock. 'Um ...', I stammered. 'I'm just kidding, of course.' Still, the folks eyed me with suspicion.

☆☆☆

I wasn't really offended. After all, I resembled a vagrant and my wine looked disgusting; it hadn't been filtered yet and there'd been no time for it to age. On the other hand, this was the real thing – wine at its most rustic stage – and I thought it was a poor connoisseur who was afraid of sampling something so pure and fresh.

This was the real thing – wine at its most rustic stage.

I entered a half-dozen tasting rooms that afternoon, yet met no one daring enough to even smell my concoction. I camped alone that night in the quiet oak forest of Bothe State Park. I ate walnuts, prickly pears, and the inevitable figs for supper, then began sipping what would be my last bottle of bike booze. Pedaling along that day I'd noticed that all the local vineyards had been stripped clean. To the commercial wine-makers, this was just another stage in the calculated process of putting poetry into a bottle. To me, though, the barren vines alluded to the end of the season, the coming of winter, and the time for me to steer toward home.

No one else in eight weeks of travel ever tasted my wine, and it's all I can do now to provide the instructions for others to make it. To anyone interested in making their own booze during their next wine-country bicycle tour, I say: do not be daunted. The materials are few, the process simple, and if you just put some heart into it, the results will be bottled poetr– well, at least it'll rhyme.

APPENDIX – BICYCLE MAINTENANCE

MAINTENANCE ON THE ROAD

At home, maintenance can be put off forever. On tour, you're covering much greater distances and need to keep your bike running efficiently. Rest days are a good time to keep up with maintenance on your bike, at the campsite or in a cheap hotel courtyard. At the very least you want to be checking the '3Bs': bolts, brakes and bearings. Maintenance can be a chore but on the road it's much more satisfying when you have no distractions or time constraints and know that your work will ensure the smooth continuation of your trip.

Cleaning your derailleur drive train

Cleaning the chain and exposed gears is an important and rewarding task. Your bike will ride a little faster and more quietly and the drive train will certainly last longer and be less messy if you keep it clean. You may have one of those chain bath gadgets to wash the chain but on the road it's easier to give the chain and gears a dry clean using an old toothbrush (or the specialist brushes from manufacturers like Park), a tiny flat screwdriver and a rag. Working with everything dry makes far less mess.

With your bike standing upright, pick away at the grime on the chain and gears; if you have some WD40 or similar solvent spray, this will help loosen any crud. Hold the flat end of a small screwdriver against the side of the jockey and pulley wheels of the rear derailleur and rotate the pedal backwards to scrape off dirt, as if you were working a lathe. If you can, do the same to the rear sprockets, cleaning each one in turn. It's harder to get in behind the largest chainring but be persistent and your efforts will pay off.

CHAIN OIL

Convenient free supplies!
Instead of carrying your own chain oil, you might look around petrol/gas stations for discarded motor oil containers. You need only a few drops and there's usually enough in one plastic container for one or two bikes. In the developing world motor oil is sold in bulk so you won't find discarded bottles but you will find fellows who will part with a few drops from their oil cans, either at no charge or for the equivalent of pennies, in roadside repair shops.

Motor oil is not the most ideal lubricant but many long-distance tourers have managed for years with this low-cost method, which also spares you the risk of an oil spill inside a pannier, if you miss tightening a bottle top!

How much chain oil to use
Sprays like WD-40 are not really good enough to properly lubricate a chain alone; they are not thick enough to protect the metal of the chain, cogs, and chainwheels. Chain oil (especially the thicker formulations, such as 'Phil Tenacious Oil') should be applied sparingly: a maximum of six drops, over the entire length of the chain (while backpedaling, by hand, 2-3 turns of the crank when the chain is in the large chainring). If a chain looks wet after you've oiled it, you've used waaaaay too much! Wipe off the excess or your chain will become a sticky magnet that attracts abrasive dirt and grit, and that defeats the whole purpose of lubrication: reducing wear.

Paul Woloshansky

Do the same with the chain itself; you need to poke and scrape every link, especially in between the plates.

Next, lay the bike down. Fold your rag in two and pull it tight to create a straight line along the folded edge. Use the rag like dental floss to 'floss' between the sprockets of the rear cassette. You don't have to remove the wheel and can use the rag to move the sprocket around when you have cleaned one side. Wipe off any excess muck and let everything dry, then add a few drops of whatever lubricant you're carrying (see box on p.266).

Checking bolts

Some riders check nuts and bolts daily, especially for their racks, but unless you're riding off-road it's excessive except if you've noticed persistent loosening (either visible loosening or a wobbling rack). Checking all bolts every rest day is certainly a good idea.

Brake maintenance

Brake pads have a much shorter life on tour – you're riding greater distances, and though there's hopefully less stop and start riding you're bike is heavier and you might be making some long descents. Wet weather is also very hard on brakes pads and so they need frequent attention.

Fine tuning, which normally means tightening the brakes as the pad wears, is done by turning the small barrel adjuster on the brake cable anticlockwise to tighten the brakes. You might find the adjuster next to the brake lever if you have mountain bike bars, or they'll be by the brakes themselves. Over time, this fine tuning is not enough as the pad becomes so worn that it does not fully engage with the rim. Check after a big descent or a rainy day that the pads have not become dislodged. Brake pads can move out of position and in the worst case rub on the fragile tyre sidewall. If the pad is wearing unevenly you won't get good braking performance and should replace it.

Replacing brake pads

Owners of V-brakes have an easy time as the rubber pads slide into the brake shoes which saves having to remove the brake shoe. The advantage is that you don't have to reposition the brake shoe every time you change the pads. Cantilever brake owners are not so lucky; the brake pad and shoe are a single unit that must be thrown away. Loosen the cable anchor bolt, most likely a 5mm Allen bolt and screw the barrel adjuster all the way back in.

Fitting new brake shoes is not easy as the pad can move around while you are tightening it, and you need near-perfect positioning. Don't feel you have to push the perpendicular bolt on the brake pad all the way into the cantilever so that the brake pad rests against the cantilever arm; the brakes will have greater mechanical advantage if you extend the brake pad out from the arm a little – try it that way and adjust later. Half-tighten the brake shoe, push the brake against the wheel and adjust the pad to where you want it to hit the rim, allowing a little toe-in (ie: the front, leading edge of the pad is a little closer to the rim than the rear). Tighten it fully, then pull the cable through the anchor bolt, holding both brake arms with your other hand almost against the wheel. With luck the cable will not slip back through the anchor bolt while you reach for your Allen key to tighten it. If it does, you either need a friend

Adjust bolt to set brake pad

Tiny Allen bolt for fine adjustment of brake pad

to help or a pair of locking pliers – but be careful not to damage the cable by clamping it too hard.

Cleaning brake pads

Brake pads build up with grit and tiny scraps of metal to act like sandpaper on the wheel rim, which reduces braking power. Using any sharp tool, carefully scrape or dig out as much grit as you can from the brake pads which you may have to remove beforehand. Occasionally cleaning the wheels is a good idea as it allows you to see any damage to the rim and also makes wheel truing easier (see p.272).

Brake squeal

Brake squeal is an annoyance but not usually a safety issue. It could be a toe-ing in problem – see p.267 for how to set cantilever brake pads. Other causes of brake squeal are dirty or damaged rims, damaged or badly worn brake pads, loose brake arms (tighten the bolt attaching the brake arm to the boss on the fork or frame), or even the type of brake blocks.

Centring brakes

Brakes touching the rim unevenly is a common problem; usually one pad is dragging lightly on the rim. It may be that one pad is out of position and catching on the rim, or the wheel was not properly centred in the dropouts when you last put it in but, most of the time, a simple adjustment solves the problem. Look for a tiny Allen bolt (usually 2mm) on the side of one or both brakes – see illustration. Tightening that bolt on the brake that is rubbing will push it away from the rim. Alternatively you may have to loosen the small bolt on the opposing brake. Experiment but be careful not to over-loosen these bolts – it can release a spring inside the brake, and you'll need to remove the brake from the brake boss, dismantle it and reset the spring.

Replacing brake cables

Not a difficult job but make sure you have the right cables you need – brake cables are longer for rear brakes and different for mountain bike and dropped bar setups. Note how your brake cable fits into the brake lever when you push it out. You may have to squeeze the brake a little to see where the cable nipple fits into the brake lever.

Weak brakes

There are many possible causes. The longer cable on rear brakes reduces power – there's more stretch in the cable and also more chance for dirt in the cable housing, causing friction. The brakes themselves could be set in a position giving little mechanical advantage, or the straddle cable (older brakes have a thick cable linking the two brake arms) may be too long. It's usually possible to set the spring inside each brake arm in two different positions on the brake boss, so remove the brake from the boss, see where the coil spring fits into a hole in the boss, and make sure it is in the hole that gives it greatest resistance. An over-tight bolt or grime in the brake could also reduce efficiency.

Derailleur adjustment

As derailleurs have become indexed (click-shifting) and built to higher standards and narrower tolerances, they've become more fussy and in need of more regular adjustment. It's minor work but you might need to make small adjustments every couple of days. For a derailleur to work well, the chain, sprockets and derailleur mechanism (or 'mech') all need to be clean. A dirty cable will also stick and cause problems, and a kink in a cable can only be rectified by replacement. Manufacturers advise not to lubricate gear cables but if they are rusty or slightly damaged a squirt of spray or oil would be a quick road fix. Common problems include:

Noisy or poor shifting Assuming everything is clean, you need to look at the alignment of the mech and check it's tracking exactly in line with the sprocket carrying the chain. A mech feeding the chain a little to the left or right will be noisy and cause friction.

Turn the bike upside down and turn the pedal with one hand. By rotating the barrel cable adjuster one way or the other, the derailleur will move up or down the cassette – a few turns of the adjuster and it will jump into the next gear. Keep adjusting it till the derailleur is centred for each gear. It's easier if someone else shifts gears using the handlebar gear control while you pedal and experiment with the barrel cable adjuster – you'll soon get the hang of it as the gears run most quietly when all are correctly aligned with the mech.

Many gear shifters have a second barrel adjuster next to the gear shifter on the handlebar. On a long straight stretch of road where there's nothing but the sound of your gears chattering, try adjusting it on the fly – you'll soon be in the habit of listening out for gear noise and doing some fine tuning to eliminate it.

Chain comes off the cassette This is caused by loose limit screws (see illustration) allowing the rear mech to move too far. These limit screws can work loose over time; tighten them so they only just allow the chain into the highest and lowest gear. The limit screws are at the back of the rear mech and are usually marked 'L' and 'H'. Screw in 'L' a touch to stop the chain jamming into the spokes and screw in 'H' to stop the chain going off the smallest sprocket (highest gear).

Rear derailleur
adjustment

Chain skipping This might be caused by a tight link not articulating fully as it goes round the sprockets; it could have got damaged by the chain getting stuck in the spokes. Lubricate the tight link and prise it apart. If the plate on the side of the link looks damaged, you may have to replace that link. Sometimes your chain and/or sprockets are so worn that the chain comes off, especially during hard pedalling. There'll be no apparent damage, but examine your chain for stretch and check your sprockets too – see 'chain stretch' below.

Front derailleur

Front derailleurs don't have the fine-tuning adjustment of a rear mech, only the limit screws, but it's usually possible to move the cage (the curved plates which sit around the chain) while you're riding if they're rubbing on the chain. If you hear a clattering sound, it may well be the front derailleur and you can look down while riding and check if the cage is rubbing. Half-shifting the gear control on the left handlebar will usually shift the cage out of the way.

To move the chain over such large jumps between chainrings, the cage has to over-shift, that is, it needs to move a little further than the ideal position in order to push the chain onto the next chainring. That's when you need to give it a click or half-click to push it to a centred position for the ring you want to use. Very occasionally an extra push is needed when going up into larger rings or a click in the other direction to pull it back. Again, let noise be your guide and adjust it any time you can hear it.

Limit screws

Front derailleur limit adjustment

Limit stop adjustment

As with rear derailleurs, tightening either screw moves the limit inwards, so if the chain is falling off the chainrings tighten the screw on that side. Note that the limit for the large chainring tends to be right on the ring, whereas for the smallest chainring you have to set the limit a millimetre or two left of the ring itself.

Don't alter the height of the derailleur on the seat tube on the road, this needs doing only if you change the chainring or fit a different size. The cage should be as close as you can get it to the curve of the large chainring without touching.

Chain stretch

Chains don't actually stretch like knicker elastic, but the rivets and collars around them wear out over time, allowing each link to lengthen and so effectively stretch the chain. Measure your chain using a 12" rule held at the centre of one rivet in the chain link. The 12" line on a new chain will be exactly in the centre of the twelfth link. More than 1/16" (nearly 2mm) over and it's time for a new chain and more than 1/8" (3mm) over, you'll more than likely need new sprockets as well. If you can see daylight between the chain and sprockets or chainring, your chain and the sprockets/rings are on the way out.

Headset maintenance

Paul Woloshansky

Headset maintenance is mostly ignored by touring cyclists, who are usually more concerned with how their wheels and drive-trains are holding up. Generally speaking, on shorter tours the bearings that allow a bicycle to be steered shouldn't require servicing or adjustment. On long journeys, however, ignoring an out-of-adjustment headset can ruin this component, damage a frame and fork, and negatively-affect your bike's handling. A bicycle burdened with very heavy front panniers exacerbates the potential for harm so you need to recognize the problem early on in order to prevent or minimize damage.

The following advice is really 'an ounce of prevention' so you won't have to look for 'a pound of cure' out in the middle of nowhere:

Threaded headsets

If your bike is equipped with a threaded headset you'll need a tool that fits the flats of your bike's headset adjusting cone to adjust or service the bearings. Wrenches much smaller than the ones bikeshops use are available and are a good choice for a touring toolkit (e.g: Park Tool's RW3, which has a 36mm headset wrench on one end and a 15mm pedal wrench on the other; make sure you get one that fits your bike!).

Ideally two wrenches are used to adjust a headset, but you can usually find an adjustable spanner (crescent wrench) in most roadside repair shops to fit a headset's locknut, which is tightened down clockwise against an adjusting cone held securely by either a 32, 36, or 40mm headset wrench.

Don't fret if your first adjustment results in an overtight headset: adjustment is by trial-and-error, try again, backing off the adjusting cone a little before re-tightening the locknut against it. To check if your adjustment is too loose, grasp the front brake lever and rock the bike forward and backward to detect any play, and adjust it out with the adjusting cone. Keep on checking and adjusting until you've got it right, but be aware that a headset that's been loose for a while will probably have pitted bearing surfaces, so the final adjustment will often be a compromise between too tight and too loose.

Aheadsets or threadless headsets

Threadless systems are adjusted from the very top; tightening down the Allen-head bolt (visible in the centre under the top cap) drives the stem downwards on the smooth, threadless steerer tube. This action compresses the Aheadset and eliminates bearing play. It's possible to over-tighten, so watch that there is no play but that the handlebar moves freely.

The golden rule is this: you must loosen the Allen-head bolts on the side of the stem (they attach the stem to the steerer) before you snug down the top bolt. This step allows the stem to move freely down the steerer. If you forget to do this, you risk damaging or dislodging the star-nut (the barbed nut that has been driven down inside a steerer tube, that the adjusting bolt screws into).

Also, before snugging down an Aheadset, check to see if any plastic or rubber seals are protruding. If they are, centre them so they aren't damaged or sheared-off during adjustment. If the seals are damaged the system will be less weather-proof.

Wheel truing

Because of the extra payload and rough roads it's normal for wheels to go out of true on tours. Squeezing pairs of spokes gives a very rough idea of spoke tension but should help identify any loose spokes. They'll also need some minor truing should a spoke require replacement. To do so without a truing stand or any tools other than a spoke key follow these instructions. Of all bicycle maintenance procedures, this essential skill is something worth learning before leaving home as it does require a certain knack.

1. With the panniers off, stand the bike upside down.

2. Spin the wheel and push one brake pad towards the wheel. As you push it closer, it will probably make contact in one or several places on the rim.

3. Select the biggest point of contact to work on first. As the wheel rubs against the brake pad, it slows down and comes to rest on the biggest bump.

4. Slowly turn the wheel back and forth to find the centre of this bump. If it looks as if the bump is on the other side of the wheel, go round to that side and start there.

Wheel truing takes a little practice. It's easiest with a proper spoke key (shown here). Turn anticlockwise to tighten; clockwise to loosen.

5. Bear in mind that though you're tightening the spokes, you're actually turning the nipples that the spokes screw into, so you tighten the opposite way. Turn the key **anti-clockwise to tighten spokes**, and clockwise to loosen them.

6. Tighten or loosen in quarter-turn increments. Turn just past 90°, then back off in order to loosen the spoke in the nipple, as sometimes the spoke twists but does not turn in the thread. Lightly lubricate the nipple if necessary. Check the rim frequently by spinning the wheel to check on your progress, so you don't overtighten and risk a broken spoke or round off the nipple so the spoke key can't grip.

7. For small bumps, turning only the one spoke at the centre of the deviation may

---

REPAIRING A BROKEN FRAME WITH GLUE

British bike designer Mike Burrows writes that two-part epoxy glue (such as Araldite in the UK) can make a good repair on broken frames or racks. First, clean the frame using petrol or something similar to remove all grease. File or scratch the surface thoroughly to give good adhesion. Wrap with strips of woven glass fibre, binding it as tight as possible on the frame. Use a knife to spread the mixed epoxy on, warming it up beforehand if necessary. PVC insulating tape can be used to bind the epoxy resin onto the frame, pricking the tape to allow excess resin to escape. A clean break in a rack can be strengthened by using a tent peg as a splint before binding with glass fibre and glue. (From CTC's *Cycle Magazine* January 2005).

work, but you may have to slightly loosen the spokes either side of it. Be careful loosening spokes as this is as dangerous as over-tight spokes in causing metal fatigue (and hence breakages) and allowing the wheel to go out of true.

8. Work around the wheel until all large deviations are eliminated. Once you can rotate the wheel and feel numerous tiny bumps, there is probably not much more you can do yourself. If you can get the deviations from true down to 1mm, that is excellent for a roadside repair.

Fixing a puncture

You'll need a pump to match your valves (these days nearly all pumps fit both Presta or Schrader valves), glue, chalk or talc, patches or old inner tube to cut a patch from, sandpaper and two tyre levers.

Most people on day rides simply fit a spare tube rather than repair a puncture on the spot and hold up their friends. It saves a few minutes. Even then remember to check the tyre for thorns or broken glass which might still be embedded.

To repair an inner tube

1. Loosen the brakes by pulling the brake cable out of its guide. Open the quick-release on the wheel and remove the wheel.

2. Remove the cap on the tube valve or locknut around the base of the valve, if there is one.

3. Loosen the tyre from the wheel by hand, squeezing the tyre as you go round it with your hands.

4. If the tyre is loose in relation to your wheel, you might be able to remove it by hands – the safest way to do so and rather satisfying too!

5. If not, use plastic tyre levers. These are soft and less likely to damage rims or tubes. The kind with a hook on the other end allows you to clip it to a spoke and free your hands to insert the second tyre lever – see illustration opposite.

6. Work your way slowly round the tyre with the tyre lever, bringing the tyre off the rim on one side only.

7. Remove the inner tube and pump it up. You can probably spot anything

Using plastic tyre levers to remove tyre.

larger than a slow leak. Mark it or hold your thumb over it and keep searching in case there are more punctures. If you can't dip the tyre in water to look for escaping bubbles, you'll have to use your ears or try to feel the air rushing out if you hold the tyre up to your eyes or wet lips.

8. Rub round the hole with sandpaper, making sure you eliminate any raised edges running down the centre of the tube.

9. Apply a thin layer of glue to an area around the hole larger than the patch. Let it cure till it becomes tacky, then apply the patch, removing any backing plastic or foil first on the side which goes on to the tyre. Hold it tight for a minute or two. If you have chalk or talc, spread a little on the excess glue. Or if there is some very fine soil around, crumble it to dust in your fingers and use that.

10. While you let the glue dry a little longer, check the tyre for foreign objects. Rips in the tyre can be reinforced with patches of old inner tube glued on the inside, though this may only work as a temporary repair.

11. The glue will be dry within five minutes. Partially inflate the tube and stuff it back in the tyre and seat the valve in its hole.

Before resorting to tyre levers refit the tyre as much as you can by hand.

12. Begin fitting the tyre bead back behind the rim. Go as far as you can around the wheel with both hands. Before resorting to the tyre levers to push the last bit of tyre bead over the rim, push the lever in between tyre and rim to make sure the inner tube is not trapped.

13. Partially inflate the tube then deflate it quickly to free the inner tube, should it be trapped. Inflate the tyre to full pressure, hope it stays that way and refit the wheel and the brakes.

TOOLKIT

Your toolkit should be chosen with your own bike in mind so that it comprises only the tools you need. It will be based around the following essential items:

> Multi-tool with sufficient Allen keys, screwdrivers, chain tool, blade
> Leatherman or similar
> Spoke key
> 2 tyre levers

It's easiest to build your toolkit around a multitool such as the **Topeak Alien II**, one of the most popular bike tools available, with 26 functions on it. Having them all in one place makes it harder to lose the small tools, such as the 2mm Allen key you may need to fine-tune your brakes. Check all over your bike to see if you have the necessary screwdriver or Allen key to fit everything. Something as big as the Alien II will have all those keys, and in long enough sizes to reach all the places you need to reach.

A few **extra Allen keys** or a small **wrench** for the most commonly-used sizes would not hurt – you may lose or damage keys and wear out their edge. You may need a particularly long Allen key to reach into certain places, such as the stem, and the short keys that multi-tools have are sometimes not long enough. Pedro's of the USA makes an excellent set of long individual Allen keys with ball ends for working at odd angles. Having a few individual 'L'-

shaped Allen keys enables you to use either end depending on whether you want extra length or leverage. You could also buy an extension collar to gain more leverage on your Allen keys. I use these in combination with an adjustable wrench to remove pedals. Pedals need a 15mm wrench to remove them, but pedal wrenches are normally about 30cm long as force is usually required. Most people balk at carrying such a long tool and my alternative is to be able to extend the length of the wrench that I carry. Grease your

A lightweight tool and repair kit: – CoolTool, hose clamps, valve adaptor and cable ties.
© Robin Wielder

pedals' threaded spindles before fitting them to the crankset, every time you re-assemble your bike for a long trip. If you are going to box your bike for a flight or train trip, (it may be required for trips on Amtrak in the USA, for instance) you must be able to remove the pedals. The right tool must be slim to fit in the gap beside the pedal but strong enough to apply sufficient force. Another great bike tool that has been around a long time is the **CoolTool** made by Gerber but it can be hard to find outside the USA. The CoolTool has an adjustable wrench opening up to 19mm that can handle pedals, and you can combine the tools to make a long lever, more so if you buy a short section of tube to extend your 6mm Allen key. Since this is a rare need, you could instead use the 10cm piece of 10mm diameter aluminium tubing you should have brought for repairing broken tent poles.

The second multi-tool you need is a **Leatherman** or something similar. This gives you good quality screwdrivers that bike-specific multi-tools usually lack, and in different sizes. It serves as a backup for several tools and has wire cutters and pliers that are essential for removing and installing gear and brake cables. It also has one or more sharp knives for emergency roadside repairs. Having good knives for working on your bike means you can keep your penknife clean for using on food. Some riders swear by a multi-tool with built-in locking pliers, such as the **Leatherman Crunch**, which is probably the best choice for a biker. I was once saved in a remote part of Wyoming by using

ESSENTIAL SPARES

- Puncture kit
- Hose clamps
- Electrical ties/zip ties
- Duct tape (may fit around your water bottles or loose around the seatpost)
- Brake cables
- Gear cables
- Cable ends
- Spokes in all necessary lengths
- Old toothbrush for cleaning gears

- WD40 or similar solvent
- Small tub of grease (use an old film container)
- Spare spokes: several of each length
- Various nuts, bolts and washers
- Glue – Loctite, SeamGrip, Epoxy
- Small patches of fabric- canvas, old inner tube or tyre wall, nylon for tent or mattress
- Sleeve piece of aluminium to repair tent poles

A fabric tool roll is a convenient way to pack your tools and keep them from rattling.

locking pliers as a clamp to hold a broken rack on my bike. Locking pliers damage nuts, bolts and cables very easily though and should not be used when a proper wrench is available.

A **dedicated spoke key** is another luxury, as you will have one on your bike multi-tool, but it is for emergencies only. When you are truing the wheel on a rest day, you will appreciate having a high quality spoke key. Even the best ones are not expensive; just make sure it fits your spokes before you buy it. A **cassette removal tool**, still sometimes referred to as the Hypercracker long after the firm stopped making them, is a necessity. When spokes break, the ones next to the gears go first and these cannot be replaced without removing the cassette. In a workshop, you would use one tool to immobilize the cassette and another to remove the lockring. On the road, you have no space for these tools. Instead, buy either of the following gadgets, either from the USA or the Netherlands: ⌨ www.sheldonbrown.com/harris/stein-mini-lock/ or ⌨ www.m-gineering.nl/indexg3.htm (and click on 'hard to finds').

GLOSSARY

Note: some of the terms used below are illustrated in the photograph on p.26

- **Anodized** Anodizing is a method of coating and hardening aluminium at room temperature. This also makes it corrosion resistant.
- **Audax ride** Long, fast ride with minimal gear. Bikes designed for audax rides have the comfort of a touring bike but are designed for speed.
- **Bar-ends** Bolt-on extensions to handlebars to provide extra hand positions to straight/mountain-bike handlebars. Available in many shapes and almost a necessity for touring on a bike with a straight (ie non-dropped) handlebar.
- **BOB** (as in 'Beast of Burden') **is a maker of single-wheeled trailers; their Yak model is the most popular among tourers, particularly for off-road use.**
- **Bottle cage** Metal or plastic drink-bottle holder that screws onto bike's frame.
- **Cartridge bearings** Some ball bearings are supplied loose and installed individually (though always replaced together, never matching old with worn bearings), others come in a cartridge.
- **Cassette sprockets** The small gears at the back, also known as cogs. Used to be fitted individually into a cluster so that you could change the sizes of individual sprockets if you wanted, but these days the cluster of gears is produced in one unit which is known as a cassette.
- **Chainrings** The large rings in between the pedals at the front of the drivetrain. Controlled by the gear shifter on the left of the handlebar.
- **Chain stays** Tubing connecting the bottom bracket to the rear dropout.
- **Cones** screw onto the axles and tighten against the bearings to hold them in place and give the wheel the minimum amount of play while allowing it to rotate freely. They rarely need adjustment but require thin (15 and 16mm) wrenches.
- **Derailleur hanger** The place on the frame immediately behind the rear dropout where the derailleur is bolted onto the frame. This is a vulnerable point because it projects and if bent in an accident or in transit will badly affect gear shifting. Aluminium frames usually have a replaceable hanger owing to the difficulty of repair.
- **Drivetrain** Sounds as if a motoring journalist made up this term but it simply refers to the gear system considered as a whole.
- **Dropouts** Dropouts are the wrench-like ends to the forks and at the corner of the rear triangle on the frame, into which the wheels fit.
- **Groupset** An anglicized version of the Italian Gruppo, referring to the entire set of gears, usually in connection to the name brand and quality, eg Shimano Deore LX.
- **Headset/Aheadset** The headset is the bearings supporting the front wheel, one set being at the bottom of the head tube and one at the top. The Aheadset is the most modern type of headset and is found on almost all quality bikes, and differs from the headset in that the steering tube is not threaded but uses a bolt instead to pull the steerer up into the head tube, making it easier to adjust. Note, however, that the handlebar cannot be raised at all on an aheadset. You have to buy a new stem to do that.
- **Quills/stems** A quill-style stem is the old style in which a narrow handlebar stem fits into the head tube rather than around the top of the steerer.
- **Recumbent** Bicycle design where the rider lies back rather than sits in the traditional fashion.
- **Sag wagon** Support vehicle; what you get when you sign up for a typical guided bike tour. It carries your bags, spare parts and emergency supplies and gives exhausted riders a lift.
- **Seat stays** Run from the top of the seat tube to the rear dropout.
- **SPD pedals** Shimano's style of pedals that lock onto cleats in the bottom of cycling shoes designed especially for Shimano SPDs. They are the most common kind of pedal designed for cleated shoes. Undoubtedly efficient but some bike tourers like them, some don't.
- **Swaged spokes** Where the metal is worked to make it thinner in some areas to save weight.
- **Threaded steerers/brake shoe posts** Where the steerer tube is threaded, as in old headsets. Bikes with large (32-36mm) nuts around the head which lock the steerer into the head of the bike have threaded steerers. Similarly, some old brakes had metal posts (the short metal piece perpendicular to the rubber pad) which were threaded.
- **TIG-welded frames** TIG welding uses electricity rather than oxy-acetylene: the metal is welded at a higher temperature.
- **Truing** The art of making a bicycle wheel true: perfectly round with no kinks or wobbles.
- **Wheel 'dishing'** Wheels are 'dished' in that the side of the wheel has a saucer shape, giving it greater strength. The left side of the rear wheel is more dished than the right side on a bike with derailleur gears, and the more derailleur gears a bike has, the less 'dish' to its shape and the weaker it will be.

CONTRIBUTORS

Jean Bell (see p.205)

Alastair Bland (see p.263)

Janne Corax has spent most of his time since 1994 travelling the world by bicycle, having cycled through over 60 countries. He has ridden all the major routes in western China and many of the minor ones and made the first bicycle crossing of the Chang Tang high plateau in northern Tibet in 2003-4 with his partner, Nadine Saulnier. He is also an accomplished mountaineer and guide. His website is 🖳 www3.utsidan.se/corax-e

Philip Davis regards himself a latecomer to cycle travel but he is now making up for lost time. His first bike adventure was cycling from Jordan through Syria and to the Lebanon. He has since cycled through much of SE Asia, and also part of Ladakh in India. He rode the Friendship Highway late in 2005 and just returned from Japan. Philip hopes to get to Kyrgyzstan on his bike before the dread 40th birthday arrives.

Sebastian Eissing skipped university in '94 to enter 'the school of travel' on his first big bike trip: cycling through Africa on an old Chinese bike. During the last 12 years of rambling and working around the globe in close on 100 countries, bicycles, always cheap ones, have been his means of seeing the world. Sebastian rode home to Germany from Korea in 2005 and now lives in a small village near Frankfurt, from where he rides out to work as a postman.

Mark Elliott is the author of *Azerbaijan with excursions to Georgia*, and *South-East Asia – the graphic guide*, both published by Trailblazer. He also co-wrote the groundbreaking *Asia Overland* and has published or contributed to many other travel guides for Lonely Planet. He lives in Belgium with Danielle, whom he met while travelling in Turkmenistan.

Edward Genochio (see p.215)

Cass Gilbert There is nothing worth knowing about bicycles and expedition-touring that Cass Gilbert doesn't know. Cass did two very long rides, Turkestan by tandem and Sydney to London, as well as countless shorter tours before beginning a successful writing career for *Cycling Plus* magazine in the UK and the CTC's magazine, *Cycle*. He spends his summers running his own tours of the Indian Himalaya (see 🖳 www.out-there-biking.com) with his partner, Cara Coolbaugh.

Anna Heywood (see p.227)

Simon Hill Retiring at the grand young age of 45 to devote his life to travel, Simon has enjoyed long bike trips around India, South-East Asia, Australia and his native Britain. He finds cycle-touring is the perfect way to travel for someone who is time-rich and money-poor.

Felix Hude is an animator, multimedia artist and lecturer from Melbourne but is well known among web-surfing cyclists for his website – 'Biking South-East Asia with Mr. Pumpy', to be found at 🖳 www.mr pumpy.net.

Alastair Humphreys left the UK in September 2001 to ride round the world. His journey promoted the work of Hope and Homes for Children through talks, interviews and his website 🖳 www.roundthe worldbybike.com. Over four years Alastair pedalled 45,000 miles across sixty countries and five continents.

Igor Kovse (see p.243)

Mark and Juliette McLean left Liverpool in July 2002 and cycled overland to reach Sydney, Australia, in December 2004. Mark is a computer programmer and Juliette has left teaching to begin a new career in physiotherapy. Their website is 🖳 www.mark-ju.net.

CONTRIBUTORS (cont'd)

Tim Mulliner has travelled in over 40 countries, many by bike. He is currently finishing his masters degree and lives in Dunedin, New Zealand. He recently published his account of his ride home from the UK, *A long ride for a pie*.

Steve Pells is a scientist and lives in Edinburgh. He has cycled extensively in Europe, the Americas, Asia and Oceania, and prefers riding in mountainous regions. His scientific background inclines him to the technical aspects of cycling and he has been building (and touring on) his own wheels for some years. He has raced in events such as the Ironman triathlon and marathon, and also climbs, skis and runs. His website is ⌨ www.sentient-entity.pwp.blueyonder.co.uk.

Luka Romih and Manca Ravnikar Luka and Manca are from Ljubliana and have done several long rides together, starting with adventurous trips in Slovenia and neighbouring Croatia and Romania and later travelling as far as Kyrgyzstan, the Pamir Highway and west Tibet.

Michele Sanna (see p.252)

Chris Scott is the author of *Adventure Motorcycling Handbook* and *Sahara Overland* and the forthcoming *Overlanders' Handbook*. He also leads motorbike tours in the Sahara and makes DVDs about off-road motorbike riding. He has a sneaking admiration for people mad enough to go adventure-touring on a 'pushie' but although he likes the idea of it in principle, Chris claims never to have cycled more than 10 miles in his life.

Luke Skinner (see p.227)

Peter Snow Cao travelled for three years on his Grand Asian Tour and met his wife in China. They live in Chengdu, where Peter runs Bike China Adventures (⌨ www.bikechina.com). Besides loving cycling, China and family, Peter admits to an interest in confluence hunting – well worth checking out at ⌨ www.confluence.org.

Laura Stone Laura's cycling career began in Cambridge, which is as flat as a puncture patch, by speeding to Classics lectures on a £5 bike. Thanks to Cass Gilbert, she graduated to the hillier polders of Holland, where she updated the *Rough Guide to the Netherlands*. In 2003 she booked a one-way ticket to India and set off on a six-month solo bike trip around the Himalaya. Since then, Laura has returned every year: in 2004 to update the Himalayan chapters for the *Rough Guide to India*, and in 2005-2006 to write *Himalaya by Bicycle – a route and planning guide* for Trailblazer (due mid 2007).

Dave Wodchis (see p.257)

Paul Woloshansky began bicycle touring in 1970, at age 16. A poorly-equipped and badly-planned trip up the Alaska Highway before it was paved turned out well, in spite of everything, and was the beginning of a life long passion. When he's off his touring bike and at home in Calgary, Canada, Paul is a bicycle mechanic and writer of cycling- and travel-related articles, with an Asian focus: *Sharing the Road: A Cyclist's Guide to India* is a current work-in-progress.

Robin and Heleen Wielders-Boerman Robin Wielders lives to be free, juggle and climb mountains, and love Heleen, his wife whom he married in Laos in 2003. Robin and Heleen recently finished a trip through the Middle East, North Africa and Europe, riding home while Heleen was pregnant.

Maya van Leemput (see p.248)

Raf Verbeelen started his cycling holidays with some friends in Belgium and neighbouring countries. Now trying to combine this with his passion for the Sahara he puts his bicycle on planes to North Africa. He has visited the deserts of Morocco, Egypt, and Tunisia.

Ivan Viehoff (see p.237)

INDEX

TRAILBLAZER

OTHER GUIDES FROM TRAILBLAZER – see p288 for full list

The Silk Roads – a route & planning guide
Paul Wilson & Dominic Streatfeild-James
336pp, 50 maps, 30 colour photos
ISBN 1 873756 53 4, £12.99, Can$29.95, US$18.95 *1st edition*
The Silk Road was never a single thread but an intricate web of
trade routes linking Asia and Europe. This guide follows all the
routes with sections on Turkey, Syria, Iran, Turkmenistan,
Uzbekistan, Kyrgyzstan, Kazakhstan, Pakistan and China.

Trekking in Ladakh *Charlie Loram*
288pp, 75 maps, 24 colour photos
ISBN 1 873756 75 5, £12.99, Can$27.95, US$18.95 *3rd edition*
Fully revised and extended 3rd edition of Charlie Loram's practical
guide. Includes 75 detailed walking maps, guides to Leh, Manali
and Delhi plus information on getting to Ladakh.
'Extensive...and well researched'. **Climber Magazine**
'Were it not for this book we might still be blundering about...'
The Independent on Sunday

New Zealand – The Great Walks *Alexander Stewart*
1st edn, 272pp, 60 maps, 40 colour photos
ISBN 1 873756 78 X, £11.99, Can$28.95, US$19.95
New Zealand is a wilderness paradise of incredibly beautiful landscapes. There is no better way to experience it than on one of the nine
designated Great Walks, the country's premier walking tracks which
provide outstanding hiking opportunities for people at all levels of fitness. Also includes detailed guides to Auckland, Wellington, National
Park Village, Taumaranui, Nelson, Queenstown, Te Anau and Oban.

Kilimanjaro – a trekking guide to Africa's highest mountain
Henry Stedman, 2nd edition, 320pp, 50 maps, 30 photos
ISBN 1 873756 91 7, £10.99, Can$22.95, US$19.95
At 19,340ft the world's tallest freestanding mountain, Kilimanjaro is
one of the most popular destinations for hikers visiting Africa. It's possible to walk up to the summit: no technical skills are necessary. This
guide includes town guides to Nairobi and Dar-Es-Salaam, excursions in the region and a detailed colour guide to flora and fauna.
Now also includes Mt Meru guide.

Adventure Motorcycling Handbook
Chris Scott, 5th edition, 288 pp, 28 colour, 100 B&W photos
ISBN 1 873756 80 1, £12.99, Can$29.95, US$19.95
Every red-blooded motor-cyclist dreams of making the Big Trip – this
book shows you how. Top ten overland machines, choosing a destina-
tion, bike preparation, documentation and shipping, route outlines. Plus
– ten first-hand accounts of epic biking adventures worldwide.
'The first thing we did was buy the Adventure Motorcycling Handbook*'*
Ewan McGregor, *The Long Way Round*

South-East Asia – The Graphic Guide
Mark Elliott 240pp, 210 maps, *1st edn.* ISBN 1 873756 67 4, £9.99
SE Asia is quite deservedly one of the most popular regions for budget travellers. Travel there is now so easy that a different type of
guide is needed: this book fills the gap, concentrating information –
more maps and less talk.

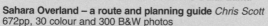

TRAILBLAZER

OTHER GUIDES FROM TRAILBLAZER – see p288 for full list

Tibet Overland – a route and planning guide *Kym McConnell*
224pp, 16pp colour maps
ISBN 1 873756 41 0, *1st edition*, £12.99, US$19.95
Featuring 16pp of full colour mapping based on satellite photographs, this is a guide for mountain bikers and other road users in Tibet. Includes detailed information on over 9000km of overland routes across the world's highest and largest plateau. Includes Lhasa-Kathmandu route and the route to Everest North Base Camp.
'...a wealth of advice...' **HH The Dalai Lama**

Sahara Overland – a route and planning guide *Chris Scott*
672pp, 30 colour and 300 B&W photos
ISBN 1 873756 76 3, *2nd edition*, £19.99, US$29.95
Fully-revised new edition. Covers all aspects Saharan, from choosing a vehicle to how to 'read' sand surfaces – it's all here along with 70 GPS routes and detailed itineraries: over 25,000kms in nine countries, from Egypt's Western Desert to Mauritania's Atlantic shore. Now with a tough hardback cover.
'Gets right to the heart of desert travel.' **Michael Palin**

Norway's Arctic Highway – Mo I Rana to Kirkenes
John Douglas 320pp, 30 colour photos, 53 maps
ISBN 1 873756 73 9, *1st edition*, £13.99, US$19.95
Norway's Arctic Highway stretches 900 miles from Mo i Rana to Kirkenes, almost all the route within the Arctic Circle. At its most northern point the road comes to within 19.5 degrees of the North Pole. This is a region of intense physical beauty – tundra plateaux, vast glaciers and magnificent fjords. Includes km-by-km route guide with maps plus detailed guides to Tromsø, Bodø, Hammerfest and other towns along the route.

Himalaya by Bicycle – a route and planning guide
Laura Stone 336pp, 28 colour & 50 B&W photos, 60 maps
1st edition, £14.99, US$25.95 – **due mid 2007**
An all-in-one guide for Himalayan cycle-touring. Covers the Himalayan regions of Pakistan, Tibet, India, Nepal and Sikkim with detailed km-by-km guides to main routes including the Karakoram Highway and the Friendship Highway. Plus: town and city guides.

Trans-Siberian Handbook *Bryn Thomas*
480pp, 55 maps, 32 colour photos
ISBN 1 873756 94 1, £13.99, US$19.95 *7th edition*
First edition short-listed for the **Thomas Cook Guidebook Awards**. Seventh edition of the most popular guide to the world's longest rail journey. How to arrange a trip, plus a km-by-km guide to the routes. Updated and expanded to include extra information on travelling independently in Russia. New mapping. *'Definitive guide'* **Condé Nast**

The Blues Highway New: Orleans to Chicago – a travel and music guide *Richard Knight* 2nd edition, 304pp, 50 maps, 30 colour photos, ISBN 1 873756 66 6, £12.99, US$19.95
The first travel guide to explore the roots of jazz and blues in the USA.
❑ Detailed city guides with 40 maps ❑ Where to stay, where to eat ❑ The best music clubs and bars ❑ Who's who of jazz and blues ❑ Historic landmarks ❑ Music festivals and events ❑ Exclusive interviews with music legends Wilson Pickett, Ike Turner, Little Milton, Honeyboy Edwards and many more. *'Fascinating'* – **Time Out**